THE C.A. LEJEUNE
FILM READER

Also from Carcanet

The Dilys Powell Film Reader
edited by Christopher Cook

The
C.A.
Lejeune
Film
Reader

EDITED BY
ANTHONY LEJEUNE

CARCANET

First published in 1991 by
Carcanet Press Limited
208–212 Corn Exchange Buildings
Manchester M4 3BQ

British Library Cataloguing in Publication Data
Lejeune, C. A. (Caroline Alice) *1897–1973*
   The C. A. Lejeune film reader.
   1. Cinema films
   I. Title   II. Lejeune, Anthony
   791.437

ISBN 0 85635 911 4

The publisher acknowledges financial assistance
from the Arts Council of Great Britain

Set in 10½pt Bembo by Paragon Photoset, Aylesbury
Printed and bound in England by SRP Ltd, Exeter

Contents

Acknowledgements

Most of the film reviews prior to 1928 are from the *Manchester Guardian*, and most of the subsequent reviews from the *Observer*. I am indebted to the Editors of those two newspapers for permission to reprint them here.

'My Story' (p.23f) and 'Head 'em off at Eagle Pass' (p.312f) were first printed in *Good Housekeeping*; my thanks are due to the National Magazine Company for permission to reprint them.

'The Real America' (p.307f) is Copyright © 1947 by The New York Times Company; reprinted by permission.

The excerpts on pp.328–54 are from C. A. Lejeune's autobiography, *Thank You for Having Me* (London: Hutchinson, 1964).

– A. L.

Preface

BY

ANTHONY LEJEUNE

I've been accustomed to say that my mother, C. A. Lejeune, was the first professional film critic. It may not be true. Somebody in Europe or America may have written regular film reviews earlier: but I doubt if anyone else's career began sooner and went on as long. She began writing about films shortly after the First World War and wrote her last weekly article for the *Observer* on Christmas Day 1960; a period which, one might say, covered the rise, full flowering and the first stages of the decline of the film industry. Certainly it covered the rise and fall of the studio system. She saw the artistic development of caption-writing in the silent cinema, elaborations of the camera, the first shining of international stars, the coming of sound, the triumph of colour, attempts – more than once – at stereoscopy, the film industry at war, the letter-box screen, the wrap-around screen and at least the seeds of most of the changes which have, more recently, transformed Hollywood. She also wrote about, and wrote for, television.

Of the tributes paid on her retirement, two are perhaps worth quoting in this context. Anthony Asquith said:

> It must be difficult for readers of this generation to realize the importance of C. A. Lejeune. Of course they recognize that she has been one of the two or three outstanding film critics writing in English, that she has a style as vivid as her perception is acute, that she has wit, humour and that peculiarly English thing, a delicious sense of nonsense and, above all, that she has that rarest and most valuable of all critical gifts, the ability to infect one with her own enthusiasm.
>
> What is difficult for the present-day reader to realize is that, when she started to write many years ago, she was almost unique. Those who wrote about films then could be roughly divided into two classes, the fan-magazine gossip columnist and the austerely intellectual theorist. Miss Lejeune was one of the first critics to write with equal seriousness and write with equal perception about all kinds of films.

Peter Sellers, whom she knew personally much less well, said:

> Her kindness, her complete integrity and her qualities as an observer and a commentator have gained her the unqualified admiration of my profession. She respects integrity in others and has no harsh words for anyone whose honest efforts end in failure. Everything she has written, I am sure, has come as much from her heart as her head, and the high quality of her writing, and the standards of film-making she encourages, have made her work a part of cinema history.

Her own life story can be summarized quite briefly, since she was a notably private woman, a non-traveller, a person of inner, not outer, weather.

She was born on 27 March 1897, in a suburb of Manchester. Her father, Adam Edward Lejeune, belonged to a Huguenot family that had settled in Germany. As a young man he came to England from Frankfurt to learn the cotton trade: he died in Switzerland before his youngest daughter – Caroline Alice – was two years old, leaving her only the dimmest memory of a stranger who once visited the nursery. Her mother, Louisa, was the daughter of a leading Nonconformist minister, Dr Alexander Maclaren of Edinburgh, a famous preacher in his day. They had three sons and five daughters. One of the boys emigrated to America, another to Australia and the third became a 'railway missionary' in South Africa; one of the girls went with her husband to Canada. In true Victorian style Mrs Lejeune kept in close touch with them all.

'I realize now,' Caroline wrote long afterwards,

> that I was a favoured child. The youngest, by ten years, I was given the best of all the good things at Christmas. My pile of presents was the biggest, and the little table on which they were laid was directly under the Christmas tree. I was allowed to decorate the pictures with the brightest sprigs of holly and the mellowest mistletoe. Everything that love and unselfishness could do was done to make my days of Christmas happy. I was too young and thoughtless to be grateful for it then, but the people who strove with trifles to please an excited child gave something of value to last a lifetime.

Mrs Lejeune was remarkable in many ways – 'the most

magnificent woman I have ever known', my mother wrote to me in a letter attached to some family papers. Two of her daughters went to Oxford and one to Cambridge, which was by no means usual then. After leaving Withington Girls' School, Caroline was expected to follow her sister Franziska to Somerville. She passed the entrance exam and had an amicable interview with the Principal but surprisingly, if perhaps characteristically, took a dislike to the place and chose to stay at home. She read English at Manchester University and gained a first-class degree; by which time she was already writing pieces for the *Manchester Guardian*, mainly about opera and particularly about the annual visits of the D'Oyly Carte Company, some of whose members became her lifelong friends.

C. P. Scott, the *Guardian*'s editor, and Mrs Lejeune had a long-standing and close relationship. He would bicycle round, several times a week, for tea. Caroline persuaded him to publish an article from her juvenile but enthusiastic pen, pleading for recognition of the kinematograph as a new art form. It had occurred to her, after seeing Douglas Fairbanks in *The Mark of Zorro*, that she might become a film critic. She was in her last term at college: she would soon need a job: she would have preferred to write about the theatre but she enjoyed films, and this was something no one else was doing, so why not? Scott agreed to consider the matter but thought it would have to be done 'from the London end'.

Accompanied by her mother, she moved to London, ostensibly to read for a Ph.D. in the British Museum. The thesis was never completed. In January 1922 the *Guardian* gave her a column of her own, 'The Week on the Screen', signed 'C.A.L.'

Three years later she married my father, Edward Roffe Thompson, also a graduate of Manchester University. He was a journalist and succeeded the notorious Horatio Bottomley as editor of *John Bull*. They built a house at Pinner Hill in Middlesex, on an estate of open fields and woods which is now a conservation area; Mrs Lejeune came to live nearby. In that house I was born, their only child, and in the same year, 1928, my mother moved, with Scott's blessing, to the *Observer*, where her column appeared every week, except when she was ill or on holiday, for the next thirty-two years.

She wrote for many other journals, ranging from the *New York Times* to the *Farmer's Weekly*. In 1931 she produced a slimmish volume, called *Cinema*, surveying the state of the art (or industry) at that stage. More historically interesting, in retrospect, is *The Private Life of London Films*, which was serialized but never published in book form; it traces the career of Alexander Korda from his early days in Europe to the building of Denham Studios. Denham was only a few miles from our house, and visits there were frequent. For a while, indeed, my father worked for Korda on future projects and as some kind of publicity director.

When war loomed, Alfred Hitchcock suggested that my mother and I might take refuge, under his care, in California, but for reasons movingly described in her autobiography, she felt it would be wrong to go. The war came. There was an air-raid shelter in the garden, which we shared with a neighbour: nothing worse than a few chunks of shrapnel fell very near us. After a week or two when all the cinemas were closed, films became part of the war effort.

From the very early days of public transmission we had a television set, a Baird, bulky as a cocktail cabinet; the screen was actually a mirror, which reflected an upright cathode-ray tube. My mother, unlike Lord Reith, the director general of the BBC, never doubted the future importance of television and its intimate relationship to films. What she could not foresee – no one, I think, did – was that, by capturing the family audience, it would change the market for films in cinemas and therefore the nature of the studios' product. When the BBC's television service was resumed after the war, she reviewed television as well as films, for a while, in the *Observer*: but the combination didn't really work. It was much more satisfying to adapt a number of her favourite books as television serials: A. E. W. Mason's *Clementina*, John Buchan's *The Three Hostages* and some Sherlock Holmes stories. She and I wrote a television play together, a gentle comedy called *Vicky's First Ball*. Since all drama productions were live, with occasional, rather ill-matching, film inserts, the craft involved getting the actors unobtrusively from one set to another.

Throughout her career my mother broadcast sporadically, but she was too modest for personal performance to come naturally to her. She produced plays for a local amateur dramatic company, and was offered the chance to direct a professional production. Although intrigued, she couldn't quite bring herself to do it. During those post-war years Lady Astor, whose husband, Waldorf, owned the *Observer*, became, if not exactly a close friend, a warm and forceful acquaintance. While visiting Cliveden, where naming Lord Astor's foals was a party game for guests, my mother was introduced to racehorses. Studying form and betting by telephone – in a very mild way, having deposited £50 with a bookie at the start of the season – became one of the minor pleasures of her life. She was particularly pleased to include in a series of 'personality pieces' which she wrote for *Good Housekeeping* magazine an 'interview', as she herself described it, with the great Hyperion on the twenty-first anniversary of his Derby win.

Newspapers and films were changing. The new trends in the cinema didn't suit her and she no longer really suited the *Observer*. Along with other old hands, she was kindly but irrevocably eased out. She received nearly 2000 letters from readers, and Durham University afterwards gave her an honorary degree. The gap in her life, after so long, was nostalgically perceptible and her pension was small, but not having to go into central London and see films was a relief. She had lost her taste for them. Except for a half-hearted attempt, in the first months of her retirement, to do a little free-lance reviewing, she never entered a cinema again. The only screen entertainment which gave her keen pleasure was *The Forsyte Saga* on television. She wrote a charming but reticent autobiography, *Thank You for Having Me*, completed a novel which Angela Thirkell had left unfinished, wrote a little book on gardening, pruned her roses, groomed the dog and read detective stories and children's stories. She died in the spring of 1973, my father precisely six months later. Both died at home, neither having suffered the slightest mental impairment.

In 1947 my mother had published a collection of her film reviews, called *Chestnuts in Her Lap*. Intending it, not for students of the cinema, but as light bedside reading, she included nothing written before 1936. The review sections of the present volume are much more comprehensive.

I have divided them into the four decades of her career. The 1920s I kept thin because much of the material – the columns were very long and leisurely – now seems quaint rather than essentially interesting to the general reader. Most of the films would be familiar only to cinema historians, while the quality of writing and the views expressed show the strengths but also the weaknesses of youth. The extracts reprinted here provide glimpses of the period and of a sharp, eager but still immature, mind.

The 1930s and '40s presented an opposite problem. There is too much material worth reprinting. Those were the golden years of Hollywood – and of the British studios in so far as they ever had a golden age. The richness, and the sheer quantity, of output are amazing; the major American studios were each releasing around fifty films a year. The youthful priggishness and overwriting which marked some of my mother's earlier reviews had gone. Style and judgement alike were fully mature, although it strikes one – well, it strikes me – as odd that she should, for example, have felt she must apologize for recommending more warmly the frivolities of It Happened One Night than the solemnities of Robert Flaherty's documentary, Man of Aran. Perhaps she thought, rightly or wrongly, that she was meeting her readers' expectations. As the decades pass, this distortion vanishes, and I should like to have included many more reviews than space permits.

The 1950s may show the first traces of disillusionment, or a faint, but distinct falling-off in the overall quality of the films. Or is it just hindsight to think so? Certainly my mother would not have liked the tendencies which have become steadily more evident since then – the violence, the noise, the crude language, the calculated lubricity. When she came to London from Manchester and saw the film industry at close quarters, it was, she said, her first experience of organized vulgarity, and it had excited her. But the vulgarity of the 1920s was very different from the vulgarity of the 1960s and succeeding decades.

As the American show-business journal Variety, overcome by a sudden access of deep thinking, observed in 1985, 'When the causes of the Decline of Western Civilisation are finally writ, Hollywood will surely have to answer why it turned one of man's most significant art forms over to the self-gratification of high-schoolers.' Modern juvenile audiences are said chiefly to enjoy three things: defiance of authority, destruction of property and people taking their clothes off. Their attention span is presumed to be fleeting and their language foul. The films made for them have surely contributed to the truth of these assumptions. Old Hollywood, on the other hand, despite its absurdities and naïveté, was genuinely an influence for good.

The values it projected were not ignoble and its picture of America – Andy Hardy's America – was justly enviable. Of course there were exceptions then and there are exceptions now. There have been recent films which my mother would have enjoyed, but the incipient cruelties and obscenities which she most disliked have become explicit, whereas wit, melody, good manners and honest sentimentality have grown rare. The spectacle of motor cars chasing each other and space-ships blowing each other up would simply have bored her.

The forty years' panorama of motion pictures painted by the reviews in this book is inevitably *pointilliste* rather than fully coherent. I have sought to include, on the one hand, entertaining reviews of films which may not themselves have been entertaining, let alone important, and on the other, reviews, whether or not inherently very interesting, of films which, seen in perspective, are obviously important to filmgoers. The inevitable result is that some of the pieces here are less amusing than some others which she included in *Chestnuts in Her Lap* but which I have been compelled to leave out. If sometimes the balance of judgement in her column appears odd, it should be remembered that she was not assessing a decade's, or even a year's, films: she was addressing each week's crop separately.

We have all been able, lately, to see a lot of old films on television, and most of us have had occasion to revise earlier judgements. Some films wear well, others badly: some were over-rated, some under-rated, by contemporary critics: and a few have the strange quality of looking better every time one sees them. Some – musicals conspicuously – possess an extra charm now because nothing like them is being made any more. There are no infallible rules; if there were, there would be no box-office flops.

My mother's view was that a bad press could never destroy a potentially successful film, but that a critic might sometimes draw attention to a good film which would otherwise pass unnoticed. I thought of including a chapter of mistakes. No critic works for a life-time without getting many things wrong. In the 1920s, for example, my mother wrote: 'Although kinematography, it is now generally agreed, was born in England, exploited in France and adopted in America, it is in Northern Europe that its real future lies. Sweden takes her kinema industry very seriously . . .' The last sentence, at least, remains indisputable.

Her review of Cecil B. de Mille's *Cleopatra*, in 1934, begins well. It was, she said, Mr de Mille's 'latest endeavour to popularize the genteel orgy. In a barge which looks neat enough from the outside to navigate the Grand Union canal, but which reveals an interior at least the size of the Crystal Palace, the elegant Cleopatra stages an entertainment designed less to stir the senses of Antony than to comfort a public threatened by an imminent purity campaign.' But she concluded that de Mille was now working 'like a tired man, straining every nerve and sinew to get an effect that he once would have achieved without labour', and she thought his career might be drawing to its end. Ahead, unforeseen, lay the Crusades and the epic of the plainsmen and Charlton Heston as Moses.

Frankenstein she dismissed in a paragraph as 'a very horrid production from Hollywood'. *Casablanca* she only quite liked: 'It's a busy film, with bright lines, a perfunctory romance and a dim message.' *The Wicked Lady* she didn't like at all: 'I found it a thoroughly repugnant picture; shoddy, amateurish, dull, ill-acted, ill-written, and unsightly; and the only comfort I derived from it was the malign reflection that actors, particularly bad ones, in Restoration costume, look exactly like caterpillars on their hind legs.'

The Wicked Lady has proved enduringly popular, but I'm not sure she was wrong. Some oddities of judgement, such as that *Grand Hotel* was 'pretty strong melodrama, and not for the school-children', merely reflect changed assumptions. *King Kong* too was 'definitely not for children'. Which reminds me of Fay Wray.

Reading Miss Wray's own agreeable autobiography and feeling vaguely that I had met her, I looked for her name in the index to *Thank You for Having Me*. She had indeed been to dinner in our house, but the only recorded comment is from Tilly, our stalwart 'daily help'. 'All the time I was servin',' declared Tilly, 'she kep' on talk, talk, talk, till my head was fair openin' and shuttin'.'

My mother met a great many actors and directors in the course of her career; she probably shook hands with every star who visited Britain. With very few, however, did she become friends. The two she liked best were Robert Donat and Leslie Howard. Donat was in the first film I ever saw being made, *The Ghost Goes West*, at Denham. And I have a vivid recollection of sitting on a lawn somewhere with Leslie

Howard and his beautiful French girl-friend, Violette, who died tragically, leaving him bereft and vulnerable. I remember him, too, seeking my mother's advice about his personal problems just before he left on the wartime journey from which he never returned. Those memories, mixed up with thoughts of childhood, of pre-war summers, of the vapour trails in the sky in 1940, render *The First of the Few*, for me, a deeply evocative and touching film.

But the film-industry figures who loomed largest in my mother's life were the two largest figures: Alfred Hitchcock and Alexander Korda. She had marked Hitch out as the most promising British director when he was a very young man, and, though he had long removed himself to Hollywood, he sent her, every year at Christmas until she died, two dozen half-bottles of champagne. Korda's most considerate gift was made during the war, when he managed to obtain for her what had become unobtainable, a black powder called *poudre d'Abyssinie* which she burnt for the relief of asthma. The whole Korda entourage, his brothers Vincent and Zolli, Merle Oberon, Perinal the cameraman, Dave Cunningham the man of business, the grandeurs and follies of London Films, Denham and 'the Claridge', were a constant theme. I hope the 'People' section of this book conveys something of them.

In a real sense, though, anyone who grew up in the film era is likely to feel a kind of intimacy with most of the names mentioned. That was the point of the star system and the effect of the repertory company of familiar faces which the studios maintained. You felt you knew them. Actors who pompously refuse to talk about their private lives, claiming that only their work matters, fail to understand the relationship on which their success depends. The intimacy was an illusion, of course, but the love was genuine and it imposed a responsibility which the true professionals always accepted. Seeing the beloved shadows now, reading the old reviews and the old interviews, is an experience both sweet and sad. We know the ends of too many stories. We know who died prematurely, whose careers petered out, who soldiered on indefatigably, and who, having bought property in Malibu, enjoy a rich retirement, making occasional appearances on late-night talk shows. I have in my bedroom a picture of Mickey Mouse, saying, with a jaunty wave of his four-fingered hand, 'Greetings to Miss C. A. Lejeune!': and I have in mind a magazine cover, when Walt Disney died, which bore no caption, just a picture of Mickey Mouse with a tear dropping from his eye.

My mother never went to America, never saw Hollywood and never considered that this was a damaging lack in her professional equipment. When I first visited America, I was pleased to find how familiar everything looked. In an article, written during the 1940s and included in this volume, she described the America which Hollywood has taught us to expect; like all good jokes, this article contains more than a grain or two of truth among the chaff. She knew little or nothing about studio politics, the exigencies of film finance, the power struggles of Hollywood, which have been fascinatingly exposed, these long years afterwards, in such books as *Inside Warner Brothers* and *The Genius of the System*. But this too she would have regarded as no great loss. She was not a business analyst or a gossip writer or an evangelist for any cause. Her job, as she conceived it, was to deal with what was on the screen; her primary function was to provide a service, guiding her readers, by consistency of judgement, on whether or not to pay their money at the box-office. But because her articles were amusing, they were read also by many people who never went to the cinema at all. To take one example at random, her review of the archetypal Dorothy Lamour sarong-drama, *Her Jungle Love*, is, by any standards, a fine piece of comic writing.

Throughout the forty-year body of her work two patterns emerge. The first shows her arguing, in the early period, that films (never 'film' in the pretentious modern style) were an art; in the later period that they are not. The gist of the iconoclastic argument is that films are a team product, assembled from the work of scriptwriters, actors, cameramen and directors, mechanically recorded and cut into shape by an editor, and that such a blend cannot, in the ordinary sense, be called art. This is not a very plausible argument and I'm not sure how seriously my mother meant it. What it signified was a revulsion from highbrow nonsense, like Alfred Hitchcock's contempt for the *cinéastes* who wove elaborate theories about his work.

The other pattern, which still recurs periodically, is a belief that the British film industry was on the verge, at last, of the great breakthrough, of challenging Hollywood. In this belief, if she did believe it, she reflected the perennial chauvinistic optimism of the industry itself. She had stated the blunt truth in that little book *Cinema*. 'It would be doing no service to the British movie,' she wrote then,

> to pretend that its achievements, even the best of its achieve-
> ments, are distinguishable in feature to any observer taking a
> bird's-eye survey of the world's screen. The British cinema has
> been handicapped in every way – with bad brains, shortage of
> money, lack of confidence, injudicious flattery, misdirected
> talent, unfortunate legislation – and it is making a tough fight
> for recovery, which may or may not eventuate in a sound-
> cinema with national characteristics and a national force of
> its own.

How often that wistful hope has been repeated and frustrated! Most notably perhaps in the Ealing comedies, the British film industry did acquire a voice of its own, but it was a very small voice. The folly of the quota system, which required British cinemas to show forty per cent British films, has been repeated over television, and we constantly hear pleas that a little more protection, a little more subsidy, will bring the elusive breakthrough. But there is surely no more reason why the British film industry should be able to match the American film industry than that British wine should match French wine.

Although, especially in the earlier years, she drew the attention of British filmgoers to Continental films, and although she emphasized the role of directors before the *auteur* theory of films had been invented, she had very little in common with writers about the cinema who think that almost any foreign-language film is more worthy of respect than the standard Hollywood fare and that directors matter more than stars. Did she really want, as some of her articles imply, films of gritty realism about 'ordinary' British people? Surely not. *Millions Like Us* was just such a wartime film: her review somewhere, I seem to recall, consisted of only three words – 'And millions don't.' What she enjoyed was high romance, warm-hearted comedy, those things which drew her to films in the first place, and a jolly tune like 'The Deadwood Stage' in *Calamity Jane*. If she under-rated, as I think she did, Errol Flynn's *Adventures of Robin Hood*, Ronald Colman's *Prisoner of Zenda* and Basil Rathbone's version of *Sherlock Holmes*, it was only because she loved the books so much.

There were generally five or six films a week to be seen, on Mondays, Tuesdays and Wednesdays, with a buffet lunch or drinks afterwards. Most were slipped into the programme at some West End cinema, a few were shown in private theatres, of which the nicest by far was MGM's small theatre in Tower Street. I can see it now, presided over by the most genial and civilized of publicity chiefs and with Saunders, the barman, leaning forward to watch the film. Among the familiar band of fellow critics were James Agate and Dilys Powell, Fred Majdalany, Campbell Dixon, Dudley Carew of *The Times*, Ernest Betts and Jympson Harmon, Paul Holt, who had been a celebrated war correspondent, and Paul Dehn, who, as an officer in the Special Operations Executive, had briefed Odette Churchill before sending her to France, and who later turned to script-writing with brilliant success. And there was Harris Deans, an undistinguished critic on an undistinguished paper, who taught me a salutary lesson about films and indeed about all artistic enterprise. He rebuked me for being dismissive of somebody's efforts. 'Never forget,' he said, 'that it's just as hard work to make a bad film as a good one.'

My mother was always glad to get home to Pinner Hill, travelling from Baker Street in the old brown trains with 'Live in Metroland' inscribed on the brass handles of the compartment doors. On Thursdays she wrote her column with a soft pencil on a pad of white paper, constantly correcting and rubbing out, not easily. The manuscript was typed by Constance Redfearn, who had been Bottomley's secretary and who lived with us, part-secretary, part-housekeeper, part-nanny to me when I was young.

From the age of about ten I went with my mother to press shows, and I continued to do so during school holidays, on leave from the Navy and in vacations from Oxford. My father having become somewhat reclusive, I escorted her to most social events. Reading her work through now, I have been surprised to find how often her judgements surprise me, how often her opinions differed from mine without my having been aware of it. We must surely have discussed the films we'd just seen and the people we met? But the young are egocentric and take much for granted. Perhaps anyone reading a detailed account of his parents' thoughts would be equally surprised.

In certain matters, nowadays considered important, my mother was remarkably unsophisticated. She never noticed the politics underlying some flagrantly political films. The obscenities which began to creep into film scripts were actually new to her; embarrassingly she asked me what one such word meant. She came, as she wrote somewhere, from 'a God-fearing King-honouring home'. Her account of why we didn't go to America in 1939 shows that *Mrs Miniver* was not as unrealistic as modern cynicism believes.

To that extent, this is a history book. The piece about *Gone with the Wind* evokes war-time London as vividly as any few paragraphs I know. The films themselves are landmarks of our time. Incredibly, more than fifty years have passed since we first heard the dwarfs 'Heigh-ho', but my mother knew as soon as she saw *Snow White*, tinkly tunes, jerky animation and chocolate-box human figures notwithstanding, that she had seen history made. But if this is a book for film buffs and historians of the cinema, it is also, I hope, a book for everyone who enjoys old films and appreciates good writing. Relax. Come with me to the Odeons and Embassies of long ago, to the palatial Granadas ('Pronounce it Grā-nā-dā,' said the advertisements), let the Mighty Wurlitzer sound and the pastel-lit curtains divide . . .

I

Autobiographical

My Story

When people ask me how I became a film critic, I am always at a loss to answer. It happened so long ago; and there was no how and why about it. It just happened, that's all.

Like most children, I always had the itch to write. My ambition was to write as well as my eldest sister, who had produced a full-length exercise-book novel about a Tennysonian young lady named Gwendoline, divinely fair and most divinely beautiful, and prone to meeting her lover in gardens scented with lilies and glowing with passion flowers. I adored it, but the only sentence I can now recall clearly is, 'Before dinner the gentlemen went to the bathroom to brush their hair and wash their hands.'

Somehow I never got down to tackling a novel myself, although I did write poems in a red leather autograph album. They were addressed to all the people on whom I had a crush; or, as we used to describe it in those days, the people I was 'gone on'. Since I was gone on at least half-a-dozen people every year (I kept two lists headed respectively, 'Nearly gone' and 'Quite gone'), there were a remarkable number of poems in the book. At the age of fifteen or so I read a cautious selection to the curate, whom I was particularly gone on at the time. He was a shy, ascetic young man, who encouraged me, nervously but conscientiously, to pursue my literary career; and went off very fast to be a Chaplain in the First World War. I marked the occasion with a tear drenched little number beginning

> Kitchener's Second Army,
> Marching, training,
> On Salisbury Plain,
> In the mud and the rain,

and promptly transferred my devotion to the school gym mistress.

It was about this time, I suppose, that I began to be interested in films, which were shown in 'electric palaces' and not considered quite proper in my mother's circle. Well-conducted young ladies were taught to hide behind cardboard cut-outs of Charlie Chaplin lest they should be spotted in the queue by Mother's callers. The only films we were encouraged to attend were such classics as the Italian *Cabiria* and *Quo Vadis* and the French *Les*

Miserables. These were considered educative, and calculated not to harm the burgeoning mind. I enjoyed them, because they were pictures, and they moved, but I much preferred such heart-clutching serials as *The Perils of Pauline* and *The Exploits of Elaine*. And presently the handsome young John Barrymore; the World's Sweetheart, Mary Pickford; and the wild and woolly cowboy, whom she was later to marry, Douglas Fairbanks.

I suppose it was Douglas Fairbanks who really determined my career. One blazing August afternoon during a holiday at Brighton I went to see him in *The Mark of Zorro*. I was nearly grown-up by that time, and the problem of My Future was becoming acute. Suddenly, as I watched Fairbanks' harlequin poses and swirling trajectories across the screen, there sprang into my mind a wonderful idea. Why should I not turn my pleasure into profit, and earn my living by seeing films?

Such an idea would not seem in the least remarkable to a young man or woman of this generation. But at that time, soon after the First World War, it was a very strange and bold idea indeed. Moving pictures were still considered not quite the thing in the best circles, and not more than two or three national newspapers recognized their existence as anything other than curiosities. The profession of film critic had not yet come into being, if one excepts the reviewers on the trade papers (one of which was still subtitled *The Magic Lantern Weekly*). But in my youthful arrogance I dreamt bright dreams of a regular column about this new art form, which would appear above my initials in some fine and authoritative newspaper.

Luck was on my side, for my mother happened to be an old friend of C. P. Scott, the editor of *The Manchester Guardian*, and his wife. Their daughter, Mrs C. E. Montague, had been at school with my sisters; her children, although slightly my juniors, were at school with me. 'Scotty', at the time I first remember him, was a widower, and one of the handsomest old gentlemen I have ever seen. He had a full white beard and keen hawk's eyes which, when he talked to children, which he loved to do, softened and grew extraordinarily kind. He affected loose, light tweeds, which had the real peaty smell. Every afternoon, wet or fine, he used to take a three-mile bicycle ride round the grimy but still open spaces of south Manchester – what we called 'the fields' – and two or three times a week it was his custom to drop in for tea. Mother always had hot crumpets ready for him, or wafer-thin, delicious pikelets, dripping with butter, and rich black Eccles cakes; or some round éclairs from a Swiss pastrycook, oozing ambrosial vanilla, called respectively Othellos (chocolate colour) and Desdemonas (white with chocolate blobs).

I don't know whether it was Mother's crumpets, or my persistence, or C.P.'s natural kindness, but already he had given me the chance to write one or two small things for the paper. There was a piece about books for children, for instance, and a notice of a minor Sunday concert; and there were three reviews of Gilbert and Sullivan operas, all signed with the modestly reversed initials, L.C.

Now, after the blinding revelation of my day at Brighton, I teased and badgered the poor old gentleman into accepting an impassioned article called 'The Undiscovered Aesthetic'. Boldly initialled C.L., it pleaded for recognition by discriminating critics of this new art form, the Kinematograph. The article reads comically today, in its faded yellow newsprint. It is shockingly priggish and precocious, full of such loose terms as 'subjectivism', 'introspection' and 'epic narrative', but there is no doubt at all as to its meaning. It meant that *The Manchester Guardian* ought to have a regular column of film criticism, and that the proper person to write it was the undersigned C.L.

In spite of this open invitation to the paper to avail itself of my services, I had to wait quite a long time before it did so. In point of fact, I had to come to London, with an introduction to James Bone, the *Guardian*'s London editor. Mother, although she was then well over sixty – I was the youngest by ten years of an immense brood of children – and had lived all her life in the north country, insisted upon coming with me; to protect me, I verily believe, against the activities of White Slavers, who might offer poisoned sweets to innocent young provincial girls in the big city. For my sake, she sold her comfortable house in Manchester, left her friends, tore up her roots, and faced the prospect of bleak years in shabby hotels, stuffy furnished flats and flea-pit cinemas in London. At the time, it all seemed very natural to me; but looking back now, as I am approaching old age myself, I can remember glimpses of Mother's tired face, the moments when she dozed off in cinemas, and the times when she said apologetically, 'You go on ahead, I can't hurry to the bus stop'; and at last I realize what a sacrifice and what devotion that move entailed.

James Bone was a Scotsman, who would put up with no nonsense about aesthetics, undiscovered or otherwise. He was Muirhead Bone's brother, and knew more about art, as well as journalism, than I shall ever fathom in a lifetime. He read the introductory letter from the Big White Chief, glanced perfunctorily at my press cuttings and told me to go away and play until I had learnt how to write an interesting paragraph of two hundred and fifty words about the way a pew-opener opens a pew.

But he had a kind heart beneath his dour exterior. Perhaps he thought I looked a bit forlorn; perhaps he realized that pew-openings in London, E.C., were infrequent. At all events, after the lapse of a few weeks, he sent me to 'cover' a floodlit mannequin parade in a Hampstead garden; where I was so overwhelmed by the magic of the million pin-point lights of London, viewed from the heights and cupped in the great hollow, that I failed altogether to notice the dresses, or differentiate the work of this costume-house from that.

Perhaps what I wrote about that mannequin parade, seen in its jewelled setting through the fascinated eyes of a stranger, may have been the equivalent of the paragraph about the pew-opener opening the pew. I don't know. All I do know is that, a short time later, I was sent to see my first film trade-show, *General John Regan*, with Milton Rosmer, at the old Alhambra Theatre, on the site of the modern Leicester Square Odeon. I shall never forget the mixture of pride and trepidation with which I walked past the doorman with a printed invitation card, and stood modestly at the back of the stalls – for the house was packed with exhibitors – inhaling the cigar smoke, watching the screen, and inflated with excitement, in the knowledge that I alone was responsible for telling hundreds of people in Manchester and Bolton and Wigan about a film they would have to wait months to see.

As it happened, the film could hardly have been a happier choice for me. I knew a good deal about *General John Regan*. My brother-in-law had played a small part in it on tour; my eldest sister, the one who had written that inspiring novel about Gwendoline, had walked on as an extra with a donkey. I managed to write something about the film, to length, to time, without ever using that dread word 'aesthetic'. Almost before I knew what was happening, the *Guardian* was sending me to do a

London letter paragraph about D. W. Griffith's *Dream Street* and my beloved Douglas Fairbanks's *Three Musketeers*.

As a Christmas present for 1921, they gave me my longed-for column, called *The Week on the Screen*, with my full initials, C.A.L., at the bottom of it. To celebrate the event, I bought myself a packet of gold-tipped Aristons, and Mother and I recklessly shared a nip of medicinal brandy, which she kept in a flask against emergencies. I was a columnist; more, I was a film critic. I had arrived.

There are some critics who enter upon every new week, every new day of films as if it were a glorious adventure, glittering with hope and promise; even though they have been watching films come and go for a quarter of a century. These are the rare ones, the men and women who have found their true vocation, and the cinema owes a large debt to them.

But I imagine that most film critics, and particularly the very young, enjoy the first years of their job intensely. I know it was so in my case. I revelled in every moment of it. The curious smells of Wardour Street, composite of gas and acetone, went to my head like wine; the stuffy, dark little private theatres, sometimes in the basement, sometimes high up under the roof, where we sat on chairs with broken springs, and listened to the whirr of the projectors showing 'silent' films, had the magic of some cavern from the Arabian Nights. The garish posters, the windows full of 'stills', were an unfailing delight, and to possess a non-transferable ticket, or better still, a private pass, to the grand morning trade-shows with an organ in the house, was as good as an invitation to Buckingham Palace.

The cinema of the 1920s was in any case an exciting affair. As a social institution, it began to settle in. A number of quite respectable persons went to the pictures now. One or two men and women of distinction even predicted a new art form. Hilaire Belloc mentioned it in lectures, and so did H. G. Wells. Colour films (many of them rather wishy-washy, some hand-painted) made a shy appearance here and there. Inventors gave private demonstrations of the first sound machines.

It was not long before super-luxury palaces, neon lights and Mighty Wurlitzers added comfort, if not always distinction, to the film-goer's lot. An orgy of affluence pervaded the Hollywood scene. Cecil B. de Mille indulged in his bath-tub epics. Elinor Glyn endorsed 'It'. A young dancer from the Argentine called Rudolph Valentino snaked his slim hips, smiled his inscrutable smile and opened wide dark velvet eyes on a world that had found its Dream Lover.

It was the hey-day of stunts and presentations. Tom Mix rode his horse up the steps of the Guildhall. A military band was engaged to play a print of a Hollywood film all the way from the docks at Southampton to the vaults of Wardour Street. Douglas Fairbanks stopped the traffic in Piccadilly by performing Tarzan antics on his hotel balcony. The Talmadge sisters sponsored a film beauty competition, in which a hundred lucky girls (selected by photograph) were brought to London, and personally touched up for their final camera test by the delicate Talmadge hand.

Madam Kirby Lunn, in black sequins, consecrated the new Tivoli in the Strand with the National Anthem, Little Tich topping the bill in the supporting programme. The lobbies of London cinemas were packed with atmosphere. Commissionaires and usherettes were pressed into fancy costume, vaguely related to the subject of the feature picture. In one lobby one could descry a monkey in a cage; in another, a hooded falcon. White roses were given to patrons of one theatre; red roses in another. A certain enterprising theatre installed a handkerchief bar, with the inscription, 'You will need this handkerchief for the tears you will shed when watching –' etc., etc.

I clearly remember being invited to attend a show at which two hundred clergymen were to be present. This was closely followed by another with two hundred politicians. Then there was something with the attraction of two hundred mothers-in-law (the real figure evades me, but two hundred is a good round number), and one with two hundred Royal Academicians. To a British film called *Comin' Thro' the Rye* trooped two hundred grandmothers (whose total age, we were told, would aggregate more than ten thousand years) with fifty Chelsea Pensioners as a guard of honour. Two hundred authors were impressed for another film; the main interest being that a majority of their number had never been lured into a picture-house before. And then there were the two hundred Alsatian wolf-hounds invited to the first performance of *Where the North Begins*. For some curious reason, contemporary journalism made no point of noting the dogs' reaction; but all this sort of thing caused great joy in the streets; crowds of onlookers collected round the doors, and not a few drifted in to watch the fun.

While this was going on at home, and we, the young, were revelling in its liveliness, a film movement of a very different, but far-reaching sort, was taking place on the Continent. First Sweden, comparatively untouched by war, began to send its charming, cultured pictures overseas.

It was not long before the best Swedish directors and players followed their films west; as far as Hollywood, in fact. One of these voyagers was a very young girl called Greta Garbo, who had played an *ingénue* part in *The Atonement of Gösta Berling*. Miss Garbo's chances were rated less promising than those of her countrymen who preceded or accompanied her; but it was hoped that good looks, combined with a certain acting ability, might ensure her at least a reasonable career.

With the exodus of its best film minds, Sweden's short day seemed to be over. But now Germany, turning hungrily to art for refreshment and rebirth after the First World War, was making film after film that teased and captured the imagination. It was the golden age of fantasy – of pictures such as *Siegfried*, *Metropolis*, *The Cabinet of Dr Caligari* and *The Student of Prague*. For the first time we heard the names of Emil Jannings and Conrad Veidt, of Fritz Lang and Ernst Lubitsch.

Almost simultaneously, a new breath of life came to the cinema in France, which had been dragging along for years with heavy costume spectacles and plushy old melodramas adapted from the stage. A group of young, keen artists – amongst whom was a newcomer named René Clair – began to experiment with films which they described as '*d'avant-garde*'. 'Little' theatres, specialized cinemas that were almost experimental workshops, sprang up in Paris, mostly on the Left Bank, and created quite a stir amongst the younger highbrows from England who could take a holiday across the Channel.

All through the early and middle Twenties I was passionately in love with French and German films, and would travel for miles by bus to seek them out in some remote London suburb – for there were no Academies or Curzons then. By the same route I became acquainted with the great pictures of Eisenstein, Pudovkin and other Soviet directors, which were frowned on by our censors, but managed to creep into this country in devious ways. Quite a vogue for Russian films was growing amongst the intelligentsia and pseudo-intelligentsia of London when the blow fell. The talkies arrived from Hollywood, and suddenly, almost overnight, the silent cinema became a dead cinema.

The year was 1928; the season early autumn. I am not likely to forget these dates, because two other important things happened to me at the same time. My son was born, and I left the *Manchester Guardian* to write for the *Observer*.

When I broke off reviewing films, in July, the dog Rin-Tin-Tin was Hollywood's most gainful star; *Ben Hur* with its chariot race was the big release in this country; and a hot summer had taken so many Londoners out of town that the appearance of a film called *The Jazz Singer*, in which Al Jolson not only recorded a song but spoke a snatch of unrehearsed dialogue, passed almost unnoticed by the critics.

When I came back to work in October, under entirely new management, the film situation had changed. The first film I was invited to review was a full-length, all-talking version of Edgar Wallace's thriller, *The Terror*; in which a masked and cloaked figure, the progenitor of the modern compère, advanced to the front of the screen, pointed a menacing finger at us, and dared us to discover the identity of the secret killer.

By all artistic standards, *The Terror* was a pretty dreadful bit of work; but to me, sharpened by my weeks of enforced abstinence from the cinema, it provided the experience of a lifetime. I was wearing a smart humbug-striped coat, I remember, with a waist somewhere round the hips, and a coal-scuttle hat, with a dashing black tassel. I had a new baby at home, and nothing much seemed to be happening in the world outside. An aurora borealis had upset the transatlantic cable. Al Smith was opposing Herbert Hoover in the American Presidential elections. Down at Savoy Hill, the BBC engineers were experimenting with the first closed circuit broadcasts of televised pictures.

On the surface, life was placid enough, and it seemed natural to expect that we were simply attending another trade-show of another rather undistinguished picture. But there was something working through that theatre like a yeast in ferment. The feeling was not normal. Too many persons were declaring, with too much vehemence, that talkies were a fad that wouldn't last. I remember going home, perplexed and excited, through the autumn twilight; breathing the keen blue smoke of bonfires, eager for the warmth and lovely *soapy* smell of the nursery; a little frightened at being out in the world alone again; and certain that history had been made in Piccadilly that October afternoon.

Everyone was asking the question, Had the talkies come to stay? The answer was prompt and positive. They had.

Within a few weeks of the day when the flower-like heroine of *The Terror* opened her rosebud lips, and uttered the memorable words, 'Say, Pop, can't you hear that turrible oirgan?', London had grown accustomed to this new thing, the talk-film. *The Terror* was quickly followed by *The Lights of New York*, *The Melody of Love* (in which we first heard the pleasant baritone voice of a young actor named Walter Pidgeon), and by Al Jolson's famous weepie, *The Singing Fool*. Half the town was whistling *Sonny Boy*, or singing it in the bath. Wishful thinkers in Wardour Street might insist until they were blue in the face that talking films were a fad that wouldn't last, but by the beginning of the new year they were coming across the Atlantic in dozens.

All over the world studios were scrapping existent material, installing sound-proof stages and recording apparatus. One after the other, picture-theatres were wired for sound. Sometimes the sound was awful, but it had to be there; even if, by some slight technical hitch, men were heard speaking with women's voices, or the needle stuck in a groove, and the star kept on madly repeating 'I love you I love you I love you.'

For a while silent films still turned up here and there. But not for long. Most silent films in production were junked, or brought up to date with dialogue sequences. Stars who couldn't talk went out, and actors who could talk, or at least talk better, came in. Elocution teachers were rushed out to Hollywood, and fading veterans of the theatre earned a new lease of life by coaching bright young starlets in the use of pear-shaped vowels.

The next ten years of film-making were so crowded, so vivid, and so vigorous, that it would be hopeless to try to describe them in any sort of order. It was a wonderful period for a journalist to live in; there seemed to be no day without its special, highly-coloured news-story. Garbo spoke. Charlie Chaplin refused to speak; then gave way to the extent of speaking some peculiar form of gibberish. Fred Astaire and Ginger Rogers formed the perfect partnership. Walt Disney made a world hero of a mouse. Walt Disney made a world hero of a duck. Walt Disney made world heroes of seven dwarfs. A girl named Marjorie Robertson changed her mind about a note she had scribbled in her diary a few years before, 'Saw Herbert Wilcox today about a film. Think I shall stick to the chorus.'

Cycle after cycle of films from Hollywood ran their course in the cinemas, and came back to the beginning again – the back-stage cycle, the gangster cycle, the crazy comedy cycle, the biographical cycle, the Civil War cycle, the cycle of the Young Man Who Won't Take Discipline. Al Jolson was succeeded by a different type of singer called Bing Crosby. Harpo Marx chewed up telephones. Dorothy Lamour immortalized the sarong.

Alexander Korda changed the whole face of British screen history by getting very fretful one fine spring morning, cramming his hat on his head, hugging his overcoat round him against the Easter winds, and loping out of his office into Grosvenor Street with long, angry strides. He was financially in a bad way, but he still thought big. He wanted to find some tremendous, national subject, that would find room in it for Charles Laughton, just home from Hollywood.

A taxi was coming very slowly round the corner from Davies Street; probably from Claridge's, where the more prosperous Korda was later to take up his habitation. It was the lunch-hour in Mayfair, and the streets were comparatively empty. The taxi's flag was up. The driver was singing, 'I'm 'Enery the Eighth, I'm 'Enery the Eighth, I am.'

Korda stopped dead in his tracks. 'That,' he said to himself, 'is the picture I should like to make. A picture about a king who has become so much a part of national legend that four hundred years after his death he can still come to life in a comic song.'

This may, or may not, have been the inspiration for *The Private Life of Henry VIII*. At any rate, nobody can dispute it, since nobody has evidence of the thoughts that were passing through Korda's mind as he stood on the pavement of Grosvenor Street on that keen spring morning. What matters is that *The Private Life of Henry VIII* was produced and marketed, and became the first really notable British prestige picture. It made a world-famous star of Charles Laughton; and got a Hollywood lead in *The Count of Monte Cristo* for Robert Donat, whom I first remember as a small, rather scrubby boy, riding a tricycle vigorously round the back streets of our native Manchester. It also found a husband for Merle Oberon, a dark slip of a girl who played the tiny part of Ann Boleyn. I can see her now, removing the necklace from her throat on the morning of her execution.

'Such a little neck' was her line, and almost her only line. But when she had spoken it on the set, she ran to Korda, and burst into tears on his shoulder. 'I don't know what's the matter with me, Alex,' she sobbed, 'but I do feel so miserable.' 'That's what it is to be an actress, darling,' he told her, and patted her hand very kindly. Later on he married her, as everybody knows.

Perhaps it is fair to reckon *The Private Life of Henry VIII* as the beginning of the great glamour era in film productions. Whether Korda's film was a direct cause of it or not, there was a constant coming-and-going of stars between England and America. Some of the Hollywood stars came to work here, others simply stopped in London for a night or two on their way to Paris and a Continental holiday. It was natural for a journalist to come across them all; at receptions, at studios, or by some means or another; and when people ask me, as they sometimes do, whether I have met any film stars, I am at a loss to answer, for there are so few I haven't met.

I can see Marlene Dietrich now, making a royal progress along the corridors at Denham; collecting eyes, left and right, extending a beautiful hand to be kissed by some temperamental foreign artist, indulging in conversation which consisted mainly of 'Yes' and 'No', with 'I lov to die' as the most expansive statement. I can see Myrna Loy's delightfully freckled, snub-nosed face, as she poured me breakfast coffee at some unearthly morning hour at the Savoy; and Gracie Fields' currently glowing orange head as she chatted to about forty people at once in her dressing-room at the Palladium. I remember meeting William Powell at Croydon Airport, and barely recognizing him because his skin was such a tanned leathery brown.

I remember interviewing Grace Moore at Claridge's, when she came to London to sing Mimi in *La Bohéme* at Covent Garden. What a superb *prima donna* entrance she made! A wisp of cyclamen tulle handkerchief in one hand, the right smile, the right pause, against a banked setting of what I am sure could only be described as 'floral tributes'. Nevertheless, there was no nonsense about Grace Moore. She had a heart as big as a football, and she was splendid to talk to, because her sense of business was as keen as her appreciation of art. It was she who warned me never, never to sign my name on any proffered sheet of paper, but always to demand an autograph book; the paler, the bluer the page the better, 'because then they can't

use it to extort money; oh yes, my dear, you'd never *believe*.'
I liked her very much, and I think she liked me. At all events
as I was leaving she looked round the room for some sort of
souvenir, and finally pressed on me an orchid with a stem at
least three feet long. Rarely have I been so embarrassed in the
Underground during the rush-hour.

I remember house-hunting with Rosalind Russell, who turned
out to be an expert on heating and plumbing; and looking at
snapshots of Paul Muni's dogs, which broke his heart, because
he believed them to be lonely. I remember Sabu, as a very small
boy, playing at electric trains with my even smaller boy; and the
face of a local handyman, clipping a hedge, when he suddenly
caught sight of Paulette Goddard, tottering in 4-inch-heeled
white sandals up my suburban garden path.

Then there was the never-to-be-forgotten time when Toscanini
was trampled underfoot by the ravening hordes of fans who
came to see Spencer Tracy arrive at Waterloo Station. They
didn't see Tracy, because the blinds of his coach were drawn,
and he was hurriedly taken across the rails to a standby train
and unloaded at a station farther back. But when the few of us
who were in the know reached Tracy's hotel, the poor man was
sitting on a sofa, greenish-white under his freckles, clasping a
cushion to his bosom, swaying to and fro and muttering in
genuine agony, 'I shall never live this down, never! What
shall I do? What *can* I do? I mean to say, guys can't trample
on *Toscanini*!'

Out of so many memories, another stands out clear. That was
a river trip down to Southend on *The Golden Eagle*, which had
been chartered by a British film company making a Galsworthy
story called *21 Days*, with Ralph Richardson, Laurence Olivier
and Vivien Leigh as the stars. Olivier and Vivien had only
recently met, on the set of *Fire Over England*, and were very
much in love. He was a rising stage star, who did films in a
savage, reluctant kind of way to add to his income; she was
a very young newcomer to the entertainment world, whom
few people yet took seriously. The idea was to shoot Thames
background scenes as we chugged along, but it rained and it
rained and it rained, and in the end a few of us retired into a
cabin to play rummy, or sat in the shelter of the deck and talked.

The conversation came round to *Gone With the Wind*, which
was the fashionable book of the time and Hollywood's current
casting problem. In a light-hearted way, Olivier remarked that

he had been thinking of putting in for the part of Rhett Butler. I can see Vivien now, rising to her feet, all five feet two or whatever it may be of her, quivering with excitement. She was certain of herself, and in that moment she was glorious. 'Larry,' she said, with the rain whipping against her face, 'you couldn't play Rhett, but I'm going to play Scarlett O'Hara.' He laughed at her; I laughed at her; everyone within hearing laughed at her. But she went to Hollywood and played Scarlett all the same.

These are the sort of memories that come back to me from the 1930s; impressions of a growing and flourishing film industry, busy with comings and goings across the Atlantic; of hundreds of famous faces, and hundreds of studio visits; of long talks in stars' dressing-rooms listening to grandiose plans for the future.

And then something happened in September 1939 that made us fear there would be no future for the British film industry at all.

I wonder how many people remember that in the first week of war, the Government shut down all the picture-houses in the country, for fear of air-raids? The panic measure didn't last long, but even when it became apparent that we were not going to be bombed out of existence in a single night, and the theatres reopened, there were doubts whether our studios would be able to carry on with production, in view of the increasing shortage of manpower, materials and space.

The way they did carry on, making fine pictures like *The First of the Few*, *In Which We Serve*, *The Way to the Stars*, *Henry V* and so very many others, is something it makes me proud to remember. I saw a good deal of film-making during the blitz, for at that time I was writing regular reports for a New York paper, and in an odd fashion I got to know and like the studio people better in those lean years than in all the fat years of prosperity and comfort.

As a rule, nobody paid much attention to sirens and aeroplane noises, except the sound engineers ('Aeroplane noise on Scene 25, Take 3 – shall we print it?') and the wardens, roof-spotters and fire-fighters. Every studio, of course, had its ducts or deep shelters, into which the employees were supposed to troop at the first warning. But after a time, interruptions became so frequent that people just went on with their ordinary work until they were hustled into the ducts by the roof-spotters. And even then there were rebels.

I remember one actor who invariably, in a raid, made straight for the rehearsal-room piano. Gershwin was his favourite stimulant, but he could make do quite nicely with Beethoven. Another used to sneak off to the river-bank and just sit there, watching the ducks. A third, who was a director too, always retired to his dressing-room with a pipe, taking it out of Hitler by slashing pages of his shooting schedule.

One raid I remember in particular, when the watchmen on the roof got really excited, and I myself had a sick feeling in the pit of my stomach, though I was too cowardly to say so. It was a foggy day, with planes – our own or somebody else's – constantly droning behind low cloud. The traffic police had worn their gas-masks on their chests for hours.

I was talking to Derrick de Marney about Lysistrata when the windows on to the rose-garden began to rattle. 'Guns,' said someone, jotting up accounts. 'Sixteen and eleven, one pound three and – that's a bomb – fourpence. What the blazes *is* the charge for lavenders?' There was the sound of hurrying feet in the corridors, the canteen girls giggling and jostling their way down to the shelters. Then seventeen crumps, tidily spaced in a long crescendo. Nobody said anything for a moment, then Derrick's Polish secretary, a pretty little brunette who worked with him for the Polish Government by day and helped to support her family by teaching English in the evenings, smiled brilliantly on the lot of us. 'Noisy today,' she remarked conversationally. 'I type very loud, then we don't hear.'

Somebody in the passage shouted, 'They're just overhead.' The man with the accounts observed composedly, 'That's all right then. Nothing can fall on us,' and went on totting up figures. The Polish girl burst into a fantasia on her typewriter. A little shamefaced, I suggested to Derrick that it might be a good idea to try the shelters. He looked at me in a compassionate kind of way, and said all right, but it would be very stuffy down there – and we compromised by strolling through the shelters. The canteen girls, in their white caps and aprons, were playing some form of musical chairs with the help of a portable gramophone. The electricians were busy round a dartboard. The extras, dressed that day as Gestapo men and stormtroopers, were sharing out pages of somebody's morning paper. Derrick took me by the elbow, manoeuvred me gently around a live wire, and resumed, 'As we were saying, about ⌐ysistrata –'

We came out into the open air at the far end of the studio grounds. Our fighters were streaking about the sky. Bill, the imperturbable commissionaire, was feeding cod's head to his cats. 'Bill,' said Derrick, 'the canteen's closed. You don't happen to have such a thing, do you, as a cup of coffee?' Bill said he was sorry he hadn't, but there was a drop of Scotch in his cupboard left over from Christmas, and we were welcome to it. As we strolled back across the lot, we ran into Leslie Howard. 'Hello,' he said in his vague, abstracted way, 'where's everybody? Is there an air-raid or something?'

Whenever I look back on those war days, it is Leslie Howard's vague and gentle figure I remember first. I can see him drifting about the studios now, slight and a little stooped, fair hair just turning grey, unlit pipe between his teeth, in the horn-rimmed glasses he always wore of late years off the screen, rather tired flannels and an old tweed coat. I think he was the most charming and modest actor I have ever known. His death, when the air-liner in which he was travelling from Lisbon to England was shot down by Nazi fighters, was a loss to thousands of people beyond his personal friends. He closed his career in the way he would have wished, giving no farewell performance, leaving no message except the evidence of his films, to hint at the passion he had for England and the English tradition.

I should like to end these random recollections with a picture of Leslie Howard in my mind. I know his death occurred eleven years ago. I know that the film critic of today is kept so busy disentangling the technical problems of widies and deepies, of stereophonic sound, of CinemaScope and 3-D, of pictures apparently seen through a gigantic pillar-box and pictures seen through polaroid glasses, that he has comparatively little time for anything else.

Whether or not we like them in practice, such things are exciting. They present a new challenge to ingenuity and offer new scope for experiment. If they enable the film-makers to say something new or even to say the old things in a new way, they will have served their turn in keeping brains working and the industry moving.

But for the film critic they have already served their turn. There is always a temptation for the critic who remembers the early 'flickers', the coming of colour and sound, to say wearily, 'This is where I came in.' It is true that the essence of his job has not changed. His excitement is still the struggle to distinguish good from bad, the ambitious effort that never quite comes off from the unpretentious job perfectly done.

In any profession, there is occasionally given an extra, the special prize for long years of application. That extra is the people you meet who somehow give purpose to a whole industry by their own vision and enthusiasm. When I look back on these years during which films have grown from an experiment to a colossal industry, it is the people I remember first: Leslie Howard, Alexander Korda, Carol Reed, René Clair, Alfred Hitchcock, Charlie Chaplin, Douglas Fairbanks. . . . But this is really where we came in.

II

Some History

Looking Back

An attempt to trace the development of the cinema might start with the Confucian shadow-plays, or the frescoes on the pillars of the Egyptian temples; with Aristotle, who observed that the sun shining through a square hole in a shutter cast a circular spot of light on a darkened wall, or with that contemporary of his who remarked that the whirling stone of the slinger, or the light of a rapidly swung torch, presented an apparently unbroken circle to the eye. It might start in the Middle Ages with the great Leonardo, who not only evolved the *camera obscura*, but anticipated the needs of emotional film stars by having an orchestra play to his lady sitters. Or it might start in 1640 with that Athanasius Kircher, whose preview of the first magic lantern performance – starring the Devil – was attended by all the nobility and intelligentsia of Rome.

It will be simpler, however, to start in 1896, the year in which Edison's Vitascope was the novelty of New York; Paul's Theatrograph was drawing the crowds to the London music hall, and Lumière's Cinematographe had carried the new thrill of the Paris boulevards as far afield as Budapest and Vienna.

There are several advantages in choosing this date as a starting point. For one thing, it is a very logical starting-point, being the first year in which large numbers of people could enjoy the new wonder – photographed and projected pictures that gave the illusion of movement. For another thing, it obviates the necessity of discussing who really 'invented' the cinema. This is admirable, since the point has never been satisfactorily decided anyway. Taking our stand firmly on the year 1896, we can turn our backs on generations of litigation and experiment; on traumatrope, stroboscope, fantascope, daedalum, zoetrope, kinematoscope, phasmatrope, zooprazoscope, and other heathenish titles. We need not seek to determine how far the course of the cinema was affected by a millionaire's bet that a horse, when running, takes all its feet off the ground together. Most satisfactory of all, we shall not be involved in any disputes over national priority. It is all one to us whether Edison got in first, or Lumière or Latham or Paul or Muybridge, or whether, as is so persistently claimed by his adherents, Friese-Greene got in ahead of all of them. So far as we are concerned, the honour may go to the United States, to France, or to England.

Let us start then, with 1896, and see how the film had developed from those first flickering, two-minute reels to the four-hour marathon *Gone With the Wind*. Let us create, for our guidance, an exceptionally gifted observer, whose memory not only serves him accurately for the details of forty years ago, but whose judgment is at no time impaired by the enthusiasm of youth and novelty. I, for example, should be useless as an observer of this type. All my early memories of the cinema are so coloured by excitement that I can barely see them for rosy shimmer. Some part of my mind is still convinced that Mary Pickford was the greatest actress in the world, that God never created a more handsome man that John Barrymore in his youth, and that a certain pulsating drama in two reels, *The Heart of a Child*, was as long and rewarding as a Eugene O'Neill play. Our appointed observer will have no delusions of this sort. Swayed neither by youth nor age, he will see things constantly as they are. His province is simply to record. And for the moment, it will be convenient to let him record facts, to trace the course of the cinema as an aspect of twentieth century public life, without lingering too long over the significant moments, or scrutinizing it too closely as an art form.

For nearly seven years our observer would have had to content himself with short trick films, incidents and newsreels; trips to the moon and men sawn in half by auto-cars; a train arriving in a station: the view from a travelling observation car; pictorial puns like 'How Bridget Served the Salad Undressed'; domestic crises such as 'The Pretty Stenographer, or Caught in the Act.'

By 1903 he might well be wondering, along with a number of his contemporaries, whether this new fad of moving pictures were going to last. It had been conclusively demonstrated by this time that still photographs, taken and projected at the rate of sixteen pictures a second, give the illusion of movement on the screen. Nobody doubted it any more. The novelty of the trick had worn off. Few people now screamed when an engine seemed to rush out at them from the screen. In Paris, one writer tells us, 'the estate of the cinema was so low at the time that movies were shown free at little cafés as an inducement to the patrons to sit longer and drink more.' In England and America the 'bioscope' had sunk to the position of last turn in the music-hall bills. In many variety programmes the film was deliberately used as a 'chaser', to drive out the audience and clear the house before the next show.

Our observer, being a man of good sense, must have asked himself, about this time: Has the cinematograph now done all it is able to do? Having photographed events so that they looked 'real', and played tricks with facts so that they looked 'magical', has it fulfilled and exhausted its possibilities as a medium? And just as he was entertaining these thoughts, along came the answer. It was called *The Great Train Robbery*, and although it ran for less than ten minutes, it changed the whole trend of criticism and ensured the future of the cinema. It is an absurd work by modern standards. It is as obsolete as the first bi-plane, as funny as the first locomotive. But it set the course of the motion picture for the next twenty-five years. It had a complete story and suddenly, in a whirl of excitement, the public became aware of the possibilities of the camera as a yarn-spinner. To the discerning it became obvious for the first time that the camera could select and emphasize, that it could present drama with greater freedom than the theatre, and point a story with a vividness independent of the spoken word.

True, the 'topical' survived, though the trick film gradually dwindled, but the great majority of films took the short story form, had a fictitious romance, and resorted, whenever they could, to the chase motif. Round about 1906, the observer might have seen his first crude colour film, and for several years after that colour pieces, of a sort, were a frequent item in the programmes.

The cinema was definitely out of the chaser class now. It was a new cult, and it had its own temples. By 1911 there were 4,000 'picture palaces' in England. Quite respectable people were known to go to the films, not just the young, and those who skylarked on bicycles. Such distinguished actors as Sir Herbert Tree, Mr H. B. Irving, Mr Frank Benson and Mme Réjane agreed to entrust a few moments of their art to what they ironically considered to be imperishable celluloid. Mme Sarah Bernhardt was advertised as saying of her three-reel *Dame aux Camélias* 'I rely upon these films to make me immortal.'

'Those who are not familiar with the picture theatres may hardly believe it,' writes one of the first film 'critics' at about this period, 'but the spectators in those places have their "stars"

just as the playgoers at the fashionable London theatres have.'
There was G. M. Anderson, the 'Westerner' who had never, it
is said, sat a horse before he went into cowboy pictures; cowgirl
Alice Joyce; romantic Florence Lawrence; funny Max Linder;
Arthur Johnson ('the Lewis Waller of the Picture Palaces'), the
English Tilly Girls, Alma Taylor and Chrissie White; two-gun
Bill Hart; golden Mary Pickford, newly-emerged from her
anonymity as the Biograph Girl; these favourites and others
won our adoration. Some of them, it was rumoured, earned as
much as £50 a week for doing just this.

I promised that our observer would be impartial, yet already
I note in him a regrettable tendency to linger over these early
days. This will not do at all. Events are moving fast, and we
shall have to hurry to keep up with them. For some years,
long historical pictures – fabulous films that take an hour, or
an hour and a half to show – have been coming across the
Channel from France and Italy. The great d'Annunzio himself
has written film scenarios. Now the fashion for longer films has
caught on in Hollywood, that mushroom estate of California to
which the industry, driven west, some say, by patent troubles,
has flitted. Fired by the Bernhardt *Queen Elizabeth* Hollywood
has conceived the idea of presenting Famous Players in Famous
Plays. A company has even been formed to incorporate that
idea.

The year 1912 may be taken as the starting-point of the
'feature' film. From that time on, no programme was complete
without its full-length drama. The slapstick comedies, the
topicals, the new-fashioned serials, added relish to the bill. Just
round the corner, less than a year off, with the irony that has
attended the whole course of the cinema, was the greatest genius
for pocket comedy – the little fellow with the baggy trousers
and the Derby hat – that the screen has ever known. But the
'big film' had become the *pièce de résistance*, and has remained so
from that day.

Came the War, as the sub-titles would have had it in black
letters on a white ground, or, more artistically, in flaming
letters on a black ground. Came four years of resolute
escapist entertainment. Pasteboard effigies of Charlie flirted
a gay cane outside the picture palaces. Signed photographs
of Mary Pickford, the World's Sweetheart, smiled down from
the walls of countless dugouts. The serial *Exploits of Elaine* and
The Perils of Pauline succeeded *The Adventures of Kathlyn* and

drew us weekly to the cinemas. An athletic young man named Douglas Fairbanks horrified the producers, and delighted the public, by his tendency to flout the script by leaping from walls and vaulting fences. A conscientious young woman named Theodosia Goodman appeared in a film called *A Fool There Was*, adopted the pseudonym of Theda Bara and obligingly posed for still photographers cross-legged, tearing her hair, above a skull and crossbones. The adolescent world thrilled in delicious horror to the advent of the first vamp.

These films were easy to take, but one tougher figure emerged from the war years. That was the director, D. W. Griffith, who startled the world in 1916 with *The Birth of a Nation*, and a year later with the unwieldy, unpredictable, unprecedented *Intolerance*. This fellow not only made longer films than anyone else, films so long and ambitious that they had to be shown at special performances, but he played tricks with narrative style that had not been rivalled in impudence since *The Great Train Robbery*. He thrust close-ups under people's noses. His pictorial chords jarred as Scriabin's music was to jar on a later generation. He broke up his story into parallel plots, and declared that he got the idea from Dickens. In more ways than one, he played the Dickens with routine.

We have brought our observer to the end of the war, and the next years were prosperous and eventful ones. The cinema, as a social institution, was settled in. Super-luxury palaces, neon lights and Mighty Wurlitzers added comfort, if not always distinction, to the filmgoer's lot. An orgy of affluence pervaded the Hollywood scene. Cecil de Mille indulged in his bath-tub epics. Eleanor Glyn endorsed It. A young dancer from the Argentine named Valentino made a film called *The Four Horsemen of the Apocalypse* and the world had found its Dream Lover.

Flaherty discovered the Eskimoes with *Nanook of the North*, and James Cruze discovered the golden west with *The Covered Wagon*. Erich von Stroheim, The Man You Love to Hate, shocked a delighted public with *Foolish Wives*. Fairbanks anticipated Tarzan with his Robin Hood. Danton rode cowboy saddle to the rescue of the Orphans of the Storm.

Meanwhile continental Europe, too, was on the verge of a screen renaissance. First Sweden, comparatively untouched by war, began to send its charming, cultured pictures over-seas. It was not long before the best Swedish directors and players

followed their films. Victor Sjöstrom made *The Secret of the
Monastery*, *My Soul Shall Bear Witness*, *A Lover in Pawn*, *The
Dawn of Love* and *Love's Crucible*, and went to Hollywood.
Mauritz Stiller made *The Atonement of Gösta Berling* and went
to Hollywood too. So did Lars Hanson, the star of *Gösta Berling*,
and a young girl in the cast, a certain Greta Garbo. Miss Garbo's
chances were considered less promising than those of the other
three, but it was hoped that her good looks, combined with a
certain acting ability, would ensure her a reasonable career.

With the exodus of her best film-minds, Sweden's short day
seemed over. But now Germany, turning hungrily to art for
refreshment and rebirth, was making film after film that teased,
and enchanted, and held the imagination. It was the golden age
of legend, history, and fantasy. A list of the German films of
the early and middle twenties is as rich as a list of Elizabethan
literature. Let our observer, if he has cultivated the useful habit
of making notes, turn up his diary for 1923, for example. He
will find that in that year he saw *The Loves of Pharoah*, *Danton*,
The Golem, *Sumurun*, *Caligari*, *Dr Mabuse* and *Destiny*. With
justification he might call it the German year.

Events pressed close on one another in the middle Twenties.
No sooner had the German film come up, than the French film
followed. Indeed, the dates overlap here to a certain extent.
Even before the great German films were on their way across
the Channel, a Belgian director, Jacques Feyder, working in
France, had startled us with a film called *L'Atlantide*. Feyder had
followed this up with *Crainquebille*, Poirier and L'Herbier had
experimented with the new expressionism, Ivan Mosjoukine
had appeared in *Kean*, before the year 1925, when a fantasy
called *The Crazy Ray* introduced the name of René Clair to
London. Our observer, being a smart man, will have noted this
name at once, and scribbled it down in his diary.

Since he is also, we assume, a typical Briton, and not in the
habit of flitting over to Moscow for his summer holidays, our
observer is unlikely to have been aware of another significant
film that was made in the year 1925 – a work called *Potemkin*
by the Soviet director Eisenstein. He could not observe what
he might not see, and it is almost certain that the panic policy
of our censorship kept him ignorant for several years of the
tremendous events that were taking place in the studios of the
USSR. It was quite late in the Twenties before the first Soviet
films began to creep into this country by devious ways. And by

that time our observer had other things to think about, for the talkies had come from Hollywood, and the film industry was changed overnight.

So hazy is memory for the events of fifteen years ago, and so many wild guesses are made as to the priority of early sound-films, that a few dates might be in order here. Talkies of a sort, of course, had always been with us. Way back in the last century Edison had designed his peepshow kinetoscope as an adjunct to the phonograph. All through the history of silent films, inventors had played periodically with the idea of films that talked. We were invited to demonstrations of this startling patent and that revolutionary device. We saw men stand up on the screen and heard them utter recognizable sounds. But it was not until the end of the first quarter of a century, not indeed, until the force of post-war American production had spent itself, and the producers needed some novelty to hold the waning enthusiasm of the public, that experiment with sound was taken seriously.

In the summer of 1926, the first full-length film with a synchronized sound and music score was shown in New York. It was *Don Juan*, with John Barrymore. Early in 1928 the sound-track, recording a song of Al Jolson's in the largely silent *Jazz Singer*, picked up by accident a phrase of impromptu dialogue. The producers, excited, left it in the finished picture. To *The Jazz Singer*, therefore, must go the credit of being the first film with a dialogue sequence. Later in the same year came the first feature-length, all-talking picture. The star was Helene Costello, and the film *The Lights of New York*.

In England *The Lights of New York* missed being the pioneer talkie by about a fortnight. A dialogue version of Edgar Wallace's thriller, *The Terror*, got across the Atlantic first, or at least got first into the cinemas. The date was October 1928. Down at Savoy Hill the BBC engineers were trying out the first broadcasts of television pictures. The transatlantic cable had been disturbed by an aurora borealis. Smart women were wearing coal-scuttle hats and waists round the hips.

Leading members of the film trade and prominent intellectuals united for the first time in greeting this Thing, the talk-film, with contumely. The film folk said it was a fad that wouldn't last. The highbrows, who were but lately denouncing the cinema as something in its infancy, insisted that sound had destroyed the international art of pantomime. They too hoped it wouldn't last. But it did last. Within a few weeks *The Terror* was followed by *The Lights of New York*, *The Melody of Love*, and Al Jolson's phenomenally successful 'weepie', *The Singing Fool*. Our observer, if he were the type to adopt such homely metaphors, must have felt as though he were watching steam escape from a nearly-boiling kettle. Every minute the jet grew stronger. Nothing could stop it. The whole industry was coming to the boil.

Painful though it was, studios all over the world had to scrap their existent machinery and install sound-proof floors and recording apparatus. Theatres were reluctantly but inevitably equipped with sound. Sometimes the sound was awful, as we can recall. Silent films in production were junked, or brought up to date with dialogue sequences. Stars who couldn't talk went out, and actors who could talk, or at least talk better, came in. In their zeal to show off the new medium, everyone talked far too much. But even when the novelty wore off, the medium stuck. By 1930 the silent film was practically obsolete.

To the generation just grown up, the word 'film' and the word 'talkie' have always been synonymous, but to our observer, the twelve years of sound form only a short watch in the long survey of the cinema. These last twelve years – uneasy, threatening years – on the whole have brought the cinema curiously little change. There have been technical improvements, naturally; refinements of sound, a marked development in the use of Technicolor, and various individual talents; but little that is comparable in historical importance with the formulae of D. W. Griffith, the European renaissance of the Twenties, and the actual change-over from silent films to talkies. Once the fact of talk was established, the form of the talkie for the next decade was indicated.

The language barrier has, no doubt, to a certain extent, conditioned the national interchange of films. No device yet discovered, neither superimposed titles nor dubbing, has made a film recorded in one tongue entirely acceptable to people of another. But the market for continental films in this country was always specialized, and even the silent French and German films of the Twenties had only a limited British distribution. More marked, perhaps, is the effect of politics on modern film programmes. It is not hard to understand, for instance, why we have seen few German films since the first gay musicals. The war, not the language, has put a period to the intelligent product of the French studios. The war, too, has given official status to the Soviet talkie, and imposed on the British documentary an importance that is sometimes beyond its modest powers.

But our observer, paying his weekly visit to the pictures, is not likely to have been troubled much by these considerations. What he has seen, in peace and war, is twelve years of technically-improving talkies; influenced in setting by the affairs and fads of the world outside, but changing very little in essential story-content. He has watched the rise of Disney, from his first black-and-white cartoon in 1928 – *Steamboat Willie* – to the Technicolor triumph of his *Fantasia*. He has noted the revival of British films, and dated it, approximately, from Korda's *Private Life of Henry VIII* in the middle Thirties. He has seen cycle after cycle of films run their course from America – the gangster cycle, the back-stage cycle, the crazy comedy cycle, the biographical cycle. He has followed the course of the stars from Al Jolson to Dorothy Lamour. He has joined in talk about John Ford and Preston Sturges, Orson Welles and Noel Coward, and un-doubtedly had his say about *Gone With the Wind* and *Mrs Miniver*. He has seen film stars mobbed by admiring crowds, and heard them speak their little pieces on the air. He has watched the screen, which had glorified show-girls, pioneers, marines, foot-ball stars and Men in White, spring with an equal zest to the glorification of democracy. Today, on the eve of 1943, he is just a little weary, perhaps, of films about the war. But he is aware, for he is a wise observer and has seen a great many changes in his time, that this is only a passing phase, a mere paragraph to the historian of the 1960s. His study must stop here, on a moment of transition, for he is not prescient.

January 1943

Collectors' Pieces

Each successive generation is inclined to think of its contemporary idiom as an advance on what has gone before, the first tide to sweep over virgin sands. In fact, it is thousands of years since the sands were virgin. They have been embraced by wave after wave in the longest and most fertile courtship in history. Everything that is created by this embrace has been created before in the same image, and will continue to be created.

Today we talk as if the cinema had suddenly sprung to life in the late 1950s, with films such as *Hiroshima, Mon Amour*. But we were talking in just the same way about the cinema in the early 1920s, with the arrival of the first post-war films from Germany and France, and with as much justification. Something exhilarating had happened. A fresh wind was blowing from the continent, and we relished the vigour in the air.

Up to this time the Swedish films had been the best in Europe. We didn't see them very often, for the Swedish export has never been abundant and the British market never markedly responsive.

But the few films from Sweden that were shown have become collectors' pieces. The people who hunt down the Ingmar Bergman films today are sons and grandsons of the people who once hunted down the Victor Sjöstrom pictures of the early Twenties: *Thy Soul Shall Bear Witness*, *A Lover in Pawn*, *Love's Crucible*, *The Dawn of Love*, *The Secret of the Monastery*; and, perhaps the most prized collectors' piece of all, Stiller's film *The Atonement of Gösta Berling*, which introduced a new girl by the name of Greta Garbo. The critics considered she was immature but promised well.

The Swedish films borrowed a great deal from literature, but went for their expression to a technique clear of literary idiom, in which the eye and curiously the sense of touch were equally involved.

Watching those old silent pictures, we almost felt under our fingers the texture of velvet and satin and lace. Our feet used to sense the roughness of the cobblestones in the courtyard. The old wood of the beams was warm to the touch and grained.

The candlelight, too, the thin sunlight, the deep, strong shadows, had an almost tangible quality. We felt the light as a physical experience, caught the chill of dark entries. Inanimate objects, as well as growing things, were invested with a secret life. They were characters in every drama.

With the Scandinavians, as with few other creative people, we get a vivid sense of private life in every stick and stone. Much of it, in films, is due to a masterly trick of photography and lighting. We get it in all the Ingmar Bergman pictures; morning light slanting through spring woods; evening mists along the harbour front. We got it in the opening sequence of Arne Sücksdorf's *The Great Adventure*, showing the beginning of a new day on the fringes of a forest.

The old personification of the elements has never left the Scandinavian mind entirely. Wind, wood and water are still alive and intimate; often more articulate than the human characters. We find a touch of this in the writing of Selma Lägerlof and Sigrid Undset. We find it in the craftsmanship of Swedish textiles. It is something indigenous, out of time and indestructible.

The Swedish cinema has always been a thing apart. It seems to be wholly uninfluenced by, and unconcerned to influence, the work of other countries. Sjöstrom, Stiller and Garbo left home for Hollywood in the early 1920s, and for more than a quarter of a century we were to hear practically nothing about Swedish pictures. The loss, however, made no perceptible impression on the course of cinema history.

Potent forces were at work in Europe. Both Germany and France were suddenly awake to the opportunities of the film medium. It was an uprush as irresistible as the thrust of spring, and an exciting time to be a critic. There was something fascinating to write about almost every week, something stimulating to look at almost any day.

Germany in particular, turning hungrily to art for refreshment and rebirth after the First World War, was making film after film that teased and captured the imagination.

My first intimation of the German riches came on a day when I was invited to an underground theatre in Wardour Street to watch 135 reels of *Dr Mabuse*, and advise whether they could be cut in such a way as to make a single feature film for British exhibition.

I realize now that the little man who showed them to me had no interest in my advice at all. He was simply interested in getting a gullible young woman to himself for something

like nine hours in a dark, private theatre. He made a number
of half-hearted passes which I was too much engrossed by
Fritz Lang's startling film to notice. When they became a
nuisance I got up and moved to a seat directly in the shaft of
light from the projector. By this time I had learnt something
of the art of self-defence in Wardour Street. It must have been
a disappointment to the little man, who was not, I learnt
later, accustomed to rebuff by unattached young females. At
all events, he went away and left me with the picture, which
struck me as one of the most exciting things I'd ever seen.
I suppose I am one of the very few people in this country
who had the chance to watch the original, uncut version of
Dr Mabuse.

The German films were not shown widely, but they created a
stir wherever they *were* shown. For the first time we heard the
names of Lang and Lubitsch, Emil Jannings and Conrad Veidt.
This was the golden age of myth and legend; of *Siegfried*, *The
Golem*, *Destiny*, *The Student of Prague*, *The Street* and *Warning
Shadows*.

Nothing could have been farther removed from the demands
of modern fashion, which call for an anti-hero, anti-spectacle
and no plot.

If one film only could be picked to represent the German
movement of the period I suppose it would be *The Cabinet
of Dr Caligari*, which had been made by Robert Wiene and
a number of theatre people – writers, painters, architects,
photographers – who called themselves the Stürm Group.
These people, were awowed disciples of *expressionismus*, and
Caligari was their testament.

I almost understood what the word meant as I watched the
picture. In fact, it seemed so obvious that I felt I must have
missed some subtlety.

Caligari was the expression of a world seen through the eyes
of a madman. When he walked down a street the houses tilted
together above his head, the roofs nudged one another and
conspired to crush him. Everyone he met looked mad and
menacing. Light was blinding. Darkness was sinister.

Eventually he took these symptoms to a doctor – the first
psychiatrist, to the best of my knowledge, to make an appearance
in screen fiction. I can't remember now what ailed the victim,
nor whether it was ever clearly stated, but I do know that the
doctor's treatment proved successful, and by the end his patient

was able to see the world just as straight as you and I do, who are presumably sane.

Wiene's film was produced in 1919, but failed to reach either England or America for several years. When at last it did arrive it caused no particular commotion in the theatres. By that time the public was licking its lips over a spectacular item from Hollywood called *Foolish Wives*, directed and played by a certain Erich von Stroheim, who was credited with drinking ox-blood as an appetizer for breakfast and billed on all the sandwich boards as 'The Man You Love To Hate'.

Caligari, however, was to have a marked effect on studio techniques. It suggested a new line in camera work. Its huddled roofs were the forerunners of Orson Welles' ceilings in *Citizen Kane*.

Psychiatry was sweeping into fashion. Before long it would seem abnormal to be normal. A tilted camera shot, with walls askew, roofs narrowing to form a funnel, could mean something solemnly significant; return to the womb, pre-natal experience, mother fixation and all that. Even if it meant nothing it *looked* suggestive; it made an impression on the audience. Wiene's film, so precisely wrought for its own purpose, was the innocent cause of some of the most vexatious tricks in movies. Even today directors are inclined to tilt their shots to draw attention to them when they haven't the wit to think of anything more sensible to do.

1963

Talking Stars

The showing of **The Terror** in London has finally brought to a head all surmise about the value of talking pictures. For years we have been guessing what it would be like if films talked. Now we have one that really does talk. Not a mere snippet of synchronized music and photography, not a single speech, an isolated programme turn, but a full-length film in which the characters speak their lines, threaten and confide in the audience, disclosing their own natural voices and voice mannerisms just as though they were figures of flesh and blood.

In face of *The Terror* it is futile to argue that, for this, that, or the other reason, talking pictures cannot be a success. We may not want them to be a success. We may regard them as a menace both to the theatre and to the screen. We may deplore limitations of language for the hitherto universal cinema. We may dread the invasion of more sound into an already rowdy world. But to condemn *The Terror* and through *The Terror* all talking pictures, for these reasons is mere prejudice. *The Terror* may be crude, but it is a maker of history. Something has been achieved here. A new chapter of film evolution is beginning. Today it is as foolish to argue that talking films cannot be successful as to declare that a man in London cannot possibly speak by telephone to a man in New York.

The question that really concerns us is not, will the talkies come, but can the talkies last? Apparently the production heads of the industry think so, and they are not given to fantastic ideal. Nearly all the big studios today are busy making talkies. Universal has equipped its key theatres in London and Manchester with apparatus for complete sound programmes. Christie Comedies are planning thirty-two short talking pictures at the Metropolitan Studios, where a new sound stage is being constructed. Cecil de Mille's first picture for Metro-Goldwyn will be a talkie. Warner Brothers are signing up the big stage stars for Vitaphone, and *The Terror* is only the first of a continuous series of sound films. Paramount is making, amongst many others, all talking versions of *The Letter*, *Interference*, and *Half an Hour*. Universal has already nine or ten talking films ready to show here, and many ambitious productions, including *Show Boat*, in preparation for

1929. Chaplin and Harold Lloyd are said to be planning to make talking comedies, and the H.M.V. Gramophone Company to be preparing to make records for Vitaphone. Altogether, in less than six months, the talking picture has not only established itself firmly in the studios, but monopolized most of the interest of producers and promoters of films.

I cannot believe that the hard-headed gentlemen at the back of the industry have accepted the talking picture from mere love of progress. They have accepted it, surely, because they know their public, and can see in the talkies an extension of the very qualities that have made the silent films an entertainment for the masses. The root attraction of the cinema, the thing that has brought it big money and protected it against all criticism, is its salesmanship of personality. Some of us no doubt go to the cinema to see beautiful scenery, some to find art in movement, some to be educated, and some to be mystified and thrilled, but the great majority pay to see one man or woman on the screen, to see him or her as often as possible, as big as possible, in as many emotional situations as the story will allow. We buy stars, in fact, and hug the delusion that in the shadow we meet the real man. Add to the shadow the echo, to the figure the voice, and the delusion is complete. I do not in the least believe that defects in the voice, twangs, burrs, flatness of tone, will shake the allegiance of the average picture-goer. We bear with these things on the stage, on the gramophone, and even find them odd and attractive. At any rate, these individualities will invest the speaker with life, and I cannot think that, once having heard the voice, we shall ever be satisfied with the dumb figures of our favourites again.

The talkies can give, cheaply, comfortably, and easily the things we find most entertaining in the cinema, with the addition of much that we find entertaining on the stage. They are the logical outcome and perfection of the star system, presenting the star from every emotional angle, in an abundance of settings impossible in the theatre, duplicating and multiplying him. They are not art, any more than the average silent film is art. They are not, without colour and stereoscopy, even a perfect example of the reproductive machine. But they do give the people who want to buy personality better value for money, and this fact alone is enough to ensure for them prosperity and long life.

4 November 1928

Britain versus Hollywood

It is a modern cliché of our native film journalism to talk about the British film as a direct menace to Hollywood, and to advertise our home studios as the potential centre of the world's cinema trade. With the recent introduction of our larger films to America this sort of talk has gone to absurd lengths. Actually there is very little chance, at least in our lifetime, that the mastery of America's most representative industry will ever go out of the hands of America. Any other view, however warming to a British heart, is merely the result of astigmatic observation.

There is this to be said for our national optimists. The British film industry, at this juncture, is undoubtedly on the upgrade of prosperity. Our films are enjoying wider markets, our producers embracing wider projects than at any other time in their history. Thanks to the protection of the Board of Trade and to the world-wide prestige of the pictures issued recently under the Korda trade-mark, the British film has escaped the fate of some of the less happy continental neighbours. It is not only on its feet, but definitely coming on. So far the optimists are justified.

Those of us who operate with Fleet Street and Wardour Street as our two centres, taking periodic trips to the studios at Elstree, Ealing, Shepherd's Bush, and elsewhere, watching the quota of British films in the local theatres creep from an official 15 per cent to 20, from 20 per cent to 23, with a voluntary exhibitor's quota of a minimum 20 per cent British, may very well be forgiven for thinking that the British film is the chosen entertainment of the world. Every circumstance of native production and exhibition is directed towards strengthening of that belief. We learn of the vast sums expended on productions such as *Jew Süss* and *The Iron Duke*, and what is more, we know that the sums mentioned frequently err on the side, not of exaggeration, but of under-statement. We are told authoritatively, and generally accurately, of the princely salaries paid by British firms to American film stars and technicians. We attend 'charity premières' of our new pictures with all the pomp of a high society gathering, and not infrequently under royal or semi-royal patronage.

But if the British film trade of today is more or less prosperous it must be remembered that it is a highly protected industry. Largely through the means of the Quota Act it has been able to reach the saturation point of its home market, and it is now occupied in making a bid for further markets overseas. England is no longer, as it used to be, an unconsidered centre of film production, but rather a Monte Cristo to the American film star or technician in search of quick money.

So much I will concede to the patriot who believes in the new supremacy of British pictures. Things certainly look well in Wardour Street for the first time since the war. There is a spurious air of ease, of security, of well-being over the whole industry that might well fool anybody who is patriotically eager to be fooled. Films are no longer the Cinderellas of entertainment. Lady So-and-so periodically visits the local studio while the younger sons of the peerage are engaged as camera assistants or in the cutting rooms. We have, too, a severely classical organization known as the British Film Institute. We have a Films Unit of the Post Office, and a Films Section of the Federation of British Industries. Most comforting of all to an honest British heart, with three more years of the quota to run our national theatres are filling their quota of British films and in many cases exceeding it, while the products of Shepherd's Bush and Elstree are beginning to appear with a fair regularity on American screens.

But there is another side to the matter. For nearly half a century America has been steadily building up a motion picture industry, pouring money into it, buying brains for it, cornering markets, acquiring patents, and accumulating personal assets, until it has assumed the rank of the fourth largest industry in the United States.

From the eight major and the innumerable minor companies in Hollywood, an average of 600 'feature' pictures emerges yearly. At a very modest estimate, the average cost of each of these is £30,000. This means that every year at least £18,000,000 is sunk in the negative costs alone of American feature films. If to this is added the exploitation costs of these pictures, it is probably safe to say that the annual capital expenditure of the American motion picture industry is not less than £25,000,000.

And this stupendous figure takes no account of short films, whether cartoons, comedies, dramas, travel films, newsreels, or definitely educational subjects. If you want an exact picture of the activity always going on in American studios, no fewer

than forty-two feature pictures were being made during the
last week in January of this year. Against this, even with rosy
optimism, we can estimate our annual capital expenditure on
feature pictures in this country at not more than £2,000,000,
representing approximately one hundred feature films from our
half-dozen major companies.

Every week in every district in England there are four new
feature films exhibited. Even with the quota operating at the
full, three of these features will be American. It is perfectly
simple, even in these days of protection, for an Englishman to
go regularly once a week to the cinema without ever seeing an
English film. The plain fact is that England's output of films,
in spite of political protection and industrial development, is
still only a pinpoint in the international cinema. Hollywood is
today, and seems likely to remain, in spite of all disabilities,
the best factory of the film industry, and American distribution
companies will continue to be the major film sales agencies of
the world.

One would like to think that this is only a temporary
distribution of power, which we shall rectify as our studios
mature and our financial assets increase. Possibly the insidious
American propaganda of the screen has warped my judgement,
but I am prepared to take my stand on the continued superiority
of America as a film-producing country. I believe that this
particular industry, so typical a product of the western
civilization of today, will remain an American monopoly just
as long as the Americans are interested to keep it. An industry
that could survive the blow delivered to it in 1929, when the
advent of the sound film destroyed all its plans and nullified
its assets in a single night, and the specialization of language
knocked nine-tenths of its foreign markets clean from under
it, is not going to be outstripped in a straight industrial race by
England, France, Germany or any other European competitor.

Film-making in America is neither an art nor a pastime. It is
a business. The making and selling of films is as organized an
industry as the making and selling of motor cars, razor blades,
vacuum cleaners or cigarettes. If anything, the marketing of
films is taken more seriously by the authorities than the activities
of these other industries, because the film as a commodity serves
two purposes – it sells itself, and at the same time it sells a
number of other home products by indirect advertisement on
the screen.

There is a significant paragraph in Ludwell Denny's book, *America Conquers Britain*, which deals with this aspect of the cinema.

Part of the rapid Americanization of world markets [he writes] has resulted nor so much from direct publicity and sales pressure as from the indirect advertising value of Hollywood films. Some estimates place the number of American films shown as high as 90 per cent. of the total. The effect on the foreign audiences is obvious; a taste and demand is created for the kind of automobile used by the motion picture star, or the style of shoes worn, or the plumbing fixtures displayed. Reports of American consuls are almost unanimous in citing this as a major stimulant of foreign trade, especially in the new industries. Foreign companies and governments are even more impressed by this form of indirect Yankee trade propaganda. Naturally they interpret the commercial penetration as a cultural and political menace.

With this justification Britain and eight other governments have passed discriminatory laws and regulations against American films, usually putting the Hollywood product on a quota basis. Popular demand abroad, however, has prevented any large scale elimination of American films.

There is no question as to the accuracy of this view of the widespread influence of the American film. Go where you please, in any city of the world, and you will see women emulating the make-up and hairdressing styles of Greta Garbo; young men dressed in the George Raft tailoring cut, shop windows advertising the soap used by Claudette Colbert, or the cosmetics favoured by Mae West, while dashing young continentals greet you with the hand–salute of Gary Cooper.

Continuing the lyrical, but unquestionably well-founded argument of *America Conquers Britain*, we find this extract from the National Geographic Society's *Bulletin*:

American movies, automobiles, dental schools, typewriters, phonographs, and even its prize fights lead in spreading American fashions and customs throughout the world. The excellence of dental schools in the United States attracts students from all over the world, who return to their people as ambassadors of the fine old American custom of brushing teeth. Typewriters have pioneered the way for a whole battalion of office equipment devices which have converted many peoples to doing business according to American methods. As long as the U.S. remained a raw products source, selling only cotton, corn, wheat, copper, and oil, the world went its own way. That way was to follow French fashions in women's clothes, jewellery and perfume, practice trade by English methods, and to look to Germany for science and music. But American invention and mass production have turned the United States into a manufacturing and distributing nation.

Although the motion picture industry is not directly specified in all these cases as the ambassador of commerce, there is not the least doubt that America's film trade has done a great deal more for its country than amuse and educate several million people for twelve hours a day. It has become so much a part of the lives of countless people, black, white and yellow, that it is going to take a great many generations and a vast revolution in technical achievement to eradicate it. Those of us who read a little, hear good music sometimes and look at 'real' pictures occasionally, can hardly appreciate fully what those other pictures, the movies, represent in the lives of the great multitude of people of every race. Once, or even twice or three times a week in England and America, a little less frequently in other countries, the average man or woman goes to the cinema, to get there the romance and relaxation, the excitement and the laughter that they cannot find in everyday life . . .

As a wise film executive once said to me: 'The American film is a luxury cruise.' It gives us just the holiday lift that helps us to get on with our workaday life better, and for that reason, if for no other, it will continue to be the dominating feature of the motion picture screen. Against this deep-seated, psychological and, it must be noted, entirely voluntary preference, the British film industry shows few signs of being operative.

No one will profit, least of all the members of the industry, by burking the present situation. We are, at the moment, enjoying the fruits of professional tariffs, and at the same time profiting in our own theatres by America's temporary disability to meet the demands of modified English speech. But this harvest festival will pass. In three years time the Quota Act expires, and unless some form of modified protection is adopted by the government, British films will have to win their place in the open market by sheer competitive merit. At the same time America, never a slow learner, is rapidly modifying the dialect of Hollywood into something approaching a standard international tongue.

I can see only two courses for us to pursue if we are anxious to enter our film trade in the race for national honours. We must either reorganize our present cinema from top to bottom, replacing the vast majority of the personnel and developing along the lines indicated by quarter of a century of American experience; or we must jump ahead and supersede the existent cinema by some new form of entertainment. Our best chance, I imagine, is to concentrate on colour, on stereoscopy, or on television, and to organize quickly along these lines of development before the pioneer genius of our transatlantic cousins has staked out every profitable claim.

March 1935

Looking In

For four days last week the television people, who have already made tours of the Pinewood and Denham studios, took their cameras to record the doings at Elstree. I sat in an armchair, by my own fire, on some of England's beastlier November days, and watched them. As a professional studio-snooper, I appreciated the chance to do my job vicariously. But beyond that I found the experience the most exhilarating thing that has happened to me since I sat in the old Piccadilly Theatre nine years ago and heard the screen crackle and boom out its first full-length soundtrack. I wondered how many picturegoers in England were sharing the fun.

I am not a technical writer. I cannot tell you just why that particular broadcast was clearer than the other studio broadcasts – why it came over sharp and undisturbed, without electrical interference from the studios' big dynamos. All I can tell you is that as the image of a studio's spirit it was brilliant. The life of the film-making world was there, restless, turbulent, hard-driving, superficially chaotic. We watched films shot on the floor, we watched the day's rushes; we spied on camera tests, we snooped into the extras' dressing-rooms, and listened to their backchat. We met the people who make the films, and the people who are made by the people who make them. A writer would have given his soul to create an atmosphere half so clear.

When the last broadcast was over I sat back and thought about what I had just seen, with a great deal of wonder and some disquietude. Television, I thought, has given the cinema the widest opportunity and the finest publicity medium ever invented. What is the film trade doing to recognize it? With a few honourable exceptions, nothing at all.

The cinema today is terrified of television. You see evidences of that terror in every evasion, every refusal to cooperate. With few exceptions, contract artists of the big American studios are barred from making television appearances. The use of film for television is made, not impossible, but very, very difficult. The way to an understanding is beset with delays, equivocations, embarrassments. Two newsreels, Gaumont and Movietone, have come to the help of the television authorities. One or two enterprising companies have provided cartoons for the television programmes. A certain amount of old film has been obtained for use in dramatic broadcasts. But on the whole the effect of television on the cinema industry has been to evoke 'curses, not loud, but deep.'

The attitude of the American firms towards our British television service is, perhaps understandable. The day may very well come when the cinema magnates in America decide to get local possession of this new magic and menace. Absolute monopoly of their stars and stock will then, conceivably, be an advantage to them. In England, however, things are different. Television is already a State service, a State amenity. Its audience is still small, its funds limited, but it has the authority, the goodwill, that the British cinema needs.

If I were a British film producer or renter at this moment, with foreign competition strong, with the bottom dropping out of the home market, I should welcome television as a heaven-sent saviour. I should not only allow but force my contract artists to appear regularly in front of the television cameras. I should dust off all the old films, short and long, from my vaults, and allow the television people to take their pick of them. I should appreciate – I hope – that all entertainment is one entertainment, and that the surest way to attract audiences to one medium is to teach them the habit of entertainment through another.

Television is the key to all the entertainments of the future. Nothing is going to stop its progress; nothing is going to limit its ultimate efficiency. The film industry may handicap and harass it, boycott and outlaw it, but in the end the film industry will have to succumb and work with it. Once the American entertainment industry is ready for such a dual combination nothing in the world will prevent its triumphant drive forward. For once, just once, in our history we English are ready before the Americans. Why in thunder can't we have the courage, the initiative, to pool our resources, and jump ahead to prosperity now?

5 December 1939

Sound and Fury

A firm in Douglas, Isle of Man, has kindly sent me six pairs of polarised glasses, for use with three-dimensional pictures. I am grateful, but hope I shall have few occasions to wear them. The gadget that would seem most serviceable these days is earplugs. I wonder if any readers would join me in a campaign for the suppression of noise in films. It was bad enough when we merely had a surplus of background music. To this has been added the menace of ill-regulated stereophonic sound, which at times almost splits the eardrums and makes the dialogue quite unintelligible. Now I read with horror that London is soon to have a cinema with forty-eight loudspeakers in the auditorium. Where will these abominations end?

22 August 1954

III

Films of the Week

The Twenties

When Lillian Gish first came to Los Angeles in 1913, she says in her autobiography, 'the city smelled like a vast orange grove'. This is by no means the case today. We can see photographs of prelapsarian Hollywood and we can see the resurrected prints of silent films, but we cannot see them with the eyes of contemporary audiences. We know that Miss Gish, Mary Pickford and other stars of that period enchanted millions of people, but we can no more judge their acting ability, or even their looks, than we could fairly judge the performances of Garrick and Irving. The whole context within which they were seen has changed too much.

The articles in this section offer just a few, rather arbitrarily chosen, reflections of that lost world. 'I am almost exactly the same age as the cinema,' my mother wrote. The earliest milestones were already past, therefore, when she began reviewing films. *Birth of a Nation*, a decade before, had pioneered many of the techniques of cinematic story-telling. Her own juvenile taste ran mainly to serials, sweetness-and-light romanticism and Westerns. What she most disliked was slapstick comedy; she loathed the Keystone Cops and fretted through the antics of Charlie Chaplin. These inclinations were overlaid in her articles by responsibility to the readers and, at first, by considerable pretentiousness. The pretentiousness drained away: the sense of a critic's responsibility remained: but traces of her original likes and dislikes are always discernible, shadow-lines in the grass.

Silent films developed their own language and constantly explored new territory. A series of British one-reelers, under the title 'Tense Moments from Great Operas', purported to skim the cream from *Rigoletto*, *Trovatore*, *Faust* and other sensational favourites. The tradition of melodrama still survived, so that a powerful, highly moral, film could still be called, with absolute seriousness, *Where Is My Wandering Boy Tonight?*

Then, at the end of the 1920s, sound came and swept an entire form of expression away. 'First singly, then in groups, part-dialogue films appeared,' wrote my mother in her book, *Cinema*. 'Short sound-films became general, as more and more theatres began to wire. The full dialogue film arrived, and after it the singing-and-dancing show. The big firms in Europe and America began to make multi-lingual productions. Silent films changed into "silent versions", grew rarer, and disappeared from the production schedules.'

– A.L.

The film **Stella Dallas** is such a feast of sentimental emotions that there will be many people who will not allow themselves to enjoy it to the full. And that seems to me a pity. I cannot agree that being sentimental brings with it any cause for shame. The real shame, to my mind, should be for the hypocrisy that denies sentiment in a world that is largely sentiment-composed. I am a little distrustful, too, of people who turn up fastidious noses at a picture such as this. It is possible, of course, that they are honest. It is possible that *Greed* and *Waxworks* and *Raskolnikov* and the other films of dry intellectual calibre make to them the only swift and sure appeal. But – so many people deceive themselves for intellect's sake. So many falsehoods are told in the name of art. And I usually find that the people who deny having been emotionally disturbed deny it in a kind of panic insurance against themselves. They are afraid to let their thinking powers be thrown even temporarily out of gear. They are afraid to feel, because they feel so much more readily than they think. They do not realise that the real thinker uses his emotions as a whetstone to make his judgments keen and bright.

Like dogs, we are born sentimental. Sentiment is the warmth that keeps us happy, the response that brings us friends. Every man jack of us is designed by nature to be a sentimentalist. The very intelligent man transfers his sentiment from human to abstract conceptions; that is the only difference between him and his less thoughtful brother. The basic emotional quality is the same, whether one grows rapt over a movement or a man, an expression or an accident of life.

I never know why people are at such pains to hide the fact that they have been sentimentally stirred by a book, or a film, or a play. It seems to me an admirable thing, a real tonic to heart and mind, and one that should be valued in direct ratio to the amount of sentiment produced. Why should we not be honest and confess that the sentiment, and not the comedy, of *College Days* was the thing that caught us on the raw? Why not own up that scenes of Mary Pickford's *Little Annie Rooney* touched us like an April day? We make all sorts of excuses for our surrenders to sentiment, mutter 'Technique', 'Tired', 'Silly of us to make fools of ourselves', and never see that thinking ourselves silly for being silly is the silliest thing of all.

To admit that *Stella Dallas* moved us is not in the least to admit our critical faculties at fault. We are not saying that the film is a masterpiece, that it makes some great advance in kinema history, that its technique is flawless, or its production a supreme creation of art. We are merely confessing that there is something, a sequence of somethings, in the film that set our own emotional imaginations free to create. Confessing to a purely physical contraction of the muscles of the throat, a curious physical sense of leap and poise. Confessing that we have lived the ordinary lives of ordinary men and women, and caught a reflection of it here. *Stella Dallas* is quite an ordinary American story of 'mother-love', told in a quite straightforward American way. Its peculiar quality is the *truth* of the people in it, a truth not only of action and of motive, but of taste, of surroundings, of costume, of mood. We are stirred into sympathy with all these people because we cannot help identifying ourselves with them, knowing that under the same circumstances we should react in just the same way. Its emotional experiences are supremely natural, arising from character and in their turn shaping character. The whole picture is full of the half-tones of which ordinary life is composed.

Stella, the mother, big and pathetic and overdressed, making up her face in the station cloakroom and streaking the rouge with tears. Laurel, the daughter, who 'likes things so darn simple,' boarding the train in her neat little travelling frock, with her long smooth hair and the face of the nicest children we ever played with when we were young. Stephen Dallas, the father, stealing back to 'borrow' for a week the daughter who is the image of his fastidious soul. Gentle, well-bred Mrs Morrison, who does everything so *right*. Young Richard, swimming and playing and dancing with Laurel – young Richard suddenly man-conscious with a faint moustache. These are all real people whose every move rings true; real people, moving in circumstances just unreal enough to give their own reality romance.

For my own part I thought that little Lois Moran and Douglas Fairbanks, jun., brought into the love story of Laurel and Richard an element of almost painful beauty, so simple and clear-eyed and young that one was almost ashamed to be caught ~oying on it. And I think, too, that this little French girl, Lois

Moran, is the freshest and most inviting personality that has hit the American screen since Mary Pickford's days began. Here is a clear personality, a frank, sensitive face. She opens the picture-house door to the open air, and brings in the washed colour of spring mornings.

Stella Dallas is a sad film, but sad with the curious quality of sadness that leaves only happiness in its train. We, watching it, are happy to be so sad. We find here a vicarious courage; a fidelity and a generous understanding that by proxy becomes ours. We suffer, but without pain. We share in a sacrifice which our own lives would never demand. We are noble – spuriously, – and gather up the emotional fervour of that nobility. For it is this proxy business that makes sad stories always so popular, the sense of something achieved that leaves the sad endings of fiction without a bitter after-taste. We want to be happy. But still more do we want to be somehow fine. And the film that, like *Stella Dallas*, can persuade us by cunning emotional experience that we have gone through fire and come out finer, can persuade us that we have gone through fire for someone else's sake, is the film that makes us happiest of all.

[1926]

I can remember no more terrible adventure in the kinema than the moment in the middle of **Chang** when suddenly the curtains divide, and the screen seems to swell and tremble and burst its bounds, and the great herd of elephants comes rampling out of the picture and bears down upon us in a multitude of tossing trunks and angry feet. There is no time to reassure ourselves with the thought that this is nothing but a technical trick; the reaction is too swift for reason; the jungle does for a moment leap out at us and find us unprepared. The whole of the auditorium arch is filled with turbulent, grey figures – no less terrible for a certain vagueness of form that is the price of magnitude, – and we seem to be crouching below them, mastered by them, helpless in a world that has no longer any reason or law. The success of the magnascope, the new American device which is used for the first time in *Chang*, is the more remarkable because we are naturally suspicious of the kinema's claims to 'development'; we have assisted at the still-birth of so many discoveries that the promise of another more or less has lost its power to excite us. The kinema makes its greatest discovery at least once a year. It may be a new kind of colour-photography, a new means to stereoscopy, or a new way of synchronizing pictures and voice. It is always the greatest, and it is always, in effect, the same. It does not help us one jot in our appreciation of the screen.

But the magnascope is like no other invention of the kinema since the kinema was itself invented. It is good both of and in its kind. For the first time energy and initiative have been brought to bear on the perfection of something vital to the kinema; something that is of the very stuff of the kinema, that partakes of its matter and form. There is no attempt here to mimic the opera, or the theatre, or the dance. There is no rejection of the limits of the camera, but a real essay of development within these limits, playing legitimately on the senses of the audience through resources that belong to the kinema alone.

I am sure that the magnascope, rightly used, can be one of the most potent forces of the screen tomorrow. It is liable, I know, to general misuse. The possibilities of magnascoped heroines are appalling. But if it is a device that can never in itself produce beauty, as a medium of terror and comedy it is unrivalled, and not the least of its qualities is its power to invest the real picture with contrasting beauty – a distant, fairy-like, ordered effect of beauty – when the curtains swing together again and the adventure is over.

[1927]

A TALE OF FIVE CITIES

[Being the moving story of Old King Cole as it might appear on the screens of five countries.]

NEW YORK. Night. The Manhattan home of King Cole, a jovial but square-jawed monarch of commerce, known to the world as the biggest power on Wall Street. His only faults, so far as we can see, are his ambitions as a social climber and his atrocious taste in suits. Dearest to him in the world – though he's a big-hearted old chap all round – is his only daughter Billie, whom he is determined to marry well. He has chosen the Earl of Belchester for the happy groom; there is the Earl, with a monocle and a slipped chin, and there is Billie, a whole portrait gallery of Billie, philandering in the garden under a full moon. Philandering, but not with the Earl. That tall, sad-eyed young man is her tutor. A title tells us that they love one another, but love in vain. King Cole, on this one point adamant, gives a ball on the eve of his daughter's wedding, and all the State of Manhattan is invited. There are candy palaces and fountains of fire, water-chutes and ballets a hundred strong, and a great many riotous young men in paper caps throwing streamers at jewelled young women. King Cole is at the top of his form tonight. A merry old soul is he. He calls for cigars, and a camouflaged bowl, about three hundred fiddles and a full jazz band. Meanwhile the tutor has been getting very busy. He has learnt a hideous scandal of the Earl's past. He has robbed King Cole's safe. He has bribed the Earl to go away for ever. The Earl has gone away for ever. The cops get the tutor. The tutor gets time. But because a successful theft never fails to arouse the admiration of businesslike America, King Cole relents at last, and Billie's lover comes out of prison to the sound of wedding bells. The film is called 'Flaming Fatherhood'.

BERLIN. Dawn. The King of a certain country in days gone by, old and pleasure-loving, passionate and greedy. Life bores him. His Queen bores him. Amours bore him. He rides out to find adventure, and finds it with a beautiful peasant girl, who fires him as no woman ever before. He murders his wife and makes the peasant Queen. For a time he carouses, triumphant. Then he learns, one summer night, that the Queen has a lover, a young Count, – English editors include here a title about youth calling to youth – and rage springs murderous within him. He bids the city to a great feast. He calls for music and wine. He drops poison into the bowl. And then, sitting on his throne above the fiddlers, he watches the Queen drink, dance with her lover, stagger, fall and die. The Count is led away to execution. The guests scatter, horrified. But the King laughs, lifts a deep goblet to the dead, and bids his fiddlers play on. Title of the film: 'The Wife of Kole'.

LONDON. Day. (Night lighting is too expensive.) Rex Coleby, hero of 'Coleby of the White Road,' is a vagabond, a merry old soul of the Regency days. His home is a bench outside a country inn, where he sits with his pipe and his pint mug, and chaffs the travelling fiddlers who come his way. Every few minutes a title illustrates his sharpness of wit. He chucks wenches under the chin. He bursts into lusty song. And then along the road comes the young Lord of Belchester, on adventure bound, and shortly afterwards his cousin, Lady Betty Belchester, disguised as a waiting-maid. Old Rex Coleby alone knows the truth of their birth. He tells them that the Path of True Love is the Open Road. And so, when Lord Belchester has boxed at three country fairs, thrashed a bully, knocked down a drunk, and horse-whipped a villain, the wedding takes place in an ivied church, and afterwards, in the inn, there are pipes and bowls and fiddlers more than three. No story! Perhaps not, but stories are not in the best English tradition. This is a picaresque film. You need not look for a plot. Nor need you inquire very deeply into the use of the name 'Rex' in Regency days. Nobody else has. Nobody else will.

PARIS. Twilight. A view of the Arc de Triomphe. (This has nothing to do with the story, but it has to come somewhere into every French film.) Old M. Colin, known as Le Roi de la Musique, sits in an armchair gazing at the city below. Tonight he is sad, but as a rule he is a merry old soul. He has come from his son's wedding. Pictures of him being merry there. Now, in his loneliness, he calls for his pipe, and his bowl of wine, and his young nephew to play the organ for him. Dreams. His own marriage. His baby daughter. His lovely wife; their misunderstanding; her flight with another man; the child's empty cot. Dreams more and more confused, wilder, superimposed. Hatred. A world out of focus. Faces. Horrified face of the young organist. Distorted face of M. Colin. Reproachful face of dying wife. Child's face. All the faces together. The old man starts to his feet, crashing the bowl on to the polished floor, and as he does so the door opens and his lost daughter stands before him. With a cry of rage he hurls her from him, and sinks back dying into his chair. The end! Not quite. He has to forgive her first, seeing in her the vision of his wife. She and the organist have to clasp hands. And then old M. Colin can die, with the organ playing ghostly music, and the pipe and bowl lying broken at his feet. The name of the film is 'The Dream of Old M. Colin.' The more pompous press will hail it as a masterpiece of kinema art. No one will book it.

STOCKHOLM. This story is unknown in Sweden. Old King Cole was a *merry* old soul.

11 July 1925

Ever since the first producer sent his hero westward behind the first film engine it has been certain that the road to adventure lies along the track of those gleaming rails. Horses may be clean-limbed and fleet. The slim racing-car may be lovely in its pride. But for the kinema only the steel trail runs right into the heart of adventure, carries its passengers through the outskirts, the romantic suburbs, of adventure to that goal where dreams are, where we are very young again, and anything may come true.

The kinema – why should it be forgotten? – is a mechanical thing. It was born of science out of industry, and its whole life runs on wheels. This, the modern medium of expression, fulfils itself most completely in the presentation of modern forms in the shaping of things industrial, the service of the machine. Wheels, piston-rods, screws of steamers, turning lathes, the glow of blastfurnaces, the polished bellies of guns, are all materials of splendour to the motion-picture camera. They and the kinema are of the same stuff and time. In expressing accurately these mechanical things, conveying into flat image their build and texture and power, the kinema is most itself, most forceful, and, because most mechanical, most nearly an art.

Of all the machines that have turned and throbbed their way across the kinema screen none is more potent, none has moved to a finer measure, than the railway engine on the track. When the camera picks up a running mail, with the great wheels flying and singing; when it catches that long, gleaming thing, smoke-capped, on a bend of line; when it boards the driver's car and plunges into the mountainside; when it stands on the rear platform and watches the bright rails for ever falling away; when it whistles with the rushing air and sways with the beating of the train's heart: then the kinema draws magic from science and shapes an art between the wheels of the machine.

It is a curious thing that we should have had to wait all these years for a film which should carry us clear through to adventure along the railroad track. The power of the engine has long been recognized on the screen. Film producers from France,

Germany and America have made constant use of it. They have gone to the rails for romance, taken spurious pace from the turning wheels. They have sent engines hurtling together in a dozen false climaxes. But, with the exception of Abel Gance, who was feeling towards something of the kind in his film *La Roue*, no director has thought, until now, of freighting his engine with an entire theme and setting it at full pace along the track to adventure's end. No director, until now, has really done his railroad honour. No director has considered that an engine might be of more arresting interest than a man. Now at last a film has come from America which trusts the railroad, and sees magic in it, and power; which honours the railroad, and holds it mightier than man; which loves the railroad, and is content to follow it into the heart of romance. It is a spacious film. It is a rather splendid film. **The Iron Horse** is its name. John Ford is its director.

The story of *The Iron Horse* is the story that every schoolboy knows, of the building of the railway across America; the fighting story of the U.P. trail. It tells about the idealists who dreamed of tracks across a continent, and Lincoln who made those dreams a possibility; about the soldiers of the North and South, the Chinese, the Italians, the Irishmen, who worked side by side felling and shovelling, chiselling tunnels and laying track; about the Indian raids that threatened every mile of the way, the hunger, and the hardship, and the cold. It tells about the great track-laying race between the workers of the east and the west, how the Union Pacific and the Central Pacific crept towards each other day by day, until at last, by superhuman effort and endurance, the tracks met seven years before their time. And it tells about 'the wedding of the rails', how the Jupiter and the One Nineteen nosed together from the two ends of the land, how the wires carried, from Washington to San Francisco, from New York to Omaha, the message 'Done', while they drove in with a silver sledge the golden spike that formed 'the last link in the girdle of a continent.'

It is the railway's film, from first to last; the dream of a railway, and the railway born; the railway's long struggle against nature; the railway's costly triumph. Nothing, nobody, is allowed to turn the interest from this central idea. Lincoln comes, does his work for the railway, passes. He is assassinated, but the rails go on. The Indians come, wreck the railway, are shot down. The work begins again, and the rails go on. The men are ambushed and killed. Others take their places, and the rails go on. And only when the tracks meet at last, forming 'one shining path from sea to sea', is the railway appeased and the drama over.

14 November 1925

THE SPHERE OF THE SUB-TITLE

The summary of the position of the sub-title in the kinema seems to be this: there is ample room in the right kinema for the right titling; it is not essential, but neither is it alien, to the true kinema; but it must be conceived and presented in a photogenic way. The title must be part of the sequence, making no break for the eye or mind to detect. Producers have begun to realize the rupture to visual continuity that comes with the sudden illumination of a title-sheet in the middle of dark photography, and have studied more or less successfully with dark backgrounds for the letters, with the printing of titles through and across the actual picture, to trick the eye into acquiescence. But that is not enough. The words in themselves should have movement, should never be unconscious of their medium. Only by keeping them well in the line of development or making them, by their fruitful shape or size, a momentary resting-point to which the action leads and from which it continues, can the introduction of titles be justified for the screen.

So far we have been concerned with the ideal – with the kinema as it might be if artists turned their hands to it and created in terms of it, with the kinema as it has been in the rare instances when artists have turned their hands to it in the past.

But the kinema that is with us day by day is quite another matter. In its realist scheme the sub-title is essential. It has been built up around the possibility of the sub-title, taught to rely on the sub-title to get it comfortably out of any mess. It is in itself an elaboration of the sub-title; an illustrated novel of which the sub-titling forms the text. Themes for the expression of which words are indispensable are chosen for the kinema every day. The producer does not think in terms of picture. He thinks in terms of illustrated print. The pictures are always an embellishment. The words, or situations that depend on words, are the core.

Under these conditions the elimination of the sub-title, a favourite device with young producers, seems to be mere folly. It reminds one of a child hurrying along the pavement with a grim determination not to tread on any of the lines between the stones. There is no reason in the world why he should not tread on the lines. But he will take all manner of complicated steps to avoid them. There is no reason in the world why the realist producer should not use sub-titles. But he will go to any lengths of tiresome device to eliminate them. I have seen a serious young hero in a wordless film at terrible pains to convey to his lady-love the news that he was going down into Kent to work on a farm. He finally achieved it by hopping round the room on one leg. And she still married him! She did more. She had a baby. And to assure you that the baby was in perfectly correct order (pressure of time bringing it rather suddenly into the film) there was a pause while the producer showed you the budding and blossoming and fruiting of a tree branch to check up the seasons of the year.

Much ingenuity, I allow, goes to the making of these wordless films, much hunting for symbols, much play with clocks and calendars, a great deal of gesture as frenzied as a child's secret sign. The producers say it with dancing; they say it with flowers; they have even been known to say it with music. And when they have finished they are no better off than if they had said it with words in the good old obvious way. They have not, with all their ingenuity, made a wordless film. They have only made a wordy film with the words missed out. It is as far removed from the true wordless kinema, which needs no words to express what has never been verbally conceived, as a game of dumb-crambo is from a harlequinade.

D. W. Griffith once told me that he considered sub-titles to be quite unnecessary, serving only to 'illumine and enheighten' the film. I could not then, and cannot now, agree with him. To my mind, in the films he was speaking of, although perhaps not in the films he thought he was speaking of, the sub-titles are the film. Everything of importance happens in them. Great resolutions are made in them. Births, deaths, and marriages take place in them. Characters are fixed in them. Secrets are revealed in them. All the wit of the production is tied up in them. Entire backgrounds are blocked in by them. Atmosphere is conveyed through them. They are the end and the beginning of the whole matter, the natural skin for clothing the body of realistic thought.

Titles in these everyday films can be, and often are, pungent; the raw American tongue has a kick in it that sends wit flying. They can be, and sometimes are, imaginative. But the most important thing about them is that they should be clear. My quarrel with kinema titles is not that there are too many of them, for the merit of that fault is that there are fewer pictures, nor that they stay too long on the screen, for one can always sleep, but that, all-important as they are to the understanding of the picture, it is often a penance to try and understand them at all.

I can see no justification for titles misspelt, titles without grammar or punctuation, titles floating as it were in mid-air, without any indication of the speaker. I dislike intensely the coloured titles, which makes the film look drab, and the 'art' title, which makes the words look tawdry. I have no patience with the 'atmospheric' title in which letters are twisted and tortured to seem Russian, or Hindu, or Chinese. I hate the impressionist title with dots between the words. And most of all I detest the smug title that says, 'I'm no coward, and I tell you to go,' when the hero has quite visibly remarked, 'Yellow nothing! You're canned!' I prefer an honest title that says what it means and says it quick. And I prefer a good plain script that does not claim to be a palimpsest from ancient Egypt or to have been carved by Moses out of stone. If we must have a kinema that must in its turn have titles, let the titles be written so that they can be read by the simplest of us, for those are the only ones of us it is necessary to consider. The others will not be there to read.

10 April 1926

'TO BE CONTINUED'

A referendum taken at Christmas-time among 10,467 picture-goers of Great Britain has arranged the various types of film in the following order of popularity: – Society drama, comedy drama, Western drama, comedy, historical or costume drama, war drama, news film, cartoon, interest (ironical word!), and serial.

And serial. Yes, times have changed. It is not so very long
ago since the serial was cock of the kinema walk, since Pearl
White, the golden-haired 'stuntist', ruled two continents with
her lipstick. It is not so very long ago since pictures of *The
Clutching Hand* adorned the bill-boards and we thrilled weekly
to *The Exploits of Elaine*. Not so long ago, but in another world.
The serial is out of favour with us today.

In France, and in many other parts of Continental Europe, the
serial picture – or the chapter-play, or the drama in episodes,
whatever name it may be given – still keeps an honourable
place. The better theatres are not ashamed to show it. Audiences
applaud its title on the screen. I have known a packed audience
in a suburban Paris kinema get to their feet and greet the brigand
serial *Mandrin* with cheering. I have passed many a doorway
where the serial, in great, pompous letters, topped the bill.

But although the American stunt stars Pearl White and Ruth
Roland can still hold a French crowd intent, are still regarded
among the great ones of the screen, the serial that France loves
best is a serial of its own making. In nine cases out of ten
the period chosen is a historical one, or the earlier half of the
story is concerned with the distant ancestry of the latter half.
The hero swaggers in doublet and hose, carries a sword, goes
buccaneering on the high seas. The heroine wears high-waisted
gowns and bonnets, or gets into breeches and mans it in the
old Rosalind way. Neither of them has ever used a telephone.
Neither of them has walked with sheriffs or talked with sleuths.
Their adventures lead them into battle and shipwreck, to the
favour of kings and the displeasure of cardinals, among armies,
among mutineers, among slaves. Their stories are for all the
world like an old chronicle of which a new page is written week
by week; a full and true account of the manners, the costumes,
and the conditions of other times, perfectly accurate, beautifully
written, and a little dry in its fine script. They are scholarly
productions, these serials of France, made with the care and
preparation that in other countries is given to 'supers' alone.
The producers are good producers. The actors are good actors.
The photography is as fine as eye could desire.

Our friend the serial of the good old days, the melodrama
that used to draw us week after week to the picture theatre
to follow up our hero's perils, had very little kinship with
these costume chronicles of France. It was a raw, swaggering,
full-blooded thing, eminently suited to the place that housed

it. Crude, as the picture palace is crude. Vulgar, as the picture palace is vulgar. There was no nonsense about it, no beating about the bush. What it wanted to say it shouted. Where it wanted to move it ran. Highly concentrated in form, with not an inch wasted on incidental matter, it crammed into one twenty-minute instalment all the drama of a dozen reels. The 'punch' that knocked you from one instalment clean into the middle of next week was nothing less than a neat finish to a tabloid melodrama that had a beginning, middle and ending all its own. Only the top of that ending, as it were, was lifted off. You went next week to try and find it. You did not find it, but another punch found you.

Every good serial began with a girl, a crook and a document. The document was invariably in two halves. The girl had one half. The crook had the other. The object of ten reels was to bring the two halves together. Every good serial ended with a girl and a document. The crook was dead.

Let us suppose that you find yourself in a picture theatre facing Part 2 of *The Power of Peril*. (Nobody has ever yet been known to chance upon the first part of any serial.) A long paragraph on the screen acquaints you with what has gone before. 'Muriel Murgatroyd,' you read, 'an actress, whose father, Thomas Murgatroyd, has left her a hidden treasure and a Peril Pact which he has hidden in a secret place unknown to Muriel but guessed at by Black Jim, the head of a gang of crooks whose headquarters are in an old mill owned by John Fraser, the father of Dick Fraser, a journalist who is in love with Muriel, and has been captured by the gang in a desperate encounter, during which she is locked up in a burning building where, unknown to her, the Peril Pact is kept.' Clear enough, isn't it? Now you will be able to sympathise with Muriel when she jumps out of the burning building of Part 1 only to be thrown to lions in Part 2, and tames the lions only to be pushed over a cliff in Part 3, and swims ashore only to be captured by Black Jim in Part 4, and escapes on the arms of the windmill only to fall down a trap in Part 5, and digs a passage out of the trap only to be threatened with dynamite in Part 6, and cuts the fuse only to be captured by motor bandits in Part 7, and drives the car to safety only to be smashed up by an express train in Part 8, and escapes with a cut finger only to be sacrificed to idols in Part 9, and finds the Pact in the idol's mouth only to be married to Dick in Part 10.

Now that is what I call a moving picture. All the old serials were. But the audiences of today would rather put Black Jim into a dress suit, have Muriel flirt with him for nine reels before she marries Dick, cut out all the action, label it 'society drama', and put it at the head of their list.

1 September 1926

THE YEAR IN RETROSPECT

Nineteen twenty-eight strikes about the average with five outstanding films: Chaplin's *The Circus*, Lubitsch's *Student Prince*, Murnau's *Sunrise*, Ruttmann's *Berlin*, and Starewitch's *Magic Clock*. These pictures are pure cinema, rightly conceived and executed, each in its way completely satisfying to the most fastidious film-goer. . . .

The prime importance of 1928 to the cinema, however, is not that it has produced any particular film or group of films, but that it marks the arrival and establishment of the talking picture in Europe and America. At the moment the talkie is a crude business at best. Amongst the various long dramas and short vaudeville turns that the sound-cinema has brought us, there has not yet been one to which we could apply any standards of art. To satisfy imagination and a desire for good cinema we must go to the silent productions of the year – to Berlin – *The Student Prince*, *The Magic Clock*. The talkies are still concerning themselves with the quality, not the content, of their speech. They are still marvelling at having found a tongue. But the important point is that they *have* found a tongue – that the millions of picture-goers who are willing to pay for personality have discovered a new way of getting value for money. Six months ago the talkies were a supposition. Today they are a fact of two continents. They have carried the cinema a definite step forward towards perfect mechanization, and in an age of pace and economy that step will not be retraced.

30 December 1928

The Thirties

The first film I saw in a cinema was *The Scarlet Pimpernel* with Leslie Howard, my previous experience having been confined to Felix the Cat and The Inkpot Men at my kindergarten school. I can still remember the brief adjustment required before I could believe that the voices from the loudspeakers were coming from the figures on the screen. The whole world, by then, had made the same adjustment.

Films had become pretty much as we know them today. Those dating from the very early 1930s have, admittedly, a slight museum-piece air. The progress in sophistication between, for example, *Frankenstein* and *The Bride of Frankenstein* or between *Tarzan of the Apes* and *Tarzan and His Mate* constitutes a giant stride. But by the mid-thirties the best films were as good as films have ever been, and the final years of the decade were, in terms both of quantity and of quality, wonderful.

Contrary to some modern mythology, the 1930s were, at least in southern England, a generally happy period. It was a good period for us. My mother was writing well and prolifically on a subject which interested almost everybody. Films were the world's most popular entertainment. Film stars were gods and goddesses. There were eight cinemas within easy reach of my home – only one of which exists now. In London the new Odeon, Leicester Square, opened with a flourish; it had leopard-skin seats. My mother took me to see its first attraction, which was *The Prisoner of Zenda*.

Television had begun but was available only within quite a short range of the Alexandra Palace transmitter. I used to bring boys home from school to watch the cricket. Since there was no form of video-recording, it's hard to know what the quality was like: but we were accustomed to films, and I don't remember thinking television notably inferior.

As 1939 approached, the shadows lengthened. European refugees in Britain and America stimulated anti-Nazi films, sometimes overt, sometimes lightly disguised.

All our summer holidays were spent at my aunt's house at Bexhill, where the beach was good for building sandcastles, and there were real historic castles to be visited nearby, and ice-cream parlours and cinemas for wet afternoons. The last summer, the summer of 1939, is, in my memory or my imagination, slightly grey, as though a cloud had come over the sun: but it can't have been so, at least not according to my mother's description.

'We all lived on borrowed time in our own way,' she wrote in *Thank You for Having Me*.

Tony and I went for our usual summer holiday to Bexhill. One day at the end of August my husband turned up in the car to fetch us home. He said the roads were thick with military traffic, tanks and guns and lorries on the move.

Nothing had happened yet, but something was likely to happen at any moment. Quite suddenly I knew what I must do with my last hour of borrowed time. I went down to the beach and had a solitary bathe. There was nobody in sight along the shore. I am nothing of a swimmer and an appalling sailor; but the sea, the fact of being in the sea, part of the sea itself, has always fascinated me. The sea comes into almost all my dreams, and in the best dreams of all I find myself moving with careless ease through temperate water into a golden sunset.

The water was temperate that day, and there was a hazy sun in a pale August sky. I floated on my back for a long time, accepting the benison, and deliberately thinking of nothing at all.

That was the last bathe I ever took. After the war I felt too old for swimming. As I dried myself, dressed, swept the wet sand from the coconut matting, and locked the hut door in what proved to be an act of supererogation, I knew quite well that this was goodbye. We never saw that foolish little hut again.

– A.L.

Miss Louella Parsons, the American film journalist, announced at a Press luncheon in London the other day that we should only enter the cinema on a real competition basis with America when we had developed something approaching the American star system.

Film journalists – even women film journalists – are sometimes right, and we don't need to go any further than the new Metro-Goldwyn picture **Grand Hotel** for a proof of Miss Parson's argument. *Grand Hotel* opened on Wednesday night at the Palace Theatre – a regular 'legitimate' theatre with regular and possibly 'legitimate' prices – and on Tuesday evening there were already a couple of dozen people waiting to see the show. By Wednesday afternoon the queue of camp-stools went half-way round the theatre, and the advance box-office was humming like a hive. This is not what is generally known as 'publicity-dope' – I saw it with my own eyes. I have been through a good many film first-nights, in which the enthusiasm was either real or cunningly stimulated, but I remember nothing to equal the curiosity, excitement, and impatience with which London prepared to sample *Grand Hotel*.

What caused all this preliminary enthusiasm? Nothing, I am convinced, but the extraordinary list of stars. Vicki Baum's novel was a good one, but stories don't bring all-night queues to a theatre door. The play, when it was produced in London, attracted interest, but caused no furore. Metro-Goldwyn have a prime reputation as movie-makers – none better in the trade – but the public doesn't waste its beauty-sleep on the credit of any firm. What drew the audience was quite simply the names of Greta Garbo, Joan Crawford, John Barrymore, Lionel Barrymore, and Wallace Beery on the theatre walls – and behind those names the whole tradition of the system they represent.

I am an old hand at the game, but I confess that even I felt moved by the magnificence of that cast-list, and found myself, as the stars crowded round the hotel desk in the opening scenes of the film, with the same sense of awed and yet critical admiration with which we, as juniors, used to regard a mass meeting of prefects in our schooldays. There they all were – Garbo, as Grusinskaya, the dancer; Crawford, as the calculating Flaemmchen; Lionel Barrymore, arguing out Kringelein's right to live; John, with the ravished charm of Baron Galgern; Wallace Beery, as the blustering Preysing; Jean Hersholt, waiting at the porter's desk for the news of his son's birth; Lewis Stone, speaking the chorus from the scarred mouth of Dr Otternschlag – meeting, passing, listening, waiting; stealing one another's close-ups, capping one another's lines; and each one, not a single figure, but the symbol of a dozen earlier romances, the type of a whole career of individual conquests on the screen.

I can imagine that it may sound crazy to the outsider to talk of the intense *excitement* in seeing these stars inter-act. But anyone who has been a regular picture-goer will understand what I mean. We are accustomed to think of any one of these people as capable of carrying a film alone – and we have been frequently satisfied with just that. And now to see Garbo, in a fine new freedom of mood – even her poses have broken down their old contours – balanced by a Barrymore who has forgotten his mannerisms; to see Wallace Beery in full control of his vast ebullience, and Crawford turning her slick youth to grim and logical purpose; to see Lionel Barrymore suddenly towering, from sheer force of argument over the rest of the cast – to be given all this in one film, is good measure for any audience, but a measure that reserves its special bouquet for the movie connoisseur.

Director Edmund Goulding has taken Vicki Baum's 'Kolportageroman', and by sheer excellence of craftsmanship made a grand film out of it. The raw material was always there. When you read *Menschen im Hotel*, you felt that you were turning over the pages of a film scenario. But Goulding has selected, adapted, and above all *cut* the material, with the authority of a man who knows his medium. The film is all broad movement, broad handling and bold pace. It is still a Kolportageroman, but there is no trace in it of a literary idiom. It is movie, movie and again movie, with the cameras driving you irresistibly round the endless circle of the theme.

Grand Hotel is Hollywood's five-star final, the last word in dramatic production for the million. The screen can do much subtler work than this. The camera can go deeper. But to grumble at it is to prove that you have never really got the essential fun out of the movies. If you've loved the cinema, faults and all, and grown up with it, faults and all; if you've found some kind of emotional escape in it, week after week, through your most impressionable years; if you've learnt your alphabet of stars in the school of Sennett and Griffith and De Mille, then *Grand Hotel* is unquestionably your picture. It is America's complete justification of the star system, and the prize for long service to the faithful 'fan'.

25 September 1932

This week we have the heartening experience of seeing a film of British life that was made in England. J. B. Priestley's story of the road, translated into a film by Gaumont-British, has come to the screen just as it was written, honest and sentimental and episodic, with the smell of the tarmac and the railway buffet, the tinny rapture of the pavilion piano, the jostling pageantry of insignificant faces.

We have waited over twenty years for **The Good Companions**. We have watched the British producers trying to copy the film manner of Hollywood. We have watched them trying to copy the film manner of Berlin. We had almost given up hope of seeing them strike out for themselves a national manner in film-making – an English manner, with the characteristic slow, packed development of the best English art – a picaresque manner, which has always been, in writing, painting, drama, and music, the English heritage.

The Good Companions does for the British cinema what Fielding's novels did for the artificial and derivative literature of the early eighteenth century. It lets in the daylight, and shows us faces that we recognize, and places that we have lived in, and circumstances that move us with the incalculable emotion of the everyday. Like all good picaresque narrative, the effect of *The Good Companions* is cumulative, and yet never completed; it depends all the time on the next twist of circumstance, the adventure just round the corner. It begins with the four chief characters separated by the length and breadth of the English counties; Jess Oakroyd in his Yorkshire mill-town, Inigo instructing the youth of Washbury Manor, Miss Trant surveying the wreck of her west-country home, Susie Dean stranded with a pierrot troupe at Rawsley in the Midlands. Slowly the roads draw them together, tramping south, riding west, driving east, until they meet in a Rawsley doorway with the casual indifference of the really important encounters of life. They have ten frenzied weeks on the road together, and then they go off on their several ways, Inigo and Susie to the London stage, Miss Trant to a honeymoon in Europe, Oakroyd to see his daughter and the 'little 'un' in Canada, and we are left with the sense of another lifetime of adventures just round the bend of the road.

The whole of the film is good, but the last reel is incomparably the best bit of corporate production ever turned out of a British studio. Director, scenario-writer, cutter, camera-man and cast have combined to give those closing scenes the very maximum of emotional effect. It is a real example of the barrage that can be brought to bear on an audience by a well-written script, a well-lit close-up, a well-handled crowd, a well-balanced climax, and a well-arranged sequence of shots.

The Good Companions should bring laurels to a number of people concerned in its production. It is a tremendous personal triumph for Jessie Matthews, who plays Susie. It is the complete justification of Edmund Gwenn, who plays Oakroyd. It suggests a long screen career for John Gielgud, who plays Inigo. It marks Victor Saville as one of those very rare directors who can make consistently able pictures and not be satisfied with mere ability. *The Good Companions* is so much the best thing that he has ever done, so much the most alert, and progressive, and generous, that we have got to acknowledge the value of those tentative fumblings in *Love on Wheels* that took him for a time out of the ranks of the 'safe' directors. I don't think Victor Saville could ever again make a *Michael and Mary*. He has matured since then, and got a firmer technical grasp of his material, a more alert interest in the niceties of the camera and the microphone. He is a grand cutter's 'feed', taking a mass of safety shots from which an intelligent contrast and continuity can be effected; he knows just how to let other people get on with their job, and whom to teach, and from whom to learn.

A good story, a wise director, a grand technical staff, a first-rate cast, and a sympathetic producer have combined to make *The Good Companions* the first real British film that this country has turned out. We want more films of this kind, dozens more. We want every British studio to produce them, and every sceptic of the British screen to see them. But meanwhile it is encouraging to find that the biggest producing firm in the country has the courage to think big every once in a while.

26 February 1933

This week England has made film history, in more senses than one. The London Films' production, **The Private Life of Henry VIII**, has been publicly shown in London, and proves to be the most significant achievement of the British industry since British films began.

The Henry VIII picture is that rare phenomenon, a film that more than justifies its preliminary ballyhoo. For months its progress has been heavily boosted. Minute details of production found their way into the Press. Douglas Fairbanks saw the rushes, and his exuberance became front page news. The film was bought for America, and shown in New York with considerable success. The American Press took it up. They were enthusiastic over it, genuinely and generously enthusiastic. The film was successfully shown in Paris – with cuts, because its political parallels to the present situation excited the authorities. The first night in London followed an intensive publicity campaign and was staged with all the munificence of a court reception. It did not seem as if any film could live up to such preliminary ardour.

It is to the joint credit of Charles Laughton, who plays Henry VIII, Alexander Korda, who directed it, Lajos Biro and Arthur Wimperis, who wrote the script, and Georges Perinal, at the camera, that *The Private Life of Henry VIII* is just as good as it was reputed to be, and a little bit better. It is more likely to bring prestige to the British film industry, both at home and abroad, than anything we have done in the whole history of film-making. Up to now, the best British films have been the sort of thing that Hollywood can do just as well or better. Their method has been English, but their material has been polyglot. Even *The Good Companions* was primarily a studio story; it was only incidentally a film of English-character. But *Henry VIII* is national to the backbone. The fact that it was directed by a Hungarian does not change its birthright. It is the British prestige picture that we have been demanding for ten years back, not pedantic, not jingoistic, but as broadly and staunchly English as a baron of beef and a tankard of the best homebrew.

The fact that the hero is a monarch of England does not

necessarily make it a national picture. We once had a film called *The Virgin Queen*, and the less said about that the better. *Henry VIII* is national because it has been seen from the typical English slant, which combines a kind of forthright and blundering honesty with a childish naivety of humour. Henry is an English hero not because he is a king, but in spite of it. His life story belongs to the people of later generations, not because it is in the history books, but because it was crude and generous and vulgar enough to establish an England about which history books could be made.

Korda might very well have made a very bad picture out of the life, public or private, of Henry VIII. He once made a film in America on the *Private Life of Helen of Troy*, and it was not so good that we want to remember it. His success in *Henry* is due to clever casting, careful detail, grand photography, good set construction, but chiefly to a very remarkable scenario, which has thrown overboard all ideas of conventional film plot and concentrated on the development of a single character under the stress of the conditions of his day. It presents a king of the herd, watched and groomed and lovingly fed by the people like a pedigree breeder, growing past the strength of the body which gave a meaning to his conquests, and hunting for quiet pastures where he can browse and sleep in the sun.

The script never departs from its straight line of development, and the acting emphasizes this unity. Charles Laughton has at last come into the rank of great screen actors with his performance as Henry VIII. For some time his future has been doubtful. He has been playing Hollywood successes too easily, getting quick effects with cheap methods, and standing out from the film not because his work was particularly good but because the rest of the work was consistently poor. Now at last his intelligence has come to grips with something bigger than himself, and won. For the first time he has broken down his stage manner and created for the screen on a broad scale – some of the spaciousness of the Tudor times has got into his bones. His only mistakes are still in the softly-spoken passages of monologue. He hasn't learnt yet to put colour and richness into the subdued voice. But at all other times, roaring, mating, fighting, jesting, and suffering, he is a terrific and generous figure, playing a Jannings part better than Jannings ever played it, with brain and heart behind every scene.

29 October 1933

An ironical situation has arisen in the cinema. The Jews are at last using their own medium as a racial manifesto to the world – turning the art which they have served so long into a plea for tolerance and recognition.

In England and America the epics of Jewry have begun. They are not blatant nor controversial. Nobody has yet made the real saga of the latter-day exodus. We are still too close to the event. In five years' time the producers may see in it the modern prototype of *The Covered Wagon*. But at present they are confining themselves to stories of individual Jews, through which the note of racial persecution rings persistently.

All the previous Jewish pictures have been small domestic comedies, or individual romances of the Ghetto. The best have been German – *Baruch, or the Ancient Law*, made more than ten years ago by the Jewish Dupont, and Paul Wegener's fantastic *Golem*. They were fine and moving pictures, but had little dynastic significance. The new films of Jewry are stories of a whole people, played against a background of endless time.

George Arliss, in America, is starting work on *The House of Rothschild*. It has been emphatically announced that this film has no modern significance. But the climax of the film is Nathan Rothschild's dictation to the Prussian Government of the decrees restoring the Jews to the full rights of citizenship. Anybody is free to draw his own conclusions from the fact.

In England, having finished *The Wandering Jew* at Twickenham, we are making **Jew Suss** at Shepherd's Bush. A silent version of the Feuchtwanger novel was contemplated more than five years ago by another company, but it is only at this significant moment that production has become a fact. *The Wandering Jew* birked the issue, but *Jew Suss* makes no such mistake. The tone is struck in the opening shot. The film begins in a medieval schoolroom, where the master is telling his boys of the persecution of the Jews throughout the ages. Suddenly there is an outcry from the court beyond. The camera tracks round the schoolroom, through the grill, and out into the crowded ghetto below. The new persecution has begun.

Lion Feuchtwanger, fresh from his own experiences of medieval intolerance, has gone over the script of the film with Lothar Mendes, the director. 'He agrees with me,' Mr Mendes told me, 'that the scope of the book should be very much expanded in the film translation. It is much bigger than a mere ghetto drama. It is still the colossal tragedy of one man played out against a canvas of medieval life. But the individual has taken on all the significance of a race.'

Mendes himself has seen *Jew Suss* as his ideal film ever since the book was first published, but modern circumstances have given the theme a fresh impetus. 'I doubt whether any other story,' he said, 'would so strongly have tempted me to come over and work in England. I have always wanted a chance to make "Suss", but as a silent picture it would not have been possible – and sometimes I feel that without Connie Veidt it would not have been possible either. We should have been forced to imagine some other actor of his peculiar personality and force before we could have begun to consider it – and there is no other quite like him on the screen.'

The strong working partnership between Mendes and Veidt has been backed up by the full strength of the Gaumont-British resources. 'I am not saying it just to be polite,' says Mendes earnestly, 'but "Suss" could not have been made better, and I doubt whether it could have been made as well, anywhere else in the world. I have never met anywhere with more cordial co-operation and enthusiasm throughout a studio. And Mickey Balcon is one of the few producers with whom you can talk story – emotionally and intelligently.'

It will not be Mendes' fault, nor Veidt's, nor the fault of Gaumont-British, if *Jew Suss* is not the protest of a whole race against barbarism. But anyone who prefers can take it as 'the colossal tragedy of one man.'

With the conclusion of *Jew Suss*, Victor Saville, also working at Shepherd's Bush, is going to direct Louis Golding's *Magnolia Street*. Saville, cornered with a direct question, will laugh off the racial significance of his material. 'Do you believe in making Jewish actors play Jewish parts?' he sidetracks. 'I don't. Have you ever noticed how a good Jewish actor goes about carrying all the sorrows of Judaism on his shoulders, until his performance becomes completely ham-like? It is so easy for a Jew to overdo the Jewish humility. The Jews are great artists by birthright, and good business men by force of circumstance – because they have always been shut off from the land and forced to take their possessions in currency. But the Jew is a very simple fellow really, and it is possible to take him far too tragically.' And yet in a serious moment Saville will talk about Louis Golding as one of the few really significant modern writers, inspired 'with all the passionate joys and sorrows of our race.'

The odd and peculiarly characteristic quality of this new Jewish movement in the cinema is its diffidence. It is the only deliberate propaganda on the screen that is reluctant to admit authority. The film propaganda of the Russians, the Americans, the Nazis and the Italian Fascists is frank and triumphant, while these Jewish stories are claimed to be primarily individual romances 'with a racial background.' Yet the Jews have the clearest claim of all to a national drama on the screen.

From its very earliest days the success of the motion picture has been due to Jewish acumen. Almost all the great figures of the film industry – actors, producers, directors, and technical men have been of Jewish extraction. Without the Jews the cinema, in all its vast modern proportions, would never have come into being. For nearly half a century they have been using the motion picture as a mouthpiece for the ideas and interests of other races. It is not unreasonable that at last, now that the right moment has come, they should contemplate using it for the justification of their own.

7 January 1934

At last, after two years of work and struggle and anticipation, **Man of Aran** is an accomplished fact, and anyone in London who has not already viewed it – I cannot recall whether Flaherty told me he had shown it to sixty or six hundred individuals to date – can see it at the New Gallery Cinema this week. Let me say at the outset that it is a beautiful film. Flaherty, as a cameraman, can never be beaten this side heaven, and six thousand feet of such fine and purposeful pictorial composition have seldom been set out upon the screen.

Man of Aran is lovely to look at – sincere, virile, and understanding. It has been made by a man who loves the place and the people, and his passion has been communicated in every shot. Everyone will go to see it – everyone should go to see it – for Flaherty has not his like in the film-making world. But it is not a great picture, in the sense that *Nanook* was great. It is superbly free of trivialities, but the struggle for existence, which is the basis of all Flaherty's films, is never made dramatically clear to an audience who are, after all, strangers to this sea-folk, and unversed in the difference between the incidents and the accidents of their lives.

Two years is too long a time to spend over any picture,

however vast in project. It is possible to get too close to a subject in two years. Feuchtwanger told me once that he saw more of the truth of a place or a person in three days than he would ever capture again in a lifetime of experience. Flaherty, I think, has come to understand his islanders so well that he has forgotten a little about the public. His film takes the islanders for granted, marches in silent comradeship with them from the start, which is a thing that we outsiders, however sympathetic, can never do.

Man of Aran has no story, not even the trace of story that was to be found in *Moana* and *Tabu*. It barely recounts the movements of a nameless father, mother and son through their daily life of fishing, seaweed-gathering, the planting of potatoes, the harpooning of sharks. It works up to a formal climax in the onset of a storm at sea, but that, one feels, is more to round off the film in proper shape than because the idea demands it. It is safe to surmise that Flaherty intended all these incidents to be illustrative of a central theme, but he is himself so familiar with the theme that he has come to believe that the bare statement of circumstances is enough to suggest it. When Flaherty sees a woman walking along the shore with a basket of seaweed on her back, it is for him exciting and dramatic, because he knows by experience the struggle for existence that that load represents. But when the audience see the same picture, they see only the woman and the seaweed. *Man of Aran* is a sealed document, the key to which is still in Flaherty's own mind.

I am not quite sure whether it is legitimate to round off a column on the classic *Man of Aran* with a note on the frank entertainment film **It Happened One Night**, now showing at the Tivoli, but in view of the fact that it was directed by Frank Capra, who is generally recognized amongst connoisseurs, cognoscenti and the what-have-you of our discerning public as the best craftsman currently working in America, I think I have a reasonable case.

It Happened One Night is the old Taming of the Shrew story on board a transcontinental bus, with Clarke Gable as a tenacious reporter and Claudette Colbert as a spoilt society heiress on the run. The train of circumstance is, to say the least of it, fortuitous, but Frank Capra has handled his players and situations with such assurance that nobody is likely to raise a quibble. His great talent is in making extraordinary people do extraordinary things in a quite ordinary way – a secret that has helped the great imaginative liars ever since Homer. It is my broad opinion as a motion picture fan that *It Happened One Night* is one of the most entertaining films that has ever been offered to the public, and I have a shrewd suspicion as a critic that Frank Capra is the only director who could elevate Mr Gable and Miss Colbert, charming and talented though they undoubtedly are, into the main body of this weekly oration.

My official tip for the week is *Man of Aran*. My unofficial tip is *It Happened One Night*. I know that this statement will bring down upon me the bitter contempt of film societies, film groups and film theorists generally, but we all have our weaknesses, and mine happens to be a preference for story over seaweed, however patiently gathered and significantly displayed.

29 April 1934

By the time this column appears in print you will, if you have followed the maxims laid down for you by His Majesty's postal authorities and others, be done with the strenuous business of getting ready for Christmas, and not averse from letting the holiday season do something for you.

Assuming, since you are reading this column, that films are your fancy, I should recommend that you make a bee-line for the Leicester-square Theatre and see **The Scarlet Pimpernel**. This exciting costume piece of the French Revolution is not only the best entertainment of the holiday season, but, I would suggest, the most skilful bit of all-round craftsmanship that has ever been evolved in a British studio. S. N. Behrman, of *Queen Christina*; Robert Sherwood, of *Reunion in Vienna*; and Messrs Biro and Wimperis, of *The Private Life of Henry VIII*, have contrived to produce between them a script that is swift and mellow, packed with beautiful English, and smoothly dovetailed. I remember as a schoolgirl creeping out of bed at four in the morning to finish the last thrilling chapters of Baroness Orczy's story. The modern film has lost none of that wide-eyed excitement, but it has, in addition, a background of authority, and a certain moving dignity of expression, that the original never knew.

This *Scarlet Pimpernel*, in spite of its romance, suspense, and occasional melodramatic devices, is a reasonable film. It introduces you to a London, a Paris, in which people lived, and died, and worked, and paid visits to their tailors; it presents a problem of contemporary history, of one nation's doings as seen and reported by the people of another. Thanks to a combination of good script, good direction, and occasionally great playing, the characters live and have individual sharpness; Leslie Howard's troubled Sir Percy and Nigel Bruce's warmly human Prince of Wales are the high spots of the cast, but all are creatures of their class and circumstances, qualified by sharply personal traits.

Hal Rosson, recently Metro-Goldwyn's ace camera-man, has made a fine job of the photography; I doubt if there is any other camera-man in the world who can do such lovely things with the texture of a woman's face. The direction is by Harold Young, who has been known, hitherto, but will certainly not be known again, exclusively as a cutter. Mr Howard's performance has already been mentioned, but I should like to stress it as one of the screen's outstanding emotional performances, finely tempered, and beautifully spoken. The production is, of course, Alexander Korda's. I am sorry to refer so constantly in these columns to Mr Korda. The reason is that he is one of the very few producers who do things that merit reference. *The Scarlet Pimpernel* not only merits reference, but a considerable amount of national pride.

23 December 1934

It is with a considerable measure of national pride, and I confess a certain amount of self-congratulation, that I find myself faced with a review of Alfred Hitchcock's new picture, **The Thirty-Nine Steps**.

I have always fancied 'Hitch' as a director, even in the latter days of his doldrums under the B.I.P. banner. Ever since a very young Hitch, fresh from art direction, made the silent film, *The Lodger*, I was confident that he would eventually come out on top of all the British-born directors in this country. Last year, with *The Man Who Knew Too Much*, he all but justified my opinion, and at last, with *The Thirty-Nine Steps*, he is really there.

Perhaps it would be as well to explain from the start that *The Thirty-Nine Steps* is not in the least faithful to John Buchan's story. The main plot remains, and many of the individual situations; the setting is still Scotland; the hero is still Richard Hannay, although a younger, and a changed, Richard Hannay. But Hitchcock felt that the story as it stood was dated with the tricks of its age, many of which have long since become banal in the cinema. For that reason the stricter conventionalities of melodrama were cut out from the start. A lighter romantic element was introduced, and the methods of escape and detection were modernized. John Buchan himself has endorsed the screen version and, by promising to write a Canadian sequel of the Hannay adventures for Hitchcock some time in the future, seems to have given both the film and the director his blessing.

I cannot help thinking that the choice of Robert Donat for the Hannay role was one of the British industry's happier inspirations. Mr Donat, who has never been very well served in the cinema until now, suddenly blossoms out into a romantic comedian of no mean order. Beginning a little heavily, and quite obviously feeling his way through this mass of new, realistic material, he strikes, before a quarter of the film is over, an easy, confident humour that has always been regarded as the perquisite of the American male star. For the first time on our screens we have the British equivalent of a Clark Gable or a Ronald Colman playing in a purely national idiom. Mr Donat himself, I fancy, is hardly conscious of it, which is all to the good. Mr Hitchcock is certainly conscious of it, and exploits his new star material with all the easy confidence of a local van Dyke or Capra.

When a picture is as good as *The Thirty-Nine Steps*, it is almost superfluous to detail its individual virtues. I could advise you of its best moments – the scene in the political meeting, where Hannay, escaping from the police, is taken for a platform speaker, the Glencoe sequences, beautifully shot in the Highlands through a movable window frame, the glimpse down from the Forth Bridge, the thrilling shot with the foreshortened finger, the charming and expertly managed section in the inn bedroom. I could explain how steadily Hitchcock has refrained from any kind of technical chicanery, how still he keeps his cameras, how adamant he has been against trick cutting. I could point out a hundred ingenuities in the picture, and enjoy doing it, because for once in the cinema recollection is a pleasure. But it will be simpler and less selfish, I think, to include everything in the one recommendation, go to *The Thirty-Nine Steps* and find it all out for yourselves.

6 June 1935

After months of preliminary publicity, the Reinhardt film of

A Midsummer Night's Dream has finally appeared this week in New York and London. Reinhardt himself sets his seal of approval on the picture by announcing, 'For the first time in my life, I have realized my own dream of doing this play with no restrictions on my imagination.' He adds that Mickey Rooney and James Cagney, as Puck and Bottom, 'have lent their amazing personalities to interpretations which are a contribution to Shakespearean tradition.' We may take it, I think, that this is the line along which the inevitable series of Shakespeare subjects is going to be exhibited in the cinema. If that is the case, I am very much afraid that Shakespeare, as a scenarist, is predoomed to failure.

A Midsummer Night's Dream is a vast, ample, and handsome production, which should considerably brighten up the schoolbooks, but adds nothing at all to the mature apprehension of Shakespeare. It has, of course, its happy moments. The clown scenes, when Bottom and Flute and the rest obviously get their own way with the slapstick comedy, have the real earthy tang. There is a long dawn sequence, when Oberon's black cloak, billowing out through the forest, catches quite a lot of magic in its folds. And the Mendelssohn score, beautifully arranged from the music of the *Dream* and other works, helps the illusion of drama a great deal.

But taking it all round as a film production, the *Dream* is muscle-bound. It is so loyal to the letter that it never has time to be loyal to the spirit of the drama's greatest showman. The text, always accurate, though occasionally abridged, sounds for the first time like a dead language. Shakespeare, who wrote for his own audience and his own medium as few other dramatists have ever done, has been ruthlessly exposed to an age and a medium that is alien to him. And that, far more than any alteration of the actual text, seems to me to be giving Shakespeare the lie.

I cannot for the life of me see why Shakespeare, because he was a great dramatist, should be expected to be a good writer of film scenarios. We all know by now how badly the straight stage play adapts itself to the cinema. Why should the plays of Shakespeare be an exception? I should have thought that the very fact that he was better than most, that his plays had more theatre sense than most, should have made him the more unsuitable subject for film performance. I am afraid that only a very snobbish sycophancy, or a very obtuse sense of cinema fitness, could really embrace the Shakespearean text as sound script-writing for the screen.

The plays of Shakespeare have, I admit, one great quality for the cinema. They have story value, and the cinema needs stories badly. They are also rich in 'character parts', and the cinema can do with those too. But they have got to be adapted for the cinema in just the same way as Shakespeare adapted his own 'sources' for the Elizabethan theatre. Otherwise they will be films without a public, stories without a listener. For people have changed in four hundred years, whatever the pedants may say.

There is one solid fact that must not be forgotten in any discussion of a cinema Shakespeare. However loyal to the text the producers may be, the play has got to be performed by modern screen players. Whether their accent be English or American is, I think, a matter of indifference. The important thing is that they are bound to speak the lines with a modern connotation, endow the situations with a modern significance. Speech changes, knowledge changes, humour changes, and each is only pregnant in the light of current understanding. No one knew better than Shakespeare the art of writing for his colleagues and his contemporaries. I hold it the highest possible insult to a great showman to insist that the style he found right for the sixteenth-century theatre should be pointed and applicable to the film players of the present day.

13 October 1935

The tonic appearances of young Mr Fred Astaire in dancing comedy – top hat, white tie, tails, and all the rest of it – are, to me, amongst the greatest joys of the modern cinema. It doesn't much matter where, why, or in what story he happens along. In the present instance it is a marriage mix-up in Venice, including comic valet, comic Italian dress-designer, the lovely but inevitable Ginger Rogers, and a vastly elaborate dance routine number to wind up the show.

Top Hat may not be Mr Astaire's most distinguished vehicle, as the phrase goes, but I doubt whether that will worry anyone seriously. Mr Astaire can get anywhere he wants to on his own feet. Watching him, you are suddenly aware that the lower half of the cinema screen has been wasted all these years. The players have been rooted in it, acting with their faces, their hands, their backs, occasionally their hips. I know of no screen stars except Chaplin and Fred Astaire who have really learnt to act volubly from the knees down.

The engaging thing about Mr Astaire's dancing is the effect of spontaneity. No one, of course, can round off a formal dance number like 'Top Hat' or 'Isn't It a Lovely Day?' with more neatness and style. But it is in the casual occasions of modern life, when he is not deliberately dancing, that his feet behave themselves with the most eloquence. They tell you, far more libellously than words, just what he thinks of the silence room in a London club; they let out all sorts of secrets about the fun of driving a pretty girl in the rain. They criticize and confess; they are sometimes caustic, often impudent, never sentimental.

Fred Astaire may not be in the leading ranks of the screen's great lovers, its foremost thespians, or even its golden-voiced singers. He is, however, one of its most talented and tonic personalities with a genius for making people happy, and the cinema would be the poorer without him by a very long way.

13 October 1935

Germany's film study of the career of France's national heroine, **Das Mädchen Joanna**, is an ingenious and significant contribution to the Nazi documentation of patriotism. Joan of Arc's earlier film historians have dramatized her trial and passion; constituted themselves lawyers for the defence in a flagrant case of miscarriage of justice. Gerhard Menzel, who wrote the present scenario, justifies Joan's execution as a stroke of brilliant strategy on the part of Charles VII, who saw that the legend of Joan dead was a far greater inspiration to a united France than the presence of Joan living. Charles is his hero, Charles his *Führer*; the Maid a pale, possessed virgin, whose fate seems to cut off a life already half rapt away.

This canonization of the Dauphin is, I think, a new point of view on the Jeanne d'Arc episode, and one that fits in neatly with the opinions of the present German regime. It is, one must own, superbly done. Every line, every action, given to the Dauphin Charles is designed to build up this figure of the lonely leader, who allows Joan the easy glory of death, while he has to live on in dishonour for his country's sake. It is a fine part, written without flamboyance, and Gustav Grundgens plays it with a kind of terrible melancholy. Even if the film were less ample and handsome, less sensitive to the physical textures of mediaeval living, I would ask you to see it for his performance. It is a haunted bit of work, spoken with pain and beauty; a masterly apology for a school of thought which you may not applaud but cannot reasonably ignore.

13 October 1935

Since this is the season of brotherhood and goodwill, I think we are justified in a fairly sentimental gesture of gratitude to America for making this British patriotic picture.

It is possible that no English picture would ever be as jingoistic as **Mutiny on the Bounty** but it is certain that no English picture has ever been quite so generous. From first shot to last bar of recording it is a love-song to this island of sea-men, to their ships, and their stout hearts, their discipline and their integrity, to the course they hold to and the stars they follow. The Americans have, in generous measure, the quality of admiration, and it does not seem to them fulsome to praise things they admire.

The Americans believe that the British Navy has always been a darn good navy. In the Bounty film they say so. They tabulate, with an onlooker's clear observation, the detailed rigours and traditions of the service, and show how, though they may have been warped and twisted to serve many men's ends, they have achieved in the end a standard compromise with authority.

Mutiny on the Bounty, highly coloured though it may be, is quite an important document in the history of seamanship. It presents with understanding the case for three men, each schooled in a different code of ethics. There is Captain Bligh, the servant and master of the disciplinary machine, who would leave the prisoners to rot in the hold, but who brought his crew three thousand miles to safety in an open boat in one of the most superb feats of naval history. There is Fletcher Christian, seaman and dreamer, who smashed the Bounty to wreck on the rocks of Pitcairn Island sooner than let his men go back to brutality and punishment. And there is Roger Byam, the lad who sailed in the Bounty to find coral reefs, and flying fish, and the bright stars at night, and who alone of all the crew of that grim adventure found the strait compromise between regiment and humanity.

Metro-Goldwyn, in attacking this triple deal in character-
ization, have been happy in their casting. Charles Laughton's
Captain Bligh has one fault. I find, and one only – he does not
love the sea so much as accept its impositions, does not live
with it so much as in spite of it. Otherwise it is a stubbornly
regimented study of a man who had no grandeur except in
pettiness; a terrible, blasted piece of screen acting, narrow in
range, but deadly accurate.

Clark Gable's Fletcher Christian is, as one might expect, a less
academic portrait, but it gives him the right to be called an actor
at last, and not a film star. Franchot Tone, I found, had many
of the most successful moments of the picture as Byam, but,
then, his part was the most readily likeable, and the best lines
of Talbot Jennings's lovely English dialogue fell to his share.

I can't pretend that *Mutiny on the Bounty* is a very agreeable
picture. If you are squeamish about lashings and other disciplinary brutalities you should not see it. But if these old stories
of tough adventure excite you, if you are in love with white
clippers and rolling water and the course set to far countries,
you will hardly be able to resist the Bounty's importunities. It is
one of America's most masculine excursions into film-making,
excellently handled – except, perhaps, in the scenes in Tahiti. I
utterly refuse to take those Tahiti scenes seriously. But what are a
few Tahiti *leis* against the solid virtues of one of the most exciting
pictures on the screen?

29 December 1935

I think it is unlikely that **The Charge of the Light Brigade**,
Hollywood's new explanation of the blunder at Balaklava, will
go unchallenged by historians, military experts, humanists, and
others in this country. In fact, I fancy that quite a lot of people
will have quite a lot to say about it, and that I can safely leave
that aspect of criticism to authorities who can quote chapter and
verse far better than I.

I will only enter a mild caveat in passing to the effect that this
justification of the order which sent the 27th Lancers to their
death in the Crimea seems to me romantic, but surprising. The
order, it seems, was forged by one Major Vickers (Erroll Flynn),
to avenge a massacre of women and children three years earlier
at Chukoti, in India. Learning that the treacherous Surat Khan,

instigator of the massacre, is present among the Russian troops at Balaklava, the gallant Vickers squares his jaw, waves on his men to the attack, and hisses, 'Surat Khan at Balaklava? This is worth knowing.' It is indeed.

The charge itself, when once we get to it, after one hour and half or so of motion picture in the tried and proved terrain of Northern India, is enormously effective. You may be a little surprised at the preliminary motives which send the Lancers charging so steadfastly on to destruction, and a little bewildered at the consequences, which make a major victory out of what was obviously a minor defeat, but you cannot help admiring the steady pace and intensity of the spectacle. When the noble six hundred, lances level and stirrups touching, pace, canter, and, finally, charge down the mile-long valley, with the enemy guns tearing great holes in their ranks, you are a dead stock if your pulses don't thunder and your heart quicken perceptibly. This scene may be villainous history, but it is magnificent cinema, timed, shot, and cut with brilliance.

It only cramps the patriotic effect a trifle that the Union Jack, nine times out of ten in the picture, is shown resolutely flying upside down.

[1936]

NOTE: Not the least remarkable thing about this remarkable picture is its apparent magical power of dormant development. At any rate, when *The Charge of the Light Brigade* was reissued a few months ago, the distributors were able to announce that 'Warners Bring it Back Bigger than Ever!' And guess who squares his jaw, revolutionizes history, and leads the Lancers on to death and glory? Right – Errol Flynn.

– *Chestnuts in her Lap*, 1947

The Man Without a Face – Featureless, I fear.

26 January 1936

It is my own personal belief that **Rembrandt**, the new film which Alexander Korda and Charles Laughton have made together with so much sweat and love and heart-searching, is one of the finest films ever produced here or in any other country –

but I am quite prepared to admit that this may be a matter of taste.

Rembrandt, I fancy, may not be everybody's picture. It is singularly austere. It lacks – which may disconcert the public – any independent dramatic plot, and is based on the assumption that man in the mass is interested in genius in the individual. Possibly the assumption is true. But it has never been proven, for the simple reason that no producer before has thought of putting it to the test.

Whatever the box-office verdict may be, *Rembrandt* remains, for me, a very keen recollection of pleasure. It is produced, set, and written with a fastidious feeling for beauty. The pictures shine and glow, the lines ring with music. Since it has also what is probably the finest acting performance ever recorded on celluloid, there is every reason for England to be rather proud of *Rembrandt*. Made in Berlin, Vienna, Paris, or even Hollywood, this picture would be acclaimed a classic. I hope we shall not be silly and self-conscious about it because it happens to be our own.

Alexander Korda, whom no one can accuse of lack of courage, has given us something quite new in cinema – a spiritual adventure. Of all his celebrated 'private lives,' this is the first that is really private. It is simply a close-up study of a genius – a man who loses all outward dignities, and finds in their place a new dignity of spirit. *Rembrandt* is the only film I know that exalts a tale of unsuccess into something like a song of jubilee.

The story begins in Amsterdam, where Rembrandt van Rijn was a fashionable painter, three hundred years ago. From the first scene, the note of prosperity goes sharply downwards. His wife, whom he loves passionately, dies, and Rembrandt finds, like the Preacher of the Testament, that two can be together and have heat, but one cannot be warm alone. He drinks, he whores. His fortune goes in debts. When he can borrow money for colours, he paints the beggars in the streets. A lonely and driven man, he goes home to his father's mill, to the peasant's bread, the lamp and the Bible and the fire corner, to try to find tranquillity.

In time he finds it, in a second union with a servant girl, Hendrikje, who has borne him a child, and is kindly and comforting. She, too, dies, and he is left destitute, but the comfort she has brought survives her. The picture closes with Rembrandt as an old man, who has lived fully, taking charity from an old pupil, and spending it on gold and cobalt and ochre.

Home in his room, before the mirror, he begins to paint his own self portrait – and the face that looks back at him is the face of a philosopher.

Through all the seasons of a long life, through sunshine and snow, while the bells of Amsterdam ring for feast-day and funeral, one man has grown old and wise – and that is all the picture. I don't profess to know how this austerity of plot will please the public. For my own part, I like it enormously. Patriotism, liberty, daring, have all in their time been the subject of the screen's encomiums, but this justification of spirit seems to me something sane and new.

In spite of a gracious and delicate performance from Elsa Lanchester as the girl-wife, Hendrijke, *Rembrandt* remains a one-man picture. It is a close-up so intimate that the other figures are thrown inevitably out of focus. Only by laying himself bare to the bone could any actor hope to play it. Only Laughton, I believe, of all screen actors, could hope to play it so movingly and well.

Carl Zuckmayer, the scenarist, and Korda, the director, between them have given Laughton a script that is rich with Biblical beauty, and Laughton has taken the golden passages like a psalmist. Rembrandt is his great part; his matriculation; full of the intimate moments that test an actor's integrity to the highest. The scene in which he paints furiously, trying to catch the lines of his dead wife's face before memory fades, the scene at the easel during Hendrikje's last illness, the scene of the homecoming to the mill – these are secret moments, fearfully conceived and painfully delivered. When an actor can do these things without faltering there is little left for his job to teach him. It is the one quality that Laughton and Korda share between them – the quality that makes their partnership unique in the cinema – that neither of them is 'afraid of that which is high'.

[1936]

NOTE FROM THE ICHABOD DEPARTMENT: I have made a special point of including this notice of *Rembrandt*, partly because it recalls a great film, and partly because it pays tribute to a fine talent which seems recently to have been withdrawn from us. One of the most painful screen phenomena of latter years has been the gradual decline and fall of Charles Laughton from the splendid actor of *The Private Life of Henry VIII*, *Mutiny on the Bounty* and *Rembrandt* to the mopping and mowing mug of *The Man From Down Under*. What has happened to Mr Laughton? I hesitate to place on an actor the responsibility for a crime that may have been the producer's, the director's, or the script-writer's. But I cannot be persuaded that if Charles Laughton had stood up and firmly said 'No,' any producer, director, or script-writer in the two hemispheres would have been sufficiently dull to his own interests to say 'Yes.' All that can be said is that Mr Laughton's performances in recent years seem, at the best, to be made up of lines and touches broken off from his old parts, and combined with the facility of an experienced actor who has long since stopped trying to get down to the core of a character, and is content to amuse himself and the audience with surface decoration. At the worst, his roles can roughly be classified under two heads: roguery-poguery and muggery-wuggery. One can picture the Laughton of today, who presumably still recognizes a class acting job when he sees it as well as any man living, standing bare-headed before a still from *Rembrandt* and saying, 'Laddie, what an actor I was then!'

– Chestnuts in her Lap, 1947

Sabotage is the cleverest picture Alfred Hitchcock has made since the arrival of the talkies. It is also, to me, the least likeable of them all.

Every shot in it, every sound, every conjunction of images, is the result of close and consummate care. It is a cold, calculated, and quite masterly piece of film technics, designed to raise suspense and horror to the highest frequency. There is no department of the industry, script-writing, direction, cutting, sound, and camera, that could not learn something from this picture. I am prepared to give it every honour in the academy so long as I am never asked to sit through it again.

The keynote of *Sabotage* is complete destruction. Not only is the main plot concerned with a conspiracy to blow up Piccadilly Circus and terrorize London, but everything that is human and innocent and ordinary in the picture seems consecrated to the needs of ruthlessness. The young schoolboy brother of the heroine, the only really sympathetic character in the piece, is smashed to pieces with a time bomb in a London omnibus. With him go a puppy, an amiable old lady, a friendly conductor, and all the most cheerful group of sentimental commonplaces that Hitchcock can gather together into one locale. Following this event, the heroine sticks her husband in the stomach with a carving knife, and a kindly old anarchist blows the corpse and himself to glory with another hand grenade, leaving the murderess free to marry the Scotland Yard detective. And all this destruction is neatly contrived from two pots of explosives kept in the back bedroom of a bird-shop, and labelled, with cherubic Hitchcock malice, 'Tomato Ketchup' and 'Strawberry Jam.'

This is, I grant you, a brilliant piece of horrification. The scene with the boy in the bus is superbly timed. With young Desmond Tester – last seen with Nova Pilbeam in *Tudor Rose* – as a human, likeable youngster, this bit is calculated to wring every wither in the audience. But I believe – and I stick to it – that there is a code in this sort of free-handed slaughter, and Hitchcock has gone outside the code in *Sabotage*. As a detective fan and an inveterate reader of thrillers I suggest that this is the sort of thing that should get a fellow blackballed from the Crime Club. Discreet directors don't kill schoolboys and dogs in omnibuses. Believe me, it isn't done.

16 December 1936

One very hot and dusty Friday two summers ago, when half the world was away on holiday and the other half was thinking of them with malice, there slipped into the Empire Theatre, quietly, a small programme picture called *The Thin Man*.

Five minutes after the film began we knew we were watching history made in the cinema. *The Thin Man* was in its own way as important as *The Birth of a Nation* or *Caligari*, *The Covered Wagon* or *It Happened One Night*. Its slick fun, its debonnair excitement, were new. Its treatment was startling. In an industry which lives by cycles – gangster cycles, backstage cycles, pioneer cycles, even Shakespeare cycles – it was long odds that the studios would snatch up the idea of a 'Thin Man' cycle. They did.

These later pictures could not catch the spirit of the original, but they got the notion. *The Thin Man* had two peculiar plot novelties. It proved that a murder mystery on the screen need not be a chill, morbid affair, and it showed that fun and romance may not always end with marriage. The imitators took hold of these two ideas and reduced them to a formula. Murder-with-a-smile became the fashion. The screen was bright with happy married couples. But still there was no successor to *The Thin Man*.

Now after nearly three years, Nick and Nora Charles, the couple that started all the trouble, are here again in another murder mystery. It is called **After the Thin Man**. It was made by the same staff, the same writers and director as the original picture. William Powell and Myrna Loy are still trying to find a minute to be alone together. Even Asta, the famous fox-terrier, is back on the trail.

The first *Thin Man* was made in sixteen days from start to finish. The second proved more of a problem to its producers. It begins precisely where the other left off, on the Sunset Limited bound for San Francisco, with Nick and Nora heading home from their eventful honeymoon, and Asta curled up in the hatbox. The last murder in *The Thin Man* took place in New York at Christmas. The first murder in *After the Thin Man* takes place in San Francisco at New Year. But actually two and a half years had elapsed since the Charleses boarded that train.

It was no easy job for the unit to recover the same props, the same costumes, the same make-up, the same personal mannerisms that were used for the earlier picture. But they did it. The westbound steams into San Francisco on time, with the baggage loaded years ago at the New York terminal. When Nick leads the barking Asta down on to the platform, even his leash is the same.

This new *Thin Man* isn't quite as overwhelming as its predecessor, because we looked for a good thing this time, and got it. But it's a treasure. It's gay, and careless and exciting, and beautifully human, with a surprise ending, strictly according to Crime Club rules, that should fool the expert.

For a time, I admit, I was worried by the family note that seemed to be creeping into it. It is all very well for Asta, the fox terrier, to come home and find himself reputed father of a black quintuplet, but when Nora, the gay and curious Nora, is seen knitting tiny garments, it seems to threaten an end to the whole series.

However, I find I am wrong. The author, Dashiell Hammett, will apparently fix everything. Metro-Goldwyn have already taken an option on the further activities of the Charleses. It seems likely, family or no family, that the happiest partnership of the screen will go on.

4 April 1937

Arithmetic has never been my strong point, so I will leave it to you to work out whether 100 men plus 1 girl equals 3 smart girls.

I can promise you, though, that young Deanna Durbin's second picture, **100 Men and a Girl**, is far and away better than most of Hollywood's recent offerings – a charming, humorous, and rather touching little tale of a child who whips together a band of workless musicians and gets them an engagement, with Stokowski conducting, on somebody's radio hour.

It is a long time since I saw so much furtive eye-dabbing at any picture. There is something about this child – just youth, maybe – that seems to make the toughest customers choky. She is singing, by the way, better and better, and she can give points to many a Hollywood diva in what to do and how to do it in the pauses between the musical numbers.

There aren't so many pauses here though, because when Miss Durbin isn't singing, the Stokowski orchestra is mostly playing (Wagner, Mozart, Liszt, Verdi). Twice, in fact, they go into action together, and in these scenes even my arithmetic can figure out with certainty that one girl equals 100 men.

5 December 1937

A young man who used to write slapstick gags for Mack Sennett comedies has just made one of the screen's most deliberately esoteric pictures. That is in order in our topsy turvy cinema. He has presented to his audience, very seriously, thoughts on life, sociology, and politics that have a curious Wellsian flavour of naive wisdom, expressed in dialogue as stubborn as anything Mr Wells has ever dreamed of. That is rather less in order, but it is characteristic, too.

There was nothing haphazard about the choice of **Lost Horizon** for Frank Capra's latest picture. Even while he was making the gay and engaging *Mr Deeds*, his thoughts were busy with the Hilton story. 'I read *Lost Horizon* when it was first published,' he says, 'and immediately I wanted to do it. I saw in the book one of the most important pieces of literature in the last decade. The story had bigness. It held a mirror up to the thoughts of every human being on earth.' With characteristic Hollywood thoroughness he commissioned his London agent to buy the original manuscript. He pressed all the resources of the studio into service. He spent a year on research and preparation. He chose his cast, with the exception of Ronald Colman, from comparatively small-part players. He cut the film himself, grudging every inch of its vast and crowded footage. *Lost Horizon*, at every point, is Capra's own deliberate film.

What is it about? About Atlantis, Utopia. With very slight alterations, approved by the author, it follows James Hilton's Hawthornden Prize story. A small group of white people, crowding into a rescue plane to escape revolution in Baskul, find themselves at the mercy of a Mongolian pilot, who swings the plane out of its course towards the Himalayas, towards unknown Tibet. Here, amongst the snow peaks and the blizzards, the plane crashes, and the five passengers are guided by secret paths towards the hidden lamasery of Shangri-La, in the warm, fertile valley of the Blue Moon.

Sickness and old age are unknown in Shangri-La, ruled over by a 300-year-old High Lama. The guiding principle of these people is moderation. Their motto is 'Be kind'. Disputes are waived in the interest of good manners. Year after year, for centuries, porters from beyond the mountains have brought to Shangri-La the books, the furniture, the art treasures of the outside world. They have even brought, it seems, a Bechstein Grand, and the published works of England's coming Foreign Secretary, passenger on the kidnapped Baskul plane.

It is the High Lama's pious belief that here in Shangri-La, when war and disease have destroyed the civilization of the old world, a new civilization will begin with the young Foreign Secretary as its prophet. It is a fantastic conception, childish but charming, something akin to Wells's idea in *Things to Come*, of a new world of airmen serviced from a base in Basra. So drowsy and pleasant is the country, so mystic its influence, and so kindly its people, that the little band of travellers come to welcome, in time, its narcotised doctrine. All but the Foreign Secretary's younger brother, a solid youth with constitutional notions, who urges his reluctant brother to make his way back to civilization through the blizzards and the mountain passes. The younger man is killed in an avalanche, the elder is rescued by British agents, but escapes and fights his way back, doggedly, to the enchanted valley. Here the book ends, and here the film should end, with a group of men in a London club raising their glasses in a toast to the lost fanatic, 'May he find his Shangri-La! May we all find our Shangri-La!'

Such a story, as you may imagine, is a showman's paradise, and Frank Capra has not spared a detail that might make it exciting and memorable. The photography is brilliant; it gleams and shines. The sound is stirring. He is less successful, perhaps, with the more delicate passages of Mr Hilton's Utopian fancy than in the violent adventure sequences that open and close the picture. The frightened crowds in Baskul, the burning hangar, the roar of rescue planes, set your heart pounding. The flight in the mysterious plane, bound God-knows-whither, above the sparse air of the Himalayas, makes you understand claustrophobia. The crash against the mountain-side leaves you bruised and shaken. All this, at least, is miraculous cinema; sound picture at its best.

Ronald Colman as the Foreign Secretary, John Howard as his Utopia-resistant brother, H. B. Warner as the Lama's deputy, and Thomas Mitchell as an American passenger make the cast interesting. Jane Wyatt and Edward Horton, romance and comedy, are Capra's concessions to Hollywood, and while they brighten the entertainment they hardly take on the colour of the story. Margo, in a Tibetan reincarnation of Rider Haggard's *She*, suggests, rather horribly, the fate outside Shangri-La, of an ageing woman. Sam Jaffe's High Lama is a little horrible, too, with his cracked face and gaunt hands, and hardly makes the longevity of Shangri-La seem enviable, but he does well, I thought, with two of the longest and most difficult monologues ever delivered in a film.

Lost Horizon is not by any means a flawless picture; not as deft as Capra's *It Happened One Night*; not as human and lovable as his *Mr Deeds*. But it is a considerable picture; an advance, in certain scenes, on Capra's earlier technique. *Submarine, Dirigible, American Madness, Forbidden, The Bitter Tea of General Yen, Lady for a Day, It Happened one Night, Strictly Confidential, Mr Deeds, Lost Horizon* – what a row of giants! The man who made these pictures is not quite forty. I suggest that the cinema industry subscribe for a ticket to Shangri-La for Frank Capra, to ensure a continuity of the best and most brilliantly varied entertainment on the screen.

18 April 1937

The Bride Wore Red

QUESTION.   Who was the bride and why did she wear red?

ANSWER.   She was the Most Degraded Woman in the Lowest Dive in Trieste, and she wore red because this is a whimsy.

QUESTION.   What is a whimsy?

ANSWER.   It is a film in which the characters suffer from spots before the eyes.

QUESTION.   What sort of spots?

ANSWER.   Usually spots in Ireland, with an orchard and a cow, sometimes spots in Paris in spring, occasionally spots in a neat little house in the Bronx, infrequently spots on an English moor with a wet wind blowing.

QUESTION.   What sort of spots did the Most Degraded Woman in Trieste suffer from?

ANSWER.   A white house with two automobiles, a bed with a swan's head on it, a white fur cover falling clear to the floor, and a white telephone.

QUESTION.   Did she get them?

ANSWER.   No, but she got a red evening dress and a fortnight in the best hotel in the Tyrol.

QUESTION.   How?

ANSWER.   Because a successful gambler wanted to Fix the Great Wheel of Life, and find out what made a waiter a waiter and a lady a lady.

QUESTION.   Did he find out?

ANSWER.   I really don't know. He disappeared from the picture at the end of the first reel.

QUESTION.   Why?

ANSWER.   Because the film stars Miss Joan Crawford, Mr Franchot Tone and Mr Robert Young, and the gambler is only a small-part actor.

QUESTION.   What happened to the Most Degraded Woman in Trieste when she reached the Tyrol?

ANSWER.   She lived for the first time. She noticed pine trees and birds' nests. She breathed in great gulps. She changed the shade of her nail varnish. She also met Mr Tone.

QUESTION.   What was he? A guest at the hotel?

ANSWER.   Oh, no, he was the village postman. He had suffered from whimsy man and boy. He lived alone in a Cottage High up on a Hill, with chickens and a cow. He played a flute.

When young he had tried to grow tall and strong, like a pine tree. Later on he learnt to laugh like a poplar.

QUESTION.   Did Miss Crawford love him?

ANSWER.   Terribly. Even in Tyrolean shorts and embroidered braces. But she had to marry Mr Robert Young.

QUESTION.   Why?

ANSWER.   On account of he had a yacht, and lots of money, and she had only a fortnight to get it in.

QUESTION.   Did Mr Tone know about this?

ANSWER.   Naturally. He read her telegrams.

QUESTION.   What did he say?

ANSWER.   He said in his whimsical way, 'I've always known there was a balustrade between the terrace and the lawn. I used to think it was to stop the people on the terrace from falling to the lawn. Now I realize it's to stop the people on the lawn from rising to the terrace.'

QUESTION.   Quite a philosopher, wasn't he?

ANSWER.   Yes, he was full of quaint thoughts like that. It came of getting up so early to greet the wind in the mornings.

QUESTION.   And Mr Young, was he a whimsical fellow?

ANSWER.   Yes, but his whimsy was of a lower order. He didn't care for early rising. He preferred night life and stars. Claimed to know Venus intimately. Said that her affair with Mars was common gossip all up and down the Milky Way.

QUESTION.   But wasn't that rather charming?

ANSWER.   No, flashy, decidedly flashy. He let himself go, too, about sardines.

QUESTION.   How do you mean, about sardines?

ANSWER.   He claimed that most people preferred sardines to caviare because they had never tasted caviare.

QUESTION.   Well, don't they?

ANSWER.   Possibly, but he shouldn't have said so. All the best whimsy puts sardines above caviare, sees heaven in a bed sitting-room and stars in a puddle. It stamped him at once as a low fellow with nothing but a yacht to recommend him. Besides, look what he said to Miss Crawford about her dancing.

QUESTION.   What did he say?

ANSWER.   He said: 'You don't dance like a débutante. You dance like a professional.'

QUESTION.   And didn't she?

ANSWER.   Of course she did. She hadn't been ten years with Metro-Goldwyn for nothing. But Mr Young shouldn't have noticed it. He shouldn't have danced with her at all. He should have been dancing with his *fiancée*.

QUESTION.   Oh, had he a *fiancée*? Why didn't you mention her?

ANSWER.   Why should I? She was a small-part player, too. All she had to do was to wear black velvet and suffer.

QUESTION.   Wasn't she whimsical?

ANSWER.   Certainly not. She was a lady.

QUESTION.   And which did Mr Young marry?

ANSWER.   The lady, naturally. Breeding is Deeper than Manners. Besides, Mr Tone came fluting into the hotel and blew the gaff about Trieste with a delayed telegram.

QUESTION.   Wasn't that rather unsporting of him?

ANSWER.   Very. But when you grow up like a tree you act like a tree. He said his love was stronger than Miss Crawford.

QUESTION.   And was it?

ANSWER.   Apparently. At any rate, she saw that the red dress was cheap and flashy. She saw that the nest was empty and the yacht more or less superfluous. She felt Free for the first time, walked lightly, without a Burden. And she put on a peasant dress and a paler shade of nail varnish.

QUESTION.   Why?

ANSWER.   Because she was Afraid.

QUESTION.   Afraid of what?

ANSWER.   How should I know? People in whimsy, when they're not Having Fun, are always Afraid. Don't ask such silly questions.

QUESTION.   But what did she do?

ANSWER.   She climbed up to the pines.

QUESTION.   Why to the pines?

ANSWER.   Because Mr Tone was waiting for her there. He wanted to take her to the stars.

QUESTION.   What on earth for?

ANSWER.   So that Metro-Goldwyn could say in their advertisements that 'Joan Crawford, in all her lustrous career, has never been in a production so glitterful and glamorful.'

1937

It is a strange and unhappy paradox that prevents the film of **The Golem**, that curious medieval legend of the Prague ghetto, from being made again today in the country that first produced it, with so much power and enchantment, as a silent picture thirteen years ago.

If ever there was a subject fitted at heart to the German talent, it is *The Golem*. Strange mixture of dogma and magic, of beauty and the black arts, of cruelty and sentiment, it is the story of a robot, compound of earth, air, fire and water, who can be brought to life at need to save the Jewish people. What a picture Paul Wegener made of this legend in the golden days of the German cinema! The Ghetto streets were curious and warped; the roofs furtive; the houses seemed to whisper to one another. It was a dark tale of the Dark Ages, and there was magic in it. I must have watched three thousand films since I saw it, but I have hardly forgotten a scene.

There is little enchantment about the present version of *The Golem*, but in its precise and handsome French way it is impressive. Harry Baur, as the fear-ridden emperor, is dry, academic, brilliant. The intrigues and gallantries of the court, the habits of hall and stable and bed-chamber, are done with relish. There is a lovely face in it, too: a young actress named Jan Holt, who gives the film occasional gleams of poetry. It is all rich and spacious, and rather exquisite, and the big scene at the end should do nicely. If one can forget that Wegener once did it so much better, with nothing but a robot, a child and a flower.

4 April 1937

The first time I ever heard of *The Prisoner of Zenda* I was nine, and I had just swallowed a cherry stone. I regret to be autobiographical, but the circumstances, you see, impressed me forcibly. Strelsau – and holidays in seaside lodgings in Yorkshire – salt-and-water in a tooth glass – and the reappearance of the cherry stone – are all mixed up in my memory in a vague and not wholly unpleasing miasma of excitement. Since then I have always claimed a certain intimacy with the Elphbergs. My favourite golden marble was christened Flavia. Rupert was a handsome blood alley. Rudolph himself was represented, regrettably, by a glass stopper out of a bottle of ginger pop.

For old times' sake, then, I find that I cannot be severely critical of the film version of **The Prisoner of Zenda**, which opened at Leicester Square's new Odeon last Tuesday. A reasonably good

'Zenda' in any medium – film, play, opera, or broadcast – is still a sentimental delight to me. Seated in my leopard-skin chair – the rich thought of the Odeon management – and dimly surrounded by hundreds of other leopards, I settled down, quite simply, to enjoy myself. And since John Cromwell's film is decidedly good Zenda, I did.

With small local variations, the film answers honourably to its original. It is a much better picture, all told, than the silent version, made fifteen years ago, with Lewis Stone as Rudolf and Ramon Novarro, a newly discovered juvenile, as the young Rupert Hentzau. It is just sad enough to be effective, and just romantic enough to be consoling. It is dressed, as it should be, in the puffed sleeves, the braided skirts, and the Norfolk shooting jackets of its late Victorian period. When Rassendyl leaps into the moat of Zenda to rescue his unhappy cousin by a split second, he swims deliberately – breast stroke. The whole thing is leisured and sentimental and bourgeois, and it makes you a little homesick for the quiet days when it was better to be good than to be clever. When ladies sent their heart's message wrapped round a rose, and gentlemen had time, even in moments of passion, to remember their subjunctives, and murmur academically, 'If Love Were All!'

The present film, of course, comes from Hollywood, where they are nothing if not cultured, pronouncing Don Juan Don Won, and Don Quixote Don Keehoty, and remembering the 'h' in Nottingham with a precision that should make us blush for our slovenliness. It is not really surprising, then, to find our old friend Colonel Sapt meticulously pronounced Zarpt by all the major players. It seems a little strange at first, but you get used to it: even find it, in time, agreeably classy. And Sapt or Zarpt, he is still the pivot of the story, the grand old devil who had never heard of the internal combustion engine, but knew enough to make a king a king.

With Ronald Colman as the two Rudolfs, Aubrey Smith as Zarpt, Douglas Fairbanks, Junior, as Hentzau, and Madeleine Carroll as the pale Flavia, the film runs along beautifully in the best Zenda tradition. Only a stage removed from the theatre school of the double stamp, the drama is emphasized, in all its high spots, by discreet music. 'He is my king – I have a feeling about my King' (loyal music). 'Rudolf – it's Michael!' (sinister music). 'You see, I've never been in love before' (sweet music). 'I haven't lived like a king, but perhaps I can die like one, and not disgrace a crown I've never worn!' (pompous music). 'Your heart will always be in my heart, and the touch of your lips on mine' (lingering music). 'Fate doesn't always make the right men kings! We'll meet again!'' (Abdication music and Colman on the skyline).

This mixture of pomp and nostalgia is all that it should be, and only once, in the whole performance, was I sufficiently shocked by a line to shudder in my fauteuil of leopard skin. That was when Rudolf, turning to Flavia with whimsy in his eyes, asked her if she had ever seen England in spring, and added, 'I know a little stream near Aylesbury I'd like to show you.' Such a thought is pure Hollywood fancy, 1937 style, and a disgrace to any Elphberg. Rudolf, who 'enjoyed an enviable social position,' whose address was 305, Park-lane, and whose 'haunt' the Tyrol – Rudolf, who could speak four languages fluently, who was a strong swordsman and a good shot, who 'could ride anything that had a back to sit on' – was about as likely to take a queen paddling in a stream near Aylesbury as I am to take a personally conducted party of readers to the Bahamas. He didn't even go to school at Harrow, and hop into an up-train to Aylesbury on half-holidays. I am grieved to disappoint the makers of the picture, who refer to 'the old school tie' on several occasions, but Rudolf was educated, man and boy, in Germany, and the old school tie was undoubtedly Heidelberg.

7 November 1937

NOTE: It was actually Fritz and Sapt to whom Ronald Colman talked about the trout stream near Aylesbury; which seems perfectly reasonable. Oh well – nobody gets everything right. – A.L.

The Last Train From Madrid – The Spanish civil war used by the commercial wizards of Hollywood as an opportunity for an up-to-date, *Grand Hotel*, all-in melodrama of assorted destinies. Politically speaking, it might as well be the last train from Crewe.

5 December 1937

The first moment that Miss Marlene Dietrich sweeps up to the reception desk of a Paris hotel in **Angel**, you feel sure that you are looking at a mystery woman. It is something about the highlight on her lip-rouge, the way her eyes peek from side to side, and the dashing way in which she tosses off the signature 'Mrs Brown' in the register. You know, of course, that she isn't Mrs Brown, but beyond that you have no notion who she may be, except possibly Miss Marlene Dietrich, the film star, practising acting. In point of fact, she is the wife of a British Cabinet Minister, who is currently engaged in representing his country at Geneva. Oh, you move in exalted circles in *Angel*, and meet the most wonderful people. There is no house with less than four upper servants kept in the whole of the film.

It is Mr Melvyn Douglas, whom she meets in Paris at a gaming-house, who thinks up the cosy name of 'Angel' for Miss Dietrich. As an upper-class Englishman 'recently returned from Government service in India,' he would have these bright thoughts, naturally. Quite naturally, too, and with a well-bred charm that robs the idea of any crudeness, he suggests to his mysterious lady that they should 'get together for the evening.' They get together. A perambulating violinist plays for them, tenderly, suggestively, right in the eardrum. Under his influence Miss Dietrich, dismissing the trifling thought of her husband, the Cabinet Minister, indicates that they might meet again, and elope, next Wednesday, at five-thirty. It is Paris, *mon dieu*, and cinema, and spring.

The next day, in England, Sir Frederick Barker, brilliant statesman, fresh from his round-table conquest of twenty-one nations, arrives home from Geneva. The papers are full of it. There is nothing else but Barker in the evening editions. Crowned with a weary charm that only Mr Herbert Marshall can achieve, he retires to his country seat just outside London. A real regular English home it is, just like yours or mine, or Mr Anthony Eden's, with a Great Dane on the hearthrug, yards of mullion round the windows, and Miss Marlene Dietrich sleeping in the best bedroom. Only, just to remind you that this is an important picture, Miss Dietrich, in swansdown, presently tiptoes in to her husband with a telegram. He reads it, and frowns, looking frightfully political. 'What's worrying you, darling?' asks Miss Dietrich. 'Is it France?' 'No,' says Mr Marshall briefly, 'Jugo-Slavia.' 'Oh,' replies Miss Dietrich, with a whole leading article in the inflection, 'I see.'

The problem of Jugo-Slavia being settled, presumably by breakfast time, life at Barker Hall resumes its proper serenity.

The Cabinet is quiescent. Sir Frederick and lady attend the races. I have forgotten why they do this, but I am quite clear why they also attend the opera. It is so that Mr Marshall may murmur to Miss Dietrich, in that rich indifferent voice which has thrilled thousands, 'Look, my dear, there's the Duchess of Loamshire on your left.'

Since it is essential, by this time, that Mr Melvyn Douglas should come back into the story, Mr Marshall meets him, quite by accident, at Lord Davington's place after luncheon. Finding that one of them was called Snooky and the other Poochy by the same Paris semptress during the war, the two men just naturally get together. Mr Marshall asks Mr Douglas to luncheon next day at Barker Hall. That's natural, too, and Etonian. 'You know, I've only known you for a day, and yet I feel ——' 'I know, old man, I feel it, too.' 'You forget, Barker ——' 'Frederick.' 'Of course, Frederick.' 'Gin and tonic?' 'Thanks. Just a spot.'

They have veal for lunch that day, at the great reunion. Angel, Lady Barker, doesn't eat the veal, but she carries off the reunion superbly. Not an eyelash flickers when she is left alone with Mr Douglas. 'Angel,' he murmurs, 'I don't understand you,' she replies, with that *savoir faire* that is only learnt in Downing Street and Hollywood. 'The lampshade may be blue,' he whispers, wildly and irrelevantly, 'but when you light it up, it's the greenest green in the world. I'll be waiting for you in Paris at 5.30 on Wednesday.' 'I shall not be there,' says Miss Dietrich firmly. Meanwhile, Mr Marshall is on the telephone to the Foreign Office. His face is again grimly political. 'Anderson?' he listens. 'Dear, dear, what's the trouble? Oh, t-t-t-t-t.'

'I'm afraid,' says Mr Marshall, sadly, to his wife over the whisky, 'that I shall have to go back to Geneva.' 'Can't Anderson do it?' 'He could, of course, but ——' Miss Dietrich is huffed at this. She has been counting, God knows why, on a second honeymoon in a little place in Vienna, up six flights of stairs and no elevator. That seems heaven to her, after the Barker place, and somehow terribly, psychologically important. 'Oh, very well,' she says in a pique, 'if we can't go to Vienna, take me with you as far as Paris. I haven't bought any clothes in ages.' I'll do a bit of shopping, she seems to hint, like any suburban housewife. Just drop me off at the Rue de la Paix and I'll make my own way home.

In the end it's the manager of Croydon Airport who tips Mr Marshall off to the domestic situation. In a scene that is all English and stiff upper lip, the three meet in the gaming-house in Paris.

Nothing is said that can be regretted. Nothing is said that can even be remembered. Angel, Lady Barker, and Sir Frederick Barker entrain for their inadequate hotel in Vienna, leaving Mr Douglas repentant and the English Cabinet to go to the devil.

This film, which you may care to add to your collection, was directed and produced by Ernst Lubitsch. It is intended, I am told, for 'the young, the gay, and the sophisticated.' It is also 'Dietrich as You Desire Her.' Finding that none of these qualifications concerns me deeply, I might have tossed off the film in a couple of paragraphs. Courtesy, however, compels me to give it a column, in view of the Chinese proverb printed so neatly on the front of the programme. 'One picture,' this states, succinctly, though rather optimistically, even for weekly journalism, 'is worth ten thousand words.'

1937

No one can claim that this latest output of Samuel Goldwyn's prodigal energy fails to live up to its title, *The Hurricane*. There's a hurricane all right. It's magnificent. It blows for the last twenty minutes of the picture, and is the biggest, the best, the noisiest, the most spectacular cataclysm ever screened.

Thousands perish, a whole South Sea island is destroyed, forests go down like mown grass, ships are smashed to matchwood, and Mr Aubrey Smith, the local vicar, dies in his church to the chords of a heavenly Wurlitzer. The rest of the principals are saved, because Mr Jon Hall, who has paddled 600 miles in a canoe to get there in time for the hurricane, knows just which kind of tree to tie them to.

Few people will bother to remember what the rest of the film is about. It goes with the wind.

30 January 1938

Alfred Hitchcock, the screen's most horny-hearted melodramatist, has reformed, or mellowed, or weakened, or whatever you like to call it when a man who has been killing off his victims nonchalantly for years, suddenly becomes interested in youth and innocence.

His new film, called *Young And Innocent* (just like that), is still a murder story, for Hitchcock's mind runs naturally to policemen. When he was a very little boy, one of his worst punishments was to be locked up, in a friendly way, of course, for a few minutes in the local constabulary. He is quite a big boy now, but the sight of a blue uniform still makes him sweat. That may be, although it probably isn't, the reason for his persistent predilection in favour of crime in pictures. When he sits down to think out a new subject, the first thing that comes zooming up into his brain is always murder, or kidnapping, or blackmail, or a neat bit of espionage. *Young And Innocent* is a typical Hitchcock subject. There's a body in the third shot, and the whole film is bristling with helmets and uniforms. But, for the first time in one of his pictures, the crime is secondary to a warm human interest. It's melodrama, but somehow cosy, too.

Hitchcock himself blames me for his change of heart. He was pained, it seems, by my comments on his last picture, *Sabotage*, in which he blew up a schoolboy in a bus with a time bomb. I like a bit of murder with the best of them, but there is a certain ethical code that has to be observed in crime fiction, and killing schoolboys is right outside it. We had a very acid talk on that occasion, and for quite twenty-four hours we didn't think well of each other. But Hitchcock apparently brooded. I have his own word for that, and his wife's, and his secretary's, which seems to make it unanimous. As a family man himself, it hurt him to think that the matrons of Harrow and Putney and Ashton-under-Lyne might feel badly about his treatment of the school-children. So he made *Young And Innocent*, which is concerned, besides crime, with a large family of schoolboys, and a heroine who is herself only just out of the schoolroom. The heroine finds a prospective husband, and none of the younger children suffers anything worse than an extracted molar, which may happen in Harrow and Putney and Ashton any day.

If Hitchcock likes to attribute *Young And Innocent* to me, he may, and I shall be delighted. For I like it best of all his pictures. It may not be, academically speaking, the cleverest. The adepts who go to a Hitchcock film to grub out bits of montage may be disappointed. Except for a few neat little things like cutting from a woman's shriek to a sea-gull's cry, and tracking up through a crowded room to the face of an unsuspected murderer, until his eyes, which give him away, fill the screen, it is not what I should call a tricksy picture. There is no sequence in it so memorable, from a cinematic point of view, as the knife scene in *Blackmail*, or the bit with Peter Lorre's death in *The Man Who Knew Too Much*. But it is exciting, and ingenious enough to satisfy any normally intelligent person, and it has something which I have missed so far from all the brilliant row of Hitchcock's pictures, and that is humanity.

I don't mean humanity in the soft, sentimental sense, like being kind to dogs and cuddling wide-eyed children. *Young and Innocent* is far too young and innocent to be sentimental. Sentiment is a perquisite of age and experience, which hits us hardest in the middle years. This film is about clear-eyed, rather ruthless young people, who haven't time to imagine much, but feel acutely. When the heroine, a Chief Constable's Girl Guide daughter, first meets the hero, a young man arrested for murder, she gives him an appraising glance and says coolly, 'He doesn't look like a murderer. He's not my type anyway.' But all the same she falls in love with him.

The real charm of the film is its eye for human values. Hitchcock seems to know, with a certainty that has sometimes evaded him, what is important and what is immaterial to a person in certain circumstances, just how far emotion can affect behaviour, just the look or the word or the withdrawal that can send bonnets flying over the windmill. He presupposes two young people thrown together by chance into a curiously intimate adventure. A man who has knocked about the world a little, a bit of a cynic perhaps, but a bit of a dreamer, too, is arrested for the murder of a woman washed up on the seashore. He escapes from the local gaol, climbs into an old car driven by the Chief Constable's daughter, and persuades her to help him. Torn between her warm heart and her parochial mind, she drives him furiously about the countryside. They shelter in an old mill, a railway siding, a disused mine, and, finally, run the real murderer to earth in a hotel orchestra. Meanwhile, the fugitive's gentleness, his grave consideration, have touched the Girl Guide heart, and she finds she has fallen in love with him, just about the time that her schoolboy brothers are speculating on her odd behaviour over the family dinner table.

The plot, as you can see, is something that could be made silly, or human, or just plain boring according to its treatment. Hitchcock has made it human.

30 January 1938

Cocoanut Grove is not about leis and hula-hula girls, as you might imagine, but about a celebrated Hollywood night-spot and the efforts of band-leader Fred MacMurray, Ben Blue, the Yacht Club Boys, a kid tap-drummer, his crooning governess, and the composer of 'Sweet Leilani' to get there.

After eight thousand feet of light-hearted misadventure they make it, and kind-hearted dance-band addicts may tell you the trip was worth it. Personally, I like Fred MacMurray in something quieter, like westerns, and prefer the Ritz Brothers to the Yacht Club Boys, because there is one less.

12 June 1938

Snow White and the Seven Dwarfs is a fairy tale for the masses rather than an exercise in draughtsmanship for the classes. It has more faults than any earlier Disney cartoon. It is vulnerable again and again to the barbed criticisms of the experts. Sometimes it is, frankly, badly drawn. But I think it will give more people more pleasure of a simple kind than any other film of its generation.

Except for the animal sequences, which are pure Disney, and pure genius of line and rhythm, the film is a straight transcript of the Grimm story in terms of modern and popular imagination. Its tunes are sweet as Friml or pat as a concert party chorus. It mingles in an affectionate way the romance of old towered castles and rich caparison with the sophistication of the nice co-ed and the charms of a radio baritone.

The scenario sticks close to Grimm. The wicked queen, the mirror, the huntsman, the hut of the seven dwarfs, the poisoned apple, the glass coffin, the prince from a far country – all of them are there. Only there is no stay-lace and no poisoned comb. The modern Snow White could not be tempted by the thought of lacing herself tight. Her slim figure, actually, has nothing to lace. And she ties up her black hair, like Ginger Rogers, with a scarlet ribbon.

The story is Grimm's, but the presentation is up-to-date, American, and popular. Its non-animal characters stem from the magazine-cover, the chocolate-box, and the motion picture studio. Snow White herself has eyelids like Betty Boop's and a mouth like a sugar plum. Her prince resembles a rough sketch of Robert Taylor on horseback. The witch has more than a touch of

Lionel Barrymore, and the dwarfs suggest a cross between Hugh Herbert and the Marx Brothers.

I am perfectly certain that the artists, the æsthetes and the intellectuals will detest the whole lot of them. I don't always like them myself. When Bashful blushes, when Snow White flutters her eyelids, and when the dwarfs tumble one another rowdily in the wash-tub, I feel embarrassed. And that is silly. I know it is silly. For Snow White is a compromise, and a deliberate compromise, between the chocolate box millions and the few who love line and form and integrity, whether in writing or painting, for their own sake. It is a shrewd attempt to use the idiom of the people as a guide to the especial treasures of the initiate. The human figures are conventionalized, because their job is to convey an unusual world to conventional people of every nation. They are, as it were, the H.C.F. of persuasion. I don't suppose Disney is any more satisfied with the human beings in *Snow White* than I am. But I am sure that he did what he did, deliberately, with his eyes open, knowing that the very things that make his picture distasteful to the experts will the more surely make it significant and appealing to the mass.

The one point, the great point, on which every type of audience will meet, is the treatment of the animals. Whenever Disney (under which generic term one lists the twenty odd animators mentioned in the credit titles) gets out into the woods and meadows he is enchanting. There is nothing slovenly or conventional about these drawings. Snow White and the Prince may have no bony structure, but there is sinew and muscle and shy, fierce life in the birds, the deer, the rabbits. It is Disney's especial conceit to imagine all living things, human, fantastic, and animal, as one great, indivisible family. In his cartoon world the raccoon is as important as the prince, the blue-bird as efficient as the huntsman. Actually, because here the draughtsmanship is bold and unconventionalized, the birds and animals are the real people of the drama. You will remember the fawn, when you have forgotten Grumpy, Doc, and Sneezy. You will feel for the two wheeling vultures the awe that you can never quite raise for the wicked step-mother. I don't think you will ever forget the moment when the animals, still and downcast, gaze through the rain-swept windows at Snow White in her glass coffin. The human figures are mere popular sketches of vice and virtue. The animals have grace, pathos, precision, character. In them the greatest artist of the modern screen demonstrates his freedom from the conventions that he is forced to own.

I have not the least hesitation in recommending *Snow White* to all the adults of my acquaintance, and in urging them to go and take their children. With all its faults, this is the sort of film that happens once in a generation. It is as necessary a part of our film upbringing as *The Birth of a Nation* or *The Jazz Singer*. Crude, tentative, and born of compromise it may be, but it is still history in the making. As for its 'terrors' for children, I don't believe in one of them. The witch would not frighten a kindergarten child. As for the scene in the wood, where Snow White is haunted by gleaming eyes, Disney himself has his own justification. Daylight comes, and the green glare is shown to be the eyes of the forest creatures, rabbits, squirrels, deer, themselves startled and bewildered. Snow White coaxes them, makes friends with them, apologizes for her terrors in words that should be pinned up over the nightlight in every nursery. 'You don't know what I've been through. All because I was afraid. I'm so ashamed of the fuss I made!'

Disney's *Snow White* ends with a cloud castle in the sunset, and 'So they lived happily every after.' Do you happen to remember how Grimm's 'Snow White' ends? I do. I have never forgotten it. 'And iron slippers were heated over the fire, and were brought in with tongs and put before her. And she had to step into the red-hot shoes and dance till she fell down dead.' The nicest mothers read these lines without a qualm to the nicest children in the nicest nurseries. Is it really very sensible after this to talk about Disney as a purveyor of horror to the young?

[1938]

NOTE: Seeing *Snow White* again on its revival in London for the Christmas holiday season of 1944–45, I found I drew from it a new and increased pleasure. It may have been an infection from the exuberance of the young audience, who followed the film with a kind of breathless excitement, very touching to watch and suggestive to study. I had almost forgotten that a wide-eyed generation of children has grown up in the years since the dwarfs' 'Heigh-ho' first echoed through the diamond mines, since the baby blue-bird essayed his first high note, and Snow White first whispered her dreams into the Wishing Well.

I am sure now, quite sure, that *Snow White* will have to be regarded as a cinema classic. When all the other Disney films are forgotten, this one is the most likely to be remembered. Admittedly it is far from being the best technical job Disney has done. It was the studio's first experiment in full-length cartoon, and has all the roughness and error of a first try. It is full of faults in draughtsmanship and animation. The Prince sadly lacks bone and sinew. Snow White herself is a chocolate-box cutie. The opening scenes jump like a magic lantern slide. But the thing as a whole has a happiness, a proportion, that has never been caught in any later Disney. *Snow White* is a *joyous* film. I don't know when I have seen a film more heart-warming. Its simple animal sketches, simple story, and simple little tunes have created between them the happiest effect of spring magic. It is one of those blessed, unpredictable things that seem to have been born under a lucky star. You have only to glance at the look on a child's face to know that it is enchantingly right for an enchanted audience. I came away from *Snow White*, after seeing it for the fourth time, saying to myself like the child in Chesterton's 'Ethics of Elfland,' 'Do it again!'

– Chestnuts in her Lap, 1947

SNOW WHITE, FLOWERS AND TREES, THREE LITTLE PIGS, THE GRASSHOPPER AND THE ANT

Speaking strictly as a film fancier and not as a radio critic, the thing I have enjoyed most during the past week is the broadcast of *Snow White and the Seven Dwarfs* which John Watt and his musical experts contrived with the help of twelve sessions at the picture, the piano score from America, and an album of gramophone records.

It is no part of my job to review *Snow White* as a broadcast entertainment. I liked it enormously, but then I had the memory of the deer, the rabbits, the lost little blue bird, the sunset castle, and the whole enchanting fauna and flora of Disney's world to help me. I did feel, though – and this is my business – that the broadcast brought out one quality of the film that has been generally neglected a little. A great deal has been written about the dwarfs and the animals, the witch and the lady, the psychology and the draughtsmanship, the censor's view and the child's reactions, but very little about the music, which is one of *Snow White*'s especial and characteristic charms.

In point of fact, very little has been said at all about the part played by music in the success of the Disney cartoons. Watching the pictures week by week over a stretch of years, we have taken for granted the trim little melodies, the perfect aptness of the scoring – a bell here, a woodwind there – that states, in terms akin and yet apart, the changing flow and rhythm of the draughtsmanship. We listen to Mickey Mouse's absurd little songs, to the faint sweet choruses of wood and barnyard, and miss, because there is so much for our eyes to see, the significance of their quaint cacophony. Yet Disney, without his score, is a ballet without music. Silent, he is witty, observant, charming, but rarely moving. His peculiar art is a product of the sound-film alone.

Pat Sullivan, who drew 'Felix the Cat' in the days of silent pictures, was a cartoonist whose whole genius lay in his interpretative pencil. Tony Sarg, too, was a pure visualizer; so was Max Fleischer, creator of the original 'Out of the Inkwell' series. The cinema piano, rattling out the rhythm of their drawings, more or less conscientiously, did little this way or that towards the success of these pictures. Disney, though, is another matter. With him rhythm, sheer musical rhythm, is always the arbiter of animation. In the Disney cartoons the sound is determined first, the picture follows. The beat is established, the musical line and accent recorded on the animators' production chart, before a single movement is drawn.

The use of original music for the Disney cartoons is a fairly recent development – six years old at the most. In the early days of Mickey Mouse and the Silly Symphonies, the days of black and white and only modest celebrity – the scores, although an integral part of the cartoons, were largely composed from borrowed melodies. The first coloured Symphony, *Flowers and Trees*, although an innovation in many ways, was still conservative with regard to music. The score owed most of its inspiration to Rubinstein. It was charming, but it caused no great stir. Nor did any of the Symphonies that followed it, until suddenly one called *The Three Little Pigs* came along and took two continents by storm, mainly owing to a bland ingenuous songlet composed for the film by one Frank Churchill, and entitled 'Who's Afraid of the Big Bad Wolf?'

'The Big Bad Wolf' was the first world-wide song-hit ever derived from a motion-picture cartoon. It was the beginning of a new régime. It made the name of its composer, and materially changed the policy of the Disney music department. From that time onward the Disney cartoons, both Mickeys and Silly Symphonies, have relied more on original compositions, less on applied excerpts from the musical classics. The Disney musical staff, with Frank Churchill and Leigh Harline as chief tunesmiths, have turned out one persuasive melody after another. 'The World Owes Me a Living,' from *The Grasshopper and the Ant* was the 'Big Bad Wolf's' immediate successor. There was 'The Wise Little Hen' and 'The Pied Piper of Hamelin,' 'Funny Little Bunnies' and 'The Penguin is a Very Funny Creature.' There was that stirring patriotic pæan from 'The Mail Pilot,' which insisted that the Mail Must Go Through with all the authority of a State documentary. There have been others; almost as many as there are Disney pictures. In fact, for all the purposes of slogan-writing, one may claim for Disney that there is No Cartoon Without a Tune.

Snow White, which is eight times as long as any previous Disney picture, has eight times as many melodies, for Disney is a man who does everything methodically. The tunes are simple, happy, popular and often sentimental, like the picture. Anyone can hum them. John Watt, who has adapted a good dozen Disneys for broadcasting, tells me that this was the easiest of all the scores he has had to handle. Coming away from the film, the dwarfs' 'Hi Ho,' Snow White's theme song, 'Some Day My Prince Will Come,' and the Prince's own heroic number, 'One Song, I have but One Song,' are the pieces that chiefly haunt you. But listening to the broadcast, divorced from the visual preoccupations of the picture, you are acutely aware for the first time of the neatness of the other numbers. 'The Wishing Well,' in particular, comes out strongly, without the Disney doves as a distraction. And the woodland creatures of the film, you realize, must have been inordinately fascinating to make you overlook the charm of Snow White's number, with bird obligato, called 'With a Smile and a Song.'

A child, who had never seen the picture, made a curious comment at the end of the Snow White broadcast. 'It's an opera, isn't it?' he said, and in a flash you realize, yes, it is an opera. An opera without a prima donna, without an impresario, done by figures two and a half inches high and made of celluloid. For five years or more the film people have been signing up Metropolitan Opera stars, whisking them away to Hollywood on prince's salaries, and inviting them to hold up the job of picture-making with bursts of their expensive and educated singing. For ten years or more the film people have been making their own dramas inaudible with 'background music' that has resolutely refused to stay in the background. During all this time, one man, and one man only, has been making sound-film that is really sound-film. Disney, alone of them all, has hit on the legitimate use of music in pictures; music as an integral part of the rhythm, the mood and the accent, sometimes only sub-consciously apprehended, but always moving the film onwards, smoothly and inevitably, towards the end he has in view.

1938

Well, Hitchcock has done it again. This master of screen melodrama has reached the point when every new film of his can be regarded as a blind date – something we can go to as safely as we would ask for a new Ellery Queen, a new Margery Allingham or a new H. C. Bailey from the library.

The Lady Vanishes is possibly the best, certainly the most successful of all his pictures. Adapted rather cunningly from Ethel Lina White's first-rate thriller *The Wheel Spins*, it tells the story of a drab, middle-aged music teacher who suddenly disappears from a trans-continental express under curious circumstances. The passengers and railway staff unanimously deny her existence. Just one English girl is suspicious.

The device has been used before in mystery tales, but it is still effective, Hitchcock plays up to the full the chill and panic of the situation – the girl's doubts, her growing obstinacy, the increasing tension of the atmosphere. He has his fun, too, and nobody who sees the picture will forget the grim couple of English sportsmen determined, at all hazards, to get home for the last day of the Test Match. . . .

Margaret Lockwood is the girl, Dame May Whitty (the victim of *Night Must Fall*) the vanishing lady, Naunton Wayne and Basil Radford the undeterred sportsmen, and Michael Redgrave, a new young man who grows into your confidence as the film develops, the casual hero.

Don't miss *The Lady Vanishes* if you want to give yourself a peace present*, and make a note of the gesticulating gentleman with the large cherub's face who hurries along the platform in the last scene at Victoria. That is Mr Alfred Hitchcock, the director, registering his trade-mark. 'Hitch' makes a point of doing a bit in person in every one of his films. He was a man in the tube in *Blackmail*, a guest in the hotel in *The Man Who Knew Too Much*, a spectator outside the courts in *Young and Innocent*. When he gets in front of the cameras he is shy, hurries past them as quickly as possible. But he is superstitious about making that brief appearance, pointing with some awe to the film in which he broke the habit as the one that nearly ended his career.

9 October 1938

★ This review appeared in the *Observer* the week after Neville Chamberlain, having returned from Munich, promised 'peace in our time'. The relief was very great. – A.L.

QUESTION.   Who was She and what was **Her Jungle Love**?

ANSWER.   She was a lovely Malayan with plucked eyebrows, geranium lipstick, and two sarongs, one red and one blue, and Baab was her jungle love.

QUESTION.   Baab who?

ANSWER.   Bob Mitchell, pan-American pilot.

QUESTION.   How did they meet?

ANSWER.   Quite simply. He was looking for a lost flyer named Atkins, and his 'plane crashed in the Malay Archipelago.

QUESTION.   Why did it crash?

ANSWER.   Because his *fiancée* rang him up in a storm to ask him if he was thinking about her.

QUESTION.   Was the Malayan his *fiancée*?

ANSWER.   Of course not. The blonde, Eleanor Martin, was his *fiancée*.

QUESTION.   You didn't mention her.

ANSWER.   No, I assumed you had seen some jungle pictures.

QUESTION.   What did Bob do after the crash?

ANSWER.   He bled first, because the film is in Technicolor. Then he saw a chimpanzee and the brunette, Tura.

QUESTION.   What did he say to her?

ANSWER.   He said she looked like a squirrel in Hyde Park. He was an English actor, you see, and they had to account for his accent somehow.

QUESTION. And did she look like a squirrel in Hyde Park?

ANSWER. She looked to me just like Dorothy Lamour, the heroine of *The Hurricane*.

QUESTION. But you said she was a Malayan?

ANSWER. Oh, no, she was English really. She had been brought to the island eighteen years before by a University graduate called Kuaka.

QUESTION. Why?

ANSWER. Because he was rich and cultured, wore sapphires and emeralds alternately according to the day's Technicolor schedule, and wanted his revenge on the white devils.

QUESTION. Rather thankless revenge, wasn't it?

ANSWER. Not at all. Tura was a great asset to the Archipelago. She played the guitar, served fruit dinners, threw a pretty knife, and sewed her sarongs beautifully. Besides, that wasn't all his revenge. He sacrificed one white man per annum to the sacred crocodiles.

QUESTION. Why crocodiles?

ANSWER. Because this is a Paramount picture, and Paramount have always been strong on crocodiles.

QUESTION. Where did Kuaka find the white men?

ANSWER. Oh, they just happened.

QUESTION. But if one year they didn't happen?

ANSWER. Don't be tiresome. With five script-writers on the story one was bound to happen. Besides, he had a white man in hand already – Atkins, the missing flyer.

QUESTION. Did Tura know about this crocodile business?

ANSWER. Certainly. Under hypnosis from Kuaka she beat the drum that summoned the crocodiles to dinner. She tried to warn Bob about it, but her English was hardly serviceable for detailed narrative.

QUESTION. Didn't she learn from Bob?

ANSWER. Oh, very quickly. In a couple of days she was singing 'There's lovelight in the starlight with you' with only the faintest trace of a Malayan accent.

QUESTION. What was Eleanor doing all this time?

ANSWER. Eleanor? Oh Miss Martin, the blonde. She was lying back in a *chaise longue* in a pink negligée.

QUESTION. Not exactly helpful, was she?

ANSWER. Give the girl a chance. Once she got over her first grief and registered a pastel triumph for Technicolor, she called out the U.S. navy and air force and went off to look for Bob herself in a neat yachting costume.

QUESTION.   Did she find him?

ANSWER.   Not for a long time. He was down in a sub-terranean temple watching Atkins being fed to the crocodiles.

QUESTION.   Didn't he interfere?

ANSWER.   He did all that a hero should. He said between clenched teeth, 'I don't like the look of this.' He registered manly horror. And then he embraced Tura.

QUESTION.   Wasn't that rather unfair to Eleanor?

ANSWER.   Oh, no. He said the two girls would be sure to like each other.

QUESTION.   And did they?

ANSWER.   Don't anticipate. Bob and Tura had to be thrown to the crocodiles first.

QUESTION.   Why?

ANSWER.   So that the publicity department should say that this picture *moves*. Against the lush background of the steaming jungle there is an increasing parade of *action*, in which hundreds of gaily-costumed natives and beasts, birds and reptiles of the jungle play their part. The climax is sensational, breath-taking, and realistic. The film is thrill-packed. The jungle is shown in all its colourful glory. There is also a big romantic appeal and much delightful comedy. Besides, what else were the crocodiles for?

QUESTION.   Did they eat Bob and Tura?

ANSWER.   You're so optimistic. Of course they didn't. The poor beasts never had a chance. There was a volcanic eruption; and the whole temple crashed down on top of them.

QUESTION.   How did Bob and Tura escape?

ANSWER.   Through a crack in the rock, apparently running on ball-bearings, and beautifully contrived by the script writers. The earthquake wiped out Kuaka and half the natives, and the surviving crocodiles advanced in mass formation and finished off the others.

QUESTION.   And then what happened?

ANSWER.   Eleanor came running up the beach in her nice blue yachting costume.

QUESTION.   What did she say when she saw Bob?

ANSWER.   You're very anxious about Eleanor, aren't you? She's only a *fiancée* really, just a nobody. No jungle glamour, no sarong style, merely the other woman. She said, if you must know. 'Look there! It's Baab!' And then, 'Hullo, Baab, what an attractive native girl.'

QUESTION.   And what did he say?

ANSWER.   He said, 'Tura, this is Eleanor Martin, and this is her father, Mr Martin.'

QUESTION.   Oh, was her father there, too?

ANSWER.   Of course, it was his yacht. It was a very nice yacht. They all went back on board for dinner, and Eleanor changed into a black tulle evening gown.

QUESTION.   Why had she brought an evening gown to look for a lost *fiancée* in the Malay Archipelago?

ANSWER.   Stupid, she had seen jungle pictures, even if you haven't. She knew there would be an attractive native girl. Besides, black tulle is always good for a renunciation scene.

QUESTION.   So she renounced him?

ANSWER.   Of course. Her heart told her to. So did the five script-writers. So did the art director, who gave her a tropic moon to do it by.

QUESTION.   And how did it end?

ANSWER.   Tura dived overboard and swam back to the island, heart-broken. She hadn't read the full shooting script. She hadn't seen any jungle pictures. Nobody had told her about the renunciation scene. She crouched by a pool, kissing a crushed camellia, and crooned, 'I fell in love. What else could I do?' without the faintest trace of Malayan. And then she saw Bob's reflection in the water.

QUESTION.   And the reflections kissed?

ANSWER.   Ah, I see you *have* seen some pictures.

QUESTION.   So he married Tura and not Eleanor?

ANSWER.   Well, considering the social conditions of the island, that is a theme I would rather not pursue.

NOTE: 'I think the cinema is the very greatest art, with the possibilities of becoming the greatest art form that has ever existed.' – Mr H. G. Wells, 23 November 1935.

1938

The Adventures of Robin Hood is a title that plucks at the heart like the pull of an arrow on a taut bowstring. I should say that it alone was worth to the Warner Brothers the two million dollars they are reputed to have spent on the picture. It promises something good to every man, woman and child in the audience, for there isn't one of us who has not, at some time, fallen under the spell of the Robin Hood legends. This was a film that was half-made before a shot was in the cameras. Tradition has been working on the script for seven hundred years.

It must have been an almost superhuman task to make a dull film on the subject of Robin Hood, but the Warner Brothers, who have never flinched from major difficulties, have almost managed it. I don't know when I have seen more money, more care and more important workmanship lavished on such a stupendous presentation of the obvious.

This Robin Hood, mind you, is full of good intentions. It isn't a blustery, carefree thing like the old Fairbanks picture. In 'full Technicolor,' with a pontifical score by Erich Wolfgang Korngold, it is less concerned with gay doings beneath the greenwood tree, and Sherwood's preoccupation with sport and catch and nut-brown ale of good October brewing, than with the taxation troubles of the oppressed Saxons – a problem that gibes with Hollywood's vague current sympathy with the underdog, wherever and whoever he may be.

The film, in which fine wrath is oddly mixed with riotous Technicolor, begins with Robin Hood (in Lincoln green) defending Much the Miller's son (in homely russet) on a charge of deer-slaying. Present are Prince John (in white and turquoise), Sir Guy of Gisbourne (crimson with blue sleeves), the Sheriff of Nottingham (grey and purple), and the Bishop of Black Canon (in clerical violet). For his friendly offices Robin is outlawed to Sherwood Forest, where he and his men swing from tree to tree like mediæval Tarzans, dropping from immense heights to the backs of horses saddled in the sweetest shades of pastel. In time comes love in the person of the Lady Marian Fitzwalter (rather costume-bound in silver and cherry), and Robin, after entertaining her with mutton, wins her by the sight of a group of distressed Saxons huddled beneath the greenwood tree.

After an attempt on Robin's life, foiled by Lady Marian (in rainbow stripes), Prince John (in black and gunmetal) decides to be crowned king by the Bishop of Black Canon (still in that trying shade of violet). Little does he guess that King Richard (black robe and cowl), fortified by a stoup of Technicolor wine, is now visiting in Sherwood. Maid Marian (silver with primrose stripes) is sentenced to death, but after a homily on home and foreign politics, she manages to send a message to Robin by her maid (in something red like an inverted flower-pot). Robin arrives, sword in hand, at the coronation, slays Sir Guy of Gisbourne (in predominantly green upholstery), rescues the lady, and briefly sums up the duties of kingship to Richard (now in a crimson surcoat with lions rampant on his chest).

This is a rough outline of the film that its sponsors describe as 'unapproachable in magnificence and scope' and 'unbeatable in box-office content.' They also suggest that 'only the rainbow itself can duplicate its brilliance,' and add, on what authority I know not, that Robin Hood is the role that Errol Flynn 'was born to play.'

I think the thing that hurt me most about the picture was a remark that I overheard in the lobby after the performance. 'That,' said one woman to another, 'is what happens when a legend like Robin Hood is tackled by Americans.' Madam, I am sorry to correct you, but that is not necessarily what happens when a legend like Robin Hood is tackled by Americans. I have in my shelves a fat, brown volume, with pages much thumbed by childish hands, and a large unformed signature across the fly-leaf. It is the best story of Robin Hood that has ever been written, done in the spare, strong English that puts to shame most of our slipshod modern phrasing. Howard Pyle, an American Quaker, was the author, and his good words cut clean through to the heart of legend. As a child I read it first, with passion, when I was seven. As a journalist I read it still, with humility, today.

1938

NOTE: The brown volume belongs to my son, and the signature is his. I like to think that my own handwriting, even when unformed, was very much better. This copy is a comparatively recent edition, only fourteen years old. But my memory goes back to a much earlier edition, bound, as was fitting, in Lincoln green. This book, in that edition, is one of the first things I remember coveting really sinfully. It belonged to an old lady, a calling-acquaintance of my mother, and was only lent to me, as a special grace, when I was in bed with one of the frequent colds I suffered from in childhood. It is associated in my mind with onion soup, popping gaslight, the hundreds of glass marbles I collected and adored, and leafless poplars creaking outside a tall old house in Manchester. I never could understand why the old lady didn't give me the book outright, knowing how much I treasured it. It is only in recent years that it has occurred to me that she, rest her soul, may have treasured it too.

– Chestnuts in her Lap, 1947

In an industry that has never been widely celebrated for its restraint in content and address, it is a pleasure to come across a film with so much natural dignity as **Sixty Glorious Years**, Herbert Wilcox's successor to his screen biography of Queen Victoria.

Sixty Glorious Years naturally covers much of the same ground as *Victoria the Great,* and there is actually one shot, in the scenes of the Diamond Jubilee, that is the same in both pictures. But the two films are so different in treatment that you never get any feeling of repetition. *Victoria the Great* was, in effect, a national newsreel. *Sixty Glorious Years* is the comment on it of a privileged onlooker. You watch it with the relish for personal detail that any honest public feels for any great figure in the limelight. Events in themselves are cold things, which only come to life for most people through some detail acutely personal. It was interesting to read that Mr Chamberlain flew to Berchtesgaden. It was far more interesting to read that he flew to Berchtesgaden with his umbrella. The legendary figure of the Queen behind the long history of the last century becomes much more vivid, when you learn that she had a 'stand-in' of the same size and figure to try on her dresses, that she liked the shades on her parlour windows lowered by so many inches precisely, that both she and the Prince Consort took two lumps of sugar in their tea.

This film, which has been made throughout with the blessing of the Court, and has been given more royal facilities than any work since the beginning of the cinema, is oddly bare of the pomp and circumstance attendant on the usual screen chronicles of princes. It is a very quiet film. There are few big crowds of players. The sets have been copied industriously from the private rooms in the royal palaces, and finally dispel the illusion that kings and queens live in marble halls and stir their tea with golden teaspoons. It is sub-titled 'An intimate diary of Queen Victoria and her beloved Consort, Prince Albert', and it is this sense of intimacy within the limits of royal decorum that gives the film its peculiar atmosphere of charm.

The title of the film is actually a misnomer. It covers sixty-one years, beginning in 1840 with the young Queen's firm announcement to Parliament of her intention of marrying Prince Albert of Coburg, ending in 1901 with the lying-in-state, four soldiers keeping watch over the Queen's coffin. It covers the years, too, in something like ninety minutes, cutting down every scene to its bare bones with an admirable economy. Life moves on in a swift but ordered parade between Buckingham Palace and Windsor, Osborne and St James's and Balmoral. Outside, in the world, they fight in the Crimea, they fight at Khartoum. They run the first 'electric telegraph' under the Atlantic. Peel and Palmerston and Russell, Gladstone and Disraeli and young Joe Chamberlain take their seats on the stiff benches of the House of Commons. Dr Lister discovers antiseptics. Mr Dickens crusades against bad housing. Prince Albert plans that 'monstrous greenhouse', the Crystal Palace. Disraeli buys the Suez Canal shares. And the echoes of these affairs, coming to Victoria through the spiked palace railings and the discreet channels of diplomacy, find her stiffening in her passionate but often obstinate championship of causes through the years.

The dialogue has been so finely written that it can be set down in cold print, as little film dialogue can, without losing any of its quality. Here, for instance, is the exchange of formalities between the Queen and Mr Gladstone over England's foreign policy at Khartoum:

VICTORIA: Mr Gladstone, I cannot conceal from you my disquiet at the delay in your measures for the relief of General Gordon.

GLADSTONE: Your Majesty, everything possible is being done.

VICTORIA: No, Mr Gladstone, everything the Government thinks possible. General Gordon has been besieged in Khartoum since March. Only in August has it been decided to relieve him, and only now, in November, has the relief force under Sir Garnett Wolsey started out. These tardy races against time are neither to my taste nor to our credit.

GLADSTONE: Believe me, ma'am, I understand your anxiety.

VICTORIA: Oh, it is more than anxiety, it is anguish, Mr Gladstone. This great Christian soldier means something to the world as well as to us. If we fail him, posterity will not forget.

GLADSTONE: Your Majesty may rest assured –

VICTORIA: I cannot rest, however much I am assured. I am haunted by the dread that we may be too late. That is the danger to which this country so often exposes itself. One day it may be our undoing.

And here is the final scene in the smoking-room of the House of Commons, where Chamberlain, Balfour, and Asquith are waiting for news of the Queen's passing:

CHAMBERLAIN: It won't be long now. Yet how long the magnificence has been. . . . A great clear stretch of time that happens to have been my life, and I'm proud of it.

BALFOUR: Yes, it was sometimes narrow in mind, but mostly great in spirit.

ASQUITH: The spirit of achievement and change.

BALFOUR: And what changes!

CHAMBERLAIN: And what achievements – the engineers and explorers.

ASQUITH: And our new saviours, the scientists and surgeons. . . .

BALFOUR: The soldiers and inventors. . . .

CHAMBERLAIN: Even a few of our own calling, Arthur.

BALFOUR: What a pageant it makes, this era of great poetry and prose and thinkers who might have given us a new landscape of thought. . . . More than a great queen is passing into history. An era.

They hear the bell tolling. All rise.

Both the passages I have quoted – and I think you will agree with me that they are good sense and good writing – are the work of Sir Robert Vansittart, whose name appears on the credit sheets, by his own request, without its official handle. Close readers of the political columns of the newspapers will remember that Sir Robert is adviser to the Cabinet, and that his name was frequently mentioned last month in reports of inner discussions on the crisis. *Sixty Glorious Years*, in which he acted both as adviser and part-author, is his first but not by any means his last association with the screen.

The first Victoria film was in black and white, with a Technicolor finish. The present film is all in Technicolor. While I find it hard to reconcile my theoretical acceptance of colour on the screen with my practical distaste for it, I am prepared to admit that in the present instance colour has its advantages. It points up, in a subtle way, the plush and mahogany quality of the Victorian era, the weight of sheer texture and tissue that surrounds a monarchy. It gives us exciting moments, too, when the young queen's gown of midnight blue billows out among the dancers – when she smooths down her skirts of willow-green, beside the baby's cradle – when Disraeli leans forward and touches, delicately, a bowl of his fabled primroses.

There are other things that stand out from the film in retrospect. The lovely little neck and head of the young Princess Royal. The magic lantern lecture (a grand period piece, this) and the tea-table scene when Victoria and Albert count their children. The haunting Elgar march that forms the theme-tune of the picture. The old Queen's tired step as she comes home from her Diamond Jubilee. The startling moment when she turns her back on the cameras and stumps away to tell old Maggie, her dress-model, all about it. The passionate sincerity of all Miss Neagle's acting. The Prince of Wales, square and heavy in his greatcoat, hurrying up the steps at Osborne to his mother's bedroom. The sharp topical flavour of the war debate in the House of Commons.

I realize that I have said very little about the players. This is a film in which you get no impression of individual acting. It has been cast, from top to bottom, with men who, given the right faces by the make-up room, are able to make one moment in history sharp and vivid for posterity. I suppose acting could scarcely have a better testimonial.

You may have gathered from the foregoing notes that I think well of *Sixty Glorious Years*, and you will not be mistaken. I like it for many things, but mostly for its three Ds – its drama, discipline and dignity. I have an inveterate fancy myself for the quiet days of life; good manners, large families, and broad acres. My own childhood was spent just outside the years this film celebrates, but close enough to them to give the record a strangely nostalgic quality. After a lifetime of films in which exuberance is at a premium, in which boy slaps girl, and girl likes it, it is a pleasure to spend an hour in this world of well-mannered serenity. I like to recall the days of the great middle class when fathers handed down an income to their children, and nannies ruled grimly in the nursery, and women had the high status of dependence. Thank you, Mr Wilcox, and you, Miss Neagle, for sixty courteous years.

1938

The Hollywood movie magnates, having temporarily glorified the American Army, Navy, Air Force, campus, theatre, hospital, film studio, police force, Treasury, Department of Weights and Measures, and even – with a conspicuous effort – the newspaper office, have honoured a new type of unsung hero in *Too Hot to Handle*.

Mr Gable and Mr Pidgeon are rival newsreel cameramen, the best, of course, in the business. They are in first at every war, death, and major catastrophe. In the pauses of personal bickering they produce newsreels of topical disaster that bring fortunes to the box-office of America's preferred subscribers. Their ethics may be shady, but their work is hot.

While faking a bombing in Shanghai they encounter Miss Myrna Loy, flying solo for a firm of airplane manufacturers. Miss Loy is also, of course, the best in the business. She seems tough in China, but you should just see her back in America – in a little print dress in her little country cottage watching her little niece swinging in the little garden. You realize that beneath the leather jacket of the aviatrix beats a woman's heart.

Miss Loy had a brother, but she has lost him somewhere on the Amazon. She knows he isn't dead, for her heart – a reliable organ – tells her so. In youth, it seems, she and brother Harry tinkered with radio together, and she keeps her set constantly tuned-in to the Amazon, waiting for his signal.

The demonstration of practical affection so moves Messrs Gable and Pidgeon that they pawn their best cameras to finance an expedition to the Amazon. Mr Gable, smartly redeeming his outfit, gets ahead of the others and locates Harry on the night he is to be a sacrifice to ju-ju. Happening to have by him – I told you he was the best man in the business – a reel of film of fire, flood, motor-racing, and other sensational exhibits, he projects this then and there on to a bare space in the jungle.

The natives flee in terror, the sun rises – rather nervously, I thought – and Harry raises his head to mutter the number of his sister's receiving station.

This startling tribute to the invention of the newsreel camera-man is something that our disciplined lads of Movietone, Gaumont, and Pathe, etc, would do well to study. It might give them quite a new idea of their romantic duty towards the preferred subscriber. And I recommend to their attention Mr Gable's pretty little speech, round about Reel Five, on the nobility of the cameraman's calling. Next time they are sent to film a fire in Peckham, or the Mayor of Somewhere throwing something open to the public, it should prove quite an inspiration to them in their work.

16 October 1938

Bluebeard's Eighth Wife begins beautifully, with Mr Cooper marching into the smartest man's shop on the French Riviera and demanding a pyjama coat without the trousers. He is out, he explains, to the scandalized staff, to break the great pyjama racket, which forces men all over the world to buy a coat *and* trousers, when what they really want is a coat *or* trousers. The panic spreads from salesman to floor-walker, from house manager to proprietor. Can a man legally buy one half of a pair of pyjamas without the other? You never discover, for just when the argument has reached its crisis, in slips the cool Miss Colbert and squares it all by buying the pants herself.

If *Bluebeard's Eighth Wife* had gone on as well as it began, it might have been one of Lubitsch's great pictures. But it doesn't. It develops into a bright, rather callous little story, with a blaze of technical fireworks here and there, and a damp squib of an ending in a mental 'rest home', of an American business man who has had seven wives already – one, two, three, four, five, six, seven, bang – divorced six of them, buried another, and come to the Riviera to acquire an eighth.

The most curious aspect of the film – apart from its passing thought that insanity is funny – is that we are expected to believe in Mr Gary Cooper as this ticker-tape Bluebeard, who picks up wives and oil-shares with equal impartiality. I don't know how you will feel about it, but I found the idea preposterous. Of course it is a pleasure to have Mr Cooper about, just to watch his rare smile, and the long lean grace of his walk, and the neat way he has with the technical details of his business. He acts, beautifully, a man doing this or that, having a shower, reading a dull book, facing an unpleasant interview. He even makes play with a telephone conversation in which he discusses the rise of oil two points, the sale of a million dollars' worth of steel and iron. But for all his experienced actor's tricks, the idea of Mr Cooper coolly arranging alimony for six wives, or playing bulls and bears on Wall Street, is crazier than any gag that Lubitsch has devised for the picture. Off hand, I can't think of any actor in Hollywood who is more brilliantly unsuited to the part.

24 April 1938

I never thought I should be devoting the top half of this column to **Stagecoach**. I had it all pencilled in for *Goodbye Mr Chips*, which I fancied, on advance reports, would be the film of the week, of the season possibly. It just shows how rash it is to anticipate. *Goodbye Mr Chips* is a good film, but *Stagecoach* is even better. In a remarkable season, which already, before we reach midsummer, includes eight first-class pictures, it looks as though *Stagecoach* were to be the film of the year.

Made by John Ford and Dudley Nichols, the same directing and writing team that produced *The Informer*, *Stagecoach* shows how a small budget, backed by ideals and intelligence, can beat all the rule-of-thumb executives. The film was cheap, has no outstanding stars, and is concerned, almost entirely, with a little box on wheels, only a few feet in capacity. It has a plot as old as the hills: grading it roughly, one would call it a glorified Western. Cowboys and Indians – saloon girls and warrant officers. The old, old story, but how brilliantly done!

Nine people, all strangers to one another, set off on a coach journey across Arizona and New Mexico in the days of the bad men. On the box the driver and a United States marshal. Inside, an outlaw rancher on his way to gaol. A girl from the saloons. An officer's wife, soon to become a mother. A drink-sodden doctor with enough skill in his hands yet to take over in a crisis. A traveller in whisky. An absconding banker. A gentleman card-sharper from Virginia. Accompanying them, a little troop of military, for somewhere on the route is Geronimo, the dreaded outlaw of the bad-lands with his band of wild Apaches.

Story, direction, acting, photography and sound-track – I wouldn't omit one of them – have combined to make that journey so vivid that you feel you yourself are taking part in it. Your life is in your hands with every hoofbeat, every puff of smoke on the horizon. Starting as complete strangers, you get to know these people intimately, crammed close between the jolting springs and the tight box-roof. With them, you are battered by dust-storms, checked by broken bridges and burnt trading posts, delayed by the birth of a baby, attacked by Indians, and finally saved just in the nick of time by the U.S. cavalry. By the end of the journey you know every feature of their faces, every trick and weakness of their behaviour. You have been through so much together. You are old friends.

This is the bare outline of one of the most exciting experiences the cinema has brought us for seasons. It is more than exciting. It is real, and nerve-wracking, and haunting. You keep thinking back on it afterwards – the way you all eyed each other in the coach, under the shadow of the dust-storm – the way that girl had with the baby – the surprised look on the salesman's face when he was struck by the first Indian arrow.

There is a minor plot, providing the journey with a tensely dramatic ending, in which the rancher outlaw is given ten minutes by the marshal to hunt down the murderers of his father and brother. (It reminds you of the climax of *The Virginian*.) There is a growing love affair between the rancher and the saloon girl, a hint of romance, very delicately done, in the card-sharper's regard for the officer's lady.

The film has no big-bracket stars, but, perhaps because of that every performance comes through real and startlingly vivid. Thomas Mitchell as the doctor, John Wayne (an honest-to-goodness westerner of many years' standing) as the rancher, and Claire Trevor as the saloon girl, may be the faces you first remember, but every traveller on that coach has character, every one is a partner in an urgent and terrible adventure.

I don't often ask you to make a special effort in the interests of any picture. I do ask you to see *Stagecoach*, if you love good cinema. This is one of the best of its kind, in the kind at which America excels.

I suppose I expected too much of **Goodbye Mr Chips**. I suppose the impressive statistics we had of its making, the high praise it received from the American Press, and the enthusiasm of experts like Spencer Tracy and Alexander Woolcott for Robert Donat's performance, made me look for a distinction that it was unfair to demand of any picture. At any rate, I was a little disappointed in it.

When first I read Hilton's gentle little book I cried, I remember. When I saw Leslie Banks's stage performance of the old schoolmaster I had a bad lump in my throat. Watching the picture version I experienced neither of these sentimental luxuries, and Mr Donat's performance of Mr Chips left me respectful, but unmoved.

Goodbye Mr Chips is a handsome film, a kindly film, and an unusual film, but I don't think it cuts quite deep enough below the surface to be a great film. It has great moments, when the smack of a ball on a bat, a passing parade of boys' faces, the constant roll-call of names, the unconscious stance of some lad in the crowd who thinks himself uncaught by the cameras, brings the whole force of memory into play, and you are seeing, not a film at all, but your own boyhood, your own boys. These moments are more dramatic than any of the set scenes in hall, in class, in chapel, or at the Chips tea-table. Real schoolboys are at once more subtle and more simple than these young actors make them.

In the end, I suppose, *Goodbye Mr Chips* will stand or fall by its leading performance. In spite of its enormous cast of characters, and the vivid grace that Miss Greer Garson gives to the short path of Chips's wife, Kathy, it is essentially a one-man story. The whole thing is told in a flash-back, as Mr Chips, at eighty-three, sits by his fire and thinks back on his forty-odd years as a master at Brookfield. His own memories presumably colour the telling, and it isn't quite necessary to believe in Brookfield, so long you can believe in Mr Chips.

I can't quite believe in him. Mr Donat's seems to me a great acting performance, that isn't quite great enough to prevent the man himself from appearing an actor. Conscientious, fastidious, whimsical, and enormously kindly, it catches all the mannerisms, but the real manner seems to elude it. Our public school education may be odd and old-fashioned, but it surely isn't odd or old-fashioned enough to tolerate forty years of the kind of diehard twitter that this Mr Chips seems likely to give it.

I am quite prepared to believe that my opinion is a minority one. I hope it is. I hope the crowds, who will certainly flock to see *Goodbye Mr Chips*, will find it the great picture that America acclaims it. I hope they will get the same quiet delight from Mr Donat's performance that I got from Hilton's Mr Chips, and from

Leslie Banks's stage re-creation of him. I wish I could recapture it myself, but I can't, however hard I try.

11 June 1939

I see that **The Sun Never Sets** is announced as A Mighty Drama of a Mighty Empire. I take it the reference is to the British Empire?

You take it correctly.

But I understand the film was made in Hollywood?

Naturally, or there wouldn't be a reference to the British Empire.

And is it really a film about empire-building?

Certainly. It begins at the court of Queen Elizabeth, and brings the whole job up to date in two minutes dead.

But that leaves a good deal of film over, surely?

It leaves precisely ninety-five minutes over.

And what are they about?

Douglas Fairbanks in flannels and a topee, Basil Rathbone in shorts and a topee, and molybdenum on the Gold Coast.

What on the Gold Coast?

Molybdenum. Element 42, a rare element for hardening steel, used in the manufacture of armaments.

You seem to know a great deal about it.

The motion picture is a great educational influence.

Who owns this molybdenum? The British Empire?

Certainly not. A sinister multi-millionaire named Zurov, masquerading as a scientist.

Russian, eh?

I think not. His Christian name is Hugo.

And what does he do with this molybdenum?

He plans to make himself a Dictator. He has a secret broadcasting station (DNXY on short wave) in a disused gold mine, by means of which he sinks ships, burns out planes, promotes strikes in the Far East, and incites the whole world to war against the British Empire.

But why doesn't someone stop him?

Oh, someone does, eventually. The Home Office, the Foreign Office, the War Office and the Colonial Office are all powerless, but they send out the Randolphs to investigate.

The who?

The Randolphs. Randolphs have been in the Service for three

hundred years. They have a motto over their front door, 'Go Forth and Return with Honour.' And when the Randolph sons Go Forth the mother stands at the door and gives them each a white carnation.

What for?

I guess just for Purity.

Are all Randolphs pure?

Of course. They are strong, silent Service people with firm jaws, square shoulders, clipped voices, and good table manners. They all Have Faith. Except John. He wears tennis flannels, scorns afternoon tea, refuses to join the Service, and thinks it time the sun did set on the British Empire.

But, of course, he reconsiders his opinion?

How could you guess? Yes. Grandfather Randolph shows him a map illustrating the movements of Randolphs all over the world. Each Randolph has his flag. When a Randolph dies his flag goes reverently into a little box. The game is called Keeping Track.

And that makes John join the Service?

Instantly. He is Assistant Commissioner for the Gold Coast in a twinkling.

Only Assistant?

Yes, his brother Clive, the one in shorts, is the Commissioner.

And they go out alone to fight the Molybdenum Menace?

Not alone. Helen – Mrs Clive Randolph – goes with them to Have a Youngster.

Isn't that a little rash?

It would seem rash, but they don't come finer than Helen. And so we leave London-Seat-of-Empire, and travel to the sinister laboratory where Zurov is nominally studying ants, while his men are secretly poisoning Carpenter, the Deputy Commissioner.

Shame. Do they kill him?

They do, although Clive hurries through the Rains to save him. Clive is suspicious of the ants. He knows all about them, you see. He once wrote a book called 'The Ant World, by Randolph.' Zurov has it on his desk, demy-oct., gilt edges, good quality binding. But Clive never reaches Carpenter.

Why not?

Because Helen visits some school children in the rain, and the Youngster arrives, and John fakes a message from the Colonial Office to bring Clive back. Carpenter dies, the Youngster dies, Clive is sent down, John, now Deputy Commissioner, takes to drink, and the family scutcheon is blotted.

Who wipes off the blot?

Phyllis.

Phyllis who?

Phyllis Ransome. John's *fiancée*. She arrives fresh from England in a cool summer dress, a topee, and long gloves, with a few necessaries tossed into a bag, and the box of flags from Grand-father.

And that pulls John together?

Certainly. He breaks three whisky bottles over his car, pretends to be drunk, and reels into Zurov's broadcasting station just as DNXY is calling the world to stand by for a six o'clock broadcast. Then he shouts 'The pudding is hot' into the transmitter.

The pudding is what?

Hot. That's a family saying of Grandfather's. All Randolphs understand it. Another Randolph, Simon, hears it in the Foreign Office in London-Seat-of-Empire. He cries 'John's in the radio station. I know it,' and they telephone Clive on the Gold Coast to blow the place up with bombing planes before six o'clock.

Why before six?

Because the world will go to war at six.

What time is it now?

Four-forty by Big Ben.

But John's in the broadcasting station?

Ah, you thought so and Clive thought so, but he isn't. Zurov has just thrown him out at 5.59. So when the bombs hit the broadcasting station everyone dies of concussion except John, who Returns with Honour with his arm in a sling.

And the world is saved for democracy?

The world, as you rightly surmise, is saved for democracy, the family scutcheon is wiped clean, the sun never sets, Mr and Mrs Clive Randolph and Mr and Mrs John Randolph arrive home in sixty seconds odd, and Mrs Randolph senior is waiting at the door with four white carnations.

1939

Quai des Brumes is the sort of powerful and joyless film that the French do so well – a study in foetid atmosphere, in which the one beauty is its uncompromising honesty.

It is set on a foggy quayside down by the Havre docks. The story covers two days, concerns only hunted people, haunted people, and frustrated people. A young French soldier, wanted for some crime unknown, arrives out of the night. In an inn by the waterfront he meets other wharf rats. A lascivious old toy-dealer, with a taste for church music. A lecherous young playboy with a taste for women. A drunken rum-smuggler, a mongrel dog with all his ribs showing, an unhappy girl with tormented eyes. A painter who sees a drowned man in every swimmer.

Slowly, almost fastidiously, the film takes these lives and twists them to their mutual destruction. The soldier is shot in the street just as his ship is leaving for Venezuela. The girl is left alone and hopeless. The toy-dealer is bludgeoned to death in his own cellar. The painter commits suicide. The dog is abandoned. The playboy kills his man and escapes, with an address that would not be allowed in any English or American picture.

Quai des Brumes is one of the most depressing films I have ever seen, and one of the strongest. Its message, if it has a message at all, is 'What's the use of anyfink?' 'Why, nuffink.' It grips you all through the telling, and haunts you later . . . B–r–rr, I can still smell the fog curling round the sand-dunes and see Jean Gabin, pale eyes in his brown face, and Michel Simon, licking his thick lips furtively, like a cat after stolen cream.

15 January 1939

At last, after a quarter of a century of waiting, the first Gilbert and Sullivan opera has come to the screen, copyrights all squared, music as written by Sullivan, words as written by Gilbert, and produced by an ex-D'Oyly Carte conductor with the blessing of the D'Oyly Carte office. Thousands of people all over the world have been waiting for just such an occasion. Is it a happy experiment? To my mind, no.

Mr Geoffrey Toye and his collaborators had a knotty problem before them when they set out to film a Gilbert and Sullivan opera. They had to decide from the beginning whom they were setting out to please – the theatre audience, who knew and loved the Savoy operas, or the cinema audience who didn't give a damn for the Savoy operas so long as they saw a good picture.

It was a risk either way, a risk that only a fanatic or a showman of enormous genius would have dared to take. Mr Toye and his colleagues didn't take it. They compromised. For their initial venture they chose **The Mikado**, not the best of the Gilbert and Sullivan operas, but the best known. They cut enough of the Gilbert dialogue and the Sullivan numbers to reduce the film to one hour and twenty minutes' running time. They left in nearly all the traditional stage 'business,' but added an original mimed prologue. Geoffrey Toye, himself, steeped in the Savoy tradition, produced, conducted, and devised the scenario. Victor Schertzinger came over from Hollywood to direct. Kenny Baker came from the American films and radio to play Nanki-Poo. Jean Colin, the Yum Yum, was brought in from British films and musical comedy; Constance Willis, the Katisha, from Covent Garden and grand opera. John Barclay, the Mikado, played the part with the D'Oyly Carte company in America; Gregory Stroud, the Pish Tush, in the company's Australian tours. Elizabeth Paynter, the Pitti-Sing, recently played soubrette parts under the name of Elizabeth Nickel-Lean. Martyn Green, Sydney Granville, and Kathleen Naylor are current Savoyards, good and true.

The result of this compromise is an odd film that pulls this way and that way and never quite gets anywhere. On the credit side must be put down the colour and the music. Technicolor has never turned out anything better than this fantastic canvas of fairy-tale colours. Like all colour films, there is too much of it, too high a revel in cornflower blue and almond green and magenta, and the crowd scenes badly need a colour choreographer. But the individual colours are clear and good, and the piece gains enormously from their selection. As for the recording, it is brilliant. The D'Oyly Carte chorus, the London Philharmonic Orchestra, and the sound engineers have done well by Sullivan, and Sullivan comes through as a melodist who was worth the trouble. I believe it is fair to say that *The Mikado* has never been so well played, and, as a whole, so well sung before.

When you have applauded the colour and the music, I think you have covered all the common ground of approbation between the film audience and the Gilbert and Sullivan audience. After that, opinions will be sharply divided.

I myself was in love with the Gilbert and Sullivan operas long before I fell in love with moving pictures. In my schooldays I was near the head of every pit-queue when the D'Oyly Carte company played Manchester. To me, spring never really came until the familiar black-and-red posters went up on the hoardings, and the sharp March evenings are still mixed up in my memory with the smell of size and dust and grease-paint.

I wrote reviews of the operas in a school exercise book, which was one way of getting the nonsense out of my system. In my holidays I followed the company to Birmingham, Newcastle, Nottingham. I made friends amongst the principals, and ate salad with the chorus ladies and gentlemen – very daring, I thought this – from a wash-bowl in theatrical lodgings. I was enraged when my friends Ruby This and Ivy That didn't get the solo bit in the opening chorus. I wrote to Henry Lytton in great indignation over some caustic review of Ernest Newman's that I read in the local reference library. I still have Lytton's kindly reply.

With all this behind me, I think I can claim to be a loyal Savoyard. As a loyal Savoyard, then, I resent the screen interpretation of *The Mikado*. I resent the cuts in dialogue and music. I dislike Kenny Baker's American dialogue, and Constance Willis's Wagnerian conception of Katisha. I have seen at least three better Yum Yums than Jean Colin, and that explanatory prologue merely annoys me. If I had not been in the theatre on a job of reviewing, I should have walked out when Nanki-Poo stole the first verse of Yum Yum's number 'The Sun and I'.

On the other hand, as a loyal filmgoer, I found the coyness of the old stage business maddening. Tricks, gestures, grimaces, that are rich in tradition on the stage, meant nothing to me in the cinema. If only the thing would *move*, I kept on thinking. Those long stretches of funny dialogue, that aren't on the whole, so funny . . . That stylized comedy of Martyn Green's, handed down from Lytton, from Workman, from Passmore, from Grossmith . . . All very well in the theatre, with the electric response of an audience all about you, but deadly in a cold screen close-up . . . What a relief to get to Kenny Baker's singing, foreign in timbre, yes, but so comfortably of our age and our cinema. As a filmgoer, I found myself surprised and delighted with Mr Baker, who seemed to me fresh and modest and vigorous, and singing Sullivan as if he loved it.

The Mikado is likely to cause so much argument amongst audiences, and so much division between the Savoyard and the filmgoer in each of us, that I really think you ought to go and see it. I insist myself that it is a bad compromise, but I am quite prepared to believe that you may think it a good one . . .

15 January 1939

For the third time in succession Zoltan Korda, until recently the odd-job man of the Korda brothers, has pulled off a big, swinging adventure film of the kind that exhibitors pray for.

The Four Feathers is likely to make as much history at the box-office as *The Drum* or *Sanders of the River*. It may make more, for it is a better film than either, and it comes at a time when these bold, patriotic, simple-hearted heroics just touch off the public mood.

The film is based, of course, on A. E. W. Mason's thirty-year-old novel, with a new script by R. C. Sherriff. It is the fourth screen version of this celebrated story, and the best by every standard. The period is the 1890s, the setting the Sudan after the murder of General Gordon. Largely shot in Africa, in Technicolor, with what Press agents love to talk about as 'a cast of thousands', *The Four Feathers* keeps the screen packed with movement, spectacle, and excitement. Beyond these obvious box-office virtues, however, it has another quality. It tells a thumping good personal story. I suppose you might roughly describe its thesis as the conquest of fear.

The hero is a Lieutenant in the Surreys, who resigns his commission the day before his regiment sails for active service. When he was an impressionable small boy, the youngest of a long line of soldiers, he had heard tales over the fruit and port that made his blood curdle. He is honestly, temperamentally panic-stricken at the thought of soldiering.

But when his three friends in the regiment send him white feathers, and the girl he is engaged to adds another, he goes secretly out to the Sudan to 'redeem' his character. Disguised as a native, he does the most blazingly stupid, heroic things, beside which the common risks of soldiering look like the misadventures of a district visitor. A fool might do them, or a good man under orders. The whole point of the story is that he does them, with his imagination working at high pressure, alone.

John Clements, whom we saw in *Knight Without Armour*, and as the consumptive councillor in *South Riding*, plays this difficult hero, and makes a man of him. There is a hint of raw nerves in his performance, a kind of spiritual delicacy, that is just right for the part.

It is a sign of grace in Clements, or perhaps just good sound acting, that his work stands up to the stiffest competition on the English screen – Ralph Richardson's. Mr Richardson plays Durrance, the soldier who goes sun-blind in the desert. This was the fat part in the book, and remains the show part in the picture. Richardson plays it on the grand scale, right to the back row of the pit and the top tier of the gallery. He uses face, body and voice to create a gigantic bedlam of blind panic. There will be people who will say that he overacts. I should say he just acts like a great actor in a medium that barely knows the meaning of the word.

With the story he had, and with two such players at the head of his cast, Zoltan Korda's film was half-made before he started. But 'Zolly' would not stop short at this guarantee. He is an odd, honest little man, with an odd, honest passion for truth in strange places. A born gypsy himself, he feels that his mission – if he were arrogant enough to believe he had a mission – in the cinema is to give people 'good travelling'.

His films, since he had the status to pick them for himself, are all about the far ends of empire. He is more at home in the Sudan, on the North-West Frontier, than he ever will be in Park Lane or Piccadilly. He likes the native peoples and understands them. Their music and their ceremonies excite him.

When Zolly takes his audience travelling in India or Africa, he isn't content to give them a tourist's viewpoint. There is no 'And so we bid farewell to colourful So-and-So' about these pictures. They live by their odd observation, their fierce, illustrative detail. If Zolly, on his travels, saw something fine, he shows you something fine. If he saw something foul, he shows you something foul.

The Four Feathers lives because it gives you the feel of a cracked, parched, blistering-hot Sudan in wartime. The water-holes are dry. The air swims at mid-day. Vultures wheel over the battlefields, tear at the carcasses of men and horses as coolly as though nobody in the audience were watching them. Little birds, in tremulous flocks, stream up from the bushes by the river. A blind man stumbles over corpses, shouts aloud in panic, and only the vultures answer him.

The film is a little clumsy in the dining-room, falters a bit on the home terrace in Technicolor moonlight. It hasn't the well-bred recovery of the Hollywood melodramas, or quite the ruthless drive of the soberer French pictures. It tries to do just a little bit too much of everything. But I don't know a film to beat it at the things it can do well.

23 April 1939

Jamaica Inn or, as one of the leading players insists on calling it, Jamaica Rinn, is a film that critics of the cinema, both amateur and professional, have been looking forward to with more than normal curiosity.

With Charles Laughton as the star, and Alfred Hitchcock as director, it brings together two of the most formidable and stylised talents in the English-speaking film world. Could they work together successfully, we wondered? Which would come out on top, the Laughton portraiture or the Hitchcock touches? Whatever sort of film, psychological study or frank chiller, popular romance or collector's piece, would these two odd collaborators make of their wrecking tale of a hundred years ago?

The odd thing is that, now that the piece is here, the first thing you notice is neither Laughton nor Hitchcock, but the new young woman, a Miss Maureen O'Hara, who plays the heroine. Miss O'Hara patently comes from Dublin, is nineteen years old and a tallish girl, rather grave, with a curiously soft strength about her face and figure. She speaks English with the faintest Irish brogue, and is as certainly destined for Hollywood as this article is ultimately headed for the pulp-mills. I don't know yet whether she can act for little green apples, but I do know that there is some quality about her, a vigorous young beauty, that makes you intensely aware of every minute her picture is on the screen.

What about the film in which Miss O'Hara makes her first appearance, Hitchcock and Laughton's picture? Well, it turns out to be a stormy, lurid melodrama rather in the style of a boy's fourpenny shocker. It might have been called The Wrecker's Revenge, or, Mary Yellen and the Periwigged Peril.

Innocent, orphaned Mary, in her neat black travelling cloak and poke bonnet, arrives at a Cornish inn to stay with her Uncle Joss (Leslie Banks) and her Aunt Patience (Marie Ney). The very first night she is there a man is hanged from the rafters. A ship is wrecked, and all the survivors butchered. Uncle Joss turns out to be a drunken bully, his associates smugglers, thieves, brutes and just plain murderers. Behind these small-time criminals Mary gradually discerns the Master Mind of Evil, that recognized licentiate of villainy, the village squire.

The squire, of course, covets Mary's fresh young charms. She is bound, gagged and abducted to the Dover packet, with the fate that is worse than death lurking round every corner. At the last moment the hero, whom we last saw trussed up and threatened with a horse pistol, rides up and saves her virtue at the head of a troop of redcoats. Uncle Joss is shot dead by the military. Aunt Patience is shot dead by the Master Mind of Evil. The squire goes mad and leaps to his death from the masthead. The wreckers are captured and taken away in irons. Mary averts another shipwreck by running up her lingerie as a beacon. There isn't a serial trick that the picture misses, except perhaps the ultimate nest of serpents, and the lovers bound helpless on the track.

It is great fun that these two, Laughton and Hitchcock, have had with *Jamaica Inn*, but I wouldn't like to call it great film-making. Using Laughton's passionate response to beauty, Hitchcock's razor-keen observation, on this sort of thing is like beating out a damascened blade into a plough-share. Certainly it does the job, but it does it wastefully. Perhaps I have an over-scrupulous mind, but I hate waste.

I enjoyed *Jamaica Inn* much as I enjoyed *Sexton Blake and the Hooded Terror*, not otherwise. It was engaging to watch Charles Laughton, as the squire, all jutting nose and squared outlines, playing a rollicking composite of all the villains from Nero to Tod Slaughter's. (Note to avoid correspondence: I know the villain was a parson in the book. The change of profession was made to placate the censors.) It was a relief to find a film that moved from the first shot to the last, that preached no sermon and carried positively no message. I couldn't help thinking though, what a grand chiller the French realists would have made of the same subject, how they would have 'planted' that brooding, murderous atmosphere of the inn until you couldn't look at a doorpost without a shudder.

I missed a sense of humour in the picture, and any warmth of human life, good or evil. Most of all, as a practising film critic, I missed what are known in the trade as the 'Hitchcock touches'. Thinking back on the picture, I can count exactly four of them, three minor ones and one major. Charles Laughton explains this apparent deficit by saying that Hitchcock's technique has developed in *Jamaica Inn*, that all his work today is richer, and the individual touches are not so obvious.

They are not, and I'm sorry for it. I liked the Hitchcock touches. I liked the bits that stuck out of his films like a sore thumb, and made us say affectionately, 'Dear old Hitch, how like him!' I miss them in *Jamaica Inn*, and believe that the whole film is the poorer for their absence.

14 May 1939

Gangster's Boy

Larry played on the football team
With the sons of Willmore's *crème de la crème*.
But that was before Judge Davis had
Taken a look at Larry's Dad.

Larry's Dad was a racketeer,
Made his pile on the price of beer.
(I hasten to add, lest the tale offend you,
Retired racketeer, *bien entendu*).

When Larry delivered the school oration,
On the joys of American education,
Nobody dared to clap the beggar
Except the son of another bootlegger.

But Dad, a man of the strictest morals,
Soon put an end to the local quarrels.
Smoked a cigar with the Judge, while Larry
Entered West Point and the military.

1939

There are two new detective debuts in the London cinemas this week. Basil Rathbone's and Ralph Richardson's. Mr Rathbone portrays – yes, I think portrays is the word – Sherlock Holmes in the **Hound of the Baskervilles** at the Gaumont Theatre, while Mr Richardson tosses off a flip sketch of one Major Hammond, a Whitehall expert with an umbrella, in a secret service piece called **Q Planes** at the Odeon. Both, we learn, are to continue the characters in a further series of pictures. Sherlock Holmes is already at work on his second adventure, and I suppose it is only a matter of time before we meet Major Hammond on the Maginot Line, at Monte Carlo, or in the night-life of Paris, where eventually all good secret agents go.

It may just be a personal opinion, but I thought that Mr Richardson, who apparently didn't give a rush for his detective's ethics or ancestry, managed his debut better than Mr Rathbone, who was obviously unflagging in his determination to do right by Sherlock.

Perhaps Mr Rathbone tried too hard. Perhaps he let his mind dwell too persistently on the responsibilities of the Holmes tradition. It could be. It might well curb an actor's flight of fancy to know that every line he uttered, and worse, every line he didn't utter, was a household word in twenty-four languages, including Tamil, Talugu and Urdu, and Pitman's Shorthand.

At any rate, whatever the reason may be, Mr Rathbone's Holmes works out as a curiously inhibited figure in a sadly colourless picture. It has neither the vigorous authority of the Doyle detective nor the crisp finality that Mr Rathbone customarily gives to his acting studies. This isn't the Holmes, you feel, who could distinguish the faint smell of 'the scent known as white jessamine' from seventy-five perfumes on a sheet of paper. This isn't the Holmes who once, 'when very young,' confused the typography of the *Leeds Mercury* with the *Western Morning News*.

Some of the fault lies, no doubt, in the omissions and commissions of the Hollywood script. It is a script that is generally – though not unfailingly – accurate in the big things, but completely alien in the significant details. Bullfrogs croak on the tor – and they don't call it a tor, either. Watson, who would sooner have died than commit the sacrilege, announces himself on occasion as Mr Sherlock Holmes, the great detective. Holmes himself, that meticulous amateur, usurps the functions of the police, brings his Stradivarius with him to the moors, allows himself to be trapped in the Hound's den by the simplest of ruses, and cuts his way out with a pocket penknife, for all the world like a good Boy Scout.

The Hound of the Baskervilles raises an old question, never yet satisfactorily decided. Can the pure detectives of fiction ever be brought to the screen convincingly? Isn't there something about their quality – the thing that marks them out from the sleuths of action like the Saint and Bulldog Drummond – that is essentially academic and literary? Isn't their power really in the words the author has spun for them – characteristic phrases, persistent mannerisms, individual lines of reasoning?

The screen hasn't exactly tumbled over itself to get them, but it has never been entirely averse to handling the great detectives of fiction. We have had a handful of Holmeses, several Philo Vances, Ellery Queens, and Perry Masons, three Hildegarde Withers, an assorted Poirot or two, a brace of Hanauds, a Nero Wolfe, and a Father Brown. We have had one Lord Peter Wimsey already, and are shortly going to have another. It is obviously absurd to anticipate Robert Montgomery's rendering of the Sayers hero, but all we can say is, he's got a tough job in front of him. Of all these distinguished characters who have been translated to the screen, only one or two have managed to be more than well-mannered strangers to the detective reader. (The best was Edna Mae Oliver's Hildegarde Withers, with Eille Norwood's silent Sherlock Holmes running her a close second.)

My own view, and I stick to it, is that the great detective, as distinct from the frank go-getter, is generally better forgotten by the film producer. In spite of a sneaking desire to see Rex Harrison as Albert Campion, I am glad of the screen's surprisingly dilatory approach to the works of Miss Margery Allingham. I hope they won't think of making Carter Dickson's H. M. a film star, although I wonder why they haven't. It is a mystery to me that nobody has snapped up the H. C. Bailey books, but it is also a comfortable mystery. I dread to think what the scenario department and the casting director between them might do with Reggie Fortune or Mr Clunk.

Mr Richardson's Major Hammond, of *Q Planes*, is a sleuth of quite a different colour. He has no literary traditions that I know of: he is a frank film conception. He bounces in and out of a tale of disappearing planes, disintegrating rays, and secret superchargers, with quiet resilience.

While all England is waiting for him to locate the enemy dredger that is menacing our air power ten miles off Land's End, he takes time to slice vegetables for a stew, or telephone his Daphne that he must postpone a dinner engagement. He has a closet full of precisely similar hats, and enough umbrellas to shelter all Europe. He is harum-scarum in the modern film way; apparently as blank as a fish and as mad as a hatter. I doubt if any author could write him accurately; his character is all visual hints, first and foremost picturable.

Q Planes, although it sometimes leans too far over in the pursuit of snappiness, is a bright, vigorous little picture, and Mr Richardson's Major is the brightest thing in it. You should see it. You'll like it. It has a savour. I don't suppose for a moment that Mr Richardson took his Major very seriously. I don't imagine that he 'grounded' the man in his heredity and environment, as Charles Laughton likes to do with every part; that he troubled to discover what happened to young Hammond at twelve, to give him that psychological kink for hats and umbrellas.

I fancy that he just took the Major as he found him, and acted him to the best of his ability. His job was to entertain the audience for so many minutes at a time, to do certain routine and trivial things in an interesting way, and he did it. Being a good actor, he gave as much care to his minor charge as he would give to any other professional engagement. It's a trick, if you like, but it's also a privilege and a pleasure to see such a thorough performance on a too often slovenly screen.

9 July 1939

NOTE: Ralph Richardson went off to fight in a real war at sea, so the promised series was never made; but Major Hammond was reincarnated twenty years later, when he provided the elegant model for Patrick Macnee as John Steed in *The Avengers*. – A. L.

In a very short time now British cinemas should be receiving a regular supply of newsreel pictures from the Western Front. Permission has at last been obtained to send a camera-man to France from each of the five British newsreels – Pathé, Movietone, Gaumont-British, Paramount, and Universal. The men left London early last week with all the equipment necessary for taking silent films. A Movietone sound van will follow later to service the five camera-men jointly.

Expenses are to be paid by the newsreels themselves. Positions will be allotted to the various camera-men by rota, as has been the rule on all official occasions in peace time. Film taken will be sent back to individual companies and then shared out among the various newsreels. Censorship will be done promptly by the War Office or the Air Ministry, according to the material shot.

This arrangement should put an end to the natural complaints of cinema proprietors in England and neutral countries that they are getting no first-hand reports of the war from Allied sources. The newsreels themselves are not to blame. All the companies, naturally, had made preparations for shooting in the eventuality of war. What they could not, and did not, forecast was the extent of official ukases as soon as hostilities should break out.

Immediately on the outbreak of war in Britain, secret defence notices were issued in connection with newsreels. These were amplified on September 10 by an act known as the Control of Photography Order. This new act, as one authority puts it, 'wiped out everything the Defence people hadn't thought of.' Shots of troops on the march – shots of troops in training – shots of buildings designed for troops – almost anything, it seemed, might give information to the enemy. Several cameramen were arrested. In the absence of any other urgent news than war-news, the newsreel people almost saw their functions at an end.

In order to satisfy, temporarily, the crying demand of exhibitors for war news, the War Office, on their own initiative and at their own expense, went out and took their own war pictures. They shot, discreetly, troops on the march and troops embarking. These pictures were handed out to the newsreels for circulation, and in the absence of any other material a certain proportion of the first batch was issued. The second batch, of troops disembarking on the other side, was turned down as 'inferior work.'

In the meantime Germany was busy sending out double-length newsreels to the neutrals. In one case they were shown, with editorial amendments, in this country. Although made entirely for propaganda purposes, they were so full of 'meat' that 'they made my mouth water,' according to one authority in this country. Our Ambassadors in neutral countries, seeing these began to press more urgently for something from Allied sources. It was recognized more particularly that a certain freedom of reporting was essential for the Colonial markets and for India.

Gradually authoritative pressure from home and overseas has brought about a modification in the rules restricting British newsreels. The Control of Photography Order still remains in being, but it is hoped that a committee will shortly be set up to waive its more hampering restrictions. In the meantime, home permits have been issued to newsreel cameramen, which will largely free them from interdiction by local police and A.R.P. authorities.

Finally, permission has been given for the dispatch of cameramen to the war zones, where their work should amplify the records taken by the official French photographers.

5 October 1939

The Forties

'Chin up, Tommy Atkins, carry on!' sang Judy Garland in a sequence about British children arriving as refugees in New York. I was not among them. Although we didn't go to America, America came to us. My cousin Michael was one of a handful of Americans who crossed the Canadian border and joined the British Army. He stayed at our house while waiting to go with his regiment to Europe.

Between Hitler's invasion of Poland and Japan's attack on Pearl Harbor, Hollywood wore two faces. One, exemplified by Hitchcock's *Foreign Correspondent*, urged America to prepare for battle, the other deliberately ignored the conflict in Europe. After Pearl Harbor, of course, everything changed. Errol Flynn was famously depicted winning the war in Burma. Meanwhile, British films achieved an individuality, and enjoyed a success in their own country, which had eluded them before. The Crown Film Unit and its documentaries were treated perhaps more respectfully than they deserved: much of the propaganda was crude: but films like *In Which We Serve* and *The Way to the Stars* are impressive still. Anyway, they suited the mood of the time.

My mother, the most unwarlike of women, sent a cheque to Lord Beaverbrook's fund to pay for more Hurricanes and Spitfires. She was asked to advise on what films should be shown at Chequers for Mr Churchill's diversion. His favourite proved to be *Lady Hamilton*.

Eventually we saw an armada of planes heading south for D-day. The V–1 and V–2 rockets were still to come. The V–1s were nasty; you could see them in the sky, and there was a pause, when the engine cut out, before you knew where they were going to fall. But again we were unscathed. Germany surrendered. I was in the Mall to see the King and Winston Churchill on the balcony of Buckingham Palace. Michael returned, and found that his civilian clothes, after five years in our attic, had been reduced to dust by the moths.

The war and its aftermath continued to preoccupy British and American films for several years. At first there were films about Allied co-operation. Gradually Russian villains began to appear, but the film industry never seemed as happy vilifying Communists as it had been when villifying Nazis. Although the distasteful performance of Senator McCarthy has rendered it unfashionable to say so, there really was a strong left-wing preponderance in Hollywood. Added to which, the film industry, even at its most serious, is not good at serious politics. If my mother held any views on these matters, except belief in simple standards of decency, I never heard her express them.

After some two-and-a-half years in the Royal Navy, I went up to Oxford in the autumn of 1949. The most Henry Jamesian of academic mystery writers, Michael Innes [J. I. M. Stewart], then a don at Christ Church, came to tea in my rooms because he wanted to meet my mother. He wanted to consult her, because MGM were proposing to make a film of his best book, *The Journeying Boy*, with Greer Garson playing what had been the male lead. Was this normal, he wondered, should he agree? The film was never made; which is rather a pity. – A. L.

The story of **The Wizard of Oz** written in 1900, is, I suppose, America's nearest equivalent to *Alice in Wonderland*. The film that has been made from it – the second film, for there was a silent version with Larry Semon round about 1925 – is, I suppose, America's nearest equivalent to an English pantomime.

The heroine is one Dorothy, a little girl from Kansas, with pigtails and a gingham pinafore, ankle-strap shoes, and a favourite puppy. Caught up in a cyclone on her Kansas farm, she finds herself deposited with a bump and a scream and a twizzle in Technicolor and the Land Beyond the Rainbow. There the people – the most important ones, anyway – have a curiously distorted likeness to the farmhands, the school-teacher, the vagrants, she knew at home. There is also a Good Witch, a perfect stranger to Dorothy, who looks and sounds to us exactly like Billie Burke, and who, in fact, *is* Billie Burke, pretty as a chocolate box, with a star in her hair.

Homesick for Kansas, Dorothy is directed to find the Wizard of Oz, who can grant one's heart's desire. On the way she meets three other clients for the Wizard, a Scarecrow who wants a brain, a Woodman who wants a heart, and a Cowardly Lion who is looking for courage. Before she gets back to sepia and Kansas again, Dorothy has assisted at the most lavish pantomime performance ever put on any screen, with giants and pigmies, jewel caves and fairy fountains, witches vanishing in a puff of flamingo smoke, cavorting choruses, and landscapes like a National Colour Chart.

Not in the same world with Disney or Lewis Carroll, *The Wizard of Oz* is an exciting tour de force that keeps the eye and ear constantly occupied, bothers the brain very little. It is hearty and unsubtle, generous and sometimes, in its high riot, intoxicating. Curiously enough, the most persuasive bits of all are the ones in good Kansas sepia, in which Judy Garland, who has never appealed to me before as an artist, is very, very good indeed.

28 January 1940

That little production genius, Joe Pasternak, who has guided Deanna Durbin wittily and wisely through her growing years, has pulled off a three-fold triumph with **Destry Rides Again**. He has brought Marlene Dietrich back to the screen with her best film since *The Blue Angel*. He has charmed out of James Stewart a performance even finer than his Mr Smith in *Mr Smith Goes to Washington*. And he has made a Western that is better than any Western except *Stagecoach*, and that has more romance, pungency, and gusto than that lovely picture.

Destry Rides Again starts with a good script, and builds brilliantly on it. When the film starts, there is no law but gang law in the pioneer town of Bottle Neck. Saloon-keeper Kent (Brian Donlevy) runs the town, with his singer Frenchy – the Dietrich part, naturally – as decoy. When the old sheriff, an honest man, asks too many questions they kill him and choose the town drunkard as his successor. But that is their mistake. Once long ago, the soak was deputy to Tom Destry, the greatest sheriff the West has ever known. Destry is dead, shot in the back, but he has a son, young Tom. And the soak sends for him.

Young Tom Destry is long, and slow, and very gentle. He carves napkin-rings for a hobby. He likes milk better than liquor. He doesn't carry a gun. 'If I did,' he drawls to Kent, 'one of us might get hurt – and it might be me – and I wouldn't like that – *would* I?' But, all the same, he cleans up Bottle Neck. In the end even the spitfire Frenchy, with a bullet in her heart, dies for him.

The film has everything that a successful film should have – pace, suspense, feeling, a delicious dry economy of dialogue, and enough frank vigour to make it salty. Miss Dietrich's husky songs have an excitement they haven't caught since 'Falling In Love Again'. Her first entrance, on what might be called a close-up of sound, is one of the most cunning technical tricks I ever remember in a picture.

They haven't bothered this time to shoot her through veils and drapes, with a soft focus lens, emphasizing those bright eyes, and those sultry hollows in the cheeks. They haven't needed to. Her Frenchy is made to stand up to saloon lights, and curiously enough, when the technicians don't try to soften it, a new and human gentleness creeps through the mask of make-up.

As for James Stewart, his No-Gun Destry seemed to me as delicate a bit of screen acting as we have seen this season. This long, drawling young man has recently worked out of a bad vein into the very aristocracy of screen players. More and more, that diffident manner of his is hiding strength, technique, and a kind of caustic wisdom. For Mr Stewart, for Miss Dietrich, for the sinister Donlevy, for the script, the songs, and the sheer skill and vigour of it. I'd give a first-class certificate with honours to *Destry Rides Again*.

11 February 1940

Possibly because I prefer my Hugo as Hugo, possibly because I have a prejudice against torture scenes in films, possibly because I still like to think of Charles Laughton as a great actor, I had hard work to sit through the screen version of **The Hunchback of Notre Dame**.

The film, which was made in Hollywood, runs for just under two hours, and has time in it for pretty well everything, from boiling lead to a medieval morality play. There is witchcraft, murder, and a printing-press; Cedric Hardwicke as a kind of monastic bogeyman; Maureen O'Hara coming from the rack as fresh as a daisy; a young poet called, as nearly as I could make out, Grangwah, and a great many close-ups of Charles Laughton.

Lon Chaney, who played the Hunchback in the old silent days was known as The Man with a Hundred Faces. Laughton's Hunchback has only one face, but it's a fairly shocking one. It has a squashed nose, one eye slipped down on to the cheek, and a mouth like a fish. The hump is as big as a young Alp, the arms swing like a gorilla's.

Mr Laughton, who has never been known to scamp a part, almost certainly felt deeply with Quasimodo, but the make-up is against him. It is practically impossible to convey any very fine shades of feeling with one eye and a few inches of face, as Mr Laughton must have found when he got down to work on his bell-ringer. The result is a performance that tries to do more with one eye than any actor has a right to do with two. It seems strenuous and over-emphatic, with a kind of coy relish, rather like Ernie Bagwash reciting his famous piece 'the tintinnabulation of the bellss, bellss, bellss, can-I-have-my-piece-of-cake-now-auntie?'

11 February 1940

John Ford is probably the finest film director now living, and **The Grapes of Wrath** is probably his finest film. It is not, like *Stagecoach* and *Drums Along the Mohawk*, an entertainment. It is a grave and sometimes quite shocking experience. Following closely, in its own native idiom, the mood of the great Soviet pictures, it lays bare for all the world to see America's flagrant tragedy of starvation, the slave-labour still rampant in a great democratic country.

The Joads, the typical Oklahoma family of the story, are driven from their farm by the land companies. They load their miserable furniture on to a truck, wash-tubs and mattresses, old tyres and wooden chairs, a stewpot and a few cans of food, and set off, three generations of Joads, on the long trek to the orchards of California. Eight hundred pickers wanted. Twenty thousand exiles on the road. The old people die by the wayside. Wherever the others camp they hear tales of starvation and misery. Groups of silent children gazing at food. Others dead of hunger. In California they do find work – at a dollar a ton for picking unbruised peaches. Starvation wages and child labour. They may not camp inside the city limits. The camps outside are burned by 'the poolroom boys.' The police move them on and on. One Joad kills a policeman, and slips away before dawn, to spread the gospel of revolution amongst these starving thousands. What is left of the family packs up its poor duds and goes on, this time towards the cotton-picking.

It is a terrible story, told with majesty. Except for Henry Fonda, there are no stars. Jane Darwell, as the fine Ma Joad, perhaps dominates the scene, but every man, woman and child in the huge cast is an actor in an equal sense. You seem to be driving with that truck, hoping for and dreading what may be round the bend of the road, seeing group after group of white, pinched faces in the beam of the headlights. Ford has used every trick of the great director in his unfolding of the drama, but, because he is a great director, the tricks are never intrusive or obvious. I don't often use the word 'art' in reference to the cinema, but *The Grapes of Wrath* seems to me the art of picture-telling in its highest form.

21 July 1940

There is no one quite like the Americans, bless them, for plugging an idea once they get one. You-know-Who and his regime have had their spot in every American pioneer film this year, and now they turn up again in Rafael Sabatini's Elizabethan romance, **The Sea Hawk**. This time it is Captain Errol Flynn and the British Fleet who stand between the tyrant and his dream of world conquest. There are Fifth Columnists in ruffs and threats of invasion, and there is a Munich-minded Queen who eventually addresses her people. 'My loyal subjects, a grave duty confronts us all: to prepare our nation for a war that none of us wants – least of all your Queen. We have tried by all means within our power to avert this conflict. We have no quarrel with the people of Spain. . . . But when the ruthless ambitions of a man threaten to engulf the world, it becomes the solemn obligation of free men, wherever they may be . . .' Does it sound familiar?

The Sea Hawk is a swashbuckling salute to England, made with one hand on the heart and both eyes on the box-office. It is lusty and yet sophisticated, nicely balanced between sea-hawks with sweating torsos and smart American girls with jewelled stomachers. You quickly get over the slight embarrassment of the fact that Mr Flynn's Gloriana is Flora Robson this time, not Bette Davis. Miss Robson makes the queen a jolly sort, prankish and yet womanly, a – er – dog amongst the sea dogs. Mr Flynn himself has learnt quite a lot about acting since he last stood in well-cut Tudor tights in front of the throne of England. He now not only raises the top lip slightly, but widens the eyes as well.

4 August 1940

I don't insist that James Stewart is the best of all the young actors on the screen today; I merely suggest it as a probability. For that matter, when I say 'young' I am speaking without the book. I haven't a notion when Mr Stewart's birthdate may have been; whether he is an Aries or a Taurus child; whether little Tyrone Power, and little John Garfield, and little Joel McCrea, and little Don Ameche preceded or followed him into long pants. I say 'young' because youth is the thing he is primarily master of. His talent is the suggestion of youth; of that gauche, fumbling tenderness that the years strip from a man; of gropings towards a plan of life rather than an achievement of it. He hasn't that grand range of Spencer Tracy's; his work doesn't cut as deep as our own Ralph Richardson's; he isn't as wise as Muni at his wisest; but he belongs with these men.

James Stewart's rise to the top in Hollywood is a testimony not only to his own good sense, but to the acumen of the cinema public. As a potential film star, young Stewart had many things against him. He came from theatre repertory. He was thin, and too tall – 6 ft 2½ – what the American's call 'a long drink of water.' Facially, he was no magazine cover. There was too much jaw. His mouth was difficult to photograph. His speech was a dry drawl.

I first saw James Stewart in the small part of the hunted brother in Jeanette MacDonald's *Rose Marie*. I called him 'a new screen actor with considerably more than average promise.' 'I think you will like him.' I wrote then, 'and I am sure you will hear more of him.' But those phrases, I recall, were something in the nature of wishful thinking. I didn't really believe that this pleasant, awkward young man would be allowed to go far beyond brilliant 'bit' parts. That startling little scene he had in *Wife v. Secretary* confirmed me in my opinion. Do you remember the 'bit' with Jean Harlow, where he sat in a car and told her how he got a five-dollar rise out of his boss? It was one of the moments that make film-going exciting. Probably it was too good. The studios, excited, pushed James Stewart into leads before he was ready for them. Some of them were pretty bad leads, and I'm afraid young Mr Stewart was sometimes pretty bad too.

We'll pass over such melancholy affairs as *Born to Dance*, *The Last Gangster* and *Navy Blue and Gold*, merely noting that everything eventually came right again. This is one of the rare occasions on which the perserverance of employers, the loyalty of the public, and the natural qualities of an actor work together to win success out of disappointment. Some time before the great *Mr Smith Goes to Washington* the blue streak was over. If there was still any doubt as to James Stewart's quality it was dismissed by *Destry Rides Again*.

These notes on a remarkable young player are occasioned by **The Mortal Storm**. This is a grim and anguished story of Nazi Germany in 1933, when the Hitler regime was in its infancy. It shows the disasters that crush the gentle home of a Jewish professor (Frank Morgan, of all surprising people), the break-up of friendships and family ties, the suspicions that lurk round every familiar corner. The Professor's daughter (Margaret Sullavan) finds that her young man (Robert Young) has joined the Party, and that even her young brothers are fired by the new ideology. She turns for comfort to a young, peace-loving farmer, escapes

with him to the frontier on skis, but is shot by the patrol led by
her former lover.

James Stewart plays the farmer. He is hardly a convincing
German type, any more than the other boys and girls of
the picture are convincing German types. But he makes the
bewildered young man so alive, so touching, that you forget
the racial issues in the personal tragedy of the story. Margaret
Sullavan, too, is a player whom I always find most moving.
Stewart played with her in *Next Time We Live*, again in *Shopworn
Angel*, and most recently in *The Shop Around the Corner*. The
two match each other step for step, make their companionship
seem human and convincing. Even those people – and they are
more in number than the producers realize – who have had quite
enough of films about Nazi Germany, will find it hard to resist
the persuasion of this couple in *The Mortal Storm*.

29 August 1940

Is it my imagination, or do all films seen during these months
of war tend to become war films in retrospect? Looking back on
them today, films, even the films that have absorbed me at the
time, seem less entities than part of the political pattern. Each
one has its associations with some outside event. *Of Mice and
Men* conjures up a picture of a hot London noon and the midday
papers carrying the story of the invasion of Norway. *Swanee River*
means the entrance of Italy into the war. *Virginia City* stands for
the capitulation of France. *Young Tom Edison* reminds me of the
first time I was woken by the sound of bombs in the night. *Gone
With the Wind* has some association that I can't quite fix, but I
know it is something to do with destroyers.

I can remember nothing like this since the days of one's
childhood, when the impressions of books one read, and plays
one saw, were sharply intermixed with the places in which one
read and saw them. *The Scarlet Pimpernel* and a picnic in the
heather . . . *Holiday House* on the top of a haystack . . . *Iolanthe*
on a Welsh pier with the distant sound of water sucking . . .
Robin Hood one Christmas Eve by gaslight.

There is nothing deliberate about this heightened sensibility.
We are not intentionally turning peace films into war films. It
just happens. It would surprise the good folk in Hollywood no
end, I fancy, to know how their gentlest offerings are being

tinged with the colour of battle. What might surprise them less, for they are a sporting community, is the way the English public are extracting fun from the air-raid warnings in cinemas. The matching of film dialogue with sirens is quite a game, I find, among the tougher element. Filmgoers compete for the most apt phrase heard in conjunction with a warning. One young lady of my acquaintance came back delighted from an interrupted session at *The Blue Bird*. 'Let there be light!' said the Fairy on the screen – and there was light – house-lights, and the manager making his brief announcement. My own family yesterday reported a riotous moment in the local show of *My Two Husbands*. The words 'All Clear' it seems, were thrown on the screen during a heated argument between Melvyn Douglas and Fred MacMurray over their legal status. The house appreciated it.

So far, the tin hat for air-raid stories goes to John Clements, the actor. He assures me, on his honour as an Intimate Theatre player, that this really happened when he went to see *Convoy* at the New Gallery. The manager made the usual announcement, a few people left the theatre, and the film proceeded. 'Gentlemen,' said Clive Brook's voice from the screen, 'we are going into action against the enemy.' Some time later the All Clear sounded. This time Mr Clements heard his own film ghost announcing, 'Everything's under control now.'

8 September 1940

THE STUDIOS CARRY ON

With the cinemas of London and other big towns re-imposing their curfew, and with film audiences everywhere in England dropping to the size of what is described as 'a really hot summer slump', people are naturally asking 'What about the studios? Is this going to be the end of British film production?' The answer is No. At the moment, under the most heartbreaking conditions, the studios are carrying on.

The responsible heads of the industry here have decided that this must not be another 1914–18. There must be British films, and big British films, for export, as well as for home consumption. The difficulties in the way of producers are stiff, but not insurmountable. Much studio space has been commandeered, but there are still good floors available in the major studios. The shortage of well-known directors is acute, but if some of our veterans are in Hollywood, that only gives an opportunity to younger men of talent. There are directors coming on in this country now who would have had no major chance in peace-time. Young actors can usually be loaned from the Forces, and as a country we are rich in middle-aged, experienced players. Air-raids and raid-alarms don't rattle these veterans. Many of them have refused fine American offers in order to stay and work in their own country in just such times as these.

At Denham, Gabriel Pascal goes doggedly on with his *Major Barbara*, with Wendy Hiller, Rex Harrison, Robert Morley, Sybil Thorndike, Robert Newton, and many others. The film is due in a New York theatre on November 15, and there is a general feeling that its completion is something of a marathon test of British endurance. Nothing is being scamped. There is no cutting-down of the schedule under present conditions. 'If Pascal can deliver the goods, as he looks like he's doing,' an executive of another company said to me yesterday, 'it ought to make some of our people who are now in America feel ashamed of themselves.'

Twentieth-Century Fox is going on the floor at Shepherd's Bush in a week's time with *Kipps*, with Michael Redgrave and Diana Wynyard in the leading parts, and Carol Reed directing. This will be followed by a biography of Pitt the Younger, a story which has many obvious parallels with the present world situation. Most topical title in the Fox programme is *Spitfire*, a film to be made in co-operation with the RAF and the Air Ministry. This will be the story of a typical fighter squadron, to which are attached airmen from all parts of the Empire. Somewhere round the hangars, too, are Naunton Wayne and Basil Radford, that perennial team of fatuous sportsmen.

At Elstree, John Corfield and his director, David MacDonald, have got as far as the Armada in a story of rural England down the ages. This is one of those group films, centred round a strip of land called Beacon Hill, opening with the Home Guard on night duty, fading back to the past and showing how these same few acres have always resisted or assimilated invasion. Emlyn Williams is the eternal farm labourer, John Clements the gentleman farmer, and the same group of village types appears in each episode – the parish priest, the doctor, the firebrand, the child, the innkeeper.

At Ealing, where Michael Balcon has come out as a real battling champion of British industry, they have another full programme.

Apart from the tonic George Formby pictures – the next will be George in the north-country play, *As You Are* – there are three serious films planned with a war-time background.

Air-raid warnings interrupt work two or three times a day. With staff and actors suffering from disturbed nights – 'blitz hangovers', as they call them – the producers who are contemplating these jobs have a man-size task in front of them. Unless conditions change materially for the worse, however, the films will be made. The closure or semi-closure of British cinemas would not affect them. There never was a time when the American market was so spontaneously open to British production. Apart altogether from the question of frozen dollar currency, these films are front-line stuff, which our friends and observers across the Atlantic are hungry to see.

15 September 1940

In the unlikely event that anyone – except, of course, Hitchcock himself – should have been anxious about the influence of Hollywood on England's chubby No. 1 director, **Foreign Correspondent**, coming on top of *Rebecca*, should reassure him.

Hitchcock is all right. Hitchcock, one might fairly say, has fulfilled himself. Like Ernst Lubitsch, and like Lubitsch alone of Europe's great directors, Hitchcock has found in the New World the full flowering of his talents. The films he made in this country were, at best, brilliant tentatives, graced by individual touches. The two films he has made in Hollywood are mature works, in which the touch is barely distinguishable from the whole.

Foreign Correspondent, grim melodrama, is a less likeable film than *Rebecca*. I still believe the Du Maurier work is the film that Hitchcock will live by, the film that scurrying reporters – 'Hitch' will forgive me for the macabre note – will headline in their obituaries. *Foreign Correspondent* is all tied up with these grisly days, a topicality that may give it a quick response and a short appeal. It is the story of an American crime reporter sent to Europe to cover the approach of war, how he tracks down a master-spy in the head of a peace organization, how he is shot down on the Clipper in mid-Atlantic, and broadcasts his final messsage to America with the bombs falling.

Only in the last patriotic rhodomontade does the touch miss. Hitchcock has been too long out of England to understand the mind of the bombed. The assault on London didn't happen this way. That may not matter. The assault on London couldn't happen this way. That does matter. In all the rest of the film, the smooth flow of fictitious narrative is only matched by the human reactions of the players. Albert Basserman is right. Laraine Day is right, Robert Benchley is superbly right, even the husky Joel McCrea for once is right. It must have delighted Hitchcock's cynical soul to make a hypocrite out of Herbert Marshall, an oily murderer of kind old Edmund Gwenn, and a chump called Ffolliatt of George Sanders, and to make them not only surprising but credible. The camera, too, is always in the right place, shooting the thing that matters, lighting the target like a tracer bullet. This is real film-making, by a man who has discarded more tricks than most directors have ever known.

13 October 1940

NOTE: It's interesting that, despite her long friendship with Hitchcock, my mother seems to have been quite unaware that *Rebecca* is the masterpiece she rightly considered it only because David O. Selznick had prevented him from totally changing Daphne du Maurier's plot in the cavalier fashion with which he usually treated the books on which his films were based. – A.L.

Once, long ago – I think it was after we had seen *Test Pilot* – I wrote an article which I called 'Thank You, Mr Tracy.' I remember the title, because it provoked a cable from Spencer Tracy, whom at that time I had never met and whom I had supposed to be quite unaware of my existence, saying 'Thank you, Miss Lejeune.' Since then I have wanted to say thank you to Mr Tracy again many times, but never more than now, when he turns his great talent to a part like **Edison the Man** just at a time when we need it most.

Remembering *North West Passage, Stanley and Livingstone, Boys' Town*, and *Captains Courageous*, I don't insist that his Thomas Edison is the greatest of the Tracy performances, but I can't think of anything more heartening that he could have done at the moment. Spencer Tracy's special quality is the suggestion of leadership that he puts into all his parts. Here, you feel, watching him as soldier, explorer, priest, doctor, or simple peasant, is a

man who is not only a man, but a light to follow. This fellow
would get you through, you feel, this is the comrade to have
in a tough corner. It may be just a film trick, of course, but,
if so, it is a curiously consistent and individual one. In *Edison
the Man* this sense of leadership is heightened by the fact of
the man's own human fumbling. This is no trained captain,
but a bewildered genius, nine thousand times wrong to his
one moment of inspiration. The whole part is a groping after
something, a quest for a truth that is beyond scientific precision.
Fiat lux.

The present film, which you can – and should – see at the
Empire this week, is a sequel to *Young Tom Edison*, in which
Mickey Rooney played the inventor in his boyhood. The two
films are quite distinct, and there is no need to have seen the
first in order to appreciate the second. With memories of *Young
Tom* fresh in your mind, however, you will find the allusions
in the new film richer. The haunting tune of 'Sweet Genevieve'
for instance, dates back to family evenings in Port Huron, when
Tom's gentle mother used to play it on the parlour piano. When
Spencer Tracy cups his hand round his deaf ear and mutters 'Eh?
What's that?' you'll remember how they had to get the doctor for
Mickey Rooney. When the struggling inventor spends his last ten
cents on milk and apple pie, you'll think of the chubby little cans
his mother used to pack for the schoolboy's luncheon. And when,
as a very old, tired man, Edison answers a reporter's query 'What
is the greatest invention?' by saying 'A blade of grass,' he is only
echoing a thought that came to him in the spring meadows sixty
years back. And it is one of the tenderest and most subtle aspects
of Spencer Tracy's performance that he can suggest the very tissue
of an old man's memories in that secret voice and smile.

Edison the Man begins and ends in 1929, at the inventor's golden
jubilee. Over the cigar smoke and the speeches it fades back to
the early years in New York, where young Mr Edison came at
twenty-three as a telegraph operator. It sketches his first failures
and struggles, his gentle romance with the lady who was to
become Mrs Edison, his invention of the stock-ticker and the
gramophone – on which his first recorded words were 'Mary
Had a Little Lamb' – and his long and painstaking search for
electric light. It is this quest of the Edison laboratory staff for
the 'flameless light', and the calculated obstruction of the gas
magnates, that really provides the bulk of the story. Once
New York is lit, and the long fantastic struggle vindicated,

the rest of Edison's experiments march past in a series of sub-titles.

I think it unlikely that this is a really accurate assessment of Edison's lifework. I am sure, though, that from the point of view of the films it is a sound, dramatic one. The search for light has always been a thing to capture the imagination, and *Edison the Man*, however dry and scientific it may like to seem, is really, in the end, an imaginative conception. Thomas Alva Edison *may* have countered the sceptic who asked him 'What good is electricity yet?' by replying, 'What good is a new-born baby?' but he certainly did not make the speech attributed to him on the occasion of his golden jubilee.

Earlier this evening I talked with two schoolchildren. To-morrow the world will be theirs. It's a troubled world, full of doubt and uncertainty. You say we men of science have been helping it. Are these children and their children going to approve of what we have done? Or are they going to discover, too late, that science was trusted too much, so that it turned into a monster whose final triumph was man's own destruction?

Some of us are beginning to feel that danger. But we have a chance to avoid it. I once had two dynamos. They needed regulating. It was a problem of balance and adjustment. I believe the confusion in the world today presents almost the same problem. The dynamo of man's God-given ingenuity is running away with the dynamo of his equally God-given humanity. I am too old now to do much more than to say, Put those dynamos in balance. Make them work in harmony as the great designer intended they should. It can be done. And then we need not be afraid of tomorrow . . .

This is a fine speech, even if Edison didn't make it. According to the records, the words on this occasion were limited to a few civilities. No one is to know, though, what was passing through his mind, and it is possible that the script writers have interpreted him correctly. At any rate, they have given the great man a great curtain speech, and Spencer Tracy delivers it with a humanity that again earns our affection and thanks.

20 October 1940

I don't quite know how the younger film public will react to the lacy charm of **Pride and Prejudice**, but I confess that I was considerably intrigued by it. It is such a comfort to find a Hollywood costume picture in which 'costume' doesn't mean just Errol Flynn in tights and jackboots, but is the outward habiliment of a world as real as ours, and much pleasanter, in which simple and logical things are happening every day.

Not that I am entirely happy about the costumes of *Pride and Prejudice*. With due respect to Adrian, MGM's dress expert, I suggest that the styles are something like twenty years ahead of time – not much, perhaps, in the whole wide pageant of history, but enough to lose just a little of the rural charm of Jane Austen's story. Doubtless leg o' mutton sleeves and full silk gowns flatter the line of a white shoulder and enhance the general sense of flurry and bustle, but I can't help feeling that the Misses Bennet and their friends would have looked just as nice, and felt more at home, in their own high-waisted, sprigged cottons and muslins.

This detail apart, I thought the film a quite delightful re-creation of Miss Austen's world, in which marriage was the highest concern of diplomacy, and a gentleman who would take a wife for £2 a week must have something questionable about him. Although not urgent in any modern sense, not intensely forceful or exciting, *Pride and Prejudice* seems to me one of the year's best film entertainments, engaging to look at and quietly satisfying to listen to. It is helped, of course, by Hollywood's remarkably good sense in retaining Miss Austen's conversation. The script, by Jane Murfin and Aldous Huxley, of all people, keeps the long story tidy, and doesn't make the mistake of trying to be cleverer or funnier than the original.

Once, when I was very young to journalism, I was sent to review the musical comedy *Lilac Time*. I came back full of theories as to what Schubert would have said about this or that number. I shall never forget the editor's comments on my copy. If he had wanted a ghost to write his notice, he told me, he would have hired a ghost. The lesson remains with me so vividly that I hesitate to suggest that Jane Austen herself might have chosen Greer Garson to play her Elizabeth Bennet – 'as delightful a creature as ever appeared in print, and how I shall be able to tolerate those who do not like *her* at least I do not know.'

For me, at any rate, Miss Garson is the perfect Elizabeth. 'There was a mixture of sweetness and archness in her manner which made it difficult for her to affront anybody.' I adore the way she cocks her head like a bird's and looks up under her lashes. I like her warm, sensible voice, and her delicate hands, and the way she skims along the ground, and her secret hint of laughter in the mind. It is rare to find a young screen actress with such a combination of wisdom and charm. When Miss Garson is on the screen it is very hard to look at anybody else, which is a pity, for some of the others are well worth looking at.

Laurence Olivier's Darcy, in particular, is a very pretty piece of work. His well-bred disdain is memorable, his spoilt impotence against Elizabeth's flashing wit makes him human and likeable. The studios need go no further when they are looking for a Mr Rochester for *Jane Eyre*. Mr Olivier can do it, and I hope he will. Edna May Oliver, too, is a tower of strength as Lady Catherine de Bourgh, and Melville Cooper as Mr Collins, Edmund Gwenn as Mr Bennet, Frieda Inescort, Karen Morley, and Maureen O'Sullivan, as Caroline, Charlotte, and Jane, are beautifully cast. I didn't think that Mary Boland, as Mrs Bennet, need have reached over quite so far for her laughs – they were practically in her hand, anyway – or that Mary, admittedly a bore, need also have been made into such a freak. But these are only small complaints against a picture that gave me a deal of pleasure, and that made me forget, for two blessed hours, that the world wasn't bounded by Longbourn, Rosings, Netherfield, and a wedding ring.

3 November 1940

Once in a while there turns up in the cinema a film that breaks all the rules. When this happens, the result may be good or bad, but it is always an event. Sacha Guitry's films are like that. *Green Pastures* was like that. *Down Went McGinty* was a little like that. **Our Town** is certainly like that. The film, which has been made from Thornton Wilder's prize play, will startle all its audiences, delight some, exasperate others. It blandly overlooks all the conventions of time, space, and script-writing. It turns a film from a third person narrative into the casual miscellany of a personal reflection. Its characters speak their thoughts out loud, and they, in their turn, are summed up by a commentator who sees the past as all of one piece with the future.

It is hard to give, so closely does it belong to the cinema medium, a clear verbal picture of *Our Town*. When the film begins you see a rangy, middle-aged American climbing to the top of a hill above the little town of Grover's Corners. He is the narrator, the town druggist. Casually, confidentially, he strolls up to the camera. 'I want to tell you about our town,' he begins. 'It's a nice town, if you know what I mean.' Population so many. Latitude, longitude, so and so. Congregational church down there, Methodist by the river across the railroad tracks.

The voice goes on, the film fades back to 1901, and takes us down into the valley into those neat frame houses. We live through the homely details of a day in Grover's Corners, attend choir practice, shell the peas with the housewives, catch a glimpse of the dawning love story of Emily Webb, the editor's girl, and George Gibbs, the doctor's son. The film moves on, punctuated by the narrator's quiet comments on his neighbours and their destinies, sometimes stopping for a snatch of back-chat between narrator and his characters. Bit by bit we see Emily and George's love story unfold; we attend their wedding, and finally, as Emily lies near death at the birth of her second child, we stray back with her to meet the dead of Grover's Corners, back to her own girlhood, seen afresh with the eyes of love and understanding. It's a tricky bit this – a hint of the metaphysical that I never remember attempted before, in pictures.

Our Town will either appeal to you as one of the loveliest films you have ever seen, or one of the silliest. To me it seems like opening a window and letting the sunshine into a dark room. It has a gentle philosophy of everyday goodness that I find most comforting. It knows and loves the little things of life, the common things – coffee, and bacon, sleep after a long day, the warmth of sunlight. It is so beautifully acted – and particularly by that flower-like creature, Martha Scott, who plays the girl Emily – that the human story shines through the most startling innovations of technique. An enchanting film, I thought – but you must make up your own mind about it. Like music and the bitter scent of chrysanthemums, it is the sort of thing that invites the sharpest personal response.

24 November 1940

NOTE: My mother presumably did not then know Wilder's play, which she later produced for her amateur company, or she would surely have mentioned – indignantly or sympathetically – the film's drastic softening of the climax. – A. L.

Film fanciers of fifteen years ago would have been startled nearly out of their wits by the suggestion that Fritz Lang, the stylish Viennese director of *Siegfried* and *Metropolis*, should make films about the wide open spaces where the mail must go through.

Yet that is precisely what he has done in **Western Union** – only it is the telegraph, not the mail, this time – and the result is extraordinarily successful. Ways of communication, whether by sea, rail, air, pony express or pigeon post, have always had a peculiar charm for men of sensibility. Do you remember the fun Grierson's young men used to have with those brief injunctions to Use the Telephone and to Post Early? Mr Lang who is distinctly sensible, has given us a lively piece, in clamant Technicolor, about the extension of the telegraph from Omaha to the Pacific. Indians and outlaws interfere with the scheme, and love is a distraction, too, though it is never really allowed to get in the way of business. This is very efficiently conducted by Messrs Randolph Scott, Dean Jagger, Robert Young, and other pioneer employees of the company, who surmount the various hardships of the expedition, that in days to come good people in Omaha may cable 'Happy Birthday to You' to their friends in Salt Lake City.

Unless you insist on a hero who wears silk pyjamas and a heroine with nostalgic recollections of springtime in Budapest, you should like *Western Union*. It isn't as good a western as *Stagecoach*, but then it hardly could be. It is, though, a very happy example of a type that for twenty-five years had ranked next to Love and Murder in popularity. In all that time, no one has ever really been able to change the western, though many people have tried to. The genre doesn't so much resist progress, as simply absorb it. Inevitably, in the end, it gets back to cowboys-and-Indians and no nonsense; the sort of thing that was proper when Bill Hart – who lived so long among horses that he almost came to look like one – rode the purple sage.

29 June 1941

But then I like Miss Hepburn.

I make this admission before recommending **The Philadelphia Story**, because I think it is only a fair caveat, and an essential part of a critic's service to readers. It is as much of a film reviewer's duty, I feel, to confess to a prejudice of this kind as it is the job of a reviewer of detective stories to admit to a weakness for Merlini, or Dr Fell, or Reggie Fortune – or a gardening expert's duty, before he tells you how to stock your rose beds, to make it quite clear whether he likes his own roses thin or fat.

It is my experience that Miss Katharine Hepburn, like Mr Crosby and Mr Cagney and the Marx Brothers, is a player who evokes no half-hearted responses from an audience. Either you like her, or you don't. Either you seek out her pictures, or you say, significantly, 'Oh, *her*', and avoid them.

As I say, I like Miss Hepburn. But I admit that the first time I saw – and heard – her, it was a shock. I don't know what I had been led to expect that fine morning nine years ago when we trooped along to a Press show of *A Bill of Divorcement*, to see the new Broadway star with the fine Scottish name. Certainly it wasn't that emphatic young girl, with the flaring nostrils, the strident American voice, and the gangling movements.

Coming out of the shock, like emerging from a cold shower, I began to feel the glow of it. There was something tingling and alive in that personality, after all. Hepburn, at least, was no cardboard girl. She had a terrible lot to learn about screen acting, and screen behaviour, and screen reserve, but you felt – or, at any rate, I felt – that she had the wit and passion to learn it.

I have sometimes wavered since in that belief. After her gallant performance in *Morning Glory* and that touching sketch of Jo in *Little Women*, things too often seemed to go wrong with her. She seemed almost to take a delight in perverseness, to find some wayward satisfaction in being noisy and brash and raw. She was shocking in Barrie, and unseemly as Mary Queen of Scots. In *Stage Door* she was outplayed by Ginger Rogers, whom few people until then had taken seriously as an actress, and in *Bringing up Baby* she was outdone by a leopard.

In *The Philadelphia Story* Miss Hepburn comes back to the sort of part she did so well in *Holiday*. Tracy Lord, the heroine, is the type of girl she obviously knows and understands. She is the eager, spoilt, emphatic daughter of a rich society home. She has good brains and a strict moral code, but reserves the right to use these things at her own time and in her own way. Her first marriage, with a man from her own social world (Cary Grant), has gone on the rocks. She is planning a second, with an up-and-coming business man (John Howard), whose style a Jeeves would hardly look on with approval. A third young man of a very different sort – a slow, forthright reporter (James Stewart) from a society magazine – is sent down to Philadelphia to 'cover' the wedding.

The film, which is mainly confined to the day before the ceremony and the wedding-day itself, studies Miss (or Madam) Tracy's reactions to these three men. It is slight in theme, has no earthly message for anybody, and deals with a social set that seems as remote as the antimacassar. But it is so engagingly done, so true to type, so superbly painless in its superficiality, that you hardly notice its slimness.

Every aspiring little actress who sees the film will covet the part of Tracy for her own. I shouldn't care to guess how often it will figure in film tests for ambitious starlets. It is the sort of part that actors call a 'natural'. Axshully, as they say, it is a natural for Miss Hepburn. It was specially written for her – by her friend, the playwright Philip Barry. She played it for two years on the American stage before taking it to Hollywood, and there isn't a gesture or a shading of the voice that hasn't become instinctive and familiar to her.

The Philadelphia Story, in spite of the usual beautiful performances from Mr Stewart, is really Miss Hepburn's show.

2 March 1941

Leslie Howard, who is at all times a master of under-statement, refers to his own *Pimpernel Smith* as 'Just an amusing piece of hokum.' In that phrase, and with all the deprecation of his race, he passes off a film that is one of the best anthologies of British character seen on the screen for seasons.

I am not going to use the word propa – no, I won't even finish it, that dull, deadly polysyllable with its suggestion of red tape and stuffy pamphlets – in connection with the Howard picture. It is, in fact, p— raised to the highest power; but it is also funny, touching, imaginative, and enormously exciting. It is a modern Scarlet Pimpernel story of a Cambridge professor of archaeology, who smuggles men of culture and learning out of Germany in the days just before the war.

The Chauvelin of the piece is Berlin's vast Chief of Police, played with rotund perfection by Francis Sullivan. The Marguerite is a Polish writer's daughter – a part to which Miss Mary Morris gives just the right suggestion of nervous breeding. Mr Howard himself is a casual, disarming Pimpernel, with tired old clothes, and the mellow crustiness of the college cellar. His Band are students, supposedly digging for relics of Aryan culture. They have no emblem, like the 'wayside flower' of the Orczy romances – that might seem pretentious, Mr Howard explained to me, out of keeping with the Professor's non-flamboyant character – but a snatch of their meeting-call, 'There is a Tavern in the Town', follows them on the sound-track wherever they go.

After many years of criticism I have grown wary of prophesying success for a picture. But I will take a chance with *Pimpernel Smith*. I think it's fine. I believe it will charm and enthral audiences everywhere. I had an illuminating experience myself with this film. I was allowed to take thirty little boys, ranging in age from ten to thirteen, down to the studios to see it. Apart from their natural excitement at being in a film studio, and a studio at that bearing marked signs of enemy action ('Was everybody killed?' they asked hopefully, and when told 'No, nobody,' they comforted themselves with the assurance, 'Well, they easily might have been') – apart from this natural prejudice in favour of the occasion they were the most rapt audience that anyone could have wanted. They sat dead still for over two hours, their gas-masks pressing into their thin boys' shoulder-blades, and at the end they said, 'Coo, wasn't that super?' One big twelve-year-old said to me sagely that it might do better than *The Great Dictator*, because it 'hadn't been advertised so widely.' And another, all boy, summed up the situation, 'Won't it make old Hitler hopping mad?'

Well, I haven't his natural optimism with regard to the Führer's chance of seeing *Pimpernel Smith*, but I wish he could see it, because I believe, if he were prepared to learn, it would teach him something. Something about the British way of thinking, something of the British character, our way of life, our way of doing things without seeming to do them. Everything that these islands mean to our people is implicit in that film for those who choose to find it. Watching it, those thirty little boys – though I hope they didn't know it – were studying a lesson as stiff as anything they would have learnt at school.

The great quality of *Pimpernel Smith* is that it makes you feel *you* could go out and do the same thing tomorrow. It makes you want to say to Leslie Howard, 'I say, Professor, next trip you make, you might take me along with you.' This, to my mind, is the very root of the democratic tradition, the certainty of every man, however small, however unimportant, that he can go out and pull off a job successfully, simply because he knows it to be right.

There is no doubt that, to foreign eyes, we English have a haphazard way of doing things. Most of us are not even sure which way up our flag should fly. We deprecate everything; effort, danger, achievement, celebrity. When our bombers come back from a successful raid, they call it a good show. When we lose an engagement, we call it a bad show. (That is one reason, by the way – quite apart from its inaccuracy – why I so much dislike the growing usage of the word 'blitz' when we mean an air raid. It represents an ignorant acceptance of the power of violence that isn't in our temperament at all.)

There is no violence in *Pimpernel Smith*. Mr Howard, strolling through the film in his dilapidated tweeds, seems oddly detached from the menace of the world about him. He gives you the sense of a man who doesn't see danger as a physical thing at all, merely as an impudent and insufferable threat to culture. Like most Englishmen, his professor isn't interested in politics. But he happens to care for wisdom, as another man might care for football, or horses, or gardening. When he sees wisdom threatened, he naturally goes out and does something about it. It is as integral a part of his way of thinking as the preparation of his next archaeological lecture. It is this casual assumption of risk, this refusal to treat melodrama melodramatically, that makes Mr Howard's 'amusing bit of hokum' such a revealingly English show.

6 July 1941

NOTE: Leslie Howard's charming girl-friend, Violette, to whom I referred in the Preface, can be seen very briefly in *Pimpernel Smith*. She is the girl behind the counter in the scent-shop. – A.L.

Mr H. C. Bailey, in his detective novel, *The Little Captain*, has a light-hearted passage in which he describes the premiere of a super-film on the life and death of Nelson. At the climax, if I remember rightly, a slim girlish figure in naval uniform clasps the dying admiral in her arms while he whispers softly, 'Kiss me, Emma.'

Some touch of the kind, I feel, would add a much-needed

liveliness to Alexander Korda's **Lady Hamilton**. Mr Korda, I
thought, was determined to make us feel as miserable as possible
over the whole Nelson-Hamilton business. Lest virtue blush, or
maidenhood refuse to see the writing on the wall, he puts the
whole tale into the porty, gibbering mouth of Lady Hamilton
when she has become a wrinkled harridan. Thrown out of a
quayside cafe in Calais for wine-stealing, she confides her story
to her cell-mate, a kindly girl with little or no grasp for current
history. 'And then?' asks her companion, brightly, when the tale,
after two hours, reaches the death of Nelson. 'What happened
after?' But Mr Korda doesn't relax his stern moral code for an
instant. 'There is no then,' says Lady H., disdaining common
usage. 'There is no after.' It puts me in mind of a theatre bill that
I saw in childhood, and which has always haunted me. The play
was *The Girl Who Took the Wrong Turning*, and the bill depicted
six stages of a drunkard's progress, with the awful caption, 'The
Beginning of the End.'

Since human flesh and blood could not long endure the sight
of the lovely Miss Vivien Leigh made up as a quayside trull, the
bulk of the film shows us Scarlett Emma Hart exquisitely taking
the wrong turning. We see Miss Emma at eighteen, trustful and
deluded. We see her sold to the British Minister at Naples, Sir
William Hamilton, in return for the payment of a gambling
debt. We see her lonely and nymphlike in her great bed, on
the morning when – *we* know, but she doesn't – the good
ship Agamemnon is bringing one Horatio Nelson to Naples.
Later we see him, convalescent after the Battle of the Nile, in
that same bed, lonely, too, you must understand, but hopeful,
decidedly hopeful.

For an errant woman whose sins have gone down the centuries,
Miss Hart, Mr Korda's Lady H., behaves, it seemed to me, quite
beautifully. We see her as a decorous wife, an obedient daughter,
and a devoted mother. We see her as diplomat, patriot, lover,
and little home woman. We see her being pretty nice, even, to
Lady Nelson. Except for a small scene at the gaming tables with
Horatio, and a hint of her mother's fondness for the bottle, there
is nothing, save one's knowledge of the Wages of Sin, to suggest
why Lady H. became a harridan.

I shouldn't, myself, class *Lady Hamilton* as one of Mr Korda's
great successes. Graceful and elegant it undoubtedly is. Settings
and groupings of figures have great decorative taste. There is
one shot of Mr Olivier as the dead Nelson – a headpiece like

an Italian study for the Crucifixion – that is superbly moving. There is a good moment when the captain of the Agamemnon casually mentions his name to Emma. And I suppose the experts will agree that the battle is a fine battle.

But all its minor graces don't somehow add up to a major achievement. Perhaps Mr Korda was bogged by his moral obligations. Perhaps he is just three thousand miles too far away from England to be able to make a true film for today about England and the English people. It is my impression that the film would have been a better job if it had stuck more to this man Nelson and bothered less about that woman Hamilton. These are not days when we have much patience for looking at history through the eyes of a trollop. And I am not at all sure that English people, who have been fighting for two years for something they like to call an ideal, will care very much for the implication that the future died with Nelson. So there's no then, is there? So there's no after? Come over here, Mr Korda, and watch the future being made.

3 August 1941

For the first time in screen history, an Australian film is top of the bill in a cinema in the west end of London. Its attractive title is **Forty Thousand Horsemen**. I hope you will see it. I can't tell whether it will satisfy you. I don't know whether it will make you want to laugh or want to cry. All I can promise is that it will provide the young people with a new film experience, and give the veterans the sort of thrill they haven't been able to recapture for twenty years.

Forty Thousand Horsemen is almost unbelievably primitive in these days of stream-lined talkies. It is also most uncannily exciting. I don't remember enjoying a film quite in this way since the first cowboys rode the range, since the elder Fairbanks leapt over six-foot walls with a knife in his teeth, or held up the west-bound mail for the engine-driver's whistle.

The story is a fabulous mixture of Ouida and a communiqué of the last war. Broadly speaking, it is concerned with the Anzac campaign in the Sinai Desert against the Germans and Turks, and culminates in that epic charge of the Australian Light Horse outside the gates of Beer-Sheba. More specifically, it deals with three Light Horsemen, three roistering, scrounging Australians, who encounter the only French girl in Sinai disguised as a water-boy. This piquant heroine, Julie, is never, mind you, excessively disguised. She won't disappoint the audience, although she fools the German High Command, who can only see with one eye, anyway, on account of monocles.

Simply by hanging around the mess-tent, hauling on the gun-ropes with her tender hands, Mlle Julie picks up all sorts of useful crumbs of knowledge. She learns, for example, that the Germans mean to throw a switch and blow up all the Australians in Beer-Sheba. This shocks her. With her native shrewdness, and a considerable grasp of local geography, she succeeds in saving Red, the most handsome and dashing of the Australians. Red saves the Australian Light Horse, and the Light Horse save the Sinai campaign. Last thing of all we see Julie, now dressed as a girl in something frilly and French, embracing her man on an Arab farmcart, while the Forty Thousand Horsemen, all three thousand of them, ride away into the horizon singing 'Waltzing Matilda'.

This story, as you will see, is unlikely to win an Academy award as the year's most distinguished piece of screen-writing. Sophisticates will raise an eyebrow over a point or two, and a generation accustomed to Ben Hecht dialogue may find the idiom odd. But there is something rather refreshing in its unself-consciousness, when all is said and done. It doesn't try to be smart. It merely tries to be clear. 'Rain makes puddles, and every puddle in the desert means a drink for a horse.' No writer in Hollywood could make that simple statement more dramatic. The story and the dialogue is simply a means to an end, a chance to celebrate the dash and devilry of the Australian soldier, and to recreate that homeric charge of the Forty Thousand Horsemen – a moment which could scarcely have been more effective had Errol Flynn himself been riding at their head.

There is no doubt that events at Benghazi and Tobruk will have given the film a special meaning for modern audiences. I think, though, that it has another virtue which owes nothing to current history. It has enormous zest. These people, these Australians, give you the sense that making films is a grand adventure. Their work has the freshness of discovery. They don't act that way, direct that way, you feel, because so might Gary Cooper have acted, or John Ford directed. They do it because it seems right to them, which is the only sensible way to approach an art, whether it be making films or chipping marble.

Louis Delluc, the French critic, once observed that what most of us needed was to *love* the cinema more. That was a wise and just saying, and is as true today as when he made it twenty years ago. These Australians, in their new young industry, do seem to love the cinema. The present film has all the crude power of people doing confidently what they enjoy doing. *Forty Thousand Horsemen* cannot be called a great work by Hollywood standards, but it is great-hearted, and there isn't a producer in Hollywood who couldn't learn something from it if he tried.

24 August 1941

It is my own private fancy that one day we shall see a 'Dr Jekyll and Mr Hyde' in which the good doctor will swallow the fateful draught and turn, not into an anthropoid ape but into some exquisite being resembling Errol Flynn, or Victor Mature, or possibly Nelson Eddy. This I feel, would give point to the screen fable and justify the eccentric behaviour of the females involved in it. Or, alternatively, the actor depicting Dr Jekyll might just swallow the dose and remain physically unchanged, exactly as he was to the eye of the beholder. After all, the natty thing about evil is that you don't know where you have it.

In the meantime, I am ready to put up with Spencer Tracy's transmutation in the present **Dr Jekyll and Mr Hyde** as the best to date, the most satisfactory hint that Hyde is not just a monster waiting to spring into anyone's cast-off body, but the grosser half of a split personality. Mr Tracy does not change into an egg, like Mr Barrymore, or an ape like Mr March. He does something to his eyebrows, something to his mouth, sticks out his jaw, laughs 'heh! heh!', looks a beast, and spits grape-skins at Miss Ingrid Bergman. Or, rather, he tries to look a beast. I had the feeling that he was making a hard fight for it, that there were moments when he was convinced, the honest Mr Tracy, that he was looking, not a beast, but just a jackass.

Too good an actor, though, to spoil the show with his own private trepidations, he quickly takes hold again, if he has ever wavered, and carries *Dr Jekyll and Mr Hyde* through by virtue of his technical authority. Thus and thus should a scene be played, and thus and thus, though he may be sweating at the collar, he will triumphantly play it. The net result is a good goose-flesh chiller, well, if conventionally, done against a background of Hollywood

Victoriana. I don't know if Miss Ingrid Bergman fancies she is talking Cockney as Ivy, the victimized barmaid. She isn't, but she has charm and intelligence, and really needn't bother. I thought Miss Lana Turner miscast as a Du Maurier goddess, who somehow wanders into the picture. These feminine types, of course, are not to be found in Stevenson, who managed to write a thundering good story without their aid.

15 February 1942

A foreword to Alfred Hitchcock's **Spellbound** contrives to tell us, in a few expository paragraphs, what psychiatry can do (just as though we had never been to the pictures). The film then goes on to illustrate, with a good deal of adroitness, one of the things psychiatry can't do: that is, prove as satisfactorily as the old-fashioned solid evidence, how and why the late Dr Edwardes, head of an elite psychiatric home, was bumped off, shoved off, shot or otherwise disposed of during a ski-ing expedition.

Spellbound, embellished with visual metaphor and recondite symbol, not to mention *surrealist* dreams by Salvador Dali, is nonsense of a high technical order, but, none the less, nonsense. The story follows Hitchcock's favourite formula, the pursuit of two hapless lovers through miles of suspense to a slightly indifferent embrace and a surprise finish. The lovers in this case are Ingrid Bergman and Gregory Peck; or perhaps I should say, Miss Bergman and the back of Mr Peck's neck, for that is practically all we see of him. Miss Bergman comes in two styles, (1) with glasses, as a psychiatrist, (2) without glasses, as a Woman. Mr Peck comes in one style only, neck or nothing. When the Misses Bergman observe Mr Peck totter and turn faint and the celestial orchestra burst into uncontrollable wailings, at the sight of forkmarks on a white tablecloth, they shrewdly surmise that all is not well with him. Miss Bergman (2) thereupon occupies the patient with a kiss, while Miss Bergman (1) diagnoses him as an amnesia case with a guilt complex. The rest of the film shows the two Miss Bergmans, always a step ahead of the police, solving the murder of Dr Edwardes, and proving, with the aid of psychoanalysis, that nothing is really amiss with Mr Peck except that he has forgotten he accidentally killed his brother long ago.

19 May 1946

One of the few luxuries left to us in these austere days is the privilege of enjoying a bonny bit of craftsmanship. A new writer, a new painter, a new actor, a new film-director, who can use his material cunningly, may not be as vital to mankind at this juncture as a new general who knows how to dispose his armies, but individuals will still welcome him with undiminished pleasure. So much of our current art, indeed, is wilfully purposive, so much slapdash work is put into drawing and writing and film-making to serve a temporary emergency, that a piece of work well done for its own sake is something to note with particular delight.

Such a film, I believe, is **The Maltese Falcon**. It is only a modest film, a mere thriller, but its director, John Huston, has taken such pains with it, and its players – Humphrey Bogart, Mary Astor, Sydney Greenstreet, and others – have given such able performances that *The Maltese Falcon* satisfies one more completely than many far more ambitious pictures. The story is by Dashiell Hammett, who wrote *The Thin Man*. *The Maltese Falcon* is about a Fat Man, a monumental villain in a morning coat, with a gold watchchain looped across his imposing façade, and a rich, rolling utterance. A mysterious beauty is involved in it, too, and a private detective, and a pleasantly assorted gang of killers. The whole-to-do concerns a jewelled image, a golden falcon, stolen centuries ago from the Knights of Malta.

John Huston, the director, is the son of Walter Huston, the actor. Mr Huston, senior, appears anonymously in a part lasting, perhaps, two seconds. This is young Mr Huston's first film, and he shows a pretty flair for the right shot, the apt phrase, the telling angle, that the cinema can well do with. His special talent lies, it seems, in giving the extraordinary event an immediate and startling impact. He takes the materials of a traditional thriller, and puts them on the screen as if a thriller had never been filmed before, as if we were observing for the first time our personal reactions to crime and violence.

The Maltese Falcon, I should say, is the nearest approach to the I-story that has ever been filmed. The whole audience is the I. Dimly at first, but with increasing confidence as the relations of the characters are established, we grope our way from the first suspicion of crime to the final round-up. We observe a stranger's shifty eyes, and draw our own deductions. We fumble for a telephone in the dark, hear a sleepy voice answering us from half across a city. Just so, one feels, would terror really stalk into one's life, insidiously and confusingly. It is John Huston's talent that he gets this effect without any fancy tricks, any fuzzy montage or off-screen reflections. He sees the old things with a fresh eye, that's all, and shows them to us from a new angle. Just plain good sense and good craftsmanship has made *The Maltese Falcon* a good picture, promising, we hope, even better ones to come.

21 June 1942

Again Walt Disney has turned out a full-length film to help us through a war-time holiday, and this **Bambi** is welcome indeed, a touching and beguiling thing, in the master's most felicitous style. Disney has sought after no new forms, pursued no social allegory here. He is happy and relaxed with the things he does best – sketches of wild life, studies of young animals and their endearing ways. No human being appears in *Bambi*. Man is the shot, the hunting-horn, the shadow 'off'. The animals take over the scene, against a background of the changing seasons.

The film follows the home-life of a deer, from his first tottering steps in a forest glade to the birth of his own fawns. A hunter's gun robs him of his mother, and hounds and forest fire threaten him in later days, but with the help of an old stag, the Prince of the Forest, he comes through, to take his place at last as Monarch of the Glen.

The later scenes are a little uneven in their draughtsmanship and invention. The Disney artists have not yet learnt how to give bone and muscle to a full-grown quadruped. The animal courtships have a touch of sophistication that is purely of man. But for sixty out of its seventy minutes *Bambi* is sheer enchantment. Nothing could be more charming than the fawn's baby days, his games with the rabbits and butterflies, his bewilderment over an April shower. Thumper the Rabbit is a great character, and the fawns themselves, Bambi and his friend Faline, have entirely beguiled their artists and will beguile the public too. And what a showman Disney is! How cunningly he uses his little tunes! How wisely he repeats and varies his formal effects! And how surely his instinct guides him in the closing scene, when he shows us a new fawn in the old glade, and the King Stag, ceding his throne to Bambi for the last curtain-call!

9 August 1942

Holiday Inn is the sort of piece that is sometimes described as 'unimportant'. If it is unimportant to entertain, relax, and amuse, *Holiday Inn* is superbly so. It has Fred Astaire's dancing, Bing Crosby's singing, a pleasant little romance, some engaging humour, and just a tear or two to give it savour. The story, about a singer who retires to a Connecticut farm and throws it open, on holidays only, for dancing, entertainment, and home cooking, gives Irving Berlin a chance to introduce eight seasonable numbers. His songs celebrate Christmas, Easter, New Year, Independence Day, Thanksgiving, St. Valentine's Day, and a couple of Presidents' birthdays. The old 'Easter Parade' still beats most of the newcomers, but it shouldn't be long before the whistlers are tackling 'White Christmas', a pretty, sentimental thing.

2 August 1942

It is probably very old-fashioned of me, but I must admit to deriving a good deal of pleasure from *The Corsican Brothers*, in which Douglas Fairbanks, Junr, performs rather indifferently in a dual role.

The Corsican Brothers, to be quite candid, is not a very distinguished film. It is unlikely to win any Academy Award or to be quoted by Film Society paragraphists as typical of this or that progressive trend. I should say that the producer, Mr Edward Small, hasn't really bothered much about trends. I should say that he has just let the story rip for all it's worth, and had the players behave in the way that players have always behaved in what is known as 'Dumas' Immortal Classic.'

What I like about Immortal Classic is that the story is such a rattling good one. There are, in fact, two good stories. There is the obvious one about the vendetta between the Colonnas and the Franchis, in which Baron Colonna, who fancies he has wiped out all the Franchis at a birthday feast, finds himself hounded, twenty years later, by a young man in a red stocking cap, who systematically knifes all Colonnas with a Franchi dagger. And there is the subtler drama of the Franchi boys themselves, who were born Siamese twins, and can never escape the ties cut by the surgeon's knife. This is a rich theme, a real Jekyll and Hyde theme, all the more inveigling because it leads, not to affection, but to hatred between the twins. Sentience, it seems, is one-sided.

Brother Mario, raised in Paris, is quite a normal young man. But Brother Lucien, reared by Corsican bandits, leads a life for two. When Mario is wounded, Lucien feels the pain. When Mario falls in love, Lucien's pulses race. This is hard on Lucien, who gets mad with his brother, and we're not surprised. Whether bio-psychology gives any support to this phenomenon, I don't know. But it certainly makes for a tensely exciting story.

Immortal Classic has been 'freely adapted' for the screen, but the initial story credit must still go to Dumas. These old romancers never funked a plot. There is nothing niggardly or hesitant about *The Three Musketeers*, *Monte Cristo*, *The Hunchback of Notre Dame*, *Les Misérables*, *A Tale of Two Cities*, *Wuthering Heights*, *Jane Eyre*, *Vamity Fair*, and the rest. They rioted in their abundance, in the richness of their fancy. They had so much to tell that it was pressed down and running over. According to modern ideas they were wickedly wasteful.

But the fact remains that generations pass, styles change, and these romances go on pleasing people. How many contemporary stories will be read, I wonder, fifty years from now? With a few exceptions, our best writers seem to have lost the touch or the taste for the fine, strapping tale. The idea nowadays seems to be to sketch out a mood or a character, or to get half a dozen people into a hotel or a bus and let coincidence do the rest. Our more distinguished stories, it seems to me, have a shrewd, parochial observation, a civilized wit, often a sense of social responsibility, and a good understanding of the human machine. They are more concerned, seemingly, with what causes people to do things than with the things themselves. What they have gained in knowledge they have lost in gusto.

This comes hard on the film producers, who mostly get their plots at second hand. There is, of course, no earthly reason why a script-writer shouldn't invent a good bold story of his own, but somehow it happens that he rarely does. Think back on the films you have seen lately. What are most of them 'about'? A woman who gets entangled with two men. A man who gets entangled with two women. A marriage that can't get consummated. A divorce that doesn't quite come off. A bad boy who does what the good boys can't. A good girl who gets what the bad girls can't.

These are some of the more lucid motivations of recent films. You can doubtless think of half a dozen that are 'about' even less. Of course, it is open to academic argument whether a film should be 'about' anything at all. There is a case, I think, for the purist who contends that a story is as out of place in the cinema as it is on canvas or in a musical score. But this is not the generally accepted view, nor will it ever be, I think, the popular view. Most people will agree that a good story helps a lot. That is why I recommend the dear old *Corsican Brothers* as a film that has got, not only one, but a couple.

1942

NOTE: A rather downmarket London cinema near the place where I used to lunch showed, for several weeks, a film entitled *She Lost Her You-Know-What*: on the poster it said, in very small letters, 'Made from the famous novel by Alexandre Dumas'. Finally I gave way to curiosity and asked the manager, who stood outside in a dinner-jacket, what novel this could be. The answer was *La Dame aux Camélias*. – A. L.

Of all the organizations engaged in the delicate work of propaganda, none earns my respect more than the Crown Film Unit. Crown has that combination, rare amongst publicists, of craftsmanship and ardour. There is always some scene that captures the imagination, through sheer felicity of design or movement. Its latest film, **Coastal Command**, is rich in these moments. Some are seascapes, some cloudscapes. One is a shot of Iceland ponies, startled by a flight of Beauforts. Another, an unforgettable shot, shows a Sunderland flying-boat, like some giant bird, skimming above a village street at daybreak.

In common with other documentary producers, however, Crown has one characteristic that chills me. There is a detachment in much of its work, an almost scandalized mistrust of showmanship, an effort, it would seem, to avoid, not only melodramatics, but any form of human appeal or persuasion. It would be unacceptable, I feel, to speak too warmly of a Crown Unit film. Crown does not want our affection. It only wants our respect.

This unemotional approach would doubtless be excused on the grounds that the official recorder is presenting history, not drama. It is this fallacy, one into which so many eminent historians have fallen, that has helped to make the past, in the main, such a dead letter. All records, even photographic records, are a matter of selection and viewpoint. There must always be the individual choice behind the viewpoint, and into every record of fact there must enter, at some time, the creative impulse of the interpreter. The best and liveliest historians are those who can convey the *feeling* of a scene to later generations. For emotion, whether of fear or excitement, elation or impatience, or even a nervous and fretful triviality, is as much a part of any historical event as the deeds done or the people involved in them. Without some hint of this intangible quality, some ghost of a message from one human heart to another, no record, however factual, can be either truthful or complete.

It is in this inner truth, rather than in any more measurable quality, that *Coastal Command* is lacking as a persuasive record. With a much wider scope than its predecessor, *Target for Tonight* – or possibly because of that – it manages a less exciting total. It describes, minutely and dispassionately, the whole vast machinery of search and attack that comes into play when an enemy raider is sighted off the coast of Norway. The scene shifts from a remote flying-boat station to Iceland, out to sea and back to Coastal Command headquarters. We go out on patrol with Sunderlands and Catalinas, watch a torpedo and bombing attack by Beauforts and Hudsons, and see the Beaufighters streak off to tackle a flight of Junkers. The whole piece is full of action, and yet it is somehow possible to watch it with imperturbability. A little more perturbation, and some humour, too, perhaps, might not have hurt this picture, which is at its best when the cameramen are having their way with it, or when Vaughan Williams's majestic music comes rolling up to pay a great Service the tribute it deserves.

[1942]

After two and a half years in London, **Gone With the Wind** was generally released. It would be graceless and irresponsible to let the occasion pass without remark. The career of *Gone With the Wind* is the current counterpart of the success of 'Chu Chin Chow' during the last war. Novelists and social commentators are noting it down conscientiously, I trust, in their little books. It is as much a part of the issue of London life in war-time as the foreign uniforms in the streets, the altered skyline, and the friendly square gardens now open to the casual strollers.

Gone With the Wind arrived in London one April afternoon in 1940, when Narvik seemed the hub of the world, and errand boys were whistling 'Over the Rainbow'. Messrs Metro-Goldwyn-Mayer, who owned the piece, suggested, with incredible daring, that it might run until Christmas, unless, of course, the air-war should come to England and bombs fall in Piccadilly. That was roughly eight hundred and forty days – I had almost written years – two thousand five hundred performances ago, and when I passed through Leicester Square last week the 'house full' boards were out, the queue was still waiting patiently round the block.

Gone With the Wind has survived, and in its own way helped to lighten, the burden of the worst succession of news this country has had to bear since the Napoleonic wars. Through the Norway campaign, the invasion of the Low Countries, and the fall of France, through Dunkirk and the Battle of Britain, through an autumn, winter, and spring of savage air-attack, through the Greek campaign, the Libyan campaigns, and the assault on Russia, through Pearl Harbor and Hong Kong and Singapore, through the Battle of the Atlantic and the Battle of the Pacific, through Rommel's drive to Egypt and von Bock's drive to the Caucasus, the sturdy British citizen has taken his place in line to find out what happened to Scarlett O'Hara in a war that is as remote as Agamemnon's brush with Troy.

What is the secret of *Gone With the Wind*'s success? It does not seem to me the greatest film ever made. It has not, to my mind, the sharp, emotional appeal of *Mrs Miniver*, the magic of *Snow White* and *Bambi*, the fertile invention of *Citizen Kane*, the brilliance of *Kermesse Heroique*, the elemental force of *The Grapes of Wrath*. It is not even the longest film ever made; I am told it would seem a mere trailer to the shows one might see in China. It provides a tremendous experience, but one which its title significantly describes. It passes. The very dispassion with which it can be examined indicates its weakness – that it lacks – shall we say? – heart, the high, noble, memorable emotion one associates with great drama.

Few people who have seen it admit – or have admitted to me – that it is their favourite film, and yet few would appear to feel defrauded in any way, few would seem to wish to have foregone the experience. I have no doubt that when it opens outside London the queues will equal those in Leicester Square. Why? Millions of people, I know, have read the book, but you cannot persuade me that the queues are preponderantly made up of Margaret Mitchell lovers.

It is my own fancy that the very characteristics which limit

Gone With the Wind as a work of art, the qualities in which it falls short of lasting worth, make it a proper and comfortable recreation for the times. There is a closer relation between pastime and the time in which it is passed than most people realize. 'The larger music, the more majestic length of verse called epics, the exact in sculpture, the classic drama, the most absolute kinds of wine, require a perfect harmony of circumstance for their appreciation' as Hilaire Belloc wrote in 'The Path to Rome'. In such days as these, when there is but little harmony and content in our own souls, the need is for something simpler, more varied, more immediate in its effects. A mind that is heavy and disturbed does not want to reach very high or delve very deep. It wants to be carried along, distracted by many and even little things. Great emotion at such a time is painful and dangerous.

For this reason, I think, *Gone With the Wind* just suits our war-time mood. It is a prodigal film, generous to overflowing with facile events. It has, alike with the book from which it is so faithfully drawn, an impersonal narrative style which evokes violence without pain. There is enough catastrophe in *Gone With the Wind* to make the last act of *Hamlet* seem a jest. But catastrophe without contemplation is no tragedy, and even amongst all these dead and dying, our emotions are seldom overtried.

What audiences will find in *Gone With the Wind* is a graphic account of personal doings and relationships, intimate details of this meeting and that quarrel, the gossip of a dozen homes, and the confidences of a host of interesting people. The film has a hundred different stories, each in its different way absorbing. Each receives and exacts the same engrossed attention, whether it be the Civil War or a domestic tiff, the birth of a nation or the birth of a baby. *Gone With the Wind* runs for three hours and forty minutes, or twice as long as many finer pictures. But few people, anxious to hear what happens to Scarlett O'Hara and Rhett and Melanie, carried along on a wave of sound and colour, and conscious only of the blessed distraction it gives them, will find this enormous picture overlong.

1942

Went the Day Well? the variant of 'An Englishman's Home', would possibly have provoked little comment twenty-five years ago, when, save for circumstantial evidence, it might have been written. Today, it would seem lax to ignore this account of how Bramley Green saved England from invasion; a film which must presumably be regarded as work of national importance since time, money, and manpower have been spent on it, and Men of the Gloucestershire Regiment appear 'by kind permission of the War Office'.

Went the Day Well? tells how last Whitsuntide two lorry-loads of German parachutists, dressed as Royal Engineers, arrived at the quaint old village of Bramley Green. Population possibly thirty, including seven children, four Home Guards, one policeman, two Land Girls, one A.B., one dog, and a Fifth Columnist. Their advent passes unnoticed by the outside world. The parachutists, although they cannot resist a tendency to twist a child's ear occasionally, mingle freely with the natives. It is easy for them to do this since all but one of them, as their Commander explains to the Fifth Columnist, would pass for British anywhere. Most of them, indeed, would pass for British actors.

Owing to the Commander's carelessness in carrying a packet labelled 'Chokolade, Wien,' and the fact that the Vicar's daughter reads German, the plot is prematurely out. The visitors cast off all pretence of being English gentlemen, although they never forget to be actors. While waiting for Hitler's sea-borne and air-borne invasion, they start a reign of terror in Bramley Green. The Home Guards are shot as they cycle home from exercise. The old Vicar is shot as he rings the church-bell. The post-mistress is shot as she kills a German with a chopper. The policeman is knocked on the head with a blunt instrument. Five children are to be shot at dawn as hostages.

But aha! they have overlooked the strength of Tom, the A.B., and the smartness of George, the Cockney evacuee. Tom breaks loose from his captors and arms the Land Girls with guns. George, no feminist, escapes and brings the Regular Army. Caught between these cross-fires, the Germans make their last stand. Men of the Gloucestershire Regiment die by dozens. All the Germans die. The Vicar's daughter, registering distaste, shoots the Fifth Columnist in the drawing-room. And Hitler's invasion is apparently off.

The oddest thing about *Went the Day Well?* is that it was produced by Ealing Studios, who made those eminently sensible war films, *The Foreman Went to France* and *Next of Kin*. Amongst other talents hidden in the picture are those of players Leslie Banks, Mervyn Johns, Valerie Taylor, Frank Lawton, and

Elizabeth Allan, not to mention the composer, William Walton, whose function seems to be to provide a couple of sinister bars on the sound-track as an indication that the scene you are watching is particularly dramatic.

After *Went the Day Well?* went I home rather sadly, turning over some reflections on war films in general. One is that a film praising the British spirit, as most British films at this time should and will, is obviously the more effective if it presents our enemies with a fair measure of continence. It is a dangerous thing to show your opponents as clowns or bullies, who only get results by treachery, brute force, or the long arm of coincidence. A director who does this merely cheapens his own countrymen, since victory over such people seems empty and meagre.

Another is that any display of hate, except in the hands of an expert director and artist, is to be avoided, since high passions without high performance are less likely to lead to conviction than laughter. A third is that the nearer a plot sticks to life at this tense moment of our fortunes, the nearer it gets to drama. And the fourth is simply that the most patriotic film can lose nothing by the exercise of a little talent and taste.

1 November 1942

I once knew a young woman who used to go completely mad when anyone threw eggs or custard pies on the screen. In every other way she was a placid type. Except for painting her piano saxe-blue to match the lounge, this was her sole eccentricity. She told me she couldn't help it. She said something come over her when she seen all that good food gone to waste.

Hers was doubtless an extreme case, but it is not by any means an isolated one. Most of us who go to the pictures regularly have had these temptations to frenzy at some time or another. Something come over some of us at the sight of an infant prodigy. Others are filled with black thoughts by stories of mother-love. A brief Gallup Poll conducted in my immediate circle reveals the following topics at best calculated to create alarm and despondency:

1 The story of the soldier, sailor, or airman who won't take discipline and wins a medal.

2 The story of the soldier, sailor or airman who dies for his buddy.

3 The story of the high-school boy who makes calf eyes at teacher.

4 The story of the collaborationist playgirl in mink who gets democracy.

5 The story of the swing-player who makes the musical classics intelligible to millions.

I don't know how it is with you, but the story of the small-town girl who wants to become a great actress is another plot situation that makes me nervous. I know that sooner or later the moment will come when she's supposed to *be* a great actress. My throat grows dry, and I keep my eyes glued to the screen. What if I miss the vital moment? Great heavens! have I missed it already? Which is she now, the small-town girl or the great actress? Blest if I know.

The problem turns up in an acute form this week in a film called **Presenting Lily Mars**. Judy Garland is the small-town girl who aspires to be a great actress. Now Miss Garland, although I sometimes think they make a mistake in comparing her with Sarah Bernhardt, is a smooth little performer in her own line of business, and her line is remarkably consistent. Personally, I could detect no change in the *nuances* of her acting from beginning to end of the picture.

Yet the *nuances* are presumably there for all to see. There comes a moment in the plot when Van Heflin, who plays the best producer on Broadway, stops covering his face with his hands when she recites, and tells her she is 'a good little actress.' True, he admits – very gently, for love has supervened – that she isn't quite ready yet to play the leading role in his current play, that of a matoor Russian Princess on her honeymoon. Nevertheless, he entrusts her with the third-act curtain line as an immatoor chambermaid. 'Go out on that stage and play that maid better than any maid has ever been played on any stage. Say that maid's lines and give them all they've got,' he whispers passionately.

She does just that, and never was deboo more electrifying. 'Yu Rexcellencies, ' she murmurs, 'yu room is ready. Goonight, Yu Rexcellencies, and may yur dreams be beoorriful.' The producer is enchanted, the audience is ecstatic, the matoor Russian Princess felicitates Miss Garland, and two minutes later she is starring with Tommy Dorsey and His Orchestra in a piece called 'Where There's Music.' It's all very odd.

1943

If the Warner Brothers and Joseph E. Davies's **Mission to Moscow** had been able to give us a survey of pre-war European politics as informed as it was enterprising; if it had been able to corroborate all its facts; if it had even stuck to the former Ambassador's book and reported his findings judicially, it might have been a pity the film is such a bore. As it hasn't, it isn't. It is well-intentioned, but misleading. Fortunately, it doesn't mislead persuasively enough to do much harm.

Ambassador Davies, you may remember, was sent to Moscow in 1936 by President Roosevelt to study the great 'mystery factor' in European politics. As a lawyer, he was to judge the evidence for and against Russia as a possible champion of collective security against the rising tide of the Axis. How the Russians ran their own country was no part of Mr Davies's business. His mission was to observe and report 'what sort of neighbour Russia was going to be in the case of a fire'.

Why did they film the Davies book, which is essentially plotless, historically incomplete, a series of cautious observations from a handful of European capitals? Obviously, to allay any existing American anxieties about Russia as an ally; to emphasize her military strength, her shrewd statesmanship, her integrity, and her superb handling of vast resources; also to explain away any little doubts they may have had about her past actions, such as the signing of the Non-Aggression Pact with Germany.

All this is admirable, although one cannot help feeling that Russia's own films have taken care of Russia's case already. But it would have been more admirable if the Good Neighbour policy of the film had embraced a more human study of the good neighbour. The references to Britain, really quite a decent neighbour of the United States, and a sizeable protagonist in this war, are so irresponsible as to raise grave doubts of the Warner Brothers' infallibility in reading the Moscow data. Has their Mr Davies conclusively solved the mystery factor of Europe? Were the celebrated Moscow trials really carried out in just that way? Were the German, Japanese and British ambassadors to Moscow such complete mugs? Was Mme Molotov's cosmetic salon really so chic? Had Mr Davies, and Mr Davies alone amongst foreign diplomats, such a hair-trigger grasp on internal Soviet politics? One small error of judgement on his part, one shrewd adversary or ally, one stupid or unsmiling Russian, even one dish of Russian food that wasn't 'delicious', might have persuaded us of the humanity of his observations, and endeared our Soviet comrades to us so very much more.

25 July 1943

The Life and Death of Colonel Blimp, by which, we are, solemnly assured in an advertisement, 'All entertainment, past, present and future, will be judged,' doesn't really deserve such a tough ordeal. It isn't as mediocre as all that. In fact, compared with most of the entertainment we get today, its standard is remarkably high. From the craftsman's point of view, it is a crisp, clean, workmanlike job. The dialogue is sensible; the Technicolor is unobtrusive; there are moments of acute imaginative perception; and the acting by Roger Livesey, Anton Walbrook and Deborah Kerr is good. You may not like it, but you must respect it as a work of quality.

'Blimp's' worst fault – apart from its title and its length, which is two-and-three-quarter hours and quite absurd – is an unclarity of purpose. It is a handsome piece. It is frequently a moving piece. But what is it *about*? Oh, I know what it is ostensibly about. During a Home Guard exercise a zealous young N.C.O., anticipating the scheduled war by six hours, captures the opposing brigadier in his Turkish bath. He insults the brigadier, his stomach, and his moustache. The brigadier promptly replies by pushing him into the swimming-pool. During the time they remain under water (2½ hours) the brigadier's lifestory is recalled. You see him as a young V.C., a Guards officer of the '90s. You see his impetuous journey to Berlin, to scotch rumours of British atrocities against the Boers. You see his duel with a young Uhlan officer, who wins his sweetheart but becomes his friend. You see their friendship broken and restored after the first World War. You see it renewed in the present war, when the Uhlan is a fugitive from the Nazi regime and the brigadier is retired for his reactionary views. You see the old man widowed, bombed out, and left alone, save for his M.T.C. driver and his Uhlan friend: he makes, it is true, the cover of *Picture Post*, but his BBC Postscript is cancelled in favour of Mr Priestley.

As the story of a forty years' friendship, as the case history of two men who love the same feminine type wherever she appears (for Miss Deborah Kerr trebles the parts of the M.T.C. driver, Mr Walbrook's and Mr Livesey's wife). *Blimp* is cleancut, sympathetic and true. But what is it *really* about? Don't tell me this colossal, considered affair is just a lovely romance. The enormous care taken with the film indicates that it has something much bigger to say, something it is burning to say. Three theories present themselves. *Blimp* indicates (*a*) that dear old sentimental Britain will always muddle through; (*b*) that an ex-Prussian officer advocating the bombing of hospitals, the ruthless destruction of women and children, is the right man to teach us how to wage modern war; and (*c*) that the experience of age and the functionalism of youth can be sensibly combined. 'A' has nothing to support it except Roger Livesey's winning acting. 'B' seems to have the script on its side. 'C' is my own idea, and I'm still all for 'C'. But A, B, C, or X, Y, Z, clarity is surely the thing. *The Life and Death of Colonel Blimp* will have to profess itself much more openly before it becomes a measuring stick for Shakespeare.

13 June 1943

Jane Eyre will positively be adored by thousands. It is a lovely romance about an orphaned governess who goes to live in a fog-wreathed, bastioned, Gothic castle, and falls in love with her black-avised employer, who keeps a mad wife tucked away somewhere beneath the battlements. Joan Fontaine makes a pretty mouse of Jane; Orson Welles, although monstrously miscast, works his way through the role of Mr Rochester by sheer dint of hard acting. The script is attributed to Aldous Huxley, Robert Stevenson and John Houseman, and we even see a replica of the opening chapter: 'My name is Jane Eyre. I was born in 1820, a harsh time of change in England.' Set up in folio and bound in vellum, this Huxley-Stevenson-Houseman *Jane Eyre* is both handsome and impressive. And yet I retain a weakness for a plain old thing of the same name by one Charlotte Brontë, beginning: 'There was no possibility of taking a walk that day. We had been wandering,' etc.

26 December 1943

Something extraordinary has happened in the cinema this week. Not only is there one good film to be seen in London this week. There are two. The Academy revives that superb, impious and gay-hearted satire of seventeenth-century Flanders, *La Kermesse Heroique*, at the mere mention of which metropolitan readers of this column will prick up their discerning ears and board the first bus for Oxford Street. At the same time, the Plaza presents a new work by Preston Sturges called *Hail the Conquering Hero*. Those who have been worried lately by Mr Sturges' insistence on the more painful forms of slapstick can discard their fears. *Hail the Conquering Hero* is a beauty. It is good film-making, good taste, good observation, and good fun.

Mr Sturges not only writes, produces and directs his own pictures, but stars in them as clearly as though he put on greasepaint and appeared before the cameras. He is one of the screen's most distinguished comedians, and his style is no less individual because it is conveyed through other actors. In this case, the medium is mainly a sensitive little mimic called Eddie Bracken. Bracken plays Woodrow Lafayette Pershing Truesmith, a timid soul from a small town, and the son of a local hero, who is discharged from the Marines for chronic hayfever and hasn't the nerve to tell his proud mother, his proud girl, and his proud fellow-townsfolk. So he hides away, supposedly fighting in Guadalcanal, but miserably working in a shipyard, until six lusty marines take him in hand, drag him back to his home town, spread the most fantastic stories about his heroism, and get him accepted as the local mayoral candidate. What happens when the phoney hero tries to tell the truth about himself, and is only received as a man with 'a natural flair for politics', makes up one of the most ingratiating pictures of the year.

Hail the Conquering Hero could not possibly have been made in any other medium than the cinema. It is film, film, film all the way, from the opening scene of crooners' rear elevations to the accelerating rhythm of determined feet at the climax. It is cut to a miracle; like the great Russian directors, like the great Chaplin, this fellow with a small, comic story to tell shaves his celluloid to a frame to keep the picture moving. Tricky little tunes twist through the film; the camera clings like doom to the figures it wants to emphasize. *Hail the Conquering Hero* is one of the few craftsman's models that I would recommend fearlessly to the layman. Every young man who wants to learn how to make films should study it. Every customer who doesn't give a hoot how films are made so long as they entertain him should see it and enjoy the fun.

29 October 1944

Noel Coward, who cared more about the Navy's opinion of *In Which We Serve* than the critics' approval, must have felt a glow of satisfaction over the release of **This Happy Breed**. For this film about the suburbs has gone out into the suburbs, and the suburbs have taken it to their hearts. All the Gibbonses of Greater London have flocked to see themselves on the screen. Women in fish queues, fruit queues, cake queues, 'bus queues, and queues for queues, have passed the word to each other over their baskets; We have been amused, touched, entertained, and edified by the film. It has gone straight to our address: or, as we say genteely in our suburb, *Chez Nous*.

Nor is the enthusiasm for the film confined to Metroland. The Gibbonses are a large family; they are found all over the British Isles. There are plenty of Gibbonses, too, serving in Normandy, Italy, and the Middle East. No film in my memory has brought in more letters of appreciation. The film itself; Celia Johnson's magnificent performance in the film; the cool, low-key Technicolor; the rich character sketches; have wrought so powerfully on the imagination of picturegoers that they have felt impelled to sit down and write some sort of ordered account of their impressions. For one astonished moment this strange film has made artists of them all.

One man speaks with a kind of flame about a smoky evening sky over the roofs of Clapham. Another refers to the solid sense of family. A third comments on the nice use of Mr Coward's 'London Pride' as background music. A Flying Officer in the Balkan Air Force writes that he has seen the film on three consecutive nights, with an enthusiastic audience of Dominion and Allied troops, who 'were seeing England, the real England, for the first time.'

At such moments as the announcement of the King's approaching death; the removal of King Edward's portrait, whether one privately agreed or not; the scene in the 'bus during the strike, and, above all, the precisely accurate statement of people's reasons for cheering Munich, there was a revelation to overseas troops of something they had heard, but not realized; that England is the common people.

It would be nice, although probably fruitless, to determine the special quality that recommends *This Happy Breed* to so many different people. Nice, because other British directors might make a conscientious effort to improve their films on this model; fruitless, because conscientiousness doth not make Cowards of us all. There needs another element. Our correspondent describes *This Happy Breed* as 'a documentary; the unembellished facts of a life that is lived daily and consecutively till it is finished.' There is some truth in this, but not the whole truth. It is true that Mr Coward and his colleagues have excelled in the exact observation of ordinary speech and behaviour. If you were to hear the dialogue without seeing the film, you could still call up an accurate impression of the Gibbons family. If you were to see the film without hearing the dialogue, you would be forced to invent some such speech as Mr Coward has given his characters.

Yet *This Happy Breed* is not just a photographic and microphonic record of suburban life in the years between the two wars. If it were, nobody would care to see it. Art does not consist in repeating accurately what can be seen and heard around us. Art must try to conjure up, with the help of familiar symbols, things that are not perceptible to human eyes and ears. It must be a kind of second sight, what Baudelaire calls a 'sorcellerie evocatoire.' And *that* I think, is the special quality of Mr Coward's film; a film that finds in a house in a row the symbol of a nation; daring to call itself *This Happy Breed* instead of, say, '17, Sycamore Road.'

1944

In reply to a question in the House of Commons recently, the Minister for War stated, 'No religious films are available for the Army as a normal procedure. Commercially produced films are, however, available and chaplains have been advised of that fact.'

This reply adumbrates a trend that will soon be evident to civilian audiences as well as soldiers. Following *The Song of Bernadette*, at least a dozen films with a more or less religious note are on the way from Hollywood. One of them is here already. **Going My Way**, with Bing Crosby and Barry Fitzgerald, is about a young Catholic priest who is sent to help an old one with an insolvent city parish. Being comely, equable, musical, and reasonably muscular, besides knowing a contralto at the Metropolitan Opera, he is able to get the place out of debt in two hours and four minutes. He forms the street gangs into a choir, and has them singing Gounod in a jiffy. He saves a young girl from going astray, and sees her happily married. He composes a song to raise money for the church funds, and gets the lady from the Metropolitan to sing it. He puts heart into the old priest by teaching him to play golf, and finally reunites him with his old, old mother from Ireland in a brisk burst of 'Mother Machree.'

The film, of course, is dripping with sentiment, and might easily have been insufferable. In point of fact, it is rather charming. Bing Crosby and Barry Fitzgerald, the crooner and the comedy character man, justify their odd casting. Their styles are as far apart as the poles. Mr Fitzgerald's is crafty, witty, dry; Mr Crosby's candid, informal, coaxing. Mr Fitzgerald acts all the time; Mr Crosby hardly ever. But their partnership is somehow felicitous. Leo McCarey's direction picks up the feeling of everyday life in the scrubbed chastity of the rectory, and moves with a lingering affection that doesn't do the film any harm.

Going My Way, with all its trivialities, seems to me preferable to *The Song of Bernadette*, for all its magnificent material. Hollywood is at its best when it is most human. The producers who are going to make religious films might do well to ponder that circumstance. Religion implies the relationship of man to his God, and can only be fully conveyed, this side of revelation, when the springs of man's conduct are rightly understood. It is not enough to put your hero into a clerical collar, or invest Linda Darnell with an aureole. It is not really enough to whistle up the Hollywood Heavenly Choir. The people of the film have got to be credible in their daily life, if we are to share in their spiritual experiences.

A clergyman wrote to me the other day. 'I think the approach to God must always be by the homely road of the commonplace. From that you climb to the heights of Sinai, the thunder and the clouds and the glory and the majesty. A 70-acre field of a summer evening – a silence you can feel – a lark singing as it goes heavenward – all homely things which you can experience over and over again in life. And you stand still – and everything round you stands still – and you *worship*. You can't help it almost! You get that on a mountain top. You get it in a back street in the East End and a group of children, many of them barelegged and bareheaded, dancing in the dark and the snow to a barrel organ.'

The clergyman happens to be my brother, but I see no reason to doubt his judgment on that account. And although I don't question the power of the great film, like the great music and the great paintings, using religious symbols, to attain the heights of Sinai and the thunder and the majesty, I feel the ordinary producer might do well to start a little modestly and begin by getting acquainted with the ways of his fellowmen.

1944

Christmas Holiday is a jolly title for a Deanna Durbin film, but it's the only jolly thing about it. Miss Durbin is an accomplished singer; so they cut her songs down to two and make them blues numbers. She has a naturally modest and ingenuous manner; so they cast her as a hostess in a seedy night club. She is at her best in simple comedies; so they give her a heavy drama about a wife whose homicidal husband believes her to be unfaithful. She has a youthful figure; so they dress her in sophisticated gowns. Her face is fresh; so they plaster it with make-up. She has a limited range as an actress; so they ask her to express, in ninety minutes, anguish, rapture, fear, world-weariness, and spiritual catharsis, apart from one or two other emotions you may find it difficult to identify. Does this seem to you the best way of making a Deanna Durbin picture? No? No.

1944

One of the jolliest things that has lately happened in the cinema has been the solid popular affirmation of interest in the revival of **A Night at the Opera**.

What is there about these old Marx Brothers' comedies that keeps them fresh? Why do we still remember the Marx Brothers, when we have forgotten other comedy teams who made quite a noise in their season? Broadly speaking, I should say it was a question of personality. And by personality I don't mean what the film producers mean when they use that difficult word of five syllables. I don't mean 'it' or 'oomph', or any other animal grunt. I mean the trick of living one's life or doing one's work with an intense personal conviction, an utter singleness of purpose – that is, as if one meant it with all one's heart.

Almost all the memorable human beings, from the saints to the poets and the political firebrands, have lived personally, and a great many of them have got themselves intensely disliked for doing so. A few have actually got themselves killed for it. Only the impersonal man, the cautious nondescript who plays safe, makes no enemies, by the simple expedient of making no mark. A strong personality is not infrequently accompanied by blunt speech or a caustic tongue, qualities that are apt to confuse weaker people, and make them suspicious and cross. The strong personality has got to put up with all this; taking full responsibility for his own actions, making no excuses for his failures, and accepting everything that comes to him in the spirit of fearlessness and humour. Alone of all the great personalities, perhaps, the saint can do all this without giving the impression of being a somewhat presumptuous person. As Chesterton says, 'He is not conscious of his superiority to others; but only more conscious of his inferiority than they are.'

Personality makes good entertainment, just as it makes good art and good living. One reason why there is so little good entertainment today, is that personality is so frigidly discouraged. It seems to be the ideal of those responsible for our modern recreation to reduce everything to a nice, dull, impersonal level. The majority of people who write, produce and perform for the benefit of the public are men without apparent personality. Any one of them could just as well be any other one. In fact, he very often is.

In the cinema, nonentity has been cultivated almost to the point of a virtue. Every new blonde must be like every other blonde. Every musical must conform to the pattern of every other musical. Every story must be the same story. It is the proud ambition of every director, after years of toil and experience, to become, in the end, exactly like every other director.

An American writer once remarked, 'The amusing thing about moving pictures is the enormous number of nonentities who work together to make something any normal half-wit would prefer not to make in the first place.'

There are, of course, exceptions, and on the rare occasions on which you do come across a film of character, it is ten to one you will find a single creative intelligence behind it. A great number of people may contribute towards the final achievement, but they work best when they have a strong personality to hold them together. Orson Welles is a creator of that temper; so is Noel Coward; Alfred Hitchcock is another; so is Preston Sturges. You may like the work of Messrs Welles, Coward, Hitchcock and Sturges, or you may loathe it, but it is emphatically their own work; you will never confound it with the work of Messrs Smith, Brown, Jones and Robinson. These men scrawl their signature across a film so boldly that no one can fail to read it. The same rule applies to the Marx Brothers, more than to any other comedians since Chaplain. Groucho, Harpo and Chico may be your delight or your anathema, but once seen – some will say endured – they are never forgotten; their three-fold personality has produced a type of comedy that is unique on the screen.

1945

Into the Odeon, Marble Arch, newly conditioned as an Egyptian temple, with figures of gods in niches, and a drop-curtain enscrolled with a map of the harbour of Alexandria; into the Odeon, with a fanfare of trumpets, comes the million-and-a-quarter-pound **Caesar and Cleopatra**, the third and most ambitious of the Shaw plays produced by Gabriel Pascal. It would be pleasant to be able to say that the expenditure is reflected in a work that is nobler, wiser or more sublime than other pictures; that it shines with a special beauty, or evokes an unusual stir of feeling. But, to my taste, *Caesar and Cleopatra* is a singularly cold triumph. It has authority, but *Henry V* was nobler. It has wit, but *The Southerner* had a deeper wisdom. It is handsome in an imperious way, but there is no beneficence in its beauty. I cannot recall one single moment that lights the screen and warms the heart like the shining candour of *Our Vines Have Tender Grapes*.

I have no doubt there are many lovely and gracious things to be seen in *Caesar and Cleopatra* if the eye were given time to discover them, but Mr Pascal is too stern a self-disciplinarian to dally with scenic effect when he has a message from Shaw to deliver. The spectacle is a mere background for the argument; time and again a flurry of movement, which seems likely to develop into action, is cut off remorselessly in the middle. It is a curious effect of this method that the scenes realized on the screen are less vivid to the mind's eye than the pictures called up by the stage directions in Mr Shaw's play.

What Shaw has created in *Caesar and Cleopatra* is a hero without a drama, and a philosophy without love. It is essentially a one-man play; for his Cleopatra is practically unactable, his Ftatateeta a grotesque, his Rufio a stooge, and his Britannus a pantomime joke. Mr Shaw's laughter is contemptuous, but his Caesar is superb. He is hewn all in one piece, without a flaw or slip, out of a cold marble block. He is not a man to be loved, but to be admired; to be admired because he is sensible, not because he is good. He is magnanimous, but there is nothing tender about his magnanimity. He does not love more than other men, he simply hates less. His kindness is not congenial; his flippancy is not gay. But there is something high and clean about this Roman soldier, and the great moments of the play are those in which the murky politics of Egypt give way before the ordered sanity of swords.

The complete Caesar is beyond the reach of all but the greatest actors, but Claud Rains manages some fine strokes in the graver passages; and by his looks, his bearing, and his voice he admits the possibility of a man who can be a hero by virtue of reason and not romance. Vivien Leigh's Cleopatra seems drained of life beside him; there was more of Cleopatra in her Scarlett O'Hara than in this pale elf. Mr Shaw has written a showy part for the gadfly Appollodorus, and Stewart Granger plays him handsomely in his flamingo reds and daffodil yellows. Indeed I could not conjecture why Cleopatra should ask Caesar to send her a Roman soldier with round, strong arms, when such a stunning Sicilian gallant was at hand, ready and apt to drape his round, strong arms about her shoulders with nonchalant *lèse majesté*.

It is not Cecil Parker's fault that Britannus is as uppish a conception on the screen as he is in Mr Shaw's play. It is against all common sense that these dim northern people, who inhabited our island before the blood had been mingled by invasion, or the tradition hardened by the industrial march of the centuries, should have been the exact prototype of the Edwardian branch bank manager. Mr Parker does what he can with the part, but there is only one proper comment on Britannus. In a word, pShaw!

1945

Meet Me in St Louis is a charming picture. There is much more in it than meets the ear. Not only are the numbers admirable in themselves, but someone has gone to a lot of pains to make sense of the bits *between* the numbers. The film is based on a series of stories by Sally Benson, which originally appeared in the *New Yorker*, very human sketches of a childhood in a provincial town in the early 1900s. The dialogue, brought to the screen almost intact, has a quick, but gentle, sense of fun that is rather rare in the cinema. There are no wisecracks; there is no slapstick; the comedy is almost demure. But a cook who remarks firmly, 'Cabbage has a cabbage smell' when her master is trying to make up to her about the tempting aroma of her dishes, seems rather funnier to me than many a comic who has been on the receiving end of a custard pie.

What is the film about? Nothing in the world except a family. There is a Mr and Mrs Smith of St Louis, who live at 5,135 Kensington-avenue, and have five children. Rose, the eldest, is patiently waiting for a proposal from a young man in New York, and eventually gets it. Esther (Judy Garland) has taken a tremulous fancy for the boy next door, and sings about it. Tootie, the youngest (Margaret O'Brien) is an irrepressible little ghoul who tells the most thumping lies with the candour of an angel. Lon and Agnes keep turning up in a nondescript sort of way, as the in-between members of the family.

What happens to the Smiths? Nothing of consequence. They have dances and telephone calls and trolley rides; they swim, eat tomato soup and huge helpings of home-made cake; they terrify themselves at Hallowe'en and grow sentimental at Christmas. They have a family feeling and family jokes and a family loyalty; and once, when they think their father is going to make them remove to New York, they have a minor family tragedy. The film is simply a Technicolor diary of the Smiths' goings-on during one busy summer, autumn, and winter. Can such a trivial record make an entertaining picture? Astonishingly enough, it can.

25 February 1945

Salome, Where She Danced

QUESTION.   Who was Salome, and where did she dance?
ANSWER.   She was a Viennese bubble-dancer, who stole

the plans of the High Command in the Austro-Prussian War, and she danced in the mining town of Drinkman's Wells, California.

QUESTION.   Why?

ANSWER.   Presumably to get a little much-needed practice before uncritical audiences.

QUESTION.   You misunderstood me. Why does she go to California to dance?

ANSWER.   Because the American journalist who loves her thinks she will be a sensation in San Francisco.

QUESTION.   Is she?

ANSWER.   I have no idea. Her heart is broken before the opening night. She says she will never appear before the footlights again. Mercifully she doesn't.

QUESTION.   What broke her heart?

ANSWER.   A bandit. He kidnaps her. He reminds her of her dead lover, Kurt, Prince of the Hapsburgs.

QUESTION.   That worries her?

ANSWER.   Not specifically. She worries because he has lost his faith.

QUESTION.   How's that?

ANSWER.   Because he got a complex when he saw General Lee surrender to General Grant.

QUESTION.   But she cures him?

ANSWER.   Naturally. She sings 'Der Tannenbaum'; the celestial orchestra plays 'Come, All Ye Faithful'; the bandit remembers Christmas in old Virginia, and gives back all the money he has stolen.

QUESTION.   What does Salome do then?

ANSWER.   She sings 'The Blue Danube' much too slowly.

QUESTION.   But she is happy?

ANSWER.   Until Count Von Bohlen, the Prussian Beast, turns up.

QUESTION.   He hates her?

ANSWER.   On the contrary, he loves her madly, but in a beastly Prussian way, so the bandit has to kill him in a duel.

QUESTION.   Pistols, presumably?

ANSWER.   Swords. The Beast says, 'I cannot cross swords with a mere boy.' And the bandit says, 'Don't worry, we had a French fencing master in our regiment.'

QUESTION.   So *then* Salome is happy?

ANSWER.   Not quite. There is still the Russian Colonel, San

Francisco's most fabulous nabob. He loves her, too. He gives her a picture.

QUESTION.   She wants a picture?

ANSWER.   She wants this one. She says, 'Is it not beautiful? Could it be a Rembrandt?'

QUESTION.   Could it?

ANSWER.   I am no connoisseur. I thought it was the Picture of Dorian Gray, After Treatment.

QUESTION.   That satisfies Salome?

ANSWER.   Temporarily. She gets out a white Oriental dress and two clean chiffon hankies to wave, and goes and waves them on the Chinese junk.

QUESTION.   You did say a *Chinese* junk?

ANSWER.   Certainly. Laden with silks and jade. The captain is a friend of hers. His teachings have cleared her mind of many doubts and fears.

QUESTION.   He loves her, too?

ANSWER.   Possibly; but between his Oriental philosophy and his Scottish accent it is hard to tell.

QUESTION.   Why does he speak with a Scottish accent?

ANSWER.   Because he has been to medical school in Edinburgh. He knows the secrets of the human heart. He and the Russian and the journalist –

QUESTION.   Ah, yes, the journalist. What happens to him?

ANSWER.   Nothing. He prudently gives up journalism in time, and becomes a theatrical producer. The Chinaman and the Russian and the journalist bundle Salome and the bandit into a Virginia-bound coach –

QUESTION.   What does Salome say?

ANSWER.   She says, 'I can't dance.'

QUESTION.   She really admits that?

ANSWER.   She really does.

QUESTION.   What does the bandit say?

ANSWER.   He says, 'None of this is any good, and you know it.'

1945

The appearance of **Blithe Spirit** in the cinema has finally convinced me that Noel Coward is, as I have long suspected, a great man. I am not at all convinced that *Blithe Spirit*, although superb entertainment, is a very good *film*. It is a straightforward version, in rather inappropriate Technicolor, of the Coward play about a happily married novelist who invites a medium to his home and is thereafter haunted by the ghost of his first wife, all done up in green ectoplasm to look like an animated acid drop. Although there are plenty of camera tricks in it, the thing is always closer to the theatre than to the cinema. Margaret Rutherford's performance of the medium has a gusto that is made for high fun and big theatres; but the rest of the acting has too much of a confidential, West End air, both Rex Harrison and Kay Hammond tending to throw away their lines in the certainty that a well-bred front row of stalls will catch them.

Blithe Spirit would probably have been a better film job had Noel Coward been on the spot to encourage the director, David Lean, and the camera man, Ronald Neame, to take greater liberties with his material. Perhaps it is true to say that they have lost some of the spirit of *Blithe Spirit* by sticking too closely to the letter. But the point is academic only, and it would seem unfair to press it, since one way and another *Blithe Spirit* gives us ninety minutes of concentrated, cultivated fun.

There is a tendency these days to suggest that any bright young person (if he had the mind) could write like Noel Coward. The obvious answer, of course, is to invite the bright young person to try. It is true that it may be easier to have wit than, in the deepest and most enduring sense, to have imagination. But it is much easier to *pretend* to have imagination than to pretend to have wit. A pretender may get away with a phoney poem, because it is the privilege of a poet to be mysterious. But a pretender cannot get away with a phoney joke, because it is the point of a joke to be seen.

Noel Coward can ease into a line of dialogue more than most punsters can stretch over a twenty-minute broadcast. He shares with Jane Austen, a wit of a very different temperament, the gift of animating his characters wholly through their conversation. The people in *Blithe Spirit*, for instance, are introduced in the most perfunctory manner, at a moment of high and unnatural tension; yet before the film is over, each has talked himself into a complete person, with individual tastes and prejudices, and an entirely private and peculiar history. If it were only for this gift of disciplined dialogue, Noel Coward would have earned his place as one of the great entertainers of the cinema. But that he should be able to encompass a bit of gay nonsense like *Blithe Spirit*, and still leave one with the confidence that he could produce another *In Which We Serve* if need be, confirms the impression that he is also a great man.

The fact is, that the whole mass of Coward's emotional and intellectual virtues has been partly clouded by his most obviously successful virtue – that of artistic dexterity. He has suffered from his versatility; not by not doing anything quite well enough, but by doing every kind of thing rather too well. As wit, sentimentalist, song-writer, patriot, and sophisticate, his mask has always been so good that many people have not been able to identify the single man behind it. If *In Which We Serve*, *This Happy Breed*, *Blithe Spirit*, *Bitter Sweet*, *Cavalcade*, and *Private Lives*, had each of them been a shade less perfectly done, it would have been easy to recognize them as parts of the same message.

The idea that motivates all Coward's work is the belief that civilization, in its most British and parochial sense, is still a romantic adventure. A sprig of suburban laurel is to him what a lei is to a South Sea islander. In his busy professional life he has never been able to rest on his laurels. But so long as there are English people old-fashioned and young-hearted enough to understand the romance they stand for, they should remain evergreen.

1945

Now that it is all over in the West; now, while our thoughts are precariously balanced between past and future; it seems to me a fitting moment to turn up the old files and jot down, for the sake of the records, a history of the war as we have seen it in terms of films.

Everyone, of course, has his personal associations of this kind, not least the Service men who have watched films in camp cinemas and under circumstances they are unlikely to forget. To me, for instance, *The Way Ahead* will always be associated with the Normandy beaches, and 'Champagne Charlie' with the liberation of Paris. After four and a half years, I still cannot listen to the tune of 'Sweet Genevieve' without a shudder. Virginia Weidler sang it in *Young Tom Edison*, and that night, a golden moonlight night, without warning, I heard my first bomb.

Broadly speaking, though, the people of this country can look back on a common experience of films as a background to their war memories. What are they? Here is my diary for 1939.

September 3; I see I reviewed *Bachelor Mother* on that Sunday morning. Then comes a week's blank. Do you remember how all the cinemas in the country closed down in anticipation of massed enemy bombing? One by one they re-opened, with staggered hours, in the West End of London. We went to the pictures again, conscientiously clutching our gas-masks. The new films were *The Four Feathers* and Deanna Durbin's *Three Smart Girls Grow Up*. *Jamaica Inn* was about, too, although its director, Alfred Hitchcock, and its stars, Charles Laughton and Maureen O'Hara, had already left for the United States.

We saw *Goodbye Mr Chips*, *Stagecoach*, *The Story of Vernon and Irene Castle* and *Wuthering Heights* that winter during the 'phoney war'. *Gone With the Wind*, on a bleak spring day in 1940, presaged the attack on Norway. *The Grapes of Wrath*, *Rebecca* and the first Preston Sturges film, *The Great McGinty*, were shown in the Dunkirk summer. About the same time there appeared a British film called *Just William*, in which a small, almost unnoticed child, called Roddy McDowall, played the part of Ginger, A Friend.

During the Battle of Britain we saw Shirley Temple in *The Blue Bird*, and Walt Disney's second full-length cartoon, *Pinocchio*. In the winter of bombing that followed we had *Pride and Prejudice* and *Quiet Wedding*, *The Long Voyage Home* and *Major Barbara*. Deanna Durbin's *Spring Parade* turned up in the same week as the Fire of London. *The Lady Eve* coincided with Hess's arrival in this country, and *That Uncertain Feeling* with the German invasion of Russia. While the Japanese were attacking Pearl Harbor our cinemas were showing *Here Comes Mr Jordan* and *Dumbo*.

My Gal Sal marked the turn of the tide in North Africa. *The Magnificent Ambersons* appeared after we had landed in Sicily. *The Way Ahead* was shown on D-Day. *Going My Way* and *The White Cliffs of Dover* were played to the chug of flying bombs. *Henry V* and *A Song to Remember* made their debut during the rocket season; *Kismet* and *Frenchman's Creek* during Rundstedt's Ardennes offensive. *The Picture of Dorian Gray* turns out to be an historic picture, sharing the luck of the victory sweep with *A Place of One's Own*.

What else has happened in the film world since 1939? Arthur Rank has happened. So have Alan Ladd, Stewart Granger, Eric Portman, Deborah Kerr, Gregory Peck, James Mason, Susan Peters, Phyllis Calvert, Jennifer Jones, Ingrid Bergman, and Frank Sinatra. Deanna Durbin, Judy Garland, Mickey Rooney and Shirley Temple have grown up, and Margaret O'Brien is the new child wonder. Orson Welles has happened; so have Preston Sturges and Noel Coward. Chopin, after a tough competition with swing, has become the symbol of music for millions. We have lost Leslie Howard, Conrad Veidt, John Barrymore, Carole Lombard and Laird Cregar. Technicolor has found its way into every other picture, The MoI have documented everything that could be documented, from the achievements of our armed forces to the offensive of a sneeze.

Above all, for the purposes of historical survey, a British cinema has happened. We can be allowed, I think, a moment's pride in that, at the end of six years of struggle for survival. It would not have been surprising if the British film industry, stripped of its manpower, its studiospace, and its raw materials, had been one of the war's natural casualties. Instead, the British film has not only survived the war but survived with honour. *Major Barbara*, *49th Parallel*, *Pimpernel Smith*, *The First of the Few*, *In Which We Serve*, *This Happy Breed*, *The Way Ahead*, *Thunder Rock*, *The Gentle Sex*, *San Demetrio London*, *Blithe Spirit*, *Colonel Blimp* and *Henry V* are all war-time pictures. Through necessitous circumstance, the British producer has had to work to find out what is indigenous to native art, and learn to cultivate it. I think this morning we can afford to hang out just a scrap of bunting for the British picture, with the customary warning against complacency in the grim struggle ahead.

13 May 1945

It is to be hoped that nobody will be beguiled into seeking an association between Laurence Olivier's film production of **Henry V** and the present war, on the grounds that the heroic actions of last summer and fall were fought so closely along the route that Henry Plantagenet followed. Such an association would be unfortunate; it would inevitably reveal in *Henry V* a touch of brassy romanticism; diminishing, by unnatural contrast with a very different sort of greatness, the stature of the play.

Henry V is not a great war play. The Elizabethans were too much in love with beauty and splendour and the heady draft of words to write great war plays; and Laurence Olivier, who produced, directed and starred in the screen version of *Henry V*, was too much in love with Shakespeare to make a great war film. The stuff of war is patience and endurance, courage in cold blood, and a kind of long, hard, impersonal anonymity. These are not qualities for the playhouse, still less for the movie theatre. What Shakespeare wrote in *Henry V*, and what the film has splendidly caught in its own fashion, is a fanfare; a flourish; a salute to high adventure; a kind of golden and perennially youthful exaltation of man's grim work.

The picture runs for two hours and a half, and retains about two-thirds of the original text. The only interpolations are a borrowed speech from *Henry IV, Part II*, used to explain the references to Falstaff, and superimposed over a silent scene of the Fat Knight's death-bed; and a couple of lines from Marlowe's *Tamburlaine*, given Pistol when he goes off to the wars. Mr Olivier and his colleagues have taken one daring license with their material. They have presented *Henry V* as a play within a play. The opening and closing scenes are represented as taking place during the first performance of the piece at the old Globe Theatre, and are played deliberately broad for comedy. Speech, gestures and make-up are formally exaggerated; players and audience mingle in a kind of stylized puppet play. As a device for emphasizing 'this wooden O' the conceit is ingenious; as a theory of presentation it is entirely legitimate; but in practice it works out a little self-consciously tiresome, a rather redundant addition to a film that is handsomely intelligible on its own account.

With the gathering of the English fleet at Southampton, however, the film breaks loose. The background opens out, the action is filled with a wide bustle, the poetry takes charge, and the audience is clearly no longer watching a stylized piece taking place on the stage of a theatre. From that moment onwards, the picture is a beauty. It moves with a flowing line, a rhythmic pattern of mass and colour, that has only been equalled on the screen in the best of the Disney fantasies. One rich composition after another fills the eye; the light, airy tracery of the French court scenes; the blazing canvas of the battlefield; the deep, whispering quiet of a darkened camp waiting for the morning; bold massed groups, single heroic figures; a quaint formal flower-garden for a fairy-tale princess; a rearing and curvetting of caparisoned chargers for a couple of kings at war.

The producers have gone to the Italian painters, and particularly to Uccello's 'Rout of San Romano', for their battle-scapes, and to Holbein and Breughel for their colours. For the superb charge of the French cavalry at Agincourt, they have relied on the tempo of a musician. Before a foot of this scene was shot, the composer, William Walton, worked out an exact musical score, to be used as a guide-track for timing. The result is a classic sequence, in which, as in the unforgettable scene on the Odessa steps in *Potemkin*, the poetry of pure mathematics is applied to the practice of drama. Music and movement gather impetus together; pulsing, pounding, quickening, loudening, until they break over you thunderously like the mountain of a wave.

It takes powerful acting to match this splendour of production, and fortunately *Henry V* has it. Mr Olivier has collected a cast of some of the finest Shakespearean actors on the English stage, so that every speech gets its due, every lightest word its measure. Leslie Banks, as Chorus, flings the gateway to romance wide open with a flourish. Robert Newton plays the Ancient Pistol with a huge Elizabethan gusto. The scenes in the French camp, always a little dull in the reading, are quickened by the beautiful performances of Leo Genn as the sober Constable, Ralph Truman as the joyous herald Mountjoy, and Max Adrian as the sleek Dauphin. Renee Asherson plays Katharine with a demure coquetry and a kind of school-girl secrecy that is altogether winning.

Laurence Olivier's own Henry is a development of the performance he gave some years ago at the Old Vic, adapted very shrewdly to the enlargement of the scene beyond the four walls of a theatre. As the central figure of a huge crowd in a vast campaign, he strikes a high heroic note, and uses the full leather of his lungs. 'Once more unto the breach, dear friends' is a war-cry; the Crispin's Day speech ends on something that is almost a brazen scream. Mr Olivier is not afraid to hint that Henry Plantagenet was unafraid of showmanship. But that is only half the portrait. He has another sort of King for another sort of occasion: a shy and tender wooer; a lonely man, watchful over his camp in the darkness. Above all, he suggests a Henry who is under all circumstances a leader; the sort of man honest men will follow till they drop.

One can pick out actor after actor for note, and still not catch the film's especial quality; which is that everyone in it, and concerned with it, from Mr Olivier onwards, seems to be in love and tune with Shakespeare. That is as it should be in a Shakespearean performance; behind the footlights and in front of them; on the screen and in the *loges*. For too long Shakespeare has suffered from being a compulsory subject in our education.

Because he has been presented to us from infancy as a classic, the Immortal Bard, a writer of set books for examinations, an author of plays to be pulled to pieces with the help of annotations and a glossary, the most exciting of our playwrights has become a bore. What we need is a little healthy hunger for Shakespeare; an absence from felicity awhile; and then a zest to make us rediscover him as something of our own, as we might discover Donne, or Vaughan, or Belloc. I think the Olivier *Henry V* has this special relish, and even if it were not such an eyeful, *that* would be good enough for me.

Henry V is, without a doubt, the most glowing film enterprise of the year in England.

June 1945

Recently I heard of a four-roomed seaside bungalow offered for sale at the modest price of £10,000. I wonder what would be the current market price of the seaside property in **The Enchanted Cottage**, which comprises grounds with historic ruins, a private foreshore, 18th century residence with all modern conveniences, a nobleman's escutcheon, silver tea-service, fine porcelain, hothouse blooms, a well-stocked wardrobe, and the power of making plain people beautiful, including a high-class hairdressing service operating while you sleep?

The film is adapted from a play of Pinero's, and is about an airman, disabled and disfigured by war-wounds, who marries out of loneliness a girl so homely that even the local soldiery won't dance with her. Hiding from the world in a New England cottage, which has been used as a honeymoon resort for two hundred years, the couple find that a miracle has been accomplished, presumably by enchantment. A physical change has come over them both. She is radiantly beautiful: he handsome and whole. By the time they learn that the transformation is merely an illusion of love, they are ready to go out together and face the world.

The Enchanted Cottage is a silly film with considerable charm. It will be liked by millions, who are fully aware of its silliness while being captivated by its charm. It will be liked for the best of reasons; because it is based on a solid and humane truth. Every sentient being in the world is more or less lonely; few can be confident of success through good looks; most would gladly give their savings for an enchanted cottage that would lay on happiness with the h. and c. Only the rare person, who goes about the world with his eyes open, realizes that the idea has deeper roots; that the enchantment of the cottage is what is put into it, not what is taken out of it; that beauty is not a matter of clear-cut profile and unblemished features, but of a grace within; that the eye of affection is a curiously selective lens; and that the happiest unions are often those of which people will say, 'Well, I don't know what in the world they see in each other.'

Bear these principles in mind, and you may enjoy *The Enchanted Cottage* with my blessing. Only don't, for pity's sake, imagine you are watching a work of art. From first to last, except in a couple of scenes in which Miss Dorothy Maguire's touching talent transcends the script, *The Enchanted Cottage* is a triumph of cheating. It has a camera, and does not use it. It has a chance to flood that set with enchantment, to irradiate it with light, to give every stick and stone a magic glow; and it prefers to line itself up solidly with the Ideal Home Exhibition. It has the imperative call to make human beings of its characters; and it presents them as ill-motivated types in a fashionable West End drama. Nobody in *The Enchanted Cottage* behaves as a human being would. The cast remains, not human, mature or dramatic characters, but juvenile lead, heavy lead, heavy mother, character woman, other woman, small-part comedian, and leading lady. Even Miss Dorothy Maguire, sitting out at a dance, like the girl whose best friends would not tell her, is not allowed to act according to the instincts of her sex. Don't tell me that any modern girl, even a nice girl from New England, would walk straight on to the dance-floor from the kitchen sink without titivating herself in the ladies' room. 'You have been touched,' says the script, when Miss Maguire ultimately becomes beautiful, 'by a power that is beyond this world.' Get along with you, script, you can't fool a woman. She has been touched by a comb, an electric dryer, an expert dressmaker, a pair of tweezers, an eyebrow pencil, a lipstick and a powder puff.

3 June 1945

A strangely attractive and tantalizing British film called **The Seventh Veil** turns up at the Leicester Square. It is beautifully acted by Ann Todd and James Mason, imaginatively directed by Compton Bennett, and brilliantly adorned by the work of an anonymous pianist (who I am assured is Miss Eileen Joyce),and for the first sixty minutes I could ask nothing better. Then comes the parting of the ways, and it is inconceivable that the clear and lively minds who had the ordering of the first two-thirds of the film could have been responsible for the tedious and tatty ending. At the beginning of the film, Francesca, a young concert pianist, is seen in a nursing home, where the doctors are vainly trying to treat her for a mysterious coma following a motor accident. A psychoanalyst puts her under hypnosis, persuades her to tell him the story of her life, from the time when she was a fourteen-year-old schoolgirl, and eventually cures her.

At the end of an hour it is abundantly clear both to him and to us that Francesca has two troubles – a terror of injury to her hands, and a deep love for her brutal guardian. The guardian has struck her across the knuckles with his cane, and he is sorry; he loves her, and she loves him; and obviously the right thing at this point is for him to break the cane across his knee, take his ward in his arms, and end the picture, with possibly a triumphant symphony concert for finale. But no, the producers have to reintroduce two other lovers – a bandleader and a portrait painter – for the purpose of dismissing them, and drag out the proceedings so interminably that we end by hardly caring if the girl goes off with the guardian, the psychoanalyst, or the butler. That is the disqualification of *The Seventh Veil* as a serious bit of cinema, but it will not prevent it from being a vast and largely merited success.

21 October 1945

BACK TO THINKING

Thinking with feeling of the hundreds of Chinese actors in Hollywood who can no longer earn their living as sinister Japanese now that the war in the Far East is over, my sympathies have been drawn to other earnest workers in the cinema fold, whose occupation is gone, or at least, seriously curtailed, by the cessation of world hostilities.

There is, for instance, the technical expert, who has kept body and soul together for the past six years by advising on everything to do with the war, from the behaviour of international spies to the specification of the London stirrup-pump. There is the impersonator of very important persons, whose character sketches of Presidents, Premiers, Ambassadors, War Lords and War Criminals have added to the enjoyment and instruction of millions. There is the British actor in exile, who has been kept so busy playing commandos, airmen, and heroes of the British Commonwealth in Hollywood that he hasn't had time to come home and take even the smallest peep at his own country.

All these will suffer professionally by the end of the war, but none will suffer more than the unhappy story-writer. With a single stroke of the pen, all his favourite fictions of the past six years have been erased. Among the stories that are inexorably doomed are the following:

The story about the honest chorus girl, who rejects her millionaire suitors for a simple sailor, only to find that he is the richest of them all, having joined the Navy to avoid publicity.

The one about the society woman who puts on knife-creased overalls, a chic bandeau, and a delicate smudge of oil, and goes into an aircraft factory for a little light war-work.

The story, so popular with our British exiles, about the experiences of an American soldier in the London air raids.

The film in which Errol Flynn pops into Occupied Europe to teach the beauties of fortitude to Czech, Polish, French, Norwegian or Belgian patriots.

The one about the beautiful spy in Lisbon, who is an anti-Nazi pretending to be a Nazi pretending to be an anti-Nazi.

The semi-documentary about (a) a bomber, (b) an aircraft carrier, (c) a submarine, that keeps on going somewhere for two hours and eventually gets there.

The piece about the war correspondent, relaxing at the Waldorf, who cannot tap out so much as 'quertyuiop' on his typewriter, but keeps the capitals of the world trembling with his powerful articles.

The story about the Camp or Canteen show, in which Five Great Bands and Fifty-nine Famous Film Stars demonstrate the principles of democracy to dazzled G.I.s.

Any film that ends with dewy eyes, celestial choir, the Vicar in full canonicals, and a squadron of bombers flying into the sunlight.

So long as conscription goes on, of course, they will still be able to make those merry little comedies in which a fat, funny man and his thin stooge, or a thin, funny man and his fat stooge, romp through an army training camp in long underwear. Spies will be busier than ever, I suppose, now that we have the peace-time boon of the atomic bomb, and there is nothing to stop the documentary boys from being as tediously informative about the building of a building as they have been, from time to time, about such things as the building of a bomber. On the whole, though, I fear that the writers of Hollywood are facing a crisis in their lives, and it will probably be best to remake all the old war-stories as anti-war stories, until they feel strong enough to do a little constructive thinking along original lines.

1945

QUESTION.   Who is tempted in **Temptation**, and in what way?

ANSWER.   Well, primarily, Merle Oberon, but you may be tempted too. The temptation in each case is to murder somebody.

QUESTION.   Whom does Miss Oberon want to murder, and why?

ANSWER.   She wants to murder her husband, George Brent, because she is bored with life in Cairo, Egypt, and all that singing is driving her crazy.

QUESTION.   All what singing?

ANSWER.   Oh, just the casual celestial choirs thereabouts.

QUESTION.   She's not musical?

ANSWER.   On the contrary, she's a sucker for *good* music. She agreed to marry Mr Brent when she heard him play Chopin by candle-light.

QUESTION.   Electricity cut?

ANSWER.   No, period picture.

QUESTION.   Professional pianist, Mr Brent?

ANSWER.   Oh, no, wealthy archaeologist. But he's very cultivated. He lives in 'a curious world of his own.' He thinks that George Bernard Shaw is a coming man.

QUESTION.   Does Mr Brent kick the bucket?

ANSWER.   How crude. Certainly not. They make him Director of the British Museum.

QUESTION.   What for?

ANSWER.   Because he has discovered the tomb of Rameses V, and being the first to see the mummy unveiled is a kinda honour, like the Victoria Cross.

QUESTION.   How does Miss Oberon hope to do him in?

ANSWER.   With poison, while the archaeologists and government officials are singing, 'For He's a Jolly Good Fellow'. With a strange Oriental poison. Baroudi sends it to her.

QUESTION.   Who's that again?

ANSWER.   Mahmoud Baroudi, handsome and attractive young polo player. He learnt to play polo at Oxford. Miss Oberon thinks about him all the time.

QUESTION.   *All* the time?

ANSWER.   Well, nearly all. When she can take her mind off her costume changes and the manipulations of eyelashes that nearly sweep the ground.

QUESTION.   Dressy wench, what?

ANSWER.   Stunning type. She isn't called Bella Donna for nothing.

QUESTION.   Why is she called Bella Donna?

ANSWER.   Because Robert Hitchens wrote a book of that name some time ago and the film people can't get it out of their system.

QUESTION.   Christian name, Bella Donna?

ANSWER.   Pet name. Christian name, Ruby.

QUESTION.   And this Bella Donna is in love with this polo player?

ANSWER.   Passionately, until she gets remorse in a black gown with a chaste chest-design of pyramids.

QUESTION.   What happens then?

ANSWER.   She starts seeing herself in double exposure. She stops murdering her husband. She finds she can't do it.

QUESTION.   Why ever not?

ANSWER.   Because it's not In Her. Deep down inside of her she's not bad, she's generous and gay. Even Dr Isaacson knows that.

QUESTION.   Who in blazes is he?

ANSWER.   Sir Meyer Isaacson, F.R.C.P., of Harley Street, London, Eng. He is Mr Brent's guiding star.

QUESTION.   I thought George Bernard Shaw was Mr Brent's guiding star?

ANSWER.   In theory, yes. In practice it seems easier for Sir Isaacson to drop everything and pop over to Cairo, Egypt.

QUESTION.   And Bella Donna tells Sir Isaacson she isn't bad inside?

ANSWER.   She does more than that. She gives him quite an earful. She pins the poor man down on the terrace and tells him the whole story in flashback.

QUESTION.   What does Sir Isaacson say?

ANSWER.   He says, rather fretfully, 'I didn't want your confidence. Why are you telling me all this?'

QUESTION.   Well, why is she?

ANSWER.   Hang it all, she's got to tell the story to someone or there wouldn't be any picture?

QUESTION.   Is there a picture?

ANSWER.   Well, there's what's known as an 'offering'.

QUESTION.   And so they live happily ever after at the British Museum?

ANSWER.   Regrettably, no. Bella Donna is unfortunately wanted by the Egyptian police for murdering Baroudi.

QUESTION.   But I thought you said murder wasn't In Her?

ANSWER.   Theoretically, no. But someone has to make a sacrifice for the Hays Code. She drops poison into his wine-glass and watches him die like a real little trouper. This Bella Donna is quite a woman. Pity she had to get crushed under ten tons of rock at the tomb of Rameses.

QUESTION.   Had she?

ANSWER.   Of course she had. Have you never heard of Nemesis?

QUESTION.   One of Mr Hays's boys?

ANSWER.   One of Mr Hays's best girls.

QUESTION.   And do you suggest that the readers of the *Observer* will be edified by this tale?

ANSWER.   I have no notion, but the film assures us categorically that the readers of the London *Times* will find this *very* interesting.

1947

Humoresque

In this long rapture of pretence
There is one moment of good sense,
When Crawford (J), a female souse,
Displays a modicum of *nous*.

On hearing Wagner's *Liebestod*
Performed the way it wasn't wrote,
She proves her musical devotion
By walking straight into the ocean.

1947

Cross My Heart

I always feel that Sonny Tufts
Is something rather large from Cruft's:
Which gives his work, in moderation,
A certain dogged fascination.

26 January 1947

In **The Romance of Rosy Ridge**, a story of the aftermath of America's Civil War, Van Johnson lends his support to the official Hollywood theory that the North was right, though the South was nicer. Introduced by a few bars on a mouth organ, Mr Johnson, as a Union soldier, vagabonds into a Southern farmstead, gives an abridged version of the standard democracy speech, hastily bundles up a Southern wife, and vagabonds out again. The film, not unpleasing, simply fugitive, has one bold merit. It holds the M.G.M. Champion Celestial Choir firmly in check for 102 minutes. The abandon, the joy, the volume of the C.C.C. boys when they are let loose in that final minute, is something that must be heard to be believed.

6 July 1947

Just in time for Easter, Herbert Wilcox and Anna Neagle have brought out **Spring in Park Lane**; a pleasant film with a pleasant name, which should almost exactly fulfil the emotional needs of most picturegoers on their first spring holiday. There is a faint echo of the early Astaire-Rogers films in this light romance, about an impoverished lordling who takes a post as footman and falls in love with his employer's niece. It is silly, but it is sunny, with a sort of artless freshness that makes old things seem new. Nicholas Phipps's script has more than its share of bright lines, and Michael Wilding, who gave a hint in *An Ideal Husband* of what he might do as a light comedian, eases his way through the story with nonchalance and charm. Altogether, the piece seems to have been made by people who are thoroughly enjoying themselves, and their pleasure is infectious.

Spring in Park Lane is the twenty-first film that Herbert Wilcox and Anna Neagle have made together, and by the very simple device of changing the names of the characters and practically nothing else in the picture, not even the postal district, it is likely to be as fantastically successful as its predecessors. The knack these Wilcoxes have of telling picture-stories that go straight to the big heart of the British public is something so calculated that it has become positively awe-inspiring. With the possible exception of *Sixty Glorious Years*, none of their films can be accounted a major work; few will be remembered for outstanding felicity of style, originality of thought, or remarkable brilliance of acting. Most of them are frank novelettes, and yet there is something in their unaffected delight in the simpler clichés of popular fiction that endears them to people not generally addicted to this form of entertainment.

The secret of their success lies in the Wilcoxes' large assumption that the world is a lovely place, where nice things always happen in the end to good and generous and loving people. This is such an acceptable formula in a world which is clearly nothing of the kind that I wonder more producers have not followed it, instead of brooding gloomily over scenes of ugliness and violence, squalor and misery and hopeless frustration. The Wilcox films are like a jolly Christmas card, embracing *every* good wish. They deal in gentle emotions, moving in pleasant places, among well-bred people. They come in two styles; the one in which the earl's granddaughter weds the youth of low degree, and the one in which the earl's grandson weds the poor little working girl. They are seldom really comfortable without a peer about the place, but even when they do mingle with the crowd, they never jostle.

The Wilcox address is always the best address, the Wilcox butler the best butler. The Wilcox man is tender, debonair and slightly sunbronzed; an upright type who will love one woman for a lifetime, and generally has to. The Wilcox girl – and this is the real heart of the secret – is not only what every young woman in the audience dreams she might be, but what every young woman in the audience feels she could be. Nature has not made Miss Anna Neagle so ravishingly beautiful, nor has practice made her so forbiddingly proficient, as to seem beyond all hopes of emulation. Watching her is like a tonic to Britain's womanhood. By minding our manners, keeping fit, thinking good thoughts, and looking resolutely on the bright side, we all, we feel, may wed an Hon. some day.

28 March 1948

The Swordsman – Clandemonium.

7 March 1948

Alfred Hitchcock is a very fat man who can tell a very good story. It is an academic point whether the story he has been telling so well for eighteen years would have been a different story had Hitchcock himself weighed a few stone less. Connoisseurs may remark that there tends to be an impulsive association between avoirdupois and the finesse of crime. The best detectives of fiction, men like Reggie Fortune and Nero Wolfe, H. M. and his alter ego, Dr Fell, are often bulky to a degree. G. K. Chesterton, who wrote of Father Brown, was no mean man. Charles Laughton, in the days when he carried more weight, was a rare one for interpreting crime. Sydney Greenstreet, of *The Maltese Falcon* and *Across the Pacific*, is not only the most sinister but probably the fattest villain who has ever appeared on the screen. There is also, of course, the Thin Man, who lent his name to one of the cinema's most famous series of crimes. Admittedly, he had no bulk at all. But he got murdered for it.

Hitchcock, who has grown from a chubby youth into a monumental man, has tried other types of story in his long career, and each time he has tried them he has conspicuously failed. His talent is to tell a story in which the security of middle-class life is savaged by fearful crime. Hitchcock himself was brought up in the security of middle-class life. He ardently seeks to preserve it in his own home. His films, Dr Freud might have explained, release a secret inhibition and embody an instinctive fear. He shows you a schoolboy taking a twopenny bus ticket for a destination at which he will never arrive. He shows you a murderer blacking his face and playing the saxophone with a troupe of nigger minstrels on the pier. Some day, he says, he will startle the picture-postcard addicts by a Technicolor shot of blood dripping on daisies in a field. The Hitchcock films stimulate by a series of shocks. They snap the associative curve of mannerliness, routine, security.

Hitchcock's new film, **Shadow of a Doubt**, is a choice one of its kind. It shows the effect on an ordinary Californian household of the visit of an uncle from New York. Uncle Charlie is charming, amusing and sociable. He is fond of them all. He brings them lots of nice presents. There are funny things about him, of course. He refuses to be photographed. He tears up father's newspaper. He shows an extraordinary aversion to the Merry Widow waltz. He avoids the two strange men who come to ask questions for some sort of Gallup poll. And it's odd the way he gets killed at last, falling off the footboard of a train. But the family, as a whole, takes Uncle Charlie's visit as an incident in the routine of going to the movies, getting books from the library, and cutting sandwiches for the Women's Club. Only his eldest niece, a nice girl nicely played by Teresa Wright, knows that she has given up her bedroom to a murderer.

There are points in *Shadow of a Doubt* which suggest that Hitchcock has been taking an intensive course of Orson Welles, unless one assumes that Orson Welles made an intensive study of Hitchcock in the first place. The overlapping dialogue, unrelated conversation carried on between several people at one time, is common to both directors. So is the tendency to shoot a scene from the ceiling, the cellars, or the plumbing. So is the presence of Joseph Cotten in the leading role.

Welles's Cotten is fine as Hitchcock's Uncle Charlie, although hardly stout enough, perhaps, for the top flight of crime. It's a pleasure in these days to meet a murderer who isn't working for the Axis, and who prefers a good square-cut emerald to the Secret Plans. His penchant for killing rich, silly women is not, perhaps, very adequately explained, but it is possible that the faces made in his own home by his own sister (Patricia Collinge) may have helped to drive him to it.

29 April 1948

The Laurence Olivier version of **Hamlet**, about which I have received enough publicity in the last few months to outweigh the fuel allotted to me by a kindly Government during the course of an entire year, has arrived on the screen at last, and proves to be a study in simplification, a handsomely illustrated, handily abridged text-book for the general.

Olivier calls his enterprise 'an Essay in "Hamlet".' Brushing aside all the theories and complexities of scholars who have argued for the last three hundred years as to what *Hamlet* really means, he states firmly at the beginning of his picture: 'This is the tragedy of a man who could not make up his mind.' The whole film is keyed to this simple schedule. Never has the dilemma of the Prince of Denmark been more practically stated. Here is a wholesome young man, born so long before Professor Freud that he has never heard of complexes, who learns from a ghost that his father has been murdered, and that his mother has married the murderer. The information so shocks and disgusts him that he forgets all about his infatuation for a young thing called Ophelia, and swears, in a fit of undergraduate enthusiasm, to revenge himself on the murderer, and keep his mother away from her new husband. In order to do this, he puts on an act of madness, which, for a time, he enjoys most thoroughly. But when the novelty of the act wears off, and he realizes that nothing more can be done by dressing up and posturing, he suffers the natural revulsion of a man who learns in cold blood that he has engaged to run a rapier through his uncle. He makes all sorts of excuses for his hesitation, doubtless picked up from first-year theology classes at Wittenberg, and is only induced to take action at last in a fit of passion when he learns that his Uncle Claudius has been practical enough to have him poisoned, and feels the chill venom running through his veins.

The Olivier *Hamlet* explains the multiple killing at Elsinore most satisfactorily to the audience, and is, in addition, an extremely handsome, tasteful, and devoted picture. It will bring an enormous amount of prestige to the British cinema, and, by its bold rejection or rearrangement of every idea, every hint, every soliloquy, that does not fit into its established order should prove a confounded nuisance to all pedagogues taking *Hamlet* as a set book for examination. Personally, I shall continue to find the play infinitely richer, a hundred times more exciting, than the picture, but if this enthusiastic little handbook will awake in the general public an interest in Shakespeare, I shall be the first to agree that it has served its turn.

The production, on a general level, is very much more mature than Olivier's *Henry V* but, in effect, less exciting. *Henry* with its deliberate pageantry, its preoccupation with lively scene and formally organized spectacle, is much the better play for screen adaptation. There is nothing in *Hamlet* to compare with the thrilling ten minutes of the French Knights' charge at Agincourt, although the final duel scene comes close to it. This passage, so often fumbled up into a brief adieu in the theatre, is unquestionably the film's high-spot. Olivier has directed it with the excitement of a man remembering his most dramatic experience. Everyone in the scene, down to the most casual spectator, is alert and aware of an event out of the ordinary. A passage which begins as a recognized court pastime quickly develops into a matter of life and death, and the whispers that cut through the silence give just the right impetus to the mounting tension. Olivier has introduced into this scene, with great effect, a device which has been little used in stage versions of *Hamlet*. The Queen, already suspicious of her husband, reaches out her hand for the poisoned cup prepared for her son, and deliberately commits suicide. This action, splendidly and grandly performed, makes the scene for the moment all Eileen Herlie's; a crowning reward for a performance that has been, throughout, the most remarkable thing in the film.

Olivier's own performance, done with bleached hair that adds no Scandinavian tincture to the piece and ages him unnecessarily, seems to me less effective than his stage work, and it is disconcerting to watch a Hamlet who might be the father of his own mother. He speaks the lines nobly, and with the caress of one who loves them, but he nullifies his own thesis by never, for a moment, leaving the impression of a man who cannot make up his mind; here, you feel rather, is an actor-producer-director who, in every circumstance, knows exactly what he wants, and gets it. Basil Sydney as the King, Felix Aylmer as Polonius, and Norman Woolland as Horatio, do good solid work in the right tradition. Jean Simmons is a nice, schoolgirl Ophelia, who can moon prettily over her first love-letters without the faintest conception of the grown-up passions that are going on around her. The film's one serious failure is the Ghost, who is introduced by a sound-device of drum beats and a singing mosquito note which I have been told was used, in a variant, in Jean-Louis Barrault's Paris version of *Hamlet*. There is nothing wrong with this introduction, but there is everything wrong with the Ghost, who manages to be both unrecognizable and inaudible. His account of the murder is illustrated by a flashback, perhaps wisely, since we can scarcely make out a word of it; his delivery being a mixture of a station announcer on the Metropolitan and a series of hearty Zulu clicks.

9 May 1948

The world has become so realistic and hard-headed these days that any critic who admits to being shocked or distressed by what he sees on the screen is in danger of being dismissed as a sentimental old fool, unable to face the facts of life and ridiculous in the eyes of the modern generation. Nevertheless, I am prepared to admit that *A Foreign Affair* shocked me profoundly and distressed me a great deal. I am not referring to the spectacle of Miss Marlene Dietrich, at an age at which such activities are not really becoming, lifting her skirts at a night-club called the Lorelei and smokily crooning about the blue angels of the Black Market; this sort of thing is an old vulgarity, too stereotyped and empty to create much of an ill-effect. What really shocks me about this Hollywood film is the attitude towards life that it reflects; the casual acceptance of irresponsibility and bad manners, of lawlessness and boorishness and mischief-making.

A Foreign Affair, I imagine, is conceived to be a comedy; a comedy about a bunch of American Congressmen and one Congresswoman who are sent to Berlin to investigate the morale of the American occupation troops. Since the subject is rather a large and tricky one even for three Paramount screenwriters to tackle, the investigation is very shortly confined to an investigation of the morale of one particular American officer, a captain who is carrying on a shabby affair with an ex-Nazi cabaret singer. So confident is his morale that in no time at all he has the Congresswoman taking off her spectacles, revealing herself as Miss Jean Arthur, slipping into a Black Market evening gown, and 'by now a little drunk', as our old friend Synopsis daintily puts it, being tossed to the ceiling by raucous GIs in a Berlin night-club. All this takes place against a background of ruined buildings and burlesque German fräulein, and I don't think I am the only member of the victorious allied nations who may find the spectacle tasteless and humiliating. Apart from the American commanding officer, who is played with a certain wry wisdom by a good actor named Millard Mitchell, the only person in this, to me, wholly foreign affair who behaves with discrimination is a former Gestapo chief, who makes his appearance very late in the picture, and arranges to be promptly shot.

29 August 1948

Fourteen years ago I wrote in this column, in a review of *Midshipman Easy*. 'I have never heard before of Mr Carol Reed, who directed this swaggering, swashbuckling, red-blooded boys' story, but I wish there were more directors like him. He has fun, and gusto, and courage, and tells a story straight from the beginning; I don't believe he has missed a single trick in his prentice film.'

I recall this notice today, not merely for the natural gratification of being able to say, 'I told you so', but as a salute to a brilliant young man who made a mark with his first picture, and has never, through a long and busy career, betrayed that initial promise. Mr Reed is one of the very few film directors in the world whom one can properly describe as an artist; not sometimes, but all the time; not only in his execution, which is remarkable, but in his way of looking at life, which is spirited; in the grace, and breadth and sensibility of his imagination. Of all his clear qualities, perhaps, humour has been the latest to develop. Some of his early bits of fun tended to be less comic than prankish. But he has it now in full measure; and humour in the true sense of *good* humour warms and quickens all his work today.

Carol Reed's new film, **The Fallen Idol**, seems to me the best thing he has ever done, because it is full of heart as well as intelligence, wisdom as well as wit, and with all the decision of its statement it manages to be curiously gentle. It is not so powerful a piece as *Odd Man Out* but some people will find it more completely satisfying, and I have no doubts at all that it was more difficult to execute, dealing, as it does, with the delicate balance of human relationships, and not with a drama outwardly imposed by plot and action. In my own mind I couple *The Fallen Idol* with that other strangely private picture, *Brief Encounter*. Both these films make a peculiar sort of intimate appeal to the spectator, whispering directly and persuasively to the individual rather than speaking to an audience as a crowd.

The Fallen Idol is based on Graham Greene's short story, 'The Basement Room', and tells how a small boy, left in charge of the butler and his wife in a big London house during his parents' absence, becomes a bewildered witness of the woman's accidental death and the man's unhappy love affair. Because the butler is his hero, the child lies valiantly to save him from a murder charge, and because he is very young and lies badly, his sheer devotion gets the innocent man deeper and deeper into trouble. It is only at the cost of the boy's painful discovery that his hero has been systematically lying to *him*, little white lies, but lots of them, that the story arrives at a more or less happy ending. 'There's lies and lies; some lies are just kindness,' the butler tells the little boy quietly; and the discussion of this argument is really the picture's theme.

The acting of this very tricky work seems to me almost perfect. Sir Ralph Richardson brings a gentleman's gentleness to the part of a gentleman's gentleman, and I don't think he has ever played a scene on the screen more moving than the one in which, in a shabby genteel Chelsea tea-shop, he is trying, under the watchful eyes of the child, to persuade the girl whom he loves not to go away and leave him. In every movement, every fumbling phrase, every guarded look, he conveys the terrible frustration of the secret meeting, and as he walks home across the square with the boy trotting gaily at his side, you can feel the agonizing weight of the limbs that drags one down after parting. Michèle Morgan gives the girl a sweetness and natural goodness that justifies the butler's devotion to her, and Sonia Dresdel plays the wife with just the right sting and savagery. Whether the remarkable performance of the small boy, Bobby Henrey, is the result of conscious art or of Mr Reed's gifted direction, it is unprofitable to try to judge, but there is no doubt that this is one of the most endearing child studies ever given in the cinema.

At every turn *The Fallen Idol* is a true picture of life as seen, heard, and interpreted through the delicate senses of an artist; true in speech, behaviour, instinct, mood and atmosphere; a very lovely heartfelt film.

3 October 1948

As a rule I cannot see much point in discussing a film in relation to the play or novel from which it has been adapted, but in the case of **Rope**, Alfred Hitchcock has deliberately, even pugnaciously, borrowed so much of stage technique that comparison seems justifiable. There cannot be many newspaper readers in this country who are not by now aware that Mr Hitchcock has discarded the orthodox method of shooting a film, with close-ups, dissolves, flash-backs, and disconnected scenes later integrated in the cutting-room, for a species of continuous action, in which the camera roves freely about a room, and records the speech and behaviour of the players in a number of long, unbroken shots. The celebrated nine-minute Hitchcock take accounts for a complete reel of film and some eleven pages of dialogue at a single go; the director having, in effect, prefabricated his film by doing his cutting on paper.

I may say at once that in the case of *Rope* the method proves highly effective. This play is essentially one that should have no time lapses; in fact, I am inclined to think that the act intervals customarily given it in the theatre are a mistake, and in producing it for the stage, I have found it a good plan to pick up the last line of each act at the beginning of the next, so as to preserve the close argument of the dialogue and sustain the mounting mood of tension.

Patrick Hamilton's *Rope* is simply an account of the last free evening in the lives of two young men who have strangled a fellow undergraduate for the danger and conceit of killing, stuffed his body into a chest, and boastfully invited his friends and relations to sup off it: a couple of nasty little sadists who are so confident they have committed the perfect crime that they give themselves away within a couple of hours of the murder. It is not at all a pleasant story, but the action is so closely knit, and the mental deterioration of the killers so swift and well studied, that it makes for wonderfully effective drama; and by keeping to the play's unity of time and place, and never allowing the characters to slip out of sight for a moment, as it were, to recover their balance, the film maintains a great deal of the quality of the original.

The point that bewilders me is why, having elected to use Mr Hamilton's structure, the producers have thrown away so much of Mr Hamilton's play. I do not complain too much that the scene has been shifted from London to New York; that the murderers have become Harvard students instead of Oxford undergraduates; that Rupert Cadell, the guest who finally breaks them down, is no longer a poet, but the boys' late 'housemaster at prep. school'. Since the film had to be made in Hollywood, it was probably less distressing to change the characters and their background than to have American actors living in some penthouse in Mayfair, and striving to get their tongues round an Oxford accent. I don't even object that Rupert's swordstick – which provides such a fine flourish in the theatre – has been exchanged for a gun, and that it is shots from this gun, and not blasts from a whistle, that finally bring the police to the scene, for the climax of the film, using these new devices, has been worked up with great skill, and manages to be tremendously rousing.

But there is one thing, apart from the rejection of a good deal of very telling stage dialogue in favour of a brand of familiar Hollywood drivel, that I cannot forgive Mr Hitchcock. It is a shocking error of judgement, as well as taste, to begin *Rope* with the murder. The author was particularly careful to avoid this blunder, and in the theatre the opening scene, in which the young men are discovered in darkness in the act of locking the chest, gains immeasurably in horror because we imagine, and never see, the victim.

Under the new Hitchcock technique, intelligent and sustained acting is a prerequisite, and, on the whole, *Rope* gets just that. The only thing that bothered me at first was that all the young men looked so much alike, owing to their splendid physiques, their beautifully tailored suits, and the tendency Technicolor has of draining the liveliness out of flesh-tints; but it was all right once I discovered that John Dall, as the first murderer, was the one in the navy pin-stripe, while James Stewart, as Rupert, had turned platinum at the temples, presumably with age.

21 November 1948

It is delightfully refreshing in these days, when it is becoming habitual to go to the pictures in order to be made thoroughly miserable, to come across an entertainment that is designed simply to entertain; and I would raise a cheer on these grounds alone for Ealing's **Passport to Pimlico**, even if it did not happen to be one of the most felicitous and funny films since the age of the René Clair comedies.

The author, T. E. B. Clarke, and the director, Henry Cornelius – I am bound to mention them together, for in a work of this kind it is imprudent to dogmatize as to where the function of one ends and the other begins – have invented a piece of educated nonsense that would reflect little discredit on the creator of *Le Million* and *A*

Nous La Liberté. Mark you, I thought for a while that they would never be able to pull the thing off, and sustain the fun of their frail notion for the whole eighty-four minutes of the picture. But I was wrong. The ball, once tossed into the air, never drops. The end comes too soon, which is something that can be said of very few films.

Passport to Pimlico is about the discovery, from a 500-year-old charter found in a bomb crater, that a certain street in Pimlico is Burgundian territory, and that all its nineteen families are technically foreigners. The implications of the fact that they are no longer subject to British law dawn slowly on the residents, and even more slowly on the best brains of Whitehall (Naunton Wayne and Basil Radford). When they do dawn, however, all hell is let loose in Pimlico, and the Burgundy deadlock becomes top priority in every Government department.

A Continental State, with its own Ministers, its own currency, its own customs, and even its own weather, springs up within a few hundred yards of Victoria Station. Ration books are torn up. Black market goods are openly cried from hawkers' barrows, licensing laws are flouted, barricades go up at street corners, and negotiatory talks on the highest level are invited from H.M. Government; while Mr Attlee and Mr Churchill hurry to No. 10 Downing Street, and Mr Wayne and Mr Radford sit up all night over their untasted cups of coffee.

So much happens in the first half of *Passport to Pimlico* that you might think, as I did, that nothing could be left for the second half. You'll be surprised, as I was, at the ramifications of Mr Clarke's invention. The acting of the countless small character parts that the plot brings together is splendid, and the only trouble is that you feel you have never really had enough of anybody. In particular, I could have done with a good deal more of Margaret Rutherford, as an abundant professor of medieval history: what a woman she is for hugging a grotesque part to her bosom, and giving it back again with warmth and generosity.

I happened to see *Passport to Pimlico* shortly after watching *Big Ben* on television, and it struck me how much Mr Clarke's humour has in common with Sir Alan Herbert's. Both men have a passion for the quiddities of law and custom; both are mellow native wits with the belief that Britain is a huge secret joke for Britons. 'We're English,' cries a resident of Pimlico, 'and it's just because we're English that we're sticking up for our right to be Burgundians.' This definition of the breed should appeal to Sir Alan Herbert, who holds that a man is comically justified in standing on his head with a tankard in his hand if he wants to, to assert his right to be British, and a beer-drinker, and free.

1 May 1949

After *Passport to Pimlico* and now **Whisky Galore**, I begin to regard Sir Michael Balcon and his associates at Ealing Studios as men with a high humanitarian purpose. Their mission is to keep people happy at the pictures, and as long as they go on making such wholly delightful entertainments as this pair, they cannot possibly fail.

Whisky Galore might be described as a film with the French genius in the British manner. Its characters are real people, doing real things under real conditions. Its scene – in this case an island in the Outer Hebrides – is so much an integral part of the texture of the film that you can almost taste the salt and feel the crunch of the sand and the spring of the turf. But the story is freaked with the sort of fancy that is half childlike and half agelessly wise: it accepts facts for what they are, and only tilts their representation, ever so slightly, towards the fantastic and the humorous. What happened on the war-rationed island of Todday when a ship carrying 50,000 cases of export whisky runs aground, tactlessly and inconsiderately, on the eve of the Sabbath; what emotions are suffered by the customs officer, the residents, the licensed victualler, and the head of the local Home Guard; what steps these people take to insure their private interests; and how the sun rides and the tide runs all the time; is described by Ealing Studios with a simplicity that is altogether disarming. I could write a column about the charms of *Whisky Galore*, and it would still do no more than peck at the edges of the picture. This is a bit of fun that I should hate to see my friends deprived of; take my tip and just enjoy it, please.

19 June 1949

Kind Hearts and Coronets is an emphatic reminder that Guinness is good for you. This delightful burlesque of Victorian melodrama takes its gusto from the fact that Alec Guinness, an actor, I need hardly remind you, of parts, plays eight of them in it without flagging. He represents the entire membership of the ducal family of d'Ascoyne, who must be eliminated before the latest upstart d'Ascoyne can inherit the coronet. He plays an admiral, a general, a banker, a vicar (easily the best imitation), a hunting duke, an amateur photographer, a masher, and even a suffragette, with the ease of a Wimbledon champion at a suburban tennis-tea, and such is his versatility that I was only sorry he didn't play, at least, every male role in the picture. In particular, I should have liked him to have had a shot at the heir presumptive, the young man from the wrong branch of the family who goes to such vigorous lengths to secure the title. In this part, Dennis Price is smooth enough – a good silk dressing-gown type – but seems pitifully outclassed every time he comes up against a Guinness. Valerie Hobson and Joan Greenwood, as the two young ladies principally involved, do pretty work – although I preferred Miss Hobson's simulation of a slight lisp to Miss Greenwood's exaggeration of a wee catarrh – and Miles Malleson is splendid as a hangman who can never again be content with hemp after using the silken rope. This British variation of *Arsenic and Old Lace*, however, remains predominantly a Guinness film, and I look forward one day to seeing Mr Guinness put on the whole affair as a one-man show. Are you listening, up there at Alexandra Palace?

26 June 1949

Dancers are getting into so many unlikely places these days, and turning their art to such diverse purposes, that it is not really surprising to find Gene Kelly appearing as D'Artagnan in the latest version of **The Three Musketeers**.

To the best of my knowledge, there have already been eight film versions of the Dumas romance, of which the two least preposterous were made in France, and the most celebrated was done by Douglas Fairbanks in the silent days of pictures. The present attempt claims to give us, for the first time, 'the full novel', which may surprise the people who got their information about the adventures of D'Artagnan, Athos, Porthos and Aramis direct from the author. For instance, I seem to remember in the novel a character named Cardinal Richelieu, an ecclesiastic of some note, who also turned up in the pages of the history books. There is no Cardinal in the film now on view at the

Mighty Empire. His place is taken by a layman known as Prime Minister Rishloo, or Reeshaloo (Mr Kelly favours the latter pronunciation), who might be any Hollywood gang boss scheming to dope the favourite or fix the governor, were it not that he does all his plotting in doublet and hose.

This Rishloo, it appears, is a chap of a single idea. He wants 'to dethrone the weakling King Louis XIII'. To this end he enlists the aid of Miss Lana Turner, whom he considers, with and slightly after himself, to be the only astute individual in France. She 'has intellect; she thinks', she also dresses seductively in *creme-de-menthe* ostrich plumes, and a parma violet number with a blue ham-frill. Miss Turner's commission is to employ her charms on the Dook of Buckingham, who has been carrying on a pale affair with the Queen of France. A nippy traveller, she crosses the Channel twice to the seat of the Bucking-hams, a rocky stronghold on the cliffs of Kent. On her first visit she removes from the Dook a couple of diamond studs, perfunctorily pressed on him by the Queen as a parting gift. On her second visit, prettily described as a 'death-dealing mission', she eliminates the Dook, a sentry, and the Queen's seamstress with a formidable bread-knife. Unhappily for Rishloo and Miss Turner, their plans are foiled by a Gascon named Dartanyon, operating from a building clearly labelled 'Musketeers Headquarters', and commuting between Paris and England even faster than Miss Turner by a series of literal leaps and bounds.

In the part of Dartanyon, Mr Kelly puts on an acrobatic display full of the sort of gymnastics that were the speciality of his predecessor, the late Mr Fairbanks. He finds it tedious to mount a horse without vaulting into the saddle from a balcony; and after a time even horseback exercise frets him, and he becomes airborne. He rarely enters a house conventionally through the door, preferring to swing down from the roof, or plunge in through the window; and there is a good deal more cut-and-run than cut-and-thrust about his duels.

Mr Kelly seems considerably more at home in these acrobatic passages, for which he wears a functional army beret, than in the scenes in which he is called upon to make love to Miss June Allyson to 'themes by Tchaikowsky'. Miss Allyson seems a little bewildered, too, by the sort of romp she has got herself into, and when she explains that she is 'just a girl who works at the Palace, and not used to being in love', we are sympathetically inclined to believe her. With the exception of Vincent Price, who plays

Prime Minister Rishloo with contemptuous ease, the cast gives singularly little support to Mr Kelly. Angela Lansbury, as the Queen, and Miss Turner, as the most intellectual woman in France, do much to explain why France was 'troubled'. Messrs Heflin, Young and Coote are no sort of help, but then they merely represent Three Musketeers.

10 July 1949

Into every artist's life there comes a moment when he is afraid; full of doubts about his work and himself, the validity of his senses and the persistence of his powers. This fear drives him to strange technical tricks, as another man might be driven to drink or drugs. If he is a good artist the fear passes, and the tricks with it, and the whole experience take a healthy place in the development of his art.

I am inclined to think that such a moment came to Carol Reed, a very good artist indeed, during the production of **The Third Man**. Mr Reed has never before elaborated his style so desperately, nor used so many tricks in the presentation of a film. The most intriguing of his tricks is a zither accompaniment, which thrums its way though the story and sends the audience away half-maddened and half-intoxicated. The most distracting is a habit of printing his scenes askew, with floors sloping at a diagonal and close-ups deliriously tilted, a device that can be used with great effect in short passages, as it was in the Marseilles sequence of *Un Carnet de Bal*, but is apt to grow tiresome with repetition.

One can see what Mr Reed is up to, of course; the creation of a nightmare atmosphere in which the most commonplace things seem unreal and menacing. *The Third Man* is a nightmare story; the experience of an ingenuous young American who goes to post-war Vienna to look up an old school-friend, finds him supposedly dead, grows curious about the manner of his death, and is gradually drawn into a horrible adventure that leaves him bereft and bewildered. Everything about the film is designed to give the sense of an unwelcome stranger in a forlorn city, and Mr Reed, like the German directors of the silent days, deliberately sweeps away every trace of normal life, every superfluous character, that might detract from this effect. His whole trick-laden film is itself a trick, and often a very brilliant one, with moments that I suspect will long be quoted as classic touches. It is imperatively a film to see, and will add to the reputation of all its players, from Joseph Cotten, Valli and Orson Welles in the leading parts to the smallest British and German character actors. Nor will it do Mr Reed anything but good so long as he gets over it quickly, treats it as a natural and transitory phase of development, and goes ahead without further fear.

4 September 1949

This has been Female Victims' Week in the West End cinemas. Appeals for indulgence have been made from the screen for no fewer than three hapless young women, who have sinned against the moral and social code through no fault of their own, we are told, but because of – because of – well, that's just the devil of it. In no case has the film made it very clear what the sin *was* because of. The suggestions given are so vague or far-fetched that it is fortunate for the defendants that they happen to be more than ordinarily attractive. Things might have been very different for three quite plain girls.

Victim number one is Lady Henrietta Flusky, played by Ingrid Bergman in **Under Capricorn**. Lady Henrietta's complaint is dipsomania and delirium tremens. The reason advanced for this distressing condition in a still young and beautiful Irish aristocrat is that something happened to her soul in the docks of Sydney, while waiting for her husband to finish his seven-year stretch as a convict. Obviously the director, Alfred Hitchcock, felt at some time during the development of this story that this vaguely-defined something was hardly enough to account for such an amazing collection of empties, for later he advances a much more practical theory: Margaret Leighton, as one of fiction's nastiest housekeepers, keeps her supplied with fulls.

I found *Under Capricorn*, in spite of some attractive colour arrangements in the interior scenes, rather embarrassing to watch, never quite knowing whether Miss Bergman were going to turn up drunk or sober. It is a lengthy, unhurried, and generally quiet picture, directed by Hitchcock with the dreamy contemplation of one embarked on a long sea voyage; and, apart from a frequent use of the tracking camera, and one brilliantly contrived shock-shot that twangs the nerves and sets the audience gasping, there is little about the treatment that overtly bears the director's signature. I can't feel that the choice of subject is a very happy one, for either Hitchcock or his actors, Joseph Cotten, Michael Wilding, Ingrid Bergman and Margaret Leighton; for to pretend that the first three are children of the green air of Ireland is as implausible as to insist that bonny Miss Leighton is a potential Mrs Danvers. It is only fair, though, to add that the film has been done with an obvious *attempt* at sincerity, and that Technicolor becomes Miss Bergman as much as it does not become Mr Wilding; who sometimes suggests to me, in colour films, a horse I used to know on our milk-round: a very kind, pale horse.

9 October 1949

The Fifties

I was still at Oxford when my mother's Sherlock Holmes series was shown on television. The only set I could find, on which to see the opening episode, was in the doctors' common room at the Radcliffe Infirmary. Reluctantly she had omitted her favourite story, *Silver Blaze*, from the series, because it seemed too difficult for a studio-based live production.

She had never wanted to write a film script, 'probably', she explains in *Thank You for Having Me*, 'because I knew too well that the original story teller of a film finds little of his work left in the final version. But television is a different thing from films. The playwriter remains the writer; his story is seldom mangled; the dialogue is more or less his own.'

A year or so earlier, David Astor, who had taken over the editorship of the *Observer*, gave her the choice of reviewing films or reviewing television. 'Somewhat to his surprise,' she recalled, 'and certainly to mine, I had elected to stay with my old companion, the cinema. Better the devil you know than the devil you don't know, was the adage that possibly affected my decision. Perhaps, too, I sensed subconsciously that a relapse into armchair viewing might accelerate the onset of old age in a woman well into her fifties.'

In 1955 I was Deputy Editor of Lady Rhondda's weekly magazine, *Time and Tide*. When I invited my mother to write something for us, she did a reminiscent article stimulated by the frequent letters she received asking how to become a film critic. 'Between the lines of almost all those letters it is possible to discern a hint of Wilfred Shadbolt talking to Jack Point about another but not wholly incompatible profession. "I have often thought a jester's calling would suit me to a hair . . . It should not be too difficult to be a good jester, seeing that thou art one." '

She had been looking, she said, through the yellowed pages of a scrapbook in which, as a girl, she pasted the programmes of every play or pantomime to which she was taken, together with the *Manchester Guardian* reviews and her own attempt at criticism.

All my views were appallingly florid and utterly lacking in moderation; for where I loved, I loved with passion, and when I hated, I hated hard. But I notice with interest that they were always independent, often in direct contradiction to the official criticism pasted up beside them. I was learning to use my own judgement, even if that judgement was often wrong.

What is more important, they gradually settled into the pattern required of all useful newspaper reviewing. I began to state facts first and give opinions second. This I am sure I learnt from a study of the *Manchester Guardian* cuttings. From them I learnt too to keep reviews in compass. I didn't count the words as I do nowadays, but subconsciously I grew to know that curtness and over-writing are both bad habits.

Sensible, characteristic, foundations for a lifetime's work. – A. L.

The shooting season opened briskly in the West End last week; the bag for two films comprising, at a rough estimate, eleven actors, thirty or forty stunt-men, and three Indians, not to mention eleven characters brought down off-screen, and a blonde slightly winged.

Although gun-play is not my favourite form of drama, I must confess to a good deal of respect for **The Gunfighter**. This very well-made film is an essay in tension and suspense, rather than a direct action study. The veteran director, Henry King, was practising this sort of thing in the days before many members of his audiences were born, and he has never quite lost his skill at it. The effect is mainly due to a firm establishment of background; in this case, the pioneer town of Cayenne, during three hours of a sunny morning.

Into the town's best saloon walks a tired man called Ringo. He is famous as 'the top gun of the West'. Three other gunmen are on his trail. He is wanted for twelve killings. Ringo, as you may guess, since he is played by Gregory Peck, is not altogether bad. Shooting so many people, even in self-defence, has made him very miserable. He intends no harm to Cayenne. He only wants to see his wife and child, who had left him eight years ago. His arrival, however, causes havoc in the town. All the little boys run out of school to gape at the celebrated bad man. They climb on to window-sills and peep under the door of the saloon. Crowds of loafers gather in the street. An out-of-town cowboy, dropping in for a quick drink, naïvely wonders why nobody is doing any work today. The housewives pause in their shopping to shake their heads and wag their tongues. The worried Marshal urges Ringo to move on. He doesn't want any trouble in Cayenne, he says.

Ringo, sitting grim and lonely in the saloon, refuses to budge until he sees his wife and child. The morning wears on. The three gunmen are getting close. The finger of sunlight moves across the saloon. We get to know, with the enhanced observation of a patient in a doctor's waiting-room, every detail of the place; the buffalo heads over the bar, the prim lithographs on the wall, the pattern of vine-leaves on the ground-glass panes. The Marshal looks anxiously at his watch. Somebody saddles Ringo's horse. The little boys in the street get quite out of hand. They know, or at least hope, that something violent is about to happen.

What we know, and they don't know, is that Ringo is going to be shot, for a man with twelve killings to his account can't possibly be allowed to survive in a certificated film. I am sometimes tempted to deplore Hollywood's exemplary code of morals, on strictly dramatic grounds. Whether the real drama of *The Gunfighter* lies in the spiritual problem of a man who has acquired a reputation for killing which he has come to loathe and regret, or in the speculation of the townsfolk as to what is going to happen to the celebrity in their midst, the knowledge that he has got to be dead in ninety minutes, or Mr Hayes and the censors won't like it, does take the edge off the film a bit. The code being what it is, the main interest of the latter half of the film lies in guessing who will shoot Ringo in the end; the three gangsters who are hunting him, the old man with the shotgun at a window across the street, or the young hooligan (splendidly played by Skip Homeier) who thinks it would be jolly to become, in his turn, the 'top gun of the West.' Under the circumstances, I can't help feeling that the director, with the help of wonderfully airy and stereoscopic camera-work, has managed his material admirably.

Colt .45, in Technicolor, has all the artistry of a picture-strip. The film is supposed to advocate the accuracy of the Colt .45, but leaves one with a fixed belief in the future of the bow and arrow. At all events, the hero, Randolph Scott, would have got nowhere in cleaning up the West, without the help of friendly Indians. His Colts admittedly account, in the end, for Zachary Scott (no relation) and a few choice friends, but an Indian merely has to utter a war-whoop, whip out an arrow, and – whango! – every time a cokernut.

Mr R Scott is a fine figure of a man, dressed in a black suit to look approximately like Hamlet, and so is Mr Z Scott, in a sprigged shirt to look approximately like wall-paper. Miss Ruth Roman, the heroine, is a spruce young lady who never looks better than when she has blasted her way out of a shed with gunpowder, or sustained a gun-shot wound between her shoulder-blades. The familiar western scene is plastered with Want Ads for coach bandits, and all the characters are so busy crossing each other that the plot resembles a Saturday each-way mixed double.

13 August 1950

The Hollywood movie-makers love to have the word 'significant' applied to their work, and this week they are fully entitled to it. In times such as these, the advent of the American war film *Sands of Iwo Jima* holds a great deal more significance than its quality as a picture warrants. This account of US Marine landings in the South Pacific, first at Tawara, later at Iwo Jima, is an odd conglomeration of studio bric-à-brac and authentic combat material, put together behind a curtain of ear-splitting clamour. It is not, in itself, a markedly distinguished film; there is nothing in the treatment to suggest that the people who made it had thought very long or very deeply about the potentialities of the cinema as a medium; but it cannot be ignored, any more safely than the cloud the size of a man's hand in the sky. It is less of a picture than a portent.

There are going to be a great many more war films like *Sands of Iwo Jima*. Hollywood has over a dozen already made or in preparation. For months to come our ears are likely to be assaulted by the din of naval gunfire, bombs, shells, tanks and flame-throwers, augmented by the music department's heaviest brass, while our eyes are savaged by the sight of death by bayonet, mine, grenade and gun, on a screen made hideous with flash and explosion.

That all these films spring from an initially humane purpose there can be no doubt. Hollywood favours a peaceful life for everybody, with liberty, prosperity and fun. When Hollywood makes war films, it does so with no deliberate intention of provoking war. But Hollywood has never been the wisest nor most sensitive of communities, and it may well be that its good intentions may lead to ill results. I admit I regard this renewed preoccupation with war with grave anxiety.

Just what is the outcome of the new series of pictures likely to be? What can it be except a further orientation of the mass mind towards war? It has been suggested that a film like *Sands of Iwo Jima* will discourage war, by making the people at home aware of its horrors, and the people abroad aware of the force of American arms. I wish I could believe in this suggestion, but

I can't. In a quarter of a century of film-going I can remember only one Hollywood war picture that might truly have proved a deterrent to war, and that was *All Quiet on the Western Front*. In all the others the horrors have been so calculatedly concealed in the heroics that they would stop a man from taking up arms, or a woman from encouraging him to do so, about as effectively as a straw could stop the flood of a broken dam. As for the effect of the show of American force abroad, I must point out that these films will not be seen in countries where such a show is presumably needed. The audience for *Sands of Iwo Jima* and the rest will be primarily composed of Americans and their allies, to whom their confidence may provide propaganda of a highly inflammatory kind.

Let us take a closer look at *Sands of Iwo Jima*. This is an officially sponsored film, containing genuine combat photographs, using Service personnel among the actors, formally dedicated to the US troops and their allies, and ostensibly recording a hard-won and dearly paid-for victory in South Pacific warfare. That is what it is meant to be. But what happens when Hollywood gets hold of it? Synopsis describes this dreadful episode as 'High adventure in the South Pacific!' Under this screaming headline it presents a picture of the sergeant in command of the expedition, captioned 'Two-Fisted Stryker will win the hearts of everyone!' Bottom page left it introduces John Wayne as Sergeant Stryker, face washed and hair neatly combed, cheek to cheek with a mild blonde whom he never even meets in the picture.

Story and screen-play would seem to justify the attitude of Synopsis. The capture of Iwo Jima, they appear to suggest, is a mere corollary to the social reclamation of Two-Fisted Stryker, who has taken to drink and bullying because his wife has left him. His rifle squad, with one exception, hates him; which is naughty of it, too, imply Synopsis, Story and Screen-play. Only in combat can these misguided souls learn life's true values, so that the sergeant dies beloved of all, even of a dimpled private who cherishes his 'God-given rights under a democratic form of government' to dislike whom he pleases. As the celestial fiddles take over from the heavenly brasses, the squad wipes away a surreptitious tear, the flag is unfurled, the firing ceases, and the private reads aloud a half-written letter from the sergeant to his son, which he undertakes to finish, having studied at two universities.

War is wonderful, Hollywood seems to suggest; almost as

wonderful as, say, psychoanalysis. And if anyone still maintains that films of this kind will discourage the peoples of the world from fighting, it might be recalled that such things as this were lately designed to keep up the morale of combatants, given priority propaganda value by all nations in the last great war.

1950

R.K.O. Radio Pictures, who control the immediate destiny of the Tarzan films, will not be affronted, I'm sure, if I give them a friendly word in season. I trust they are not going to grow self-conscious about this unique series, and spoil its beautifully artless nonsense by adding another sort of nonsense that is neither artless nor beautiful.

For the first time, in *Tarzan's Magic Fountain* I detected a faint note of sophistication in the fun, as if a grown-up, or at least an adolescent, were condescending to join in a children's game. For the first time a Tarzan film, which should always be played with intense sobriety, tended to turn into a rag at moments, and even the animals were guyed occasionally. This won't do at all. For more than a quarter of a century, these films have been among the innocent delights of the cinema. They have charmed us by their mixture of unblushing nonsense, wonderful acrobatics, animal spirits and strict morality, combined with dialogue so simple that the smallest child could follow it. Hands off the Tarzan pictures, please.

With this one reservation, I must say I enjoyed the twenty-fifth Tarzan thoroughly. The new Tarzan, Lex Barker, is said to be , in private life, a gifted artist in oils and charcoal, who 'enjoys smoking a pipe,' speaks fluent French, and 'understands' Italian and Spanish. He is not called upon to display any of these gifts in *Tarzan's Magic Fountain*, but his English vocabulary seems to be an advance on Johnny Weismuller's, and his arboreal work is impeccable. I also loudly applauded his taste in declining to guide visitors to the Blue Valley, where a rejuvenating spring turned everybody into Hollywood blondes or lithe young men in leopard-skin toques and loin-cloths.

Brenda Joyce, who plays Tarzan's mate Jane for the sixth time, has introduced marked social refinements into the part, as well as a touch of temper. Her comment on finding a couple of skeletons transfixed with arrows – 'This was as far as they got' – and her ladylike request to the villain, after a tough day hewing down undergrowth with a machete – 'Mr Trask, are you familiar with this part of the jungle?' – are among the highlights of the picture. It is noteworthy, too, that she now receives regular supplies of handkerchiefs and magazines as well as correspondence, by parachute. I longed to see her curled up in some cosy tree-top with a handkerchief enjoying the *Saturday Evening Post*.

Paid In Full is one of those works classified in the trade as 'women's pictures' and is aimed straight at the lachrymal glands, if it can be said to be aimed at anything. The dialogue is appalling ('Marriage used to be something holy.' 'I suppose it was,' is a sample), but the idea is novel, not to say startling. Two sisters, played by Lizabeth Scott and Diana Lynn, are hereditarily disposed to die in childbirth. Miss Lynn achieves a baby and miraculously survives, but Miss Scott, driving her roadster in a tantrum, inadvertently runs over the child and kills it. To her natural, straightforward mind there is only one proper course for her. Casually remarking to her brother-in-law, 'How's your Spanish?' she rushes him across the Mexican border and bears him another infant. This she bequeaths from a hospital bed to her bereaved sister and, somewhat arbitrarily adopting the pseudonym of 'Mrs Millikin', pops off to join the celestial choir.

3 January 1950

The Blue Lamp, as you have undoubtedly heard by now, is Ealing Studios' tribute to the Policeman's lot, and it is a singularly happy one. There have been half-hearted attempts in other places from time to time to 'do' something about the British bobby on the screen, but none has hit off with such exactitude and felicity his place in national life; his relations with colleagues, children, Scotland Yard, big crooks, little crooks, and ordinary law-abiding citizens. The story is concerned with a crime in Paddington, where a desperate young hooligan, caught in the act of holding up a cinema cashier, shoots the constable on the beat, and Londoners will have a wonderful time, during the chase that follows, identifying familiar landmarks; but *The Blue Lamp* is not in any real sense parochial, and speaks for the work of the police force in any British town.

The cast, which includes Jack Warner, Jimmy Hanley, Dirk

Bogarde and others, is exactly right, and T. E. B. Clarke's crisp script is a delight. There are minor faults in the picture, but so few that it would be ungrateful to dwell on them. I do not hold the leisurely pace of the earlier scenes a fault, for British audiences prefer not to have their films taken at a rush, and nobody can complain that the final chase is laggardly. All in all, a beautiful job, of which Ealing can be very proud indeed.

Le Roi is the sort of bed and board-room comedy that the French are famous for doing well, and in this case it is done delightfully. It tells, in a tone so light that it is little more than a whisper behind a hand, what happens when a Ruritanian monarch pays an official visit to Paris, at a time when his country and France are trying to negotiate a trade treaty. A programme of balls and pheasant shoots is laid on to entertain him, but while the Ministers are donning their Norfolk jackets and check caps and other costumes for 'le sport' the King is enjoying sport of a different nature with a Deputy's wife and mistress. These enlightened women, admirably played by Sophie Desmarets and Annie Ducaux, are clearly the type that every Minister should have about the house, for, with their help, the trade treaty is signed without a murmur.

Maurice Chevalier, as the King, isn't quite the agile young man we remember in *The Love Parade* but his talent is no less nimble on account of the snugger waistline. He is still the master of the amatory *nuance*, an artist with a mercurial style and perfect timing. Perhaps he ought to leave the sentimental numbers to more honeyed voices, but when he strolls through the park on his jaunty way, singing of Paree and *le printemps*, it would be a sour heart that couldn't feel, for a moment that all is right with the world.

1950

Bagdad is silly, but not in the least muddle-headed. The producers are fully aware that all the customers want to see of Bagdad is Maureen O'Hara, with a touch of leopard-skin at the throat to warm up a generous decolletage. They toss in a bit of local insurrection, and rely, for the most part, on Miss O'Hara's Irish readiness. 'If I leave, how will you keep the soldiers entertained?' she very properly observes.

26 February 1950

When an artist of the stature of Orson Welles associates himself with a film of the crudity of **Black Magic** it is hard to know whether to laugh or cry. The picture might well provoke either action, being at times a grotesque, and at others a melancholy spectacle; including one scene of humiliating burlesque at the expense of physical disability that is as vile as anything I have witnessed in a cinema. But on the whole, absurdity predominates, and one must grin if one is to bear it. Whether Mr Welles deliberately enhanced the joke by adding bad acting to bad material is between him and his own soul.

Black Magic is based, we are told, on Alexandre Dumas's 'Memoirs of a Physician', and sets out the story of Cagliostro, the man 'whose eyes streaked across Europe like a meteor.' Periodically we can see them streaking, not across Europe, of course, but the screen, and finally adjusting themselves in a cut-out head of Mr Welles, reminiscent of the star-bursts so popular in cinema advertising. This Cagliostro is a gipsy youth who is early advised by the physician Mesmer (played as well as may be by our Charles Goldner) that he has remarkable powers of hypnotism. Dr Mesmer wants him to use them for the good of mankind: Cagliostro has quite different notions.

His peculiar fancy is for revenge, on an aristocrat named the Count Dee Montaine, who hanged Cagliostro's mother. Cag. (the name springs naturally to the lips as a typical cross between opera's Cav. and Pag.) starts his vindictive career with a real stroke of luck. He finds a beautiful blonde in a coma, and learns she has got that way through being abducted by Dee Montaine, who is plotting to pass her off as Mree Antwarnette. Her resemblance to Mree (understandable, since Miss Nancy Guild chins her way forcibly through both parts) is so marked that Cag. throws himself into the conspiracy heart and soul. His idea is that by discrediting Mree, he can win the girl, ruin the Count, and make himself undisputed master of France.

But Cag. has underrated the strength of the opposition. In his flurry to escape from a clean young man named Jillbair, who loves the schizophrenic blonde, and conceives it to be his duty to report the affair to the Minister of Security, he has entirely overlooked the continued existence of Dr Mesmer. The good doctor, although unseen, has not been idle all these years. In his researches into the control of the human mind, he has worked out a trick worth two of Cag's. He has learnt all about the use of shining objects to induce hypnosis, and at the climax of the film he traps Cag. into a confession of his duplicity by dangling the Queen's diamond necklace before his eyes. Nothing is left for Cag. but flight, and in one of the great unrecorded scenes of history, he drags Mree Antwarnette to the dome of the Palais de Justice, fights a duel with Jillbair, and falls headlong to his death.

The whole of this story, it might be noted, purports to be told by Dumas Père to Dumas Fils in front of the *de luxe* section of the family library. Raymond Burr, who plays the younger Dumas, may console himself for an inconspicuous part by the reflection that he has by far the most sensible line in the picture: 'Father, it doesn't sound like you at all.'

19 March 1950

South of St Louis is a post-Civil War western, distinguished by the fact that all the good men wear bells on their spurs in contradistinction to the bad men. This determines character without benefit of acting, as well as making a jolly noise.

19 March 1950

If anybody tells you that **She Wore a Yellow Ribbon** is 'just another western', ignore him, for it is clear that he doesn't really love pictures, and is as false in his general assumption as he is faulty in the particular. This new John Ford work is a splendid example of the sort of thing the cinema has always done best; something, moreover, that only the cinema can do; a combination of effects and materials in which it is unique. Television will never be able to manage the western with such aplomb; the theatre has never been able to do so; radio can only give a blind impression; and one recalls the strained strategy that was needed to bring *The Girl of the Golden West* to the opera stage. The western demands film; the broad view and long sight, the free air and keen cutting power of film. And, by the same token, the film demands the western, for only by getting out-of-doors once in a while, and stretching muscles cramped by drawing-room drama, can it keep its health.

She Wore a Yellow Ribbon, out of *Stagecoach* by *Fort Apache*, is one of the most rousing films I have seen for years. It is also not without subtlety. At first glance, this story of a grizzled cavalry officer (John Wayne), who leads his men on a hazardous patrol within a few days of his retirement, would seem to be a straightforward affair of troopers and Indians. But all manner of odd adventures are quietly touched on as the picture unfolds. It is possible that British audiences may not catch all the allusions to the aftermath of the Civil War, and the beautiful scene in which a hard-bitten army wife sews a red flannel petticoat into a flag for the grave of a trooper who was once a Confederate general may go awry. Nevertheless, through all the thundering gallop of the action, the hard riding, the sharp shooting, the ferocious raids on outposts by shrieking Cheyenne dog-warriors, creaking wheels, bugles sounding, dogs barking, harness jingling, there is a sense of personal relationship with a long back-history. This, you feel, is really a story with roots in the nation, not just a fiction snatched out of the busy air.

John Ford and his camera-men in the past have made such lovely pictures with black-and-white photography, that *aficionados* may be disappointed to find the present film in Technicolor. But anything else would seem foolish in view of the title. *She Wore a Yellow Ribbon* is all tied up, as it were, with yellow ribbon; the troopers wear it on their uniforms; Joanne Dru, the belle of the troop, wears it in her hair; it streams proudly across the credit titles; and there is a jolly little theme-song about it, 'She wore it for her lover in the U.S. Cav-al-ree'. Even apart from the yellow ribbon, the colour, although occasionally bloodshot, is frequently significant, and gives us magnificent cloud effects over tawny rock-chimneys, distant blue ranges, milky green rivers, and lightning snaking down venomously from a jagged sky.

16 April 1950

The complaint that there isn't enough swimming in the new Tarzan series will only be made by people who take their notions of the character from Johnny Weissmuller's Tarzan, not Edgar Rice Burroughs's. The author was content to get his hero into hot water; it was the Olympic champion who plunged him so assiduously in cold. The present incumbent of the role, Lex Barker, is a pleasant-looking young man who can take his swimming as it comes, and it doesn't come at all in **Tarzan and the Slave Girl**. The new film invites Tarzan to investigate an abduction of nine young women, including his own wife,

Jane, by an ancient tribe known as the Lionians, who live in the jungle's greater metropolitan area amongst heavy tombs and temples. The film is nothing if not lively, but I couldn't help feeling that a statistician might have been a help to the Lionians. We are solemnly informed that the nine young women have been kidnapped 'to replenish the Lionian population, decimated by a mysterious malady.' On the figure provided, a bookmaker would quote the Lionian chance of survival at long odds.

10 September 1950

The moment chosen to tell the audience *All About Eve* is the one at which this singular and single-minded young woman is handed the Sarah Siddons Award for distinguished achievement in the theatre. Smiling, radiant, but prettily modest, as becomes a débutante actress who has just been voted the woman of the year, she stretches out her hand to receive the trophy. The news-cameras flash; the photograph is frozen into a 'still'; and, in what is probably the most authentic flashback in cinema history the account of Eve Harrington's spectacular rise to fame is shown through the eyes of the five people at the ceremony, two women and three men, who have most cause to know her intimately.

These are an ageing Broadway actress; her best friend, who has taken pity on a stage-struck girl and introduced her to the great star; a director; an author, and a critic. All five of them have played their parts in Eve's success, and to all five, in her shy speech of thanks, she pays becoming tribute. That is all I am going to tell you about the plot, because I intend to follow the example of the film and play fair with the audience. The great charm of *All About Eve*, apart from its wit and genuine understanding of human nature, is the story's gradual unfolding. A stranger is introduced into a close group of people, who have worked together for years in a world of their own. She has sufficient quality to make a vivid first impression on them all, but it takes them a long time to get to know her well. *All About Eve* is an intriguing case of *solvitur ambulando*, and a reviewer who would spoil its calculated development is a cad indeed.

Anne Baxter, as the subject of the inquiry, is a shrewd enough actress to keep her secrets to herself and reveal them in her own good time, and her playing has a candid innocence which makes Eve's popular triumph not incredible. George Sanders is splendid as a critic with an X-ray eye, a clever beast of whom our profession can feel justly proud and ashamed; Gary Merrill and Hugh Marlowe ring true enough as director and writer; and Celeste Holm manages to make a thoroughly nice woman seem nice, without ever making her seem silly.

When all is said and done, however, the film belongs to Bette Davis. There are few actresses on the screen today who can beat Miss Davis at her best, and she is at her flaming best in this one. As a hard-working, impulsive, nerve-ridden theatre star of forty, who looks every year of her age and knows it, she uses no false aids to persuasion, nor pretends to a youthful beauty she has lost if she ever had it. By sheer integrity of performance, by thinking deeply about the woman she is playing, by using all the technical tricks she has learnt in her long career as a public entertainer, she magnificently suggests an actress who must inevitably dominate any stage, and still, with all her tantrums, inspire loyalty and affection off it. When Miss Davis disappears from the screen, a reel or so before the end of the film, the fire seems to go out and the embers die, although they flare up again at last with a teasing little splutter.

10 December 1950

This is My Affair is concerned with two things exclusively: dresses, and the ownership of Susan Hayward. Miss Hayward, a costume designer of what is claimed to be extraordinary talent, wants to belong to herself alone. Dan Dailey, the best and apparently loudest salesman in the garment business, wants her to belong to him. George Sanders, 'dictator of New York's fashions,' has the same idea. Since Mr Dailey comes from Seventh Avenue, and Mr Sanders from England, probably Eton and Oxford, it is not very difficult to guess which of her suitors an honest American girl will settle for.

Some of the dresses are nice to look at; others are clearly introduced for Miss Hayward to tear to pieces. Since we are forced to look at an awful lot of them, it is just as well that the first should outnumber the second. There is nothing remarkable about the film, except perhaps the carefree abandon with which pearl necklaces are broken, and the curious sidelight that is cast on the ethics of cutters and salesmen. It hadn't occurred to me before that the male partners of a modest costume house would go into voluntary bankruptcy sooner than let their dress designer live in sin and make their fortunes, but I haven't moved much in wholesale circles of the garment trade.

1 March 1951

When Dana Andrews, as the battered policeman hero of *Where the Sidewalk Ends* is asked by his young lady, 'What did they hit you with?' he replies, very accurately, 'Various objects.' What with the people he hits, and the people who hit him, the film is a pretty beefy affair, not calculated to the taste of customers who shrink from the sight of the male fist contacting with the male or female jaw-bone. In a rather roundabout way the message is conveyed that a detective officer on duty ought not to wallop a hoodlum, unless he has to. This is admirable: nevertheless the glimpse that is offered of the official American necessity to wallop is rather startling. How different from the home life of our dear Metropolitan police!

The Great Caruso sounds like a recorded programme of excerpts from Operas You Have Loved; which indeed it is. If you like to nibble here and there at bits from the more popular arias, this film is a feast. Mario Lanza, a very good tenor with a voice of flexibility and range, does his best to revive the memory of a very great one, and fairly succeeds; using most of the legitimate Caruso tricks, including the Pagliacci sob. Dorothy Kirsten and Jarmila Novotna, of the Metropolitan, are gracious enough to feed him his musical cues, and the miracles of modern reproduction adjust the difference in volume.

The story that goes with these gems from Italian opera is based on a biography of her husband by Caruso's widow. As such, it must be accepted as substantially correct. We are entitled to a private opinion that the film seems gaudy and sentimental, but it is not for us to claim that Signor Caruso did not dress up as Father Christmas at a children's party; nor sing Gounod's 'Ave Maria' at a midnight Mass; nor confine his major engagements to the Metropolitan, New York; nor declare that a crowd of democrats chanting 'Happy Birthday to Yew' was 'the nicest thing that ever happened' to him. It is not for us to question that Signora Caruso, being great with child, indulged in an impromptu rendering of 'When You're in Love' during a dance with her husband, on the grounds that 'every mother ought to be able to sing a lullaby'. All we can say is that the artist remains bigger than the picture; the memory is stronger than the imitation. *The Great Caruso* according to the bills, 'is G-R-E-A-T from May 13'. I wonder if he was not just as G-R-E-A-T, if not G-R-E-A-T-E-R, before?

13 May 1951

When Walt Disney brought little Bobby Driscoll from Hollywood to appear in a version of **Treasure Island** with a British cast, we wondered what would come of the combination. There were objections, of course, that Jim Hawkins ought to have been played by an English boy, but these could hardly be sustained, in view of the fact that Stevenson dedicated his *Treasure Island* to 'an American Gentleman, in accordance with whose classic taste the following narrative has been designed': the American gentleman in question being young Lloyd Osborne, the author's future stepson.

There is no valid reason why an American boy should not play, as he did in the dreams that gave the story birth, the part of Stevenson's young hero. The problem is rather whether Master Driscoll is the right lad for the job. I am inclined to think not. He is a good child actor, with a pretty and touching line of his own. But in style, voice and appearance, he is still very much a child. He seems too small and frail to be the hero of an 'I' story in which thousands of boys have seen themselves for generations as the equal of fierce, full-grown men. Jim Hawkins was young, but Jim Hawkins was confident enough to suggest the man every boy believes himself to be. Bobby Driscoll is more inclined to suggest the tender child that every boy hopes he has outgrown, and *Treasure Island*, centred round this pale and curiously defenceless figure, seems less of a buccaneer adventure than a thoroughly well-organized party game.

It is Master Driscoll's party, and all his jolly uncles are present at it. Some of them pretend to be bad uncles; some of them good. The bad uncles roll their eyes and make hideous faces; the good uncles just dress up and look benevolent. The most hideous faces are made by Uncle Robert Newton as Long John Silver, although Uncle John Laurie, as Blind Pew, runs him a close second. Every now and then the bad uncles laugh horribly, 'He–heh–heh!' and cross their eyes somewhat. The biggest joke of the party is Uncle

Geoffrey Wilkinson, as Ben Gunn, who scampers about in long whiskers and a haphazard hearthrug. Somebody has borrowed a pot of raspberry jam from the kitchen, and smears it on people's clothes to suggest nice blood. Lots of relations have brought fireworks, and a kind aunt has even lent a parrot. The result is an absolutely super party, but not 'the world's greatest adventure story'. Walt Disney may have, as Synopsis suggests, 'much in common with Stevenson'. But not this; shiver my timbers, not *Treasure Island.*

1951

How proud we ought to be of Ealing Studios! Time and again this modest little company, housed in its small, prim building behind a neat, suburban grass-plot, has sent out films that catch, more consistently than the work of any other outfit, the spirit of contemporary, middle-class England.

Ealing not only gives us fun: it gives us folk-lore. It reflects our native way of life from a native angle. It looks at English people *Englishly,* and finds them most united when they appear to be most singular. It is, in the full sense of the word, a family company. Its films, one feels, are always made by a family, for the family. There are limits, of course, to the sort of thing this self-imposed discipline can do. It is hard to imagine an *Intolerance* or an *Open City* coming out of this doll's house of a studio. Ealing is not quite grand enough to offer pain, but it is good enough to provide an extraordinary amount of pleasure; and to go on doing so, year after year, picture after picture, argues a merit that is extremely rare.

The family at Ealing seem to be at home in any sort of British scene, from the Kent marshes to the Western Isles, but their happiest playground is London. Their London is not the visitors' London, the London of the West End, smart restaurants and shopping centres, but an older and more indigenous London: City streets, docks, inner suburbs, school crossings, faded crescents. **The Lavender Hill Mob** is one of these real London films. It is outrageous comedy, of course, but the observations of detail and character are so true, the sense of a familiar place so sharp, that few will resent the gusto with which the outrage is perpetrated.

The story is about a meek little man, trusted servant of the

Bank of England for twenty years, who suddenly decides that
it would be nice to make away with the gold bullion it is his
duty to transport. The keen brain under his bowler hat tells him
that it is absurd for a potential millionaire to go on living at the
Balmoral Hotel in Lavender Hill, on a salary of eight pounds
twelve shillings per week (less deductions). So he enlists the help
of a frustrated fellow-lodger, a grandiose and 'artistic' gentleman,
who groans under his hideous occupation of designing gewgaws
for the tourist trade. Between them they conceive a scheme for
robbing the bullion van, melting down the gold, using it to
coat paper-weights of the Eiffel Tower, and shipping them
as export goods to France. Since the job requires hands more
skilled in burglary than theirs, they ingeniously recruit two more
members of the Lavender Hill mob; utterly reliable old lags who
can produce Press cuttings of their court convictions.

This is only the beginning of a picture that goes from one
extravagance to another, including a giddy swirl down the spiral
staircase of the real Eiffel Tower, a wild game of hide-and-seek
among the crowds at the Metropolitan Police School Exhibition,
and a wonderful chase, in which all the radio police cars in London
are bidden to proceed as fast as possible, north, south, east and
west, towards a certain road junction – and, catastrophically, do
so. Nothing could be more sedate that the manner in which this
nonsense is played by the two leaders of the gang: Alec Guiness,
meek, shrewd, inconspicuous, humdrum; Stanley Holloway,
rich, massive and portentous: a combination described by the
junior members of the mob as 'as straight a pair of gentlemen
as we ever worked for'.

The picture is obviously contrived for the talents of these
matched comedians, but it is also contrived, beyond a doubt,
for the full use of the London scene, the London habit, and the
people and institutions of London. In employing these ready-
made materials, T. E. B. Clarke, who wrote the screenplay of
Hue and Cry and *Passport to Pimlico*, has again shown his quality.
Mr Clarke is the 'author' of his films in a way that many more
distinguished 'authors' are not, in the sense that he takes as large
a share in the final shaping of the picture as the director himself.
The present director, Charles Crichton, knows his little ways,
and between them, in *The Lavender Hill Mob*, they scarcely miss
a trick. Possibly more might have been made of the moment in
which the two conspirators get their first sight of the real Eiffel
Tower – a grave doffing of the hat, perhaps, a pause of silent

tribute? Otherwise I can hardly think of a single improvement
to this very happy, very native picture.

1 July 1951

Anyone who is interested in the progress – forwards, backwards
or sideways – of the composite artist known as Walt Disney
will find matter for speculation at the Odeon, where the highly
debatable cartoon of *Alice in Wonderland* is shown with a 'true-
life adventure' called *Beaver Valley*. Nobody could be in two
minds about this latter brilliant little picture. It is certainly the
best thing Disney has done for a decade, and may be the best
thing he has ever done.

The point that occurred to me while watching the programme
is this. Has a metamorphosis taken place, by which the design and
invention that were wont to animate the Disney cartoons have
been transferred, in a heightened form, to his real-life pictures?
Beaver Valley is an account of a year in the life of the wild creatures
– bird, fish and animal – who inhabit the neighbourhood of a
beaver pond. The seasons pass; a good commentator speaks a
notably good commentary, while a patient, affectionate, and
miraculously sensitive colour-camera catches details as tiny as
the chirruping shiver of a cricket, the pulsing of a frog's throat,
and the wink of an owl's eye. All this is exciting observation and
felicitous description, but the film has something more to give:
a rhythmical structure of sound and image that sets it apart from
all other nature-study pictures, with the possible exception of the
spring sequence from the French film *Farrebique*.

Beaver Valley is a little beauty; but the oddly suggestive thing
about it is that it is beautiful in much the same way as Disney's
'Silly Symphonies' used to be beautiful. It is drawn direct
from life, but composed directly for the cinema. The skill
and innocence that once went into the presentation of cartoon
animals have been applied, with a new vigour, but without the
new vulgarity, to the new sort of picture; and a sequence such
as the one in which the orchestra of night-sounds and the drama
of night-work by the river is accelerated to its microscopically
tremendous climax is superb film opera; a thing that one would
like to look at and listen to again and again.

Alice in Wonderland is a far less stimulating achievement, except
in the sense that it may drive lovers of Lewis Carroll to frenzy,

but let it be said at once that there are some delightful things in it. Nothing could be better in its kind than the drill of the pack of cards on parade; Alice's long fall down the rabbit-hole; the choreography of the flowers in the Queen's garden; and the figures taking frail shape and dissipating in the smoke from the caterpillar's hookah. The three gardeners spraying the roses red come straight out of the Tenniel drawings; so does the Rocking-Horse fly; so do Tweedledum and Tweedledee; and if the cat Dinah seems to have dwindled rather startlingly into the Black Kitten, she is at least endowed with every feline charm, and has clearly been created by one who knows just what cats are up to.

I have no doubt that people who do not know their *Alice* books – for the film is a combination of the two – will find Disney's *Alice in Wonderland* a jolly way of spending an afternoon. The trouble for the rest of us is that Disney's notion of a jolly afternoon seems to be constitutionally different from Lewis Carroll's, and he omits to invite so many of the people we should like to meet again. Where is Humpty Dumpty? Where is the White Knight? Where are the Duchess, the Pig-baby, the footmen? And where, above all, is the sense of summer peace, the comfortable, drowsy Victorian quietude, that used to brood over these magic stories?

To Disney's credit it must be said that he has used a preponderance of English voices for his speaking characters. Some of them are a little prissy, but they are at least, and properly, native. The music-track, however, is another matter, and here the hullabaloo is indescribable. Neither the new songs that have been composed for the occasion, nor their rendering, are likely to commend themselves to admirers of the late Dr Dodgson. It is true that Dr Dodgson indulged his donnish fancy freely in the creation of *Alice* just as dons of today indulge theirs in the writing of detective stories. But his imagination was fastidious, and there was always a method in his madness. One might say that, in the world of fantasy, the book and the film suggest a sharp distinction between what is don and what is not don.

We have had to wait a long time to see that flashing sword-stroke of the theatre, **Cyrano de Bergerac**, bite its way into the soft flesh of the screen, but it was worth the wait. Again and again, in the last fifteen years, this actor and that has been about to play Cyrano. Something has stopped him every time. What we may have lost in interpretation by the delay we shall never know. What we have gained is sun-clear. We have gained José Ferrer.

Mr Ferrer is an American actor of Spanish parentage, who has played Rostand's hero in the theatre in New York. Now we have the chance of seeing how he plays it for the films. This is a translated Cyrano, a performance exactly calculated for the medium in which it appears. I say without hesitation that it is one of the most superb performances I have ever watched on the motion picture screen. Other film actors might have played Cyrano as well in their own particular ways. None, I believe, could have played it better.

Cyrano, as you will remember, was a romantic grotesque with a preposterous nose. In order to carry off that nose with glory on the screen, losing not a whit of dignity nor pride; in order to be moving without ever descending to pathos, quixotic without braggadocio, tender without weakness, and comic without absurdity, it is necessary for an actor both to be filled with passion for his character, and to know all the tricks of his trade. That is the sort of actor that Mr Ferrer is. In the understanding of Cyrano he uses both heart and mind. In the performance of the part he uses all his members: hands, feet, body, eyes, lips, brow, even the delicate skin of cheek and eyelid, and the fine nerves under the skin. He has a splendid sense of humour, and a glowing voice. His timing of line and pause would make any broadcaster green with envy.

As a production *Cyrano de Bergerac* is vigorous, respectful, full of lively movement, and pictorially well-composed. It uses the Brian Hooker translation favoured by the Old Vic, and, although it cuts one or two of the best speeches, is largely loyal to the text. The fencing is fine. The Naafi scenes at the front are no more foolish than those we are accustomed to see. The film's chief drawback is that we are frustrated, by the exigencies of the medium, in watching Mr Ferrer all the time he is on-stage. The camera keeps cutting away to other characters, whose notion of playing makes our interest in them dim. It is bad enough that Mala Powers's Roxane, for instance, should be responsible for the death of two good men. That she should also deprive us of a moment of Mr Ferrer's acting is insupportable.

30 September 1951

The Lady Pays Off is the sort of thing that people who shun the
cinema imagine all films to be. In it Miss Linda Darnell appears as
an oddly dressy schoolmarm who is so startled at finding herself
on the cover of *Time* as the Teacher of the Year that she rushes
off to Reno, where she proceeds to get gloriously tipsy and runs
into debt to a gambler to the tune of 7,000 dollars. This naturally
qualifies her for a post as governess to the gambler's daughter, a
child who is off her feed because she hasn't got a mother. The
film eventually rectifies this state of affairs, since the gambler
is 'all man' even if he does affect fancy shirtings covered with
large clumps of narcissus. *The Lady Pays Off* ends with the filial
blessing, 'I hereby pronounce you my mummy and daddy,' in
what *Time* may well describe, with the support of this corner of
the *Observer*, as the Pay-Off Line of the Year.

14 September 1951

The Japanese film ***Rashomon*** won the Grand International Prize
at last year's Venice Festival. On seeing it at the Rialto (ours, not
theirs) some of us may be inclined to wonder on what grounds the
judges based their decision. Did they award the first prize to this
savage, strange and startling film because they honestly believed
it to be the best entry in the Festival, or because they dared not
be sure that it wasn't? It may seem to us that in a matter of this
sort, where a work is utterly outside our round of experience,
true judgment is imperilled by lack of standards of comparison.
Few Westerners, we might suppose, are qualified to say whether
the extraordinary form of acting employed in *Rashomon* is really
good of its kind, or simply vivid and impressive to us because
the style is unfamiliar. Dare one declare with any certainty that
this performance is *better* than the performance of some European
or American picture? Can we be sure, really sure, that we are
looking at a work of genuine quality, not admiring something
as meretricious as a gewgaw from Birmingham? Does *Rashomon*
satisfy the more discerning tastes of its native country, or are the
best Japanese critics, on learning of our enthusiasm, laughing up
their kimono sleeves?

   That the film is striking there is no doubt. The whole thing
comes upon a Westerner as a blinding surprise. Contrary to any
inherited belief that Japanese drama would be formal, elegant
and leisurely, and that Japanese performers would perform

inscrutably, *Rashomon* is a film of astonishing vehemence: rapid, violent, sudden, brutal, and about as restful as a race with the hot breath of a wolf behind one's shoulder. It takes the form of a story within a story, in a framework, as wiry as a Jo Mielziner theatre set, of a ruined city gate twelve hundred years ago.

Three men are sheltering from the relentless rain: a wood-cutter, a coarse and jocular servant, and a Buddhist priest. Famine and civil war have reduced them to a level, so that the servant is able to drag from his companions the story they don't want to tell. Three days earlier a horrible thing has happened. A nobleman and his bride have been attacked by a bandit while travelling through the forest. The woman has been raped before her husband's eyes; the husband's dead body has later been discovered. Who stabbed him? The bandit and the woman have different tales to tell. The dead man, speaking through the mouth of a woman medium, has a third. The servant in the outer story maliciously suggests a fourth. We never learn who killed the nobleman. Nor do the shelterers in the gate. Their argument is ended by the discovery of an abandoned baby, and in the attitude of the three men towards it the film would seem to repeat, develop and resolve its earlier theme.

I say 'would seem' because I honestly don't know. I can't pretend to understand *Rashomon*. I know it is a film of unusual shock and impact; wildly acrobatic; speeded up with camera tricks that whirl it past us like a flying saucer; feverish with animal grunts, pants, screams, sobs and gibbers, and wild with maniacal laughter; the fever intensified by a relentlessly percussive score: something combining the candour of the barnyard with a hint of spirituality. I have never seen anything like it before, and so feel unqualified to say how good it is. I can only assure you that it is memorable.

16 March 1952

The code of the Western has always been a simple one: all the bad people die violent deaths, and all the good people (save possibly some minor character whose taking-off provides the hero with an excuse for a manly tear) live and prosper. So when I tell you that the casualty rate of **Rancho Notorious** is practically one hundred per cent, you will appreciate that this is not a namby-pamby picture. I say 'practically', because one or two auxiliary characters, such as sheriff's men and porch loungers, presumably survive, but all the people with sizeable parts, including Marlene Dietrich, Arthur Kennedy and Mel Ferrer, the stars, are eliminated or about to be eliminated by the end of this luridly red-blooded melodrama.

Rancho Notorious makes no bones about warning us what we are in for. Behind the credit titles a boding baritone voice, singing to a guitar, bids us listen to a tale of 'hatred, murder and revenge', and he certainly does not exaggerate. Within a few minutes a girl has been assaulted and murdered by a bandit, and her lover, a cowboy, is riding off alone to find and kill the killer. The cowboy does not know the killer's identity, and the only clue to his whereabouts is the name of a mysterious place called Chuck-a-Luck, whispered by a dying confederate, and the name of a woman called Altar Keane, muttered by a stranger who is due to be bumped off shortly.

Now where and what is Chuck-a-Luck?

Nobody knows, and the dead won't tell observes the singing compère. Fortunately the film is not so reticent. Chuck-a-Luck is reached after a series of properly violent adventures, and proves to be a hidden ranch near the Mexican border, where the elusive Altar Keane (once a saloon singer and a 'glory girl') runs what amounts to a luxury hotel for criminals; no questions asked, unlimited bedroom accommodation, all modern conveniences (for 1870), riding, rough shooting, indoor games, and a good cuisine. One of Miss Keane's guests, the cowboy knows, is the quarry he is seeking; or possibly it is the debonair gambler, Frenchy, Miss Keane's keeper? The rest of the film is occupied with the business of identification and revenge, which ends, since all the characters have earned the death penalty according to the Hollywood code of morals, with a general massacre of almost Elizabethan magnitude.

Lurid is the word for *Rancho Notorious*. But curiously enough, it left me – and you know how much I hate violence – feeling not in the least depressed, but exhilarated. I have been wondering a good deal about this unexpected effect, and have come to the conclusion that it springs from the fact that the film makes no attempt to be realistic. Everything about it is stylized, slightly remote, and composed with cool calculation.

The sung commentary bears a strong resemblance to the same device used in the war-film *A Walk in the Sun*, but it succeeds better, because it is a deliberate artifice borrowed from a place and a period. It belongs to the school of 'Frankie and Johnny'. It is a conceit, admittedly, but a conceit conceptively used. Fritz Lang's direction seems to me the most successful piece of work he has done for many years. Always a fastidious director, he has not disdained to be fastidious here in his pursuit of the lurid, and nothing could be better than his bold use of the few remaining crudities of Technicolor, the close-up detail of faces that are not quite living faces: masks, rather; hiding, as is proper to the mystery of the story, the character behind them. I like the fine pace at which he spanks the tale along. I like his economic use of flashbacks. I like his decision to play a bloody melodrama like a bloody melodrama, without conceding an inch to the people who ask, on the one hand, for documentary treatment, and, on the other, for sweetness and light. In short, I like *Rancho Notorious* for being exactly what it sets out to be.

13 April 1952

It is an established fact that certain persons are allergic to the charms of Irish humour, just as others are allergic to cats, strawberries, or the scent of antic hay. To such sufferers **The Quiet Man** will be agony, for director John Ford, who was born in Portland, Maine, but has always had a soft spot for the brogue, has here been antic about Ould Oireland for more than a couple of hours.

The quiet man is an American boxer, who has accidentally killed his partner in a fight, and comes back to Innisfree, hag-ridden, to find peace in the whitewashed cottage where he was born. The manoeuvre proves to be of small avail, since Innisfree becomes a centre of turbulence from the moment he arrives. Everybody, he finds, is busy fighting somebody. His deliberate non-belligerency makes him seem peculiar. He has the greatest trouble in persuading his childhood sweetheart to marry him; and having achieved the ceremony finds he has gained nothing, since the lady refuses to cohabit until he has drubbed the bullying brother who is holding back her dowry. In the end the quiet man is forced to fight for his wife, in a riotous free-for-all that lasts for a whole afternoon (with pauses for refreshment).

The Quiet Man is conceived as a mixture of stage Irish comedy and robust Western cinema. Both conventions are strongly represented, with Barry Fitzgerald, as a marriage broker who is also the local bookie, taking care of the one aspect, John Wayne, as the quiet man, of the other. The small parts are exuberantly filled, and Maureen O'Hara and Victor Maclaglen, although distinctly outclassed, are bent with some skill into the director's pattern. The running fight is fine, so is a steeple-chase across the sand-dunes. Most of the film was shot in summer Ireland, and you can always console yourself with green fields, soft skies, and ox-eye daisies, when the Hollywood blarney turns too roguey-pogey and the couple's bedding problems prove a bore.

8 June 1952

It can be no exaggeration to say that those of us who have spent our lives west of Suez have never seen anything like the Indian film **Aan** even in our wildest dreams. The rare films that came to England from India in the silent days in no way prepared us for this fantastic irruption of melodrama, sound and colour. *Aan* is utterly preposterous, enormously long (it was originally a whole hour longer), violently noisy, febrile, lurid, acrobatic, voluptuous and inclined towards sadism, but it possesses in abundance the first quality of a moving picture – movement. It is impossible to convey its full effect on paper; but you may get a rough idea of it by imagining a composite of *Robin Hood*, *The Arabian Nights*, *Il Trovatore*, *The Taming of the Shrew*, any Soviet picture, *Quo Vadis*, Douglas Fairbanks Senior, Bengal lights, the Lilian Harvey musicals, the acid colours of the latest billposting, and *The Perils of Pauline*.

The title, I am told, means 'Pride' or 'Dignity', and the intention of the film, apart from its obvious purpose of entertainment, would seem to be a comparison of the simple pride of the people with the haughtiness of the ruling classes. *Aan* is described as 'a folktale of love and greed, of cruelty and passion, of murder and vengeance, of bravery and sacrifice.' The story is set in 'one of the princely States of India in the past' – but not so very far in the past, since the villain conducts several of his machinations from a streamlined maroon Cadillac. The cast is huge, but the protagonists are few and neatly balanced. On the one hand, we have the peasant, Jai, a hero equally handy with a sword or ploughshare, and the peasant girl, Mangana, who is in love with him; on the other hand, a lascivious Prince, and his sister, an imperious Princess. Operating between them is the King, a good old man who takes the fancy to sham dead, put on a false beard, and go about like Haroun-al-Raschid discovering what's what, finally abdicating in favour of the People. The plot has countless ramifications, but the gist of it is that the Prince practises his evil designs on Mangana, in return for which Jai sets out to break the haughty spirit of the Princess.

It would be impossible to enumerate the spectacular and melodramatic attributes of *Aan*, but at random I can recall a royal tournament, a pitched battle, a dream sequence, the Festival of Colours, an illuminated swimming pool, a dungeon flanked by seduction room and den of lions, suicide, murder by sharp and blunt instrument, a rodeo, lots of attractive song and dance, wedding, funeral pyre, and a terrific finale in which a minion with a pocket saw hacks off the lock of a prison just in time to save the People from destruction by dynamite; what time the fuses are burning, the Princess roasting at the stake, and the hero and villain hacking at each other in mortal combat. Whew!

20 July 1952

In considering Charlie Chaplin's film **Limelight** one must be exceedingly careful not to let judgment be coloured by old admiration for the greatest individual artist of the cinema, by courtesy to a welcome visitor who has shown himself courteous and friendly to the people of this country, or by a sturdy British sense of what Shaw's Doolittle would call 'fairity' to a public man who is going through a tough time.

Limelight must be judged on its own merits, irrespective of our attitude towards its maker. The task becomes the more difficult, in that Chaplin appears to have put more of himself into *Limelight* than into any previous picture. Or perhaps it would be clearer to say, more of Mr Chaplin and far less of Charlie. Like all great clowns, Charlie Chaplin has always been a *doppelganger*. There is Charlot himself, and there is the creator of Charlot. For nearly forty years the little tramp with the cane and boots and bowler hat has been, in the public eye, the predominating figure. Now, at long last, the other Chaplin – the one who, from the background, has fostered and sustained and disciplined the tramp, the one who longs to play Hamlet – *he* has come forward. Although, on the surface, *Limelight* doesn't differ much from the tradition of *City Lights* in its account of the tender relationship between an elderly, broken-down music-hall comedian and the young, broken-up ballerina whom he saves from suicide and deliberately drives towards hope and triumph; it seems radically a story devised, and a situation created, to allow Mr Chaplin to discourse on art, beauty, comedy, popularity, show business, the life-force and himself.

The result, to my taste, is not altogether happy, and even occasionally embarrassing. The art of Charlie Chaplin has always been to say a lot without words, or with a bare minimum of words. In *Limelight* he says less than usual with a lot of words. Between the opening scene, with the Great Calvero drunk, and the closing scene, with the Great Calvero dead, this past-master of dumb-show seems reluctant to give up talking. In a cultured voice of comparatively small range Mr Chaplin delivers flowers of platitude which Charlie, the fastidious pantomimist, would have sniffed at delicately and tossed away.

Should one see *Limelight*? Of course one should. Imperfect though it is, and uncomfortable at times, it remains a film of character; the character of something offered generously and after full consideration from one man's mind and heart. There are lovely things in it, fine things and funny things: the freshness of Claire Bloom, the stirring effect of a drama seen from the flies, the humour of moments when Charlie the tramp edges out Calvero the Great Comedian; moments when there comes a shrug, a shuffle, or a primming of the clown's mouth behind the trick moustache, and all is right again.

But there are not nearly enough of these moments. It is difficult to put one's finger on the underlying fault in *Limelight*. Too much talk, certainly; a hint of strain, of forcing, in the set comedy numbers; most of all, perhaps, self-pity. For the first time in *Limelight* Chaplin permits himself to wear his motley as mourning for the clown he has created. His heavily made-up eyes, in close-up, stare blindly at the audience. They are not looking at *us*, we feel, but are turned inwards to some unhappy vision. In another moment we expect to hear the Pagliacci sob. We are spared that, as it happens, but there is an uneasy moment when Chaplin kneels and prays behind a flat, in the middle of an Empire ballet. For all its brave words about courage and the life-force and the beauty of fighting for happiness, the film has a sense of thin blood, parting and renunciation. The fire still glows, but now it seems the fire of winter: as though the old Charlie had tuned his back for the last time on the people who laughed with him, and, in a gentle mockery of the Chaplin fade-out, softly and silently faded away.

19 October 1952

'Is it the same as the book?' is one of the first questions likely to be asked about the film Noel Langley, with tremendous daring, has adapted and directed from **The Pickwick Papers**. The answer must come promptly, 'No, it's not.' Nor is it intended to be. You can't transpose a book of Pickwick's magnitude just like that, from nearly a thousand pages of close print to less that two hours of screen running-time.

Something is bound to be lost, and anything lost from Dickens is certain to be missed. The book is crowded with characters, large and small. There is no room in the film to house them all. The cast-list contains the names of forty-seven characters, but inevitably some of the names we look for (Bob Sawyer, for instance) are not there. The book is also rambling and episodic, and the plot without much form; a style which has never been unacceptable to the English reading-public, who don't ask for shapeliness in their favourite authors, but is less satisfactory on the screen. Mr Langley has made a bold attempt to give the picture form, by simplifying the action into a contest between Pickwick, Winkle, Tupman and Snodgrass, the four gullible representatives of the Pickwick Club, and the arch-guller, Jingle.

That this deliberately dramatic arrangement, which sturdy Dickensians may understandably deplore, really *works* on the screen, is largely due to Nigel Patrick's bang-on, irrepressible performance of Jingle, who would need at least four good men to hold him down. Clear, crisp, gay, fastidious, a vagabond actor to the gloved finger-tips, he lets the book's lines go as though they were bubbling fresh from a strong, natural spring. His may not be the precise Jingle of The Pickwick Papers, but it is the very dickens of a character.

And that, I think, represents the prime quality of Mr Langley's Pickwick Papers. The film is not the same as the book in detail, but in spite of all the cuts and shifts in emphasis, remains not unlike the book in spirit. Less polished, perhaps, less distinguished for passages of pure cinema than most of the early Dickens films (there are no shots in it, for instance, to equal the opening scenes of Great Expectations and Oliver Twist), it does catch something of what Chesterton called the 'godlike horseplay' of *Pickwick*; it does manage to suggest the huge, warm-hearted vulgarity of an author who failed to draw live people only when they were life-size; a literary impresario whose passion lay in producing crowds, and whose favourite flower was the common red geranium.

It is clear that the casting of *The Pickwick Papers* has been done in no casual way. It was a shrewd stroke to give the thunder of Sergeant Buzfuz to Donald Wolfit, to commit the charge of Miss Tomkins' Seminary to Hermione Gingold (straight out of Phiz by way of Ronald Searle), and to entrust Joyce Grenfell, triumphantly tridented, with the conduct of one of Mrs Leo Hunter's literary breakfasts.

James Hayter's Pickwick seems to me just right. It gives no suggestion, at any time, of an actor 'interpreting' a celebrated part; but comes straight out to shake us by the hand; a dear old boy, the sort of simple, friendly, welcome soul who, in the double sense of the phrase, will eternally be taken in. Young Harry Fowler catches the gaiety and sharpness, if not quite the wisdom, of Sam Weller. (His split-second timing is something for pantomime and revue producers to note. This smart lad has prospects.) James Donald, as Winkle, has been given far more than the part warrants of the plot; but he does what he has to do with this shy, ingenuous, helpless sportsman so charmingly and comically that few will accuse him of having pulled his tricks, less out of Dickens, than out of stage experience with *You Never Can Tell*, *The Heiress* and *Captain Carvallo*.

Perhaps this *Pickwick Papers* makes a mistake in working so realistically on the Fleet Prison scenes. What is read is one thing, what is seen another. I am quite aware that these incidents are essential to the plot. I appreciate that at this point, Dickens's story changes shape. It isn't so much that Pickwick, with his experience of the debtors' prison, turns into a different sort of man, as that *The Pickwick Papers* turns into a different sort of book. This change, in any truthful translation, must be shown. But I can't help feeling that Mr Langley might have been better advised to press less heavily on his prison scenes, to *suggest* their impact on Mr Pickwick, rather than note so exactly every cough, and wail, and groan. Ruthless though it may seem to say so, these are not the things about *Pickwick* that we want to remember now. The film is at its best when it sticks to jolly music, genial acting, the comradeship and adventures of the road, and a roaring fire and mug of mulled ale at the end of the journey.

16 November 1952

It is a great piece of good fortune, on the Sunday before Christmas, at the threshold of the season of good will (though if good will were treated rather less as a seasonal commodity, and spread over 365 days in the year instead of lumped into two or three at the end of December, it would be a better world for all of us); it is a real stroke of good fortune that this column this week should have the pleasant charge of discussing **Hans Christian Anderson**. For, contrary to the general belief that critics are never so happy as when they are tearing someone's work to pieces, the satisfaction of being able to praise something warmly is one of the greatest that we have.

I had been ill for ten days before I went to see *Hans Christian Anderson*. It was my first day back at work, and a bitter cold one. I admit that when the film began my mind was still dwelling lovingly on the thought of bed and a hot-water bottle. But in less than five minutes the pictures on the screen and the music on the sound-track had begun to hold me quite enchanted. I found it such a charming entertainment, full of happiness and pathos, expert in interpretation yet swinging along with a gay holiday spirit that, when it was all over, I wanted to sit still for a minute and think about it, and then go away and sing its praises. And here I am, singing its praises still.

Samuel Goldwyn's film, it must be plainly understood, is not primarily a children's entertainment. Its niceties, which include a good deal of brilliant ballet from Roland Petit and his *prima ballerina*, Renée Jeanmaire, are addressed to adults and adolescents rather than to the junior spectator; its numbers, by Frank Loesser, who did the music for *Guys and Dolls*, are not schoolroom tunes by any means, and although catchy, sometimes (as in the Copenhagen market scene, with their street cries) get near to the complex operatic structure of something like Charpentier's *Louise*. The film has a 'U' certificate, and I should hesitate to say that children won't love it. But it would be misleading to suggest that Mr Goldwyn has bunched a number of fairy-tales on the screen with an eye towards the Christmas market of *Peter Pan*, *Where the Rainbow Ends* and the perennial pantomimes. It would also be misleading to suggest that the biographical background of this picture is anything more solid than the take-off needed for a flight of fancy. 'Once upon a time,' the film begins, 'there lived in Denmark a great story-teller named Hans Christian Andersen. This is not the story of his life, but a fairy-tale about the great spinner of fairy-tales.'

What you will see at the Carlton is a piece of make-believe about a dreamy young cobbler who gets into such trouble in his native village for distracting the children's minds with songs and fairy-tales that he goes off to Copenhagen to seek his fortune. In the busy life of the capital city he falls in love with a ballerina, for whom he writes the 'book' of 'The Little Mermaid'; and while vainly waiting for her favours, strikes off for a couple of children 'The Ugly Duckling' and 'Thumbelina'. This done, and the ballet performed without any proper recognition to the author, Hans Andersen goes back again, with his cobbler's tools and his fairy-tales, to his village audience, who join in singing all his favourite songs in one glorious reprise.

Jeanmaire's dancing is superb; the colour arrangement is one of the most delicate we have seen in a picture yet; the tunes flow; the children with solo parts have been selected with wonderful tact; but to me the real miracle of *Hans Christian Andersen* is Danny Kaye. I had not imagined that it was in his power to play a part so gently; to resist every temptation to exaggerate voice or gesture; to scale his performance tenderly to a young audience. Probably it is the child, as much as Mr Kaye, who is responsible for the extraordinary pathos of the 'Ugly Duckling' number, but the man makes no mistakes in a part that, with its seemingly amateur simplicity, is about as trappy for a professional entertainer as a part can be.

21 December 1952

There should have been no particular reason for a film as indifferently realized as **Cosh Boy** to merit more than a passing mention, with perhaps a note of wonder that Hermione Gingold, Hermione Baddeley and Betty Ann Davies should have submitted themselves to taking comparatively small parts in such a sketchily written and undistinguished picture. *Cosh Boy* is a record of the activities, and eventual arrest of a lecherous young coxcomb with little education and fewer principles and guts, who organizes a gang of juvenile delinquents in the Hammersmith area of London, carefully passing the cosh to a junior at the crucial moment.

No one could expect a story like this to be exactly pleasant; but there is something about this film which goes beyond the sordid nature of the subject, and leaves a peculiarly distasteful impression. Whether by design or accident, there is a feeling about the piece that this sort of behaviour is not a deadly public menace, but a half-humorous escapade of youth; an extravagance to be tolerated, if not quite condoned, like the adventures in a 'comic'. Several members of the audience at the first performance were apparently under this impression. They giggled happily at every piece of violence, relished the seduction scene, thoroughly enjoyed the hero's progress from a cosh to a razor to a gun, and laughed fit to split themselves when his stepfather finally gave him a thorough belting.

I find this horrible. Serious sociological problems are quite proper subjects for the screen, so long as they are treated as serious problems, and not as entertainment. Picturegoers of long habit cannot fail to have noticed with alarm a slow, sure change that is creeping over the screen, reflecting a similar change in public attitude; a tendency in almost every country to treat abnormality as the normal thing, to accept violence as a fact of life which, since it cannot be escaped, may legitimately be applauded.

Mr Gordon Mirams, Chief Government Censor and Registrar of films in New Zealand, recently claimed that less than one-sixth of English-speaking films are free from any display of crime and violence, and at least one-half of all features contain at least one murder. Commenting on this statement, Dr Geoffrey Wagner, of New York, writes:

> Surely something more should be done to limit first not only the increase in acts of violence on the screen, but the type and length of violence indulged in. The metronomic socks on the jaw, the slugs in the stomach . . . all these have annually to be made more titillating and prolonged to whip up the jaded appetites of the modern movie-goer. Fights in films are now carefully worked out and artistically staged, from the kick in the kidney to the final rabbit-chop or punch over a balcony.

He then quotes beatings-up in two recent films, which he describes as showing 'a balletic design which was obviously the work of someone behind the scenes who had brooded endlessly on this subject'.

This is not a state of things that should leave any thinking person in complacent mood. Appetite grows by what it feeds on, and a film exhibitor today is not without justification in claiming that he gives his customers violence, because violence is what they seem to ask for. But the longer-sighted will appreciate that it is false kindness, to put it mildly, to treat the problem of cosh boys or any other gangsters with misguided sentiment or indolent thinking. And when, as in the present film, there is a covert implication, however accidental, that boys will be boys, and kids are always up to something, the matter ceases to be one of private opinion and becomes a case for public concern.

8 February 1953

It seems only fair to Walt Disney to remember that his **Peter Pan** is primarily intended for people unfamiliar with the Barrie play. To them, perhaps, this comic-strip interpretation will be a pleasure. To those of us who have grown up with *Peter Pan*, taken our children to see it, and hold it in affection, the film can seem only a painful travesty.

This is not our *Peter Pan*. Gone is the cosy feeling of the Darling home; the absurd Eliza, who slaps the scene into magic with her harlequin's wand, the doodledoo, the frisky plank, the miserable Starkey, the awfully big adventure, the house in the trees, the Crook score, and the spirit that enables Peter to challenge Hook, without affectation, with the cry that he's youth, he's joy, he's a little bird just out of its nest. What remains is 'a new achievement in cartoon entertainment', cute, raucous, skilfully animated; with fascinating flying sequences and a well-observed child-study (Michael); about an alleged London family who get mixed up with pirates, Indians, and a gang of Dead End kids led by a juvenile delinquent named Peter. Quite the nicest thing about Disney's picture is the thought that the play is likely to survive it. 'With the spring comes Wendy', wrote Barrie. With each Christmas, mercifully, comes *Peter Pan*.

19 April 1953

NOTE: There used to be a new production of *Peter Pan* in London every Christmas, as a rival to pantomime, which is why so many actresses earned their wings in the part. – A.L.

Western films, although a delight to many, are, as a rule, conspicuously artless. They yield their last secrets at first sight, as simply as they distinguish the bad men from the good men by the colour of their shirts. There are not many westerns one could see again and again, and each time see a new subtlety of effect, a fresh distinction. *Stagecoach* was one of the rare few. So was the first version of *The Virginian*, *The Gunfighter*, *High Noon*, and a handful of others. To the best of my belief, **Shane** belongs to this select company.

George Stevens's impressive picture tells the story of a farming family – father, mother and nine-year-old son – on the borders of Wyoming, who are threatened by a professional gunfighter, hired by cattlemen greedy for their land, and saved by the transit of a mysterious stranger.

Shane, who rides out of the blue in the opening scene and rides off again as quietly when his work is done, is a hero of no common order. A figure without other than his single five-letter name, he is a champion deliberately presented as the instrument of destiny. He can draw a gun faster than the worst when occasion demands, but he is strong and handy, too, in a tussle with the soil. To understand him, and his place in the story, we must recognize the almost mystical attitude of the Americans towards the ritual of opening up the west. It is Shane's commission, whether as farmer or gunman, to help those who are taking pains to develop the new lands. Much as Hercules once passed through Thebes, Shane passes through Wyoming; righting wrongs, leaving his friends at last to their productive labours, because there is more work for him beyond the hills. In another twenty years, we fancy, the community he helped to build will be known as Shanetown, but only one small boy, grown to manhood, may cherish a true image of its founder.

It is clear that a highly sophisticated and intelligent mind has gone to work on *Shane*. The experience of thirty years of westerns is here, with all the old tricks self-consciously heightened. There are moments when the self-consciousness perhaps gets the better of the picture, but wonderfully few.

Scene after scene catches with the most telling detail the feeling of life in those frontier homesteads; the thud of an axe against a stubborn tree-stump; preparations for a Fourth of July party; a group of little girls gravely watching the behaviour of a sow with her sucklings; a wide-eyed little boy abstractedly licking a stick of rock while watching a bloody fist-fight.

There are also numerous strokes of strong dramatic invention;: a quarrel intensified by an uproar of barking dogs, neighing horses and stampeding cattle; the impulse which makes a child turn away and pat a young calf in his embarrassment during a funeral; the single repeated drumbeat which brings up the climax; the echo that repeats the boy's unavailing calls for Shane as he rides away into the mountains.

The performances, by Alan Ladd as Shane, Van Heflin and Jean Arthur as the parents, and Brandon de Wilde as the boy who idolizes the stranger, give the unusual sense of a ripening association. No character, however small, fails to leave a true mark on the picture. The scenery is glorious, and there can be little doubt that these views of the wide-open spaces gain in effect by the use of the new wide screen.

6 September 1953

At the Odeon, Marble Arch, you can see a 3-D film called *Inferno*.

I must admit to considerable difficulty in regarding these stereoscopic pictures as other than freaks, made to astonish and startle rather than engage the mind. I find it hard to concentrate upon a scene in which an arm, apparently capable of infinite extension, reaches out from the screen to the back rows of the circle, and a series of what look like monstrous cut-outs appear to rotate slowly against a painted distance. I strongly resent having objects hurled at me by strange acting persons (an incivility I should not brook even from my closest acquaintance), and I dislike both the feeling and the faint, quaint smell of polaroid glasses, in spite of repeated assurances from the management that they are decontaminated before issue.

So when I tell you that, after some slight initial confusion due to the director's whim in mixing up the plot with the credit titles, I liked *Inferno* almost as much as if it had been a 2-D picture, you will appreciate that it is something out of the ordinary. Its chief merit is a strong and simple story, in which an injured man, presumably soft and unable to look after himself, is casually left to die in the desert by his wife and her lover. Thanks to enterprise, sheer guts, and a philosophical nature, he manages to drag himself back to safety. It says much for Robert Ryan's acting that he never allows a part which largely consists of talking to himself while inching slowly from rock to rock to become in the least degree tedious. Direction is by Roy Baker. Rhonda Fleming and William Lundigan play the guilty lovers, and the supporting cast of cacti is fine.

27 September 1953

It is very right and proper that the story of the Savoy opera, if it is to be made into a film at all, should be made by a British company, to whom the authentic records are accessible, and by persons who, even if they are not willing or able to accept the Savoy tradition in its entirety, have at least grown up in the knowledge of the Savoy idiom.

Stalwart followers of the D'Oyly Carte Opera Company, who are versed in every trick of the business, familiar with each twist of score and inflection of dialogue, may find themselves impatient, quite often, with *The Story of Gilbert and Sullivan*. But I do beg them to remember that if Messrs Launder and Gilliat, had they been full-blooded Savoyards, might have done a far, far better thing than *Gilbert and Sullivan*, there are others, in other countries, who might have done far, far worse.

What is the film *like*? That is the question. It is like a sound radio scrapbook, combined with a television passing show. It is bright, swift, and bitty; faintly sentimental, enormously good-natured. Excerpts from eight Savoy operas are the important things in an unconvincing story about Mr Gilbert and Dr Sullivan; how they met, collaborated, quarrelled and reunited, with Mr D'Oyly Carte acting as a stiffly Victorian *deus ex machina*. Some attempt has been made by film producers conscious of their responsibilities to draw a visual parallel between incidents in the operas and situations in the lives of the protagonists, but the astute observer will quickly recognize that these are simply plot contrivances, designed to keep the personal narrative abreast of the musical drive.

Through no fault of the actors the story of Gilbert and Sullivan is the least absorbing part of *The Story of Gilbert and Sullivan*. Robert Morley and Maurice Evans, working conscientiously within the limits of script and direction, do succeed in breaking through the ampersand in the combination of Gilbert & Sullivan; establishing the one as a petulant fuss-pot and eccentric, the other as a rather oily social fawner. Neither, to my mind, suggests a man who might have been capable of creating half *The Yeoman of the Guard*, or *The Mikado*. Peter Finch, as D'Oyly Carte, strikes me as coming off more happily. True, he has less to do; in point of fact, he has nothing to do but *be* there. Nevertheless, he leaves the quiet impression of a man of force; a performer who doesn't need to say 'Look, no props!' to draw attention to his presence.

When all is said and done, however, what matters in *Gilbert and Sullivan* is the music. It is inevitable in a work of such compression that somebody's favourite number will be omitted from each opera. I can't help feeling that a great deal must have been left on the cutting-room floor which might have been helpful in the cinema. One catches snatches of tunes, like a customer in a gramophone shop. *Ruddigore*, for instance, seems scurvily treated, with the recitative leading us right up to the introduction to 'The Ghosts' High Noon', and then the music fading. The short extract from *The Sorcerer* might well have been discarded in favour of something from the neglected *Patience* and *Princess Ida*. I thought *Trial by Jury* came out of the picture best, with the quartet from *The Yeomen* ('When a Wooer Goes a-Wooing'), beautifully sung and rather cleverly presented as an item in rehearsal, running it a close second.

The voices, mainly dubbed, are rather heavier, and belong more to the world of concert and grand opera, than those to which we are accustomed in the performances of the D'Oyly Carte Company. One notices it most markedly, perhaps, in the singing of the light comedy and soubrette parts, which have always been the pivot on which the Savoy operas have turned. I don't suppose Savoy opera has often been better sung. But if it *were* to be sung like this, often, I shouldn't want to hear it. Lightness and dryness are essentials of these comedy parts. Henry Lytton, with practically no voice left, could rock you with laughter or draw the heart out of you, by sheer dint of technical skill and clear articulation.

On the orchestral side, *Gilbert and Sullivan* is as near as can be to perfection. Sir Malcolm Sargent conducts the London Symphony Orchestra, with the cinema's own Muir Mathieson as Associate Music Director and Conductor. Somebody (and I suspect Mr Mathieson) has arranged cross-cutting of sound between Sullivan's serious works and his Savoy operas with a wonderful combination of musicianship and tongue-in-the-cheek fun; as well as composing linking music, in the form of a Victorian pastiche, which is simply, and I mean *simply*, brilliant.

10 May 1953

When the small knot of fairy godmothers gathered for my christening, one of the many gifts they forgot to bring was the gift of hearty laughter. The omission has been a grave handicap to me in my chosen career. It does not greatly matter that a film critic should lack grace, beauty or a golden voice, the ability to swim like a fish or to do mathematical computations like a calculating-machine; but that he should be unable to laugh out loud when everybody round him is splitting his sides with merriment, is a deprivation to himself and an embarrassment to his neighbours. It also makes it difficult for him to write with passionate enthusiasm of a comic show.

I used to feel this acutely in the early days of movie slapstick. I dreaded films in which actors slipped on banana skins, sat down in buckets of whitewash, wiped a sticky mass of custard pie from their faces, or crowned each other with handy bits of furniture. Even now I cannot raise the ghost of a smile when a character is pushed into a swimming-pool or gets entangled with a bear-skin hearthrug.

Comic antics, as distinct from comic dialogue and comic situations, don't amuse me; which is why I am at pains to be fair about them. I was one of the very few people at the Curzon who did not laugh immoderately at Jacques Tati's comedy, **Monsieur Hulot's Holiday**. The opportunity is yours: the loss was mine.

Jacques Tati, who wrote, directed and starred in *Jour de Fête*, has performed the same triple function for *Les Vacances de M. Hulot*. This time he has set his scene in the small hotel, and the slight, sweet surrounding countryside, of a tiny *plage* near Caen. Here his types gather for a brief seaside holiday. They put on holiday clothes, and conscientiously attempt the holiday spirit, but instinctively cling to the habits and pattern of everyday life; submitting with docility to the discomforts of travel, the scrambled loud-speaker announcements, the tyranny of wireless and gramophone, the draught, the wet feet of children, the hearty organization of born organizers, and the bleak dining-room with up-tilted chairs.

The only thing that ruffles this placid surface is accident, in the long, ungainly person of Monsieur Hulot. M. Hulot arrives out of nowhere in a spluttering museum piece of a motor-car, achieves nothing but interference in the most good-natured manner possible, and, having blundered with the best intentions into every situation, object and personage within sight, withdraws in his spluttering little car to another year of nowhere.

Jacques Tati's Mr Accident is a great gawk of a young man in tennis flannels, gaudy striped socks, and a Tyrolean hat. His teeth grip an unlit pipe at a pert angle, and he walks splay- footed, with a stiff leg. He is shrewd enough to keep his gambols, as a rule, in the background of the picture; happily and properly allowing people to go on doing things solemnly downstage. His timing, or rather, his own direction of the timing, does not seem to me yet in the senior class of clowning. But there is a great deal to like and admire about it. M. Tati is a clean comedian; he is also a silent one; his only dialogue consists of grunts and puffs; he is at once very large and very kindly.

I find I have talked myself into enjoying *M. Hulot's Holiday* very much more in retrospect than in experience. One thing I question; the wisdom of dubbing so much of the scant dialogue into English. Command of comedy invention is best understood, it can be well understood, and perhaps better appreciated, in the original French. In the original version Tati used his sparse scraps of English for a deliberately comic purpose. In the new version, English has become the normal form of speech, French the foreign one; which makes nonsense of the background, the setting and the continuity. We are left to infer that this delicious little *plage* hotel is hourly exposed to perorations from the BBC and polyglot gabble from allegedly English-speaking visitors. Somehow I cannot feel this is altogether fair to M. Tati, who has clearly balanced his dialogue with exactitude, obviously loves his little French boys, clumping down to the shallow sea-pools with their shrimping nets, and must have caught the sense of this comedy out of some sharp, simple memory of childhood. Nor do I think it much of a compliment to the Curzon audience, which has never shown itself reluctant to take a good foreign film in any language.

At the Leicester Square Theatre there is an American film called **From Here to Eternity**, which includes in its cast Burt Lancaster, Montgomery Clift, Deborah Kerr and Donna Reed. In my opinion, this is not an export picture. Its terrible exposé of conditions in the United States Army before the attack on Pearl

Harbor; its frank outlay of brutality; its complete indifference to world affairs; its acceptance of drunkenness as an endearing part of American army life; its completely amoral outlook; all these would make me, if I were responsible for the maintenance of American prestige abroad, ban this picture out of hand, before it has a really disastrous effect in foreign countries.

15 November 1953

Wisely, in a week when the horse will be a common topic of conversation, Ealing Studios have sent a racing film to London. *The Rainbow Jacket* is probably the best racing film ever made; certainly the most complete, in that it not only provides gaily coloured and exciting spectacle and a story entertaining in itself, but takes the audience behind the scenes and shows us in fascinating detail the *workings* of training stable and race-course.

In essence T. E. B. Clarke's script is a study of the relations between a warned-off jockey (Bill Owen), a boy whom he trains to ride (Fella Edmonds) and the boy's widowed mother (Kay Walsh), who is equally interested in both of them. In effect, it suggests a cross between documentary and Nat Gould; never shying at the possible improbable, nor denying that the rainbow jacket has its seamier side, but describing with accuracy the course of a young jockey's life, from the moment he 'does' his first horse to the day he wins the St Leger.

Director Basil Dearden has taken his cameras to the race-courses themselves; to Newmarket, Lingfield, Epsom, Sandown Park and Doncaster; and sudden surprise shots show Sir Gordon Richards riding for the film and even speaking a few characteristic lines; which, I may add, he does beautifully. To me the most fascinating scenes are those which steady fiction with a touch of fact; the outfitting of the apprentice with a pair of Manny Mercer's old boots; the painting of his name on a number board to be stacked amongst the labels of the great; the jockeys' changing-room, with one old mackintosh hung against the tapestry of brightly coloured silks; the starter's foot pressing down the lever for the off; the glimpse into the darkroom where the films from the photo-finish cameras are developed; the lovely shots of schools of horses out at exercise in the misty morning.

There is no space to mention all the good actors appearing in the cast, but the joint presence of Robert Morley, Wilfrid Hyde-White and Michael Trubshawe as Stewards of the Jockey Club provides a real delight. Charles Victor, as the head stable-lad, has the pick of Mr Clarke's funny lines, and in telling the apprentices just where they get off if they don't get on he never wastes a syllable.

30 May 1954

Successful as a television play, successful on the stage, **Dial M for Murder** seems certain to continue its career of profit in the cinema. It has been singularly little changed in translation from play to film. Federick Knott, the author, adapted it for the screen. Alfred Hitchcock, the director, has known how to leave well alone. He has had the good sense to abstain from melodramatic chases, abjure antics, and keep the action more or less strictly confined to a one-room setting. The result is to concentrate the attention of the audience on detailed evidence of word and behaviour; an operation of incalculable value to a close-knit subject of this kind.

The central figure of *Dial M for Murder* is a fading tennis player (Ray Milland), who decides to kill his wife (Grace Kelly) for her money. Since he feels squeamish about doing the deed himself, he finds an admirable proxy in an old college friend (Anthony Dawson), who is in no position to resist a threat of blackmail. The ingenious scheme falls through when the wife, grasping a handy pair of scissors, kills the murderer by mistake. With a rapid change of plan, her charming husband then contrives to get her judicially hanged. He is only foiled on the night before her execution by a Scotland Yard Inspector (played with delightful dryness by John Williams), whose thought processes are slower than his, but surer.

Dial M for Murder is one of the most distinguished screen thrillers that have come our way for a very long time. The plot is extremely intricate, but admirably fair. The performance is kept a little under life-size. The direction is unobtrusive, but wonderfully firm. I have only two complaints to make against the film. I don't believe that a woman in such circumstances would have been sentenced to death, or not reprieved, under British law. And I'm quite certain it would occur to no London bobby to say 'Break it up' to a small pavement group, comprising a man with a gamp, a few housewives, and a perambulator.

18 July 1954

Soon after the war an American newspaperman, Malcolm Johnson, wrote a series of articles called 'Crime on the Waterfront' for the *New York Sun*, which won him the Pulitzer Prize for Reporting, and, it is said, prompted a State investigation into his discoveries. Not long afterwards a Jesuit priest, Father Corridan, long known for his great work on behalf of the longshoremen of the Port of New York, sent out a pamphlet reprinting one of the articles, and passionately denouncing the gang system that was holding the docks under a reign of terror. 'Where I was cautious and merely implied, Father Corridan blasted,' says Johnson. Their joint disclosures form the basis of the script which Budd Schulberg has written for *On the Waterfront*, one of the grimmest and most formidable films about organized crime since Hollywood turned its attack upon Al Capone and his men.

The film has had the good luck to be directed by Elia Kazan, and to get Marlon Brando as its leading player. The story that Mr Schulberg and Mr Kazan have put together deals with a longshoreman who has grown up in the knowledge, which he has come passively to accept, that the healthiest people on the waterfront are those who see nothing, hear nothing and say nothing of what is going on around them. Although no brighter than his neighbours, there is a strain of something dogged in him, and gradually and painfully he is brought to realize, through love and a series of brutal 'accidents', that the protective System to which he has subscribed is nothing but a form of terrorism.

It will surprise me very much indeed if a finer performance than Brando's is seen on the screen this year; the character grows achingly under your eyes. Karl Malden is excellent as the battling priest who dares to believe that the hold of a ship, beside the body of a murdered man, is as good a place for a sermon as any pulpit. The newcomer, Eva Marie Saint, has a face with thought in it as well as beauty. I have only two complaints to make about the film, and both are small. It struck me as rather alarmingly inconclusive, which is perhaps not to be wondered at, for reformation, if it is to be stable, must come slowly. And I could have done without a great deal of the background music, particularly the gluey ballad before the titles, which seemed to me an intrusion in a fine film.

12 September 1954

Whether you happen to care for it or not, you have to admit that the Americans have a rare way with a big, swinging, coloured, high-speed musical. **Seven Brides for Seven Brothers** comes from the studio that produced *An American in Paris, On the Town, Annie Get Your Gun* and *Kiss Me Kate*. The family likeness is unmistakable.

Seven Brides can briefly be described as a variation on the theme of the rape of the Sabine Women. In the backwoods of Oregon, a hundred years ago, there live seven brothers, all red-haired, fiery and 'tall as church steeples.' They have no women to look after them, so the eldest brother, Adam (Howard Keel), drives into town to get him a wife. He brings back Milly (Jane Powell), who barely reaches to his shoulder, but is as spirited as she is diminutive; and she brings with her a volume of Plutarch's *Lives*.

While Milly house-trains the brothers – they badly need the discipline – Adam applies himself to Plutarch, and conceives the idea of a raid on the town to carry off wives for Benjamin, Caleb, Daniel, Ephraim, Frank and Gideon. On a bright winter's night the raid is executed, and as soon as the sleigh-load of struggling, sobbing women gets through the pass, the brothers shoot down an avalanche of snow to block the way behind them. The girls are prisoners until spring, and the rest of the film shows how the indomitable Milly so disposes that the subject has a happy ending and wins the Universal blessing of the British Board of Film Censors.

Perhaps this outline is enough to give a slight idea of what to expect from *Seven Brides for Seven Brothers*. It has its faults. It is sometimes ballad-sentimental, occasionally facetious-vulgar. But it does have a plot, it does have imagination, it fairly explodes into life, and many discerning people will find the dance arrangements – exact, insidious, acrobatic, graceful, slipped in as if they were a natural development of the story action – wildly exciting. Director Stanley Donen and his team have contrived a musical film with strong, local atmosphere, good voices in the leading parts, and a first-rate chorus line or corps-de-ballet to support them. This is the type of indigenous

American entertainment that other countries have tried to copy quite in vain.

26 December 1954

The first week of the New Year brings a most exciting film to London. Its name is **Carmen Jones** and it is a modern American version of Bizet's opera, with an all-negro cast.

The scene has been changed from Seville and Madrid to Florida and Chicago. Carmen no longer works in a cigarette factory, but is employed in packing parachutes. Don José is an Air Force corporal called Joe. Escamillo has become a prize-fighter named Husky Miller. Lillas Pastias's place is now Billy Pastor's Desert Cafay. Micaela is plain Cindy Lou, and the smugglers' molls, Frasquita and Mercedes, have turned into Carmen's friends Frankie and Myrt, big-hearted gals with a load of superstition and a weakness for skin-tight gowns, feather boas and rhinestones.

The music, let it be said at once, is Bizet's. With only a modicum of cuts and rearrangement, the melodies are heard in their original form and their accustomed order. There has been some hot re-scoring in the café scenes, but Bizet's melodic line is never broken, nor is the essential rhythm changed.

The book and lyrics naturally are new. They are the work of Oscar Hammerstein the Second, who wrote them for the Broadway production of 1943. If they lack romance and poetry, nobody can deny their ingenuity and zest. 'Stand up and fight until you hear the bell' roars the prize fighter to the refrain of the Toreador's song. 'Carmen Jones is goin' to jail' chant the chorus of piccaninnies, apeing the military and their drill. 'De nine of Spades – dat ole boy,' whispers the horror-stricken Carmen, as she turns up the fatal card. 'Beat out that rhythm-on-a-drum,' goes the Gipsy Song, transferred from Carmen to Frankie in the desert café, and sung by Pearl Bailey with a fever that seems to set all the tom-toms in all the jungles throbbing.

Negro films have never been very successful in England. The beautiful *Hallelujah* died of sheer neglect. So did *Green Pastures* and *A Cabin in the Sky*. It would be a pity if the same thing should happen to *Carmen Jones*, and so I ask specially that from the start it should not be overlooked by discerning persons who care for cinema entertainment a little out of the ordinary. As a technical job (director Otto Preminger) it is first-rate. Dorothy

Dandridge's Carmen, a study in pale ebony and flame, is the most delicately ordered affair. They call her Heat-Wave, but nothing she does is crude. More than most Carmens whom we see on the operatic stage, she goes back to the Carmen with her point of honour, the Carmen of Mérimée, the gipsy of a gentleman's imagination. Above all, she suggests a woman of such parts that a man might fall in love with the better things in her before the worse.

Harry Belafonte's Joe is interesting and pitiful to watch. Not often does one see a Don José fall to pieces so shockingly before one's eyes. Joe Adams's prizefighter, has the look of a coloured Clark Gable; one can understand why this boy keeps a place in the stronghold described as the Gym of Champs. The singing voices of the three leading players are dubbed with admirable exactitude, but the characters are never falsified, and the music is never debased. I have seen many Carmens in my time, but not a more exciting one than this; except perhaps the ballet version with Roland Petit and Jeanmaire.

9 January 1955

This is handkerchief week in the London cinema. Two of Hollywood's most eminent directors, George Cukor and John Ford, have contributed films of inordinate length and staggering size, designed to wring the withers, claw at the heartstrings and act with violence on the tear ducts. One of the two, at least, **A Star is Born** succeeds triumphantly in this design.

Mr Cukor's film is a new version of a prize tearjerker of 1937, with James Mason and Judy Garland in the parts originally taken by Fredric March and Janet Gaynor. The plot, like most good plots, is simple but not original. A film star called Norman Maine, at the top of fame's escalator, sees a girl called Esther Blodgett, who sings with a dance band, at the bottom. With an insight none the less shrewd because it is alcoholic, he recognizes the shining quality in her. He makes her a star. She makes him her husband. The rest of the film depends on the shifting balance of that exchange.

It must be made clear at once that *A Star is Born* is not a great film, but a great show. Its genius lies in going with the stresses. It uses what it finds for its own purpose. Because Hollywood is loud, brash and vulgar, *A Star is Born* is loud, brash and vulgar. Because Judy Garland has been through a good deal of life's rough and tumble, it presents her as a heroine unabashedly rough and tumbled. Because James Mason can model to perfection the manners of a seedy, raffish gentleman, it plays him as a seedy, raffish gentleman.

So far so good. But what the film has extra is a spring of feeling in both players, which makes the private life of these public characters extraordinarily human, and keeps their relations clear, moving and fresh. The performances are fine. Mr Mason's is a fine, mordant bit of acting. I still deplore some of the noises emitted by Miss Garland in the alleged process of her singing, but for me she can sit on the edge of the stage, dangling her long legs into the orchestra pit for ever, and tell how she was born in a trunk in the Princess Theatre, again and again and again.

Sergeant Marty Maher retired nine years ago from America's military academy at West Point, after fifty years as a physical training instructor. *The Long Gray Line* purports to be an account of his experiences, as related by the Sergeant to President Eisenhower, himself a West Point alumnus.

The President's patience during his long recital is a tribute to his early training. For nearly two hours and a quarter – and at breakfast, too – he allows the old gentleman to ramble on, describing his early days in the mess as a greenhorn from Ireland, his wooing and wedding of an immigrant colleen, his misadventures in the swimming pool, his thoughts on first seeing the forward pass at football, the arrival of his daddyo from the ould country, the birth and death of his only child, his rage at being kept out of the firing line in the First World War, his emotions on learning of the attack on Pearl Harbor, the death of his wife before he can fetch her medicine and shawleen, his weak eyesight, the injustice of being asked to retire from physical training instruction at the mere age of seventy.

Not until the Sergeant is embarked on an account of a Christmas Eve party, which seems likely to go on for ever, does the President firmly but politely lift the telephone and arrange for his visitor to be flown back to West Point, where a full-scale military parade has been laid on in his honour. By the time he has been rushed on to the field, taken and given the salute, heard the band playing his especial airs, watched the wheeling columns and the Big Brass wiping away a surreptitious tear, the old gentleman is reduced to a state in which he is capable of seeing anything, even ghosts. He sees them.

The film has been directed by John Ford with every trick

of sentiment that Hollywood can devise, from the snippets of black ribbon in the class-book to the spangles on the Christmas tree. The leading characters are played by Tyrone Power and Maureen O'Hara in the style proper to persons burdened with such dialogue as 'Is it sorry you are already, Martin Maher?', 'It's sorry I'll never be, Mary O'Donnell.' There are moments when the real strength of the subject triumphs over the weakness of the narrative; but in his efforts to drive the Point home, Mr Ford has overdone the sentiment, and it is hard to distinguish the long, gray line among all the shamrocks and corn.

6 March 1955

Lucretia Borgia – Martine Carol, as a misunderstood lady of medieval days, takes a hot bath in a barrel.

The Caprice of Caroline – Martine Carol, as a misunderstood lady of Napoleonic days, takes a cool bath in a scallop shell.

4 April 1955

It is not often that we discover a masterly new actor in a musical show, but this agreeable surprise occurs in the case of *The King and I*. Yul Brynner is not only one of the most exciting personalities to appear on the screen since James Dean and Marlon Brando. He is an actor of tremendous power and discipline. I cannot tell you whether his performance bears any likeness to a real King of Siam, never having encountered such a person; but I do know for certain that it suggests the right kind of king for this particular play, bears out the clear intentions of the script, and makes a whole man, a huge man, a man one must believe in, out of this odd mixture of pride, barbarism, warmth, eagerness to learn and 'puzzlement'.

Springheeled Mr Brynner, with his sudden, strong gestures, clicking fingers, magnificent stance, voice that can sound like a gong or the tearing of calico, and tight, thin lips that break so disconcertingly into a smile, dominates *The King and I*, but I thought the whole thing (apart from the incident of the runaway lovers, which, however, is a plot-hinge) quite delightful. Deborah Kerr, back in the sort of part she does so well, makes a real gentlewoman of the Victorian English

governess, sings the easier songs in a very taking way (the others
are dubbed, but deftly), is prettily dignified in her scenes with the
King, and plays her scenes with the children ('Getting to Know
You') with a charming kindness that becomes her.

There is much to be said – there always was – for the stylized
oriental conception of 'The Small House of Uncle Thomas', but
my own favourite passage in the film is the touching entrance
of the royal children, presented very comically and sweetly,
without mawkishness. Fine, too, is Terry Saunders's quiet but
compulsive management of the Head Wife's song, 'This is a man
who thinks with his heart, And his heart is not always wise.'
Perhaps the film is spun out a bit too long. There comes a point
about two-thirds through when the attention begins to wander;
but Mr Brynner and Miss Kerr swing it quickly back again with
'Shall We Dance?', and no real harm is done. To my mind *The
King and I* is an altogether better film than *Oklahoma!*, although
less homespun and more theatrical; and I assure you that, if you
are interested at all in the art of acting, this Yul Brynner is a
man to see.

16 September 1956

In *Love Me Tender*, a post-Civil War Western, with Richard
Egan and Debra Paget, is peremptorily pushed about to make
room for a young man named Elvis Presley, who represents,
so I have been told, the latest thing, the tops, in Rock 'n' Roll
entertainment. Mr Presley is unfortunately cumbered with a part,
which he nibbles at perfunctorily when he happens to remember
it. But his *raison d'etre* in *Love Me Tender* is to sing; to sing in the
Presley way, with contorted features, heavy breathing, galvanic
jerks, eyes closed in agony, legs writhing and buckling, head
flung back like a dog howling at the moon, banjo clasped to
heaving bosom. I understand this performance is tame compared
with the one Mr Presley can put up when not handicapped by
a moving picture. My concern is with a moving picture made
nonsense of by him.

16 December 1956

On referring to Synopsis I discover that there are only seventeen

Rock 'n' Roll songs in **The Girl Can't Help It**. I am surprised.
They felt like many more. However, all seventeen are guaranteed
to be 'sensational', and are performed by persons of such renown
that 'Cats' recognize them with shrill screams of delight, and it
is necessary to describe them in the cast-list only as Themselves,
Himself or Herself. (Five Thems, seven Hims and two Hers,
though one Her is comparatively stationary.)

The Girl Can't Help It, which is in CinemaScope and Eastman
Colour, adds to its Rock 'n' Roll a trace of story, and a new
platinum blonde named Jayne Mansfield. Taking Miss Mansfield
first, as most people are likely to do, she appears to be a girl who
has come to the fore by reason of her physical geography. Her
face, when you get to it, seems kind, and her voice no more
offensive than a thousand others. But her measurements are
the most striking things about her. Above a handspan waist
she carries a structure which would have been no discredit to
Mae West. The chassis is well-sprung, and the whole model
supported on tiny, mincing, high-heeled feet. She is required
by the film to do a deal of walking, and there were times when
I felt it must have caused her pain.

I find it impossible to say yet whether she can act, though I
notice that one of my braver brethren of the trade Press has put
it on record that Miss Mansfield 'establishes herself as a genuine
comedienne by happily guying herself'. I seem to remember
much the same words used in connection with Marilyn Monroe
and Sherree North, not to mention Jane Russell, Lana Turner and
Diana Dors. If Miss Mansfield really yearns to act, she might do
worse than take a study course in Judy Holliday.

The story introduces Miss Mansfield as the fiancée of a
racketeer (Edmond O'Brien), who once had a corner in slot-
machines, spent his time in prison composing such far-sighted
little numbers as 'Rock Around the Rock Pile', and now wants to
come back into show business as the husband of a top disc-seller.
To this end he engages a talented but alcoholic agent (Tom Ewell)
with the simple injunction, 'All you've got to concentrate on is to
turn this dame into a big canary in six weeks.' Mr Ewell complies.
Fortunately he finds that the canary, who apparently can't sing,
can make a really splendid noise resembling a police siren.

From this point the film slips easily into Rock 'n' Roll. And
since it is clear that we are in for a mort of Rock 'n' Roll films,
which will still be rocking round the cinemas long after our
dancing sons and daughters have turned to some other form

of activity, I propose to make this the occasion for a brief homily.

A great deal of profitless nonsense has been talked about the mock battle of the generations over Rock 'n' Roll. I don't know which it insults the more, the sensible parent or the sensible child. Rock 'n' Roll is not an exercise which naturally recommends itself to balanced men and women of middle age. They dislike Rock 'n' Roll for various reasons. It is ugly, untidy and makes the dancers look so gormless. It sounds horrid. It is desperately old-fashioned, recalling the drearier dances of the 1920s, even though the grip and beat are different. It suggests an origin of rhythmic mass hypnosis, developed in the jungle, recognized and tabulated by all modern psychologists and medical practitioners. A fool can excel in it and frequently is indeed the best performer. But there is one great thing to be said in its favour. It exhausts energy. By the time a couple of men and maidens have spent an evening doing it, they are generally too tired to go on and make themselves a nuisance as Teddy boys and girls.

The person whom I pity is the adolescent who is happy at home and school; does not want to be a teenage rebel; will rock in moderation, but relies for a background on good books, plays and pictures. What on earth has the modern cinema to offer such a person? The gentlemen of the film trade constantly complain that they are losing custom. They blame the loss on entertainment tax and television. Have they, I wonder, overlooked another possibility; that every film shown lays a foundation, sure or shifting, for the future? I am a middle-aged rebel, and I look back more in sorrow than in anger on a cinema which once made films exciting in their own right, not a mere filmed record of some popular entertainment. Many films we saw twenty years ago are more vivid than the ones we saw yesterday. And this is not, I am convinced, a consequence of senile decrepitude. It is simply because they were making films better twenty years ago, giving substance for the older people to recognize, and the younger to recall.

3 February 1957

Without any hesitation I should rank *The Curse of Frankenstein* among the half-dozen most repulsive films I have encountered in the course of some 10,000 miles of film reviewing. Indeed, at the moment I can think of only two which sickened me more (leaving newsreel records and factual reports of such horrors as the concentration camps and the Hiroshima business out of count). Both of these alleged entertainments were versions of the same story, *The Mystery of the Wax Museum*, in which a waxworks show takes fire, and you see the coloured figures melt and smear into gruesome simulacra of corruption.

It must be twenty-five years since I watched the first 'Wax Museum' film, but I have never quite got over the experience of that afternoon. There has remained something indefinably foul to me, something almost obscene, about the effect of molten wax. The other evening, to avoid the rush hour, I was walking through the quieter streets of London, and passed a little café where candles stood in wine bottles in the window. Down the side of each bottle was a deliberate cascade of wax, in dripped, mergent colours. I have no doubt at all that it was a very decent little café. But I hurried past that window as if the devil were at my heels.

The 'Wax Museum' films were made in Hollywood, the second one essaying a new Guignolite effect in a 3-D version. *The Curse of Frankenstein* is all our own work. Under the heading 'Horror Has Its Own Hues' it is presented as 'Britain's very first horror film to be made in colour'. The leading players are Peter Cushing, Hazel Court, Robert Urquhart and Christopher Lee. The censors' certificate is X. The screenplay, by James Sangster, is 'based on the classic by Mary Shelley'.

Mr Sangster sets his scene in pseudo-nineteenth-century Switzerland. He takes as central character Victor, son of the celebrated Baron Frankenstein. Victor is a far-from-endearing youth who applies himself from childhood to the pursuit of the more recondite sciences. Debarred, by some copyright difficulty, from creating a Monster, he employs Papa's formulae and Papa's wealth in the evolution of a Creature, assembled from the body of a hanged highwayman, the hands of a dead sculptor, the brain of a murdered scientist, and a couple of ill-matched eyes bought cheap from a Municipal Charnel House. Apart from its slightly ramshackle ensemble (and, as Baron Frankenstein explains, you can't have everything) there is nothing pragmatically wrong with his Creature except that the brain has been knocked about a bit in transit, so that the poor wretch is hopelessly and homicidally mad.

We are told that the director, Terence Fisher, set out to chill our marrow 'in a quietly sinister manner, rather than by blatant crudity, although there are plenty of thrills, such as the final sequence, when The Creature crashes to his death in a bath of acid, through a skylight window, while a blazing mass of flames.' 'More – more', Mr Fisher is quoted as insisting while they smeared The Creature's clothes and make-up with petroleum jelly, 'I want him like a human torch – or, rather, an inhuman torch.' he added carefully.

Ideas of blatant crudity differ, and it would be stupid to ignore the morbid streak in human nature. 'The morbid,' James Agate once said, 'has an extraordinary attraction for many people, not because they like it but because they fear it.' And A. B. Walkley wrote with truth, 'We all have our Guignolite moments, moments of Taine's ferocious gorilla surviving in civilized man, when we seek the spectacle of torture or physical suffering or violent death; but we are careful to aesthetize them, refine them into moments of poetry or art.' It is not apparent that anyone has experienced such care in *The Curse of Frankenstein*. In this whole chronicle of horrors I could not discern one moment of art or poetry, except for a single instance of artful relief: when Baron Frankenstein, between murders, turns to his betrothed at the breakfast table, and asks her, in Peter Cushing's shock-absorbent voice, to be so good as to pass the marmalade.

5 May 1957

There used to be a schoolroom joke about Toulon and Toulouse. I'm often reminded of it, rather grimly, while watching modern films. Nowadays I associate it with the words too large and too loud. I wonder if I'm alone in thinking that a sojourn at the cinema today, what with the monstrous size and noise of everything, is apt to suggest a glimpse of the inferno?

Amplification is the vogue, and I suppose it won't be long before we hear Bach adapted for a musical on well-tempered Hi-Fi, and see Sophia Loren animating the romance of the Mona Lisa in slightly concave Technicolor at least ten feet high. The latest example of Hollywood's belief that size will always make up for lack of content is **South Pacific**, the first film to be shown in this country in the Todd-AO system. What a monstrous visual riot! What a din!

The Rodgers and Hammerstein stage show from which the

film was culled had one of the better scores of the recent crop of American musicals. 'Happy Talk', 'I'm in Love with a Wonderful Guy', and 'Gonna Wash that Man Right Out of My Hair' remain memorable numbers. There are those who still swoon dreamily to the strains of 'Some Enchanted Evening', and the off-screen voice of the New York Metropolitan's operatic baritone Giorgio Tozzi beautifully emits the sounds mouthed on the screen by Rossano Brazzi. The score is full of sound, popular things, though many of them are too loud and too sharp for my liking. (Nonsense, to my mind, to talk about 'natural sound'. Amplification is useful, but seldom natural.) Anyway, the score is loud but good. It takes more than Hollywood presentation to smash up a catchy tune.

The wrongness lies in what we are now taught to call 'the visuals'. The Todd-AO screen is a huge, in-curved affair, rather like the other side of a monstrous broken cup, which gives the director heaps of room to move about in. It's all of a piece, not a triptych like the Cinerama affair (and why in the world Cinerama doesn't show something different on its side panels, I have never understood), and sometimes the big curve proves too much for an intimate subject, and there is a nervous huddle in the middle, involving grotesque close-ups, with every skin-pore showing.

The director of *South Pacific*, Joshua Logan, has striven to overcome this difficulty by fogging his picture round the edges, and suffusing the actors' faces with coloured filters. Hope turns a young girl yellow; love strikes a young man purple. Vermilion slides in constantly, and so does orange; and in its quieter moments the film turns bloodless green, shading into that awful tone you see in your companion's face when you walk at night under those lamps that give no shadow. I find the colours dreadful and most distracting from the story, which deals, in a scant way, with American marines and nurses posted to a bunch of islands in the Pacific. Mitzi Gaynor, John Kerr, Rossano Brazzi are the stars, and France Nuyen prettily mimes the 'Happy Talk' number; Juanita Hall, as Bloody Mary, the devilish old native trader, is the one member of the cast who makes her presence strongly felt.

27 April 1958

'A nauseating week is finished, I'm relieved to say. Critics have been invited to review just two new films, both of them X-certified for horror. Both of them come from Hollywood, both of them seem to me morbid, ugly and repellent, and in my own mind I distinguish them as the Big Nasty and the Little Nasty.

Big Nasty is called *The Fly*. In Cinemascope and Eastman Colour, with stereophonic fly-sound, it describes the experiments of a young scientist who has almost perfected, in the laboratory of his bijou home, a method of disintegrating matter, transmitting the molecules, and reintegrating them elsewhere in their original form. Almost, but not quite. He suffers a temporary set-back when trying to reintegrate Aunt Somebody's priceless wedding gift, an ashtray upon which the words 'Made in Japan' reappear in something like looking-glass language. And there is a bad business over the attempted transmission of the family cat, which vanishes in 'a stream of cat atoms', leaving only a miaow behind. Nevertheless our scientist learns from his mistakes, and does so well with the reintegration of a guinea-pig and a bottle of champagne that he presently decides to transmit himself; not noticing that a common housefly has got into the mixer.

I don't propose to describe what happens when the machine reintegrates the two objects fed simultaneously into its maw. The advertising provides an ample hint. 'If she looked upon the horror her husband had become,' it prattles, 'she would scream for the rest of her life!' It might be possible, I suppose, to take this preposterous piece of merchandise as a monstrous joke. Even so, it would be a joke in deplorably bad taste; shown at its worst in the tender passages set to celestial music, involving the incomplete scientist and his panic-stricken wife. There's a maggot eating somewhere into the imagination of *The Fly*. Al Hedison (scientist), Vincent Price (brother), Herbert Marshall (police inspector) and Patricia Owens (potential screamer) are the players chiefly concerned in the performances of the Big Nasty.

Little Nasty is called *Macabre*. A bit of pseudo-Monk-Lewis Gothic, in black and white, it deals with the frenzied hunt through graveyard and funeral parlour for a doctor's child, supposed to have been kidnapped and buried alive. 'Her funeral', says the mocking voice over the telephone, 'has just taken place, and she is with the dead.' Working their faces something frightful, doctor and nurse assistant rush from grave to grave, shovelling a few tablespoons of earth, and from coffin to coffin, snapping up the lids. They find nothing more rewarding than the body of the doctor's sister-in-law, which is due for burial at midnight anyway, and an automatic pump in the funeral parlour which conveys the effect of heavy breathing. ('So life-like for the bereaved', explains the undertaker.)

Production is poor, although swirls of fog hide a number of deficiencies. No actor in this nasty little item is familiar to me except Philip Tonge, a rich old gentleman conveniently shocked to death with heart disease. I do know him because I happen to possess a glossy picture postcard showing 'Master Philip Tonge' as Michael in *Peter Pan* (Zena Dare as Peter), bright-faced and wielding a pillow as if he were boy eternal. Alas, poor Tonge.

3 August 1958

NOTE: What *would* she have thought about the re-make of *The Fly*? A Bigger Nasty still. – A.L.

Ingmar Bergman's new film from Sweden, **Wild Strawberries**, can be taken to mean this, that or the other according to the mind that receives it: or it can simply be absorbed as a wonderful experience, in gratitude that such skilled, such lovely and such tender work should still flower in the cinema.

In the past, Bergman's films have often been inclined to wrath; *Wild Strawberries* is merciful. It describes a day in the life of a very old man, who, between sleeping and waking, meets himself face to face for the very first time, and reproaches himself for what he has been and what he hasn't done.

Professor Borg has been a doctor for fifty years; now he is to receive an honorary degree at the University of Lund. He decides to drive to Lund from Stockholm by car, taking with him his daughter-in-law, fitting-in a call on his incredibly aged mother, turning aside to look at an old house with a tangled garden where he used to spend his summers long ago. On the road they pick up strangers: a bickering married couple, a trio of young hitch-hikers bound for Italy; the old man dozes fitfully, and dream, memory and actuality merge in his imagination.

Wild Strawberries could have been a desperately sentimental film. It isn't. It could have been ragged and perplexing. It isn't. Magnificently but very quietly played, in the grand style, by Victor Sjöstrom, the first of the great Swedish film directors, it mixes dream, memory and actuality so smoothly that one is only aware, at the end of it, of life as a continuous thing that touches, takes, releases and then passes on.

26 October 1958

Once upon a time, a couple of generations ago, Walt Disney, still a simple barnyard artist and the happy contriver of the Silly Symphonies, astonished the world and delighted most of it with his first full-length cartoon in colour, *Snow White and the Seven Dwarfs*. Even where we criticized, we felt that Disney had the root of the matter in him. Here was a splendid new way of telling fairy stories, which should grow even better as the years went on.

Twenty-one years have passed since *Snow White*, and now Walt Disney Inc., master of many enterprises, presents us with Snow White's sister **Sleeping Beauty**. The two films have a great deal in common, apart from the marked family resemblance between the heroines, and the question naturally arises, has Disney's work developed from that time to this time? So far as techniques are concerned, yes, undoubtedly. In all that affects the imagination, regrettably but definitely no.

The new film is a large and lusty infant endowed with Todd AO, Technirama 70, Technicolor and six-channel Stereophonic Sound. The animation is much smoother than it used to be. The prince's horse gallops almost like a horse. The characters walk as if their limbs co-ordinated. The embraces have a certain cosy comfort. The subject is presented in the form of illustrations from the pages of a child's richly ornamented story-book, and some of the medieval pageantry is charming. The score, adapted from Tchaikovsky's 'Sleeping Beauty Ballet', slows for at least one divagating pop song, and one or two visual effects come off with brilliance: the scene, for instance, in which the court is plunged in sleep, the fountain dies and the lights along the castle battlements blink out in a diminishing crescent.

But the story, adapted by no fewer than seven pairs of hands from 'Charles Perrault's version of the medieval tale', is a sad and sorry business. It attempts to describe how the Princess Aurora, cursed at her christening by the witch Maleficent, is brought up as a peasant in the forest by three good, homely fairies, Flora, Fauna and Merryweather, and saved from the sleep of death by the kiss of one Prince Philip, a cartoon hero bearing a marked resemblance to Elvis Presley. The fourteenth-century dialogue is notable for such remarks as the prince's whisper to his horse 'Y'know, Samson, there's sumpn mysterious about that voice, too byootiful to be reel,' and the anguished cry of one fairy to her sisters, 'It's Melluficent! She's got Prince Fillup!'

The forest scene, which gives us a glimpse of Disney's special animals, is much too short and serves chiefly to remind us that the same sort of thing was done more happily in *Snow White*. The drawings on the whole suggest a combination of *New Yorker*, comic horror strip and chocolate box – the special Disney chocolate box assortment with hard centres and soft centres. *Sleeping Beauty*, we are told, 'is indeed the ultimate of Disney studios' constant striving for perfection in the art of animated story-telling.' Too bad, but one can hope.

2 August 1959

In the old days we went to a Hitchcock film in order to be startled. Now we go in order to relax. We know exactly what to expect. A smoothly expert drama of flight and pursuit. A case of subtly mixed indentities, with an ambushed hero, a concealed villain and a heroine as glossy as a burnished chestnut. A bizarre and utterly fictitious thriller, leading towards a sensationally unlikely climax.

We know, too, what not to expect. A story with a social message. 'The most outspoken picture of our times.' A 'significant' film. A 'starkly honest' film. Hitchcock himself is honest as the day, but he is old-fashioned enough to believe that the first purpose of the screen is to endue its customers with pleasure.

For almost four-fifths of **North by Northwest** my feeling of well-being lasted. Scriptwriter Ernest Lehman has provided Hitchcock with an exciting story. About an advertising man (Cary Grant) who is mistaken for a Federal agent by a suavely sinister exporter (James Mason) of Government secrets. So, regrettably, he has to be eliminated. And the party chosen to lead him towards elimination is a lovely but ambivalent creature played by Eve Marie Saint.

The story goes wonderfully well up to the point at which Mr Grant is destined to be murdered in the middle of nowhere. He has had orders to meet a mysterious stranger at a bus-stop in a lone reach of country. The scene is flat ploughland, ochre-brown; empty as far as the eye can see. A main road cuts straight through it like a sword. The bus-stop seems a frivolity in this immense, dun waste. A local wayfarer, waiting for the bus, points out an oddity to Mr Grant. A low-flying aeroplane, dusting crops where there are no crops to dust. The bus arrives and the wayfarer departs. Mr Grant is left at the mercy of the aeroplane.

This sequence is likely to be remembered as a classic. For drama, suspense, colour and sheer cinema thrill Hitchcock has never done anything to excel it. I would recommend *North by Northwest* for the bus-stop scene alone. The trouble is that it marks the high point of the film. And there is still half an hour or so to go. Most of what follows seems an anticlimax.

This is a long picture (136 minutes). To my mind too long. By the time we reach the intended climax – a typical Hitchcock scene of vertigo, on the face of Mount Rushmore, a memorial where the heads of America's dead Presidents are carved in rock – some of us have lost the sharp edge of appetite. To read a thriller is one thing. To watch it is another. I sometimes wonder whether Hollywood has seriously enough considered the point of audience exhaustion.

Too long or not, *North by Northwest* is a film to see. You get a lot of entertainment for your money. You get a couple of clever, sophisticated screen actors and an elegant actress with a fine-drawn, exciting face. You get one scene that will be talked about as long as people talk about films at all. And everything for little more than the price of a glossy, colour-plated magazine, which in many ways this much resembles.

18 October 1959

A new film by Alfred Hitchcock is usually a keen enjoyment. **Psycho** turns out to be an exception. The story, adapted from a novel by Robert Bloch, has to do with the fate of one Marion (Janet Leigh), an uninhibited secretary who steals $40,000 from her employer and drives off in the night to meet her lover (John Gavin). During a storm she arrives at a sinister motel, owned by a crazy taxidermist (Anthony Perkins), whose even more demented mother lives in the adjoining mansion.

There follows one of the most disgusting murders in all screen history. It takes place in a bathroom and involves a great deal of swabbing of the tiles and flushings of the lavatory. It might be described with fairness as plug-ugly, although I'm told that our British Board of Film Censors has expunged a lot of blood.

This isn't the end of the tale by any means, for the victim has a sister (Vera Miles) who is, not unnaturally, anxious to discover what has become of sister Marion. *Psycho* is not a long film, as films go nowadays, but it feels long. Perhaps because the director dawdles over technical effects, perhaps because it is difficult, if not impossible, to care about any of the characters.

The stupid air of mystery and portent surrounding *Psycho*'s reputation strikes me as a tremendous error. It makes the film automatically suspect. 'The manager of this theatre has been instructed, at the risk of his life, not to admit any person after the picture starts,' 'By the way, after you see *Psycho*, don't give away the ending' – signed, Alfred Hitchcock.

I couldn't give away the ending if I wanted (though it can be guessed at without much difficulty), for the simple reason that I grew so sick and tired of the beastly business that I didn't stop to see it. Your edict may keep me out of the theatre, my dear Hitchcock, but I'm hanged if it will keep me in.

7 August 1960

NOTE: She wasn't alone in reacting to *Psycho* with what may now seem excessive distaste. I was working on the *Daily Express* at the time, and I remember a blistering account of its unpleasantness sent by René McColl, our worldly and battle-hardened chief Foreign Correspondent, after he had seen the film in New York. – A. L.

IV

Points West – and East

The Real America

The United States of America is a cozy little country consisting
of three small States, California, Kentucky and Texas; a vague
area known as the Middle West; a rather demodé section called
the Wild, or Woolly, West, and New York. There used to be
another State called Georgia, but that was away back in history
days. Its capital city was a place with a Greek name, where they
fought some battle or other – Atlanta or Atlantis.

California is where the film stars live: it has one town called
Hollywood, and a lot of empty space. Kentucky is used for raising
horses; the best people to raise horses are adolescent boys. Texas is
populated by very tall men in white hats and plaid shirts, who roll
their cigarettes and talk with a drawl. Their job is a bit indefinite,
but whatever it is, they take their time over it, and get outside
their territory a lot.

The Middle West is sort of an innocent place; all the inhabitants
look kinda naive. The boys chew straws, and take a helluva
time to get hold of a simple thought. The girls look fresh and
blossomy, like Jeanne Crain. They dream a lot, dress in gingham.

The Wild and Woolly West isn't what it used to be. It still
offers one startling natural phenomenon. It's always sunset in
the West. But the place has grown sissified since they got rid of
the Indians. Nowadays even the cowboys are vocalized.

New York, tucked away behind the Statue of Liberty, consists
of two parts; Brooklyn and Broadway. Everyone in New York
is either terribly rich or frightfully poor. The terribly rich live in
things called penthouses. The advantage of living in a penthouse
is that you can look out of your window and see Brooklyn
Bridge, beyond which people live in tenements. In New York
nobody starts to do anything until it gets dark. Then the terribly
rich slip into mink, or white tie and tails, and set out to work
their way through the night clubs and bars. The frightfully poor
start their day's hard work, too. The working men in New
York are mostly policemen and keepers of delicatessen stores.
The working girls are all show-girls.

These constitute the main geographical sections of America.
Other outstanding spots are Chicago, where gangsters tear
up and down the streets in black bullet-proof cars, mowing
people down with machine guns; Boston, an old-fashioned,

rather stuffy place; Washington, stolid and overcrowded; San Francisco, where private inquiry agents operate along the waterfront in a perpetual fog; Atlantic City, where business men go on conventions with Blondes; the Painted Desert; West Point and Annapolis, at one of which they throw pennies at a statue, but I can't recall which; Carvel, where the Hardys live; Carnegie Hall, and Tombstone.

The history of America is short and easy to remember. There have been two internal wars: A dull skirmish with the English about tea, which was all right once they got rid of Benedict Arnold, and a really dressy struggle between the North and South. The North won, and were right, but the South, who lost, were nicer. After that, nothing happened until 1916, when some people called doughboys went to Europe and won a war. On Dec. 7, 1941, the Japs attacked Pearl Harbor, and some people called GIs had to go out to the Pacific and lick the pants off them. Any American who survived the Pacific war came home with a Purple Heart and an amnesia complex.

America is governed by a President and Senators. There have been three Presidents of the United States: George Washington, Abraham Lincoln and Theodore Roosevelt. Pardon me, I am wrong: it has lately transpired there was another President called Something Wilson, who was devoted to his family, and liked to stand by the piano, listening to old songs. He was shockingly misunderstood, and wore eyeglasses.

The Senators are smooth, well-kept men in double-breasted suits. The ones that aren't long-winded bores are frightfully corrupt. All politicians in America are corrupt. The most corrupt are called Governors, and they earn their living by protecting racketeers. Attorneys, known as Mouthpieces, are corrupt too. The higher police officials are either corrupt or bullies and brutes. Nobody is ever taken to police headquarters for questioning without being grilled, sweated, or bashed to a pulp. The only policeman in America you can trust is a street cop, and then only if he's called O'Sullivan.

The population of the country is remarkably small – not more than a few hundred people, sometimes not more than a few families, to each town. The average family consists of Pop and Mom, Grandma, son and daughter of college age, and Junior, who looks best asleep. Junior is a great one for saying his prayers. He also says 'Go jump in a pond', 'G'wan, kiss the guy', 'Mom, why doesn't Pop come home to us any more?' 'Aw Mush' and 'Jeeper Creepers'.

The people of America are always beautifully dressed. On an average, they change their clothes every ten minutes. Everything they put on is new, perfectly tailored and crisply pressed. Even the cowboys wear fresh shirts all the time. You never see anybody in a garment with a darn or patch. Nobody has to tend the household linen, mend the stockings, let down Sis's skirts, make over Pop's pyjamas, or put a new seat in Junior's pants. They simply throw the things away and start again. The only needlework done in America is the knitting of tiny garments.

The houses are built on a curious architectural plan, with no back elevation, sections of staircase, and none of the usual offices. The main articles of furniture are the ice box and the telephone. The telephone system in America (invented by Don Ameche) is one of the seven wonders of the world. In storm and snow, lightning and national emergency, it never breaks down. Nobody ever dials a wrong number, finds his correspondent is out when he calls, gets a busy signal or a bad connection.

Another of the fine things about this country is the domestic servant problem. There is no domestic servant problem. Every house has a hired help, and every hired help is a happy hired help. She sings around her work, she requires no days off, she doesn't break a thing, and she never quits. She neither gets, nor expects, a raise. She does all her chores for love, not wages.

Maybe that's because the catering for the average American household is such a simple job. Except in the Middle West, folk don't have to eat much. They simply keep going on champagne cocktails and inexhaustible supplies of scotch. Sometimes, for the look of the thing, a good cook will whip up a couple of dozen eggs in a bowl. But a light breakfast of orange juice and coffee will sustain the average adult until the evening, when he or she can drink out. The main meal is held in the middle of the night in the kitchen, and consists of a glass of milk and cold chicken from the icebox. The younger members of the family, of course, live on ice cream exclusively.

The fauna of America consists mainly of the horse and the Cairn terrier; now and then the discerning eye may detect, in the distance, a stampede of cows. The flora is largely confined to the orchid and the long-stemmed rose. The rose is a peculiarly interesting variety, having extraordinary lasting qualities, and no thorns. You can pluck it with the bare hand, or clasp it to the bare bosom without being pricked. It never opens beyond the bud stage, and will stand in a vase without water for days. We have also been told that in certain parts of the country the grass is blue, but personally I haven't seen it.

The leading national pastimes are baseball, jive, riding on roller coasters, and necking. Necking is the most important, and can't be started at too early an age. As soon as a child is big enough to be kissed by the boy next door and whistled after in the street, she is sent to school to study necking properly.

College, which follows school, and is practically indistinguishable from it, is simply designed to offer a more advanced course in necking. The curriculum is so arranged that nothing is allowed to interfere with the main pursuit. A little light practice in carrying books, and possibly a mild crush on the English Literature professor, are the most that can be required of the necker who is positively determined to make the grade.

Most of the colleges provide football captains to help the enterprising necker along. A few colleges even supply a chapel and minister to solemnize marriages at short notice.

A smart girl, by the time she's through with school and college, has learned all there is to learn, and is ready to face the world. Besides necking, she can jitterbug, ride, skate, mix a highball, and croon a throaty torch-song. She knows the two ways of life, the American Way and the wrong way, and can read the larger headlines in a newspaper. She has heard of Shakespeare, Hitler, Superman, Lincoln, Frank Sinatra, Robin Hood, Benny Goodman, Freud and Mickey Mouse. If she's really smart, she can toss off a line or two of Keats' more celebrated odes, manage a few simple bars of Debussy or Chopin, and recognize the balcony scene from 'Romeo and Juliet'. She's got all the culture a girl needs, and doesn't have to open another book in her life. Since books are not provided in American homes, mostly she doesn't.

Around this time, she's ready for marriage. She gets married in the early twenties, at latest, to a handsome, suntanned young man not more than seven feet high. He has a whimsical smile, hair with the cutest crinkle, a dimple in his cheek or chin, and a rather bumptious manner. She doesn't notice the bumptious manner, because all she's marrying him for is to Have Fun. By profession he is an artist or an architect, a scientist or a secret agent, or maybe he just has a yen for building bridges. In any case, deep down inside of him, he knows that Having Fun is the thing he's always needed.

Having Fun, in the last instance, is the inalienable right of every American citizen. It means a prolonged and hilarious bender for two, pursued without inhibitions through half-a-dozen noisy night clubs. It may end in a police cell, an automobile crash, a trip to Reno, a blessed event, or simply a hangover with an icepack. But, however it works out, Having Fun is the great tribal ceremony of America, the crowning ritual of national life.

18 May 1947

Head 'em off at Eagle Pass

The wheel of the wagon is broken,
And the days of the West are through.

Thus mourn the singing cowboys, secure in the knowledge that they are voicing a thundering lie.

The Golden West is as golden today as ever it was; thanks to television, radio, the gramophone, the wide screen, colour, the musical stage, the pulp magazines, the comic strip and even the ice show.

Hardly a day passes without somebody, somewhere, singing or playing the tunes from *Calamity Jane*, the gayest of all modern Westerns; 'My Secret Love', 'The Deadwood Stage', 'The Black Hills of Dakota'. Even in these days of science fiction, Hopalong Cassidy is a greater favourite with the world's small fry than any hero in a space-suit.

The appeal of the Westerns is elemental. They have been standard fare for more than half a century. I see no reason why their popularity shouldn't last for ever. It will certainly be a long time before the thrill of the flying saucer supersedes the thrill of flying hooves.

The Golden West has become America's Golden Legend. Every country needs its legends, but the younger countries have been forced to create them faster than others. The legend of the West is the more intensified in that it has sprung up in quick time, in a simple, handy form that can be easily developed and widely propagated. The Western appeals to people of every race and age, because it combines manly achievement with the magic of a fairy-tail. It soothes the nostalgia of every country-man. It provides a means of escape for city-dwellers, yearning in their hearts for wide-open spaces, blue mountains in the distance, the company of rangy men with guns and sparse conversation, a meal cooked over a camp-fire beneath the stars, and lots of lovely, limber horses. Its confident cowboys conquer the atavistic fear in all of us; they give us assurance, even though we don't consciously expect to be held up on the Watford By-pass or the Great West Road by Redskins in full war-paint.

The Western has changed in make-up and presentation, but very little in character, since *The Great Train Robbery* of 1903. As an indigenous part of American folklore, it is deeply rooted, and possesses marked characteristics. Its development can be traced back from a full-sized beauty like *Shane*, through *Red River*, *Stagecoach*, *The Plainsman* and *The Iron Horse*, to the early silent films of William S. Hart and Douglas Fairbanks Senior, who once delighted my young heart by holding up a trans-continental express, because he wanted the engine-driver's whistle.

By its nature, the Western is an artistic convention with a very narrow range. It rings the changes on a few situations, a few sentiments and a few broad types of character. Its people are symbols of virtue and vice rather than clear-cut individuals. It goes in quite a lot for symbolism, which the customer learns to recognize just as a child learns to read his alphabet. Even *Shane*, a classic among Westerns, makes use of this rudimentary picture language. Everyone, everywhere, knows what is meant in spiritual values when the mysterious stranger from the blue mountains hangs up his gunbelt in a farmer's cabin, buckles it on again for the moment of destiny, and finally rides away into the blue.

The Western may sometimes seem to be the most uncouth and haphazard form of film, but it is governed by rules as strict and traditional as those of the Morris dance or the morality play. Whenever it transgresses these rules, it loses its nature, and audiences are down on it like a ton of bricks.

For instance, there is an unwritten rule that, for purposes of identification, the hero should wear the white hat of virtue, while his enemy sports the black fedora of villainy. In the book from which *Shane* was adapted, the hero was dressed in black from top to toe. This was considered too complicated for moving-picture audiences. The producers put Shane into light buckskins, reserving the symbolic black for the leader of the bad men. Immediate identification of the good ones and the bad ones is as important in the enjoyment of Westerns as a recognition of colours in a football match.

Nobody in his senses goes to see a Western in search of novelty. There have been changes in the mode, of course. New rackets, new romances have replaced the old plain bank hold-up, the train or coach robbery, the cattle rustling. New technical dodges have brought the old melodrama into line.

Cowboys have been encouraged to sing; or, if such an accomplishment is beyond their powers, auxiliaries have been impressed to help them out.

Catchy, haunting theme-songs have become tremendously important in Westerns. It took at least a year for customers to recover from the hangover from the inspired theme-song in *High Noon*. The records from *Calamity Jane* are still doing a brisk trade. I shall be very much surprised if there isn't a strong demand for the Marilyn Monroe numbers in *River of No Return*. My own particular favourites from Westerns are 'She Wore a Yellow Ribbon' and 'The Man in the Saddle', although I am horribly haunted by the grim ballad from *Rancho Notorious*. It should be remembered, too, that it was a Western that introduced to us that prince of guitar singers, Burl Ives, with 'Love's a Cherry Without a Stone'.

Nevertheless, the pattern of the Western has remained unaltered, through half a century of film-making. Seen in 'quickie' or in epic alike, the general features of the Western have never changed. Customers resent change. When the news got around that some bright boy in the scenario department had decided to cut the classic line 'When you say that, smile,' from the second film version of *The Virginian*, the force of public opinion brought it back.

Rigid rules govern the conduct, dress and dialogue of the performers. The hero must never draw a gun except in defence of self or friend; although in a case of emergency, he can always draw it faster than the other fellow. He never smokes, and hardly ever drinks, except to mislead the villain at the far end of the long bar.

Neither he nor the heroine may utter any lie. Only the slightest prevarication, when the plot calls for it, is admissible. One of the neatest prevarications I can recall occurred in some Western or other where the good girl had to convince the bad man that she loved him.

A downright declaration to that effect – for everyone knew she really loved the hero – would have shocked all Western fans. So the line was evolved 'You are a man; he is only a boy.' The customers were full of admiration for a girl who could outwit a cad so smartly.

Love, in a Western, must be convincing enough to impress the blossoming minds of the under-tens, but neither exotic nor 'soppy' enough to over-stimulate or bore the sixteen-year olds. The hero is not supposed to kiss the heroine until just before the last fade-out. Indeed, there is one school of thought that holds that Shane or Tex or Steve should ride away into the blue horizon, leaving only a secret memory and a legend behind. Blue horizons, incidentally, have come on splendidly with Technicolor.

Dialogue is simple, and there isn't much of it. These tough, outdoor men are not great talkers. What they do say has altered very little since the days of sub-titles. The story goes that Charles Bickford, who played a standard villain in Westerns for many years, was carrying on his dastardly work one morning when the director handed him his dialogue for the day. Without looking at it, Bickford stuffed the script into his pocket.

'Aren't you going to study your lines?' asked the director, somewhat huffily.

'I know what they are,' replied Bickford, 'I turn to the gang and say, "We'll head 'em off at Eagle Pass." '

Astonished at this display of mind-reading, the director asked for an explanation. 'Listen, buddy,' said Bickford. 'For fifteen years I've been heading 'em off at Eagle Pass, and this is no time to change.'

Just occasionally one gets a really fine line from a Western. I have never forgotten one in *Red River* (the film that introduced Montgomery Clift to the screen). 'Prayin' and plantin', prayin' and plantin', that's all we ever do.'

But then *Red River* was something of a super-Western, one of the most memorable of the outdoor pictures.

When I pause and think back carefully over all the hundreds of horse operas I have seen since Bill Hart first rode the purple sage, there are just a few that stand out in a class by themselves, individual and durable.

Three of them belong to the silent films era: *The Covered Wagon*; *The Iron Horse*, that early masterpiece about the building of the Union Pacific railroad; and the first version of *The Virginian*, with Gary Cooper and Walter Huston as the black-hearted, black-clad Trampas.

Then came Cecil B. de Mille's tremendous work, *The Plainsman*, with Cooper again as Wild Bill Hickock, and Jean Arthur as the first Calamity Jane, the formidable young woman who loved him.

Two years later there followed John Ford's classic *Stagecoach*, with a younger and less weather-beaten John Wayne than we are accustomed to seeing nowadays; and round about the same time the glorious *Destry Rides Again*, with Marlene Dietrich asking what the boys in the back room would have, and a comparative newcomer, James Stewart, as the reluctant gunman.

We had to wait until after the war for *Red River*; *The Gunfighter* (directed by Henry King), a brilliant and underestimated piece with Gregory Peck; John Ford's splendid film *She Wore a Yellow Ribbon*, with John Wayne and Joanne Dru; Fred Zinnemann's *High Noon*, with Gary Cooper and Thomas Mitchell; and recently, what is perhaps the best of all the out-door epics, *Shane*. These, along with *Calamity Jane* and *The Far Country*, are up to now the successive nails on which I would hang my largest wreaths.

The Indians Have a Word for It

The other day I was sitting in front of a blank sheet of paper, wondering how I could pass over the painful topic of the week's new films humanely, when I was interrupted by the postman with a letter from India. The letter has nothing to do with this article, but I was grateful for it. For it reminded me of an Indian magazine that I had received some months ago and filed away as a model of reviewing. I got it down from the 'I' files, between 'It Happened in Flatbush' and 'I Want To Be An Actress'. A few newspaper cuttings fluttered out of it; advertisements of cinemas in Rawalpindi. They have a charming, direct style with these things in Rawalpindi. 'Transcendent Blessing!' for instance, seems to me a nice way of advertising *Fantasia*. 'Merciless sun! Endless sands! Ceaseless battles! Matchless thrill!' covers practically everything except the democratic message in *Sahara*. There is something refreshing, too, in the naïvety with which the exhibitor includes the renters' selling hints in his advertisements. 'Trigger fast interestnabber!' cries the proud exhibitor of *Belle Starr*. 'Points up the spectacular show qualities in Belle Starr! Shoot them out and around town before and during your playdate!'

The magazine itself is published in New Delhi, and is called *The Caravan*. A special feature is the review of current Indian films by a gentleman who signs himself Reflexion. Reflexion is a critic after my own heart, a stunner. His films are graded in six groups: Extraordinary, Excellent, Good, So-So, Poor, and Rotten. So far I haven't found one that has risen above So-So.

Reflexion writes fluently, bluntly, sparing no one and nothing, with a high disdain for punctuation. 'The story,' he says, 'is of the same sickening old pattern which now deserves to be hounded off the screen for its distorted presentation of life and society.' 'Vatsala, though unattractive from outside' (that's the stuff to give the stars) 'really possesses a sweet throat, even though she sings old-fashioned songs.' 'The heroine' (is she really one?) 'is like the Japanese rubber doll which pipes out when pinched. The other girl which dances and makes romance all the time might have suited better a sanatorium than a motion picture.' 'The hero will never learn how to act except as a bully and a battering-ram and talk in a frog-like croaking voice and play havoc with even good pictures.' (Look out, Mr So-and-So, there's a chiel in the corner taking notes.)

'One thing is difficult to understand,' adds this honest fellow, 'and that is the bridge over the brook where all the boys and girls depart to make love and indulge in romance. This whole episode is absurd; can't love be made where people live and move about?' (Brooklyn Bridge by moonlight?)

'This theme has been repeated so many times and in such disgusting manners that one feels like playing the mad man for a moment and tear the screen on which it comes in lights and shadows. God alone knows why such foolish things are allowed to appear on the screen,' runs the impassioned peroration. Next to this appears a polite editorial note, 'If you have any suggestions for improving the Caravan, please do not hesitate to tell me.' I have no suggestions for improving *The Caravan*. It's doing fine.

V

Some People

In recent years I have come to know and enjoy Southern California: but I never see those tall palm trees without wondering what my mother would have made of it all. She had absolutely no prejudice against things American. She was fond of American children's books and American detective stories (Rex Stout and Erle Stanley Gardner, not Hammett or Chandler), and she might well have found the homely streets and tidy lawns of Pasadena congenial. If she had gone there in 1939, sponsored by Alfred Hitchcock, the British colony, led by the formidable C. Aubrey Smith, would no doubt have welcomed her. But she would not have been easily transplanted. Home meant much to her.

Hitch, despite his English roots, worshipped happily enough in the church he described as 'Our Lady of the Cadillacs'. Korda, on the other hand, never lived in Hollywood. His nephew, Michael Korda, himself thoroughly Americanized, although in the New York rather than the California style, was once asked on television why not. 'A guy like that,' he said, 'who used to lunch with Brendan Bracken and dine with Winston Churchill, what would he do in Hollywood? Talk grosses with Louis B. Mayer?'

Alex was the staunchest Briton ever to speak with a Hungarian accent. When he became a British subject, he gave a party at Denham and made a very short speech. 'I haf only vun thing to say,' he said. 'To hell with ze bloody foreigner.'

Michael Korda is Vincent's son. The end of his book, *Charmed Lives*, encapsulates precisely what I would wish to say, on behalf of my family, about his family. He is describing his last meeting with the third Korda brother, his uncle Zoli:

He took us out to dinner, a table of ten at an Italian restaurant, where he ordered more food than we could eat, then went to sleep over his wine. When the bill came, he woke up suddenly, took me by the arm, and said, as if he had been thinking of Alex and the old days, 'It's not been such a bad life, my boy, has it? We had some good times, no?'

He paused, while he fished through his pockets for his money and glanced at his family, so grown up now that they must have seemed like strangers to him, since he always thought of his children as infants.

Then he sighed, as he struggled into his shabby overcoat, and closed his eyes. 'Vat the hell,' he said. 'Alex vas a very nice man.'

–A. L.

Rubáiyát of Robert Taylor

Readers, I owe you an apology. I am afraid I may have been neglecting the softer virtues of a film correspondent. I have not passed on to you, as I should, the domestic news about the stars with which their Press agents so regularly keep me posted. I have selfishly kept to myself, for instance, some sixty folio pages describing the homely activities of Mr Robert Taylor. Luckily, it is still not too late. Mr Taylor is yet with us. Here, then, is a brief résumé of an English day in the life of Mr Taylor, so far as I can condense the sixty splendid pages into one.

Today in rural England the village of High Wycombe, red-roofed, in a sleepy hollow of the Chiltern beech forests, stirs early. Apple-cheeked village maidens gather in the dawn mists in a certain lane, the farmworkers make an extra detour to pass a certain house, the postman lingers longer at a certain gate. Whose gate? Robert Taylor's gate.

Daily he rises in a bedroom built before Henry VIII was born, knocks his head on a mighty oaken beam, jumps into a cold tub that gives him a glow for the rest of the day, no matter how the wind blows, and eats his good old British breakfast of bacon and eggs.

Outside, in the lane,

the gathering and the lingering culminate in the flash of a roadster down the drive of the fifteenth-century farmhouse, the wave of a hand, and the glimpse of a smile. But the flash, the wave, and the glimpse draw the cheers and the ooh's and aah's from the faithful company, and they go their rural way, honoured and satisfied till they pay homage again next morning. Pay homage to whom? To Mr Robert Taylor, English country squire!

Having given 'that wave and smile to the country maidens, the farmworkers, and the schoolchildren,' he 'sweeps off through the woodland' to the giant concrete film plant at Denham. After that, until he 'drinks his afternoon cup of tea,' the scene varies. One day Mr Taylor may be seen sitting, 'clad only in shorts

and singlet, in a rowing eight on the River Colne at Denham.'
Although 'ice-laden winds chill Taylor and his fellow-oarsmen
to the marrow . . . Taylor daren't pull for the shore and the
warmth of his portable bungalow, lest the sun should come out
at the critical moment.' Another day, 'Taylor, tall, dark, and
finely-proportioned, in his boating shorts and singlet, becomes
the sudden victim of a rag . . . goes head-first into the water.
Does he disappear? No.' He 'rolls in the shallows and rises with
mud in his hair and frustration in his eyes. He staggers to the
bank and takes a weed out of his singlet. Laughter rolls along
the Elizabethan lawns, and in it Taylor joins.'

Yet another day, and 'beneath the willows, idly punting down
the stream, go Robert Taylor and Maureen O'Sullivan. Maureen,
in white piqué, laughs at the quips of Robert, in white flannels.' A
'mid-morning snack' is brought out to Mr Taylor in a canoe, but
does he eat it? No, he 'scatters his biscuits on to the water' to lure a
line of white swans back into camera range. 'Maureen adds a little
chocolate.' The swans, more fortunate that the apple-cheeked
maidens, 'throng round the punt'.

Lest you might suspect our hero of frivolity, I must tell you
that beside the river, 'the red Tudor brick mansions' are 'standing
age-old in the sun,' and that Mr Taylor finds time, amongst his
aquatic activities, to appreciate their history. 'Robert Taylor,
modern youth in a modern age, realizes as he treads the flower-
bordered avenues of this location that his heels are lighting on
Queen Elizabeth's ground.'

After this brief pause for homage Mr Taylor proceeds to an
indoor set of Cardinal College, in which 'filmgoers will sense
a touch of Magdalen, a feeling of Christchurch, a suggestion
of Balliol'. Wearing a blazer with a college crest designed by a
great great grandson of Lord Tennyson, he continues, it seems,
his ornithological studies. ' "The North Wind doth blow and we
shall have snow, and what will the robin do then?" asks the
classic English nursery rhyme. Robins at Denham in this cold
spell know just what to do. They flit inside to the warmth of
the sound stages. Robert Taylor and Maureen O'Sullivan find
perfectly contented robins hopping round their feet and pecking
at the acre of real grass laid down for a giant Oxford quadrangle
setting.' Does Mr Taylor offer them his afternoon cup of tea and
more biscuits? I don't know. I hope not. He has had nothing
to eat, you remember, since that good old British breakfast of
eggs and bacon. The swans appropriated his mid-morning snack.

Wasps 'devoured his box lunches on location'. No wonder 'he has acquired a taste for Yorkshire pudding' and 'intends to teach his cook in Beverley Hills how to cook steak and kidney and . mushroom pie'. No wonder 'the custom of stopping everything at 4.30 in the afternoon for a cup of tea' no longer seems 'pretty silly' to him, and he has become 'the most confirmed tea-drinker on the set'.

What Mr Taylor does between his cup of tea and bedtime is left largely to our imagination. One presumes that he flashes home, through the age-old English lanes, giving that smile and that wave of the hand to the still waiting village maidens, manoeuvres his car through the crowds of farmworkers, dislodges the lingering postman from the gate, and retires, knocking his head again on the mighty oaken beam, to the bedroom built before Henry VIII was born. So much, though, is conjecture. What happens next is known. Although he is secure at last from swans, robins, village maidens, wasps, and ice-laden winds, a final visitation awaits him in the shape of mosquitoes. 'I'd always been told there were no mosquitoes in England,' he laughed. 'Say, there are a dozen out at the house that try to go to bed with me each night.'

And so ends the day of a popular film star, now 'a typical English squire,' while out there in the dawn mists of sleepy, beech-clad, age-old, historic, woodland, red-roofed, Bucking-hamshire lanes, the faithful band of rustics is gathering anew.

1937

NOTE: Mr Taylor, of course, was making *A Yank at Oxford* – an engaging film, although not entirely to be relied on as a picture of undergraduate life. – A.L.

End of a Harlequinade

The death of Douglas Fairbanks, in California last week, has robbed the movies of a bit of themselves – a drop of the life-blood that first made them gay, and great, and indomitable.

If Fairbanks had lived, he would have been fifty-six next spring. He came into the movies in the first year of the last war. In the years between he made something like thirty silent films and five talkies, all of them strenuous.

Every film that Fairbanks tackled was a miniature marathon. When he was twelve he could ride and fence and box, swim like a fish, and jump like a cat. When he was over fifty he could still swing from roof to floor of the studio on a roll of fish-net, leap down from a 12-foot wall with a naked rapier in his teeth, and scale an 80-foot tower without a double.

He never pretended to be an artist in the sense that his friend Chaplin was an artist. Minutiae of acting didn't trouble him. He had directors to see to that; it was their department. He had just one belief in film-making – that a film should move – and one ideal for himself – to be as fit in body and mind as sound sinews and rigorous training could make him.

Fairbanks never really knew how good he was. Behind those acrobatic stunts and that schoolboy exuberance there was a real genius. His leaps, and fights, and swift, violent trajectories were thrilling to watch, but they were inventive, too; they had in them the quality of beauty and surprise. He was an unconscious harlequin. Everything he did had poise and rhythm.

He ought never to have made talkies. Speech hampered him. Like Chaplin, he came straight out of the great days of pantomime. When he talked, he was apt to be abrupt and confused. When he moved, every limb and sinew and nerve spoke for him.

Nobody who saw the great Fairbanks films will ever quite forget them. It is a privilege of middle age to be able to look back and remember – 'Doug' swinging down that vast black curtain in *Robin Hood*, 'Doug' prowling catlike through the gardens of old Baghdad, 'Doug' entering meekly under his umbrella in *The Mark of Zorro*, 'Doug' swaggering up to heaven with the musketeers in *The Man in the Iron Mask*.

All these scenes are as vivid as if they had been seen yesterday.

And some of us can go back still further, to the days when 'Doug'
held up the fast express for the conductor's whistle, and leapt over
the sedate chairs of the Lambs' Club. We may have forgotten the
names of the pictures, but that tough, stocky little figure, that
friendly grin, and the sense of almost illimitable mastery of space
and time stays with us.

Everything Fairbanks did is touched with acute memories of
our own youth, when picture-going was still an adventure,
when there were few reviews to guide us, when the films
hadn't discovered culture, and the culturists hadn't yet found the
cinema. The man was perhaps lucky in his moment. Harlequin
grace, the sinews of a Hercules, and a large schoolboy delight in
simple things might not be enough for the present generation
of picturegoers. But a man's greatness lies in his relation to the
moment, and Fairbanks was a giant in his day.

1939

Favourite Director

One day in the spring of 1925 there came to London a strange film by a young and unknown French director, René Clair. The film was originally called *Paris Qui Dort*. Then the title was changed to *Le Rayon Invisible*. In England it was put out as *The Crazy Ray*, a cheapjack title almost guaranteed to keep away the people who would like the film and understand it.

Under any name it told the story of a night watchman on the Eiffel Tower, who comes down from his lofty post one morning to find the whole of Paris struck into a trance. Or so it seems at first, but presently he discovers four other animate beings: the pilot and passengers of an aeroplane just arrived from Marseilles. This is the beginning of a series of adventures in a spellbound city which are freely and fantastically imaginative, often funny, sometimes touching, always close to human nature, told with an individual and distinctive charm.

I was fascinated by this film, and later, when René Clair had become a family friend, even more fascinated by his story of the way he made it.

We were talking in the half-dusk after dinner, by our living-room fire. René was speaking English, as he always did in courtesy to his English friends, although with equal courtesy he always wrote to them in French.

It was not hard in the dusk to make inconspicuous notes of what he said, and I have just dug them up from an old file. The pencil-writing is faded, but still decipherable. The phrases are so typical of Clair that I should like to quote them verbatim.

'Always the trouble with a young man is no money,' he said. 'With an old man too. With me the trouble will always be no money. I cannot keep it. And always the people I meet who are nice, who would have me work with them, are just the same. They have no money too. That was how I got my first real job as a director.

'I wrote a story, *Paris Qui Dort*, and found a producer who wanted to use it. He had no money, so he was willing to take me, because I was cheap and wanted to make my own films. So we started and I was very happy. But presently he said, "We can't go on." The salaries stopped. I asked one day to pay a taxi at the office, going on location, and this man told me, "Can't, no cash".'

There was a long pause of bitter memory as he gazed into the fire. I think he had no knowledge of my flying pencil.

'Then I found out. In the office was no one but creditors. The producer had an arrangement with the bank by which he got so many francs' credit for every film he started. So of course he started them. Dozens of them. He was always starting, never finishing.' A shrug of the thin shoulders. 'It was natural, yes?'

I said yes with all my heart and added, 'So what did you do next?' to keep the story going.

'So we went on with the film for nothing,' he said. 'I was young and a little romantic and I suppose I believed in it. And there was Albert Préjean too, who was just starting as an actor. We used to wander about Paris together, dreaming and planning and talking about our ideals.

'Some days we ate and some days we did not eat.

'When my family were in Paris we ate often, but in the summer when they were in the country we were very hungry. They were not quite pleased with me, you see, for going into the cinema. So I could not ask for money. You understand that, yes? You have a son. You would not like for him to go into the cinema?'

I agreed that I would not like for my son (who was at that time of a very tender age) to go into the cinema, and René went on, with seeming illogic:

'But we were very happy. I think those were the happiest days. We worked when we could afford it. But although we were on the picture eight months there were only twenty working days.

'There was one thing that was very difficult. We had to shoot from the platform of he Eiffel Tower, and to go up there cost four francs a head. Sometimes Préjean had the money, sometimes I had. But seldom both together. When we did have it we were so happy that we wanted to stay up there all day, looking over the roofs of Paris and eating nothing at all, or perhaps all day only a *madeleine*.'

It would be nice to be able to say that *Paris Qui Dort* brought riches and réclâme to its young director. It brought neither. Only a few mad foreigners rejoiced in its felicity. In its own country it passed almost unnoticed.

Clair was never to have much honour in his own country, nor

to achieve the highest honours anywhere. He must have made
something like forty films by now. His name is one to gabble
öff when talking about the cinema. His record is on file in all
newspaper offices. He is recognized as having been one of the
big names in the cinema, but not one of the giants: Griffith,
Eisenstein, Chaplin, De Mille, Hitchcock.

'My films,' he said to me when he was in England directing
The Ghost Goes West for Korda, 'have always lost money and I
suppose they always will. When I make them in order to make
money,' and he shuddered at the memory, 'they lose always more
than ever.'

I believe him. It would surprise me very much to learn that
Clair was ever a rich man. He had never been happy working
outside his own country, but even at home he has missed the
common touch. His nearest success was built on an accordion
tune. And even that has since been outclassed by a success built
on a zither tune. He has failed either to be the rage of cocktail
parties or the favourites of the boulevards.

Perhaps the secret is that his work has never been contemporary. In the beginning he made collectors' items before
there were collectors ready to collect. His later films have
been collectors' items too, but the collectors have passed on
to other more competitive markets.

Clair has always been a gentleman in an industry largely
operated by vulgarians. A few years ago I found myself
reluctantly locked in conversation with a sharp, successful little
showman who had thriven on the belief that the cinema should
be violent, sexual, neo-realist or even neo-decadent.

'Who is *your* favourite director?' he asked me, and before I had
time to answer added, 'I know; René Clair.' He made the name
sound like a dirty word, and the allegation a smear on both our
characters.

Up to that time I had never played the game of picking my
favourite director, or choosing which films of his I would take
with me to a welcome desert island. After a night's consideration
I decided that this shrewd and sneering little person was quite
right. René Clair *is* my favourite film director, and the pictures
I would choose to take are *Paris Qui Dort, Un Chapeau de Paille
d'Italie, Sous les Toits de Paris, Le Million, Les Grandes Manoeuvres*
and *Porte de Lilas*.

There have been greater directors than René Clair, but none
of whom I have been quite so fond. I have liked him in his green

spring, his golden summer and his mellow autumn. His nonsense is my kind of nonsense, his melancholy my kind of melancholy. There has never been another film director with quite his gift to offer; this special, rather private, mingling of compassion, gaiety and grace.

Alex

On a bracket in one corner of our living-room stands the carved head of a young African woman, about life-size, in ebony. Her hair is piled high and intricately braided. Her lips, full but demure, are not quite smiling. The delicate ears lie close against the small, neat head.

She comes from the Congo, and was a present from Zoltan Korda, who found her there in some small village when he was making *Sanders of the River*. He had a special fondness for the carving, and was pleased when we put it in a place of honour. The last time I saw him, not long before his death, we were talking about old times and suddenly he asked me, 'The Congo lady, be she still with you?' He was as happy as a sandboy when I said she was.

'Zolly' was the easiest of the three Korda brothers to get to know, although as the years went on he became an infrequent visitor to England. He suffered from tuberculosis, a legacy of war gas, and our climate didn't suit him. His later life was divided between California and Switzerland. Many of his letters are dated from a sanatorium. But, wherever he might be, he remembered his old friends. Always, at Christmas, one might expect a case of wine from some London merchant, with the compliments of Mr Zoltan Korda.

There was a boyish eagerness and candour about him which endeared him to shy people and to children. He had young sons of his own, and was splendid with small boys. I remember how patient he used to be with Sabu, who was brought from India to play in *Elephant Boy*, knowing only a few words of English.

Zolly had a fellow-feeling for bewildered and uprooted people. He was shy at heart, I think, a good-natured, uncomplaining fellow, with no very positive habit of self-assertion. He saw himself as the mediocre member of the brilliant Korda family. In that he did himself less than justice. Alexander Korda thought the world of him. 'Everybody in the film industry has brothers,' he once said to me; 'that of course is customary. What is not so customary is to have brothers who can *do*.'

What Zoltan Korda did, as well as directing his own films, was to act as an invaluable *aide* in cutting, editing and doctoring the films of others. It was the trade to which he had been apprenticed as a boy in the old barn studio in Budapest, and the cunning never left him.

What Vincent Korda did was to design sets for almost all the Korda films; sets that were at the same time educated, imaginative, exact to period and practical. He was a 'real' painter, who liked to mess about at peace in his own studio in Paris, happy and free amongst his paints and canvases. He had no love at all for motion pictures. 'Alex,' he once said to his elder brother, 'you are all in a crazy trade. I hate your bloddy industry. I was an honest man, now you try to make me dishonest. I design this one picture for you; then I go.'

He kept his word. But it was not to be the last word. A few months later Alex telephoned to him in Paris. 'Vincent,' he said, 'I make now a new company of my own. I am taking a great risk and I need you as art director. You must come and help me.' And because no Korda ever said no to another Korda after the first hundred times, Vincent came to London; and there he stayed.

He was the silent member of the family. I remember his room as the last resort of peace in all the turbulence of the Korda empire, the calm spot in the centre of the hurricane. He lived apart from the reeling studios in a world of his own philosophy. His corner of the art department was unmistakable, a place peculiar to Vincent.

You would find a coffee percolator dripping beside a glass of paint-water, long oil-brushes soaking in a pot next to a jar of wild flowers, a hat flung on the floor under a plan of ancient Rome, a wall of sketches for his current picture. And somewhere, vaguely, there was Vincent, laconically glad to see you; pleased to talk on any subject except films, without looking up from his drawing; ready with the unexpected comment; hiding a world of wisdom behind his slow, Cheshire Cat smile.

Alexander Korda's 'new company' was called London Film Productions. The trade mark, soon to be known all over the world, was Big Ben. It came into existence in the spring of 1932 with a light comedy known as *Wedding Rehearsal*.

That was when I first made the acquaintance of the amazing Mr Korda. During the next twenty years I was to see a great deal of him. I came to know him well; or as well as he would allow anyone to know him outside the circle of his family and what he always described (in invisible capitals) as 'My People'.

When he died in the January of 1956 the world seemed a duller place. I missed him, and shall continue to miss him. He still seems more alive than many living people.

I miss his stimulating talk, his high enthusiasms, his shrewd anticipations of things to come. I remember how amusing he could be, and how exasperating. I remember the black days when he was 'terribly tired' and the golden days when he was 'wonderfully happy'. I remember our stubborn quarrels, and the soft, purring voice with which he contrived to make them up: 'We are too long friends for this sort of thing.' It was impossible to stay aggrieved with a person who bore so little malice.

The Hungarian land agent's son who became a British knight was a great man in his way. Everything he did was on the grand scale. Even his failures had to be colossal failures. Like all great showmen, he made big mistakes, and frequently spent too much money. But he had the resilience of a rubber ball, and bounced back triumphantly after every tumble.

He was a man of taste and culture, a scholar and a natural spell-binder. A Hollywood executive once said of him, more in puzzlement than chagrin, that Korda could 'make the folks run after him, just like the rats of Hamburg ran after the Pied Piper.'

He drew towards him the best talents, in writing, acting, direction, design and music. The world was his field. He was intensely patriotic about his adoptive country, but his view was never insular. He could speak six languages fluently and inaccurately, with a charming indifference which was all part of the set-up. Even his native Hungarian occasionally appeared to fail him, but the charm never did.

Of all the figures in the British cinema, Korda's is the one around whom legends gather thickest. Alex in his heyday was the best film 'copy' in England. Physically colourless, with pale hair, pale eyes which looked naked when he took off his spectacles, pale skin, pale clothes, he was the most flaming personality in a highly coloured profession. No journalist had to go around hunting for Alexander Korda stories. They fell into his hands each day.

Alex had been a journalist himself, and knew exactly what each paper wanted.

You went to him and said: 'Alex, I need a story for next Sunday. Can you help me?'

He would start prowling up and down his office, with his soft panther tread. 'Darling,' he would throw over his shoulder, 'I am so tired, I cannot think today. We buy the rights of *Jungle Book*' (or *The Four Feathers*, or *Knight Without Armour*). 'I persuade to come here Marlene Dietrich' (Or Gigli, or Fairbanks, or René Clair). 'I talk on the telephone to Orson about a musical version of *Around the World in Eighty Days.*'

'Can I print that?'

'Certainly you print it, darling, but it is not for you. That is an evening-paper story' (or 'That is better for the *Daily Mail*'). 'It is so difficult, and I am so exhausted. Last night I talk with Charles Laughton about *Cyrano de Bergerac*. He is trying some new noses. He has gone nuts over new noses. You want to talk to him? We fix it.'

He would stop his prowl and pick up one of the multitude of telephones on his desk. 'You get me at once Charles Laughton,' he would say, and you knew he had got Charles Laughton from the friendly profanation that singed the wires between them. 'That is all right,' he would observe as he put back the receiver, 'we fix it for tomorrow. Don't believe anything that old skunk tells you.'

He always fixed it and we always got our story. Alex knew his newspapers as intimately as he knew his books. I never went to see him and came away empty-handed.

It was wiser to take most of his stories with a pinch of salt. He had far too many plans for all of them to ripen. I have lost count of the number of times he told me, 'So-and-So' (and it was always a different So-and-So) 'will play for us next year Lawrence of Arabia.' London Films never made *Lawrence of Arabia*. Laughton never made *Cyrano de Bergerac*, but he was extremely amusing about the noses. Korda's dream castles were always splendid copy, even when they turned out to be castles in Spain.

The narrow house in Grosvenor Street, which provided London Films with their first headquarters, was so busy and crowded all day long that you could hardly set foot on stairs, or corridors, or in the bumpy little lift, without treading on the toes of some celebrity. There was a waiting-room, to be sure, but except for a torn copy of *Spotlight* and a basket chair that creaked, it was always empty.

People who knew the ropes slipped in through the mews at the back and went straight upstairs to Korda's ante-room. People who didn't know the ropes, but were known to the commissionaire, pushed open the glass door at the front and also went upstairs to Korda's ante-room. It was a small room, in which a dozen made a crowd, and it was always packed with

People in the News, most of whom were old friends or eager to be friendly. In the middle of the hubbub sat Korda's secretary, small, grey-haired Miss Fischer, imperturbably tapping at her typewriter and dealing with the telephone in various languages.

Informality was the keynote of 22, Grosvenor Street. Sometimes Korda would push open the green baize door and join the party in the ante-room, leaving the visitor in the office to his own devices.

Sometimes in the middle of a conference, he would fling open the office window and call to some friend in the street below. Opposite No 22 was the establishment of one of the most fashionable couturiers in London. History records the day when Alex, bored with some trivial business argument, leant out and shouted to Robert Sherwood across the street: 'Don't go in there, Bob! They're bloody robbers!'

This did not deter the customer, nor was it intended to. It was simply an ejaculation, highly actionable of course, but uttered as a vent for tedium and high spirits. It may have surprised the passers-by in Grosvenor Street, but neither couture nor conference was affected by it.

Alex was what they call 'a masterpiece' for disposing of the unwanted caller, for saying hail and farewell in a single, painless operation. 'Hallo, how are you, old boy?' he would purr, shaking hands as he urged his visitor towards the door. 'I cannot think just now, I am so exhausted. Come and see me tomorrow at five and we will talk. Goodbye.'

And so great was his charm and authority that hardly anyone felt slighted, and almost everybody did come back tomorrow at five.

It was always good copy for a journalist to join the rush-hour crowd at 22, Grosvenor Street. You never knew whom you might meet there, and most people talked freely, as waiting people will.

But if you wanted to learn something about Korda himself you had to meet him on his own stamping-ground. Sometimes, after a late-night run-through of a picture, he would ask a few friends home to supper at his house near Regent's Park.

Alex was at his best in his library at midnight, with a good fire blazing; cold meats and a noble ham on the side-table; whisky, cognac and coffee bubbling in a big percolator. He would prowl softly up and down the room, cigar in hand, talking over ideas for pictures with his brothers and his old Hungarian friend and scriptwriter, Lajos Biro; calling up New York or Hollywood or Paris; discussing books and politics and people into the not so small hours of the morning.

Korda had a multitude of books, in English, French and German; many of them first editions. They were kept on his shelves not for show, but because he enjoyed reading them and liked to have them close at hand.

He had a valuable collection of paintings: half a dozen Renoirs, three or four Cézannes, a couple of Canalettos, a Degas or two, a Monet and several others. But I sometimes think the picture he liked best was a photograph, roughly framed, which he always kept in his office.

It showed a back alley in Paris; a broken fence, with torn papers flying; and a draggled poster, announcing '*Charles Laughton dans La Vie Privée d'Henri VIII*', peeling from the hoarding.

'That is right, that is as it should be,' he used to say. '*Sic transit gloria* . . . a private end to the public life of a notorious film.'

I was in a good position to keep an eye on Korda and his activities. After a few years of making films in other people's studios he decided to build a studio of his own. He bought an old property called The Fisheries at Denham, in Buckinghamshire, a maddening spot to reach by train from London, but only a few miles away from our house in the north-west tip of Middlesex. You could do the journey by car in fifteen minutes; and how useful that was to be when the war brought petrol-rationing! At a pinch you could even walk.

It takes a long time to build a film studio, and Denham took longer than most. Alex was determined not to spoil the character of the place, for he had bought it largely for its woods and water. 'Not a tree shall be touched,' he declared, when first he walked along the river-bank on a wintry afternoon. And he very nearly kept his word.

We had the freedom of the place from the beginning, and often went there and picnicked on a Saturday afternoon. I have always had a passion for old houses in tanglewood surroundings, and, with the curiosity of the odious Mrs Elton in *Emma*, I liked, of all things, to go mildly exploring.

The Fisheries must have been a friendly place to live in once, deep in the Buckinghamshire countryside. It had a family feel; I think a number of generations must have loved it. The unofficial way we used to reach it was across a humpbacked bridge, and then, parking the car on what is known nowadays as The Verge, through a gap in the hedge into a little coppice, where hazels covered and bluebells carpeted a forgotten dogs' graveyard.

There were headstones with the names of Tim and Bob and Nero and some fifteen other dogs who had hunted and ratted and spent their busy lives at The Fisheries before the First World War. Beyond this touching graveyard you struck the footpath by the river. On our right was the placid water, with its reeds and islets and hundreds of nests of wild fowl. On your left was a fringe of steeply hanging woods, with a fox-hole in the bank. In front was the old house, with its stables and outbuildings. Beyond lay broad acres of pasture land and arable.

As the studios grew, a great deal of the flat land was naturally gobbled up. But the old house itself remained, with a number of home fields and a long stretch of wooded river-bank. We saw them for many years in scores of pre-war British pictures.

For that matter, thanks to television, we can see them still, although films are no longer made there, and the place has been turned into a store for the United States Air Force. Not long ago I.T.A. showed us a revival of *The Ghost Goes West*. Looking at the ruins of Glourie Castle, later to become a Flemish market place for *Rembrandt*, I felt quite sentimental for a moment. *Ehu fugaces! O tempi passati!* Gone, gone, gone with lost Atlantis! Dear, absurd, vainglorious old Denham!

Television showed us *Fire Over England*, and we recognized the meadows beside the river where an extremely nervous Flora Robson, in the stiff robes and ruff of Queen Elizabeth, rode down to Tilbury, and just managed to sit her white cart-horse long enough to harangue the troops before the Armada.

It showed us *The Scarlet Pimpernel*, with Merle Oberon and Leslie Howard, and as I watched the Blakeney coach drawn up in the stableyard of The Fisheries to carry Marguerite to Dover I idly wondered what they'd done that morning with the cats, all hundred of them, who were grossly pampered by the old and somewhat lonely commissionaire.

Whenever I went there the yard was cluttered up with cats: thin cats, fat cats, old cats, young cats, cats of every shape and colour. They monopolized the place and spurned it too, turning up their whiskers at saucers of canned milk and kipper-heads, loudly demanding fresh sandwiches from the canteen and top milk from the bottle.

It was never a surprise to meet animals at Denham. Apart

from the indigenous cats and visiting dogs, both professional and amateur, there was a herd of goats, which had been imported to habitate the ruins of City Square in the Wells film *Things to Come*, and remained there with their offspring for years, perfectly content, and apparently quite forgotten.

At one time there was a resident tiger, and elephants were almost common. They lived in a compound down beside the river. I was told by one old gardener that them elephants was masterbits for fertilizer. His hothouses and nursery beds had never done so good, he said, as when Mr Zoltan and that other gentleman (Bob Flaherty) were taking that picture they called *Elephant Boy*.

The studio buildings themselves looked gargantuan to me, but the Hollywood architect who came over to design them described Denham as 'just a decent-sized little place, handy, with enough elbow-room to move around in'. A London Films publicist, with greater exuberance, informed a breathless world that Denham's power plant 'generates enough electricity to light the whole city of York'; though heaven knows why it should be required to do so.

There were seven stages, miles of concrete corridors and fifteen star dressing-rooms.

The corridors were memorable for their peculiar smell: a combination of cellar clamminess with hot radiator and varnish. The walls were decorated with what looked like crazy maps of some Underground railway system, with lines, blobs and arrows in assorted colours, directing you to get nowhere fast. Above your head, at intervals, red signs commanded SILENCE, while the air was clamorous with sawing, filing, hammering, the rattle of tea-trolleys and a babble of talk in half a dozen languages.

The star dressing-rooms had the perfection of exhibits in some ideal-home exhibition. Each of them was equipped with bath, shower, telephones, couch for exhausted artists and refrigerator. Picture widows, delicately framed in chintz, gave a view of trimly formal gardens.

These dressing-rooms suggested bedrooms in a luxury hotel. They changed hands, but seldom character. Hundreds of guests passed through them as the years went on, but only a few people managed, or cared, to endue them with a personal touch during their brief tenancy.

Elisabeth Bergner's sanctum always smelt of fruit; she adored munching at ripe apples. Charles Laughton's room invariably had a single vase of flowers, which he brought up from his Surrey garden and arranged most beautifully. I remember bluebells, just enough, no more, tenderly gathered without touching the white of the stem; and a low bowl of very small, sweet-smelling Penzance briers.

Flora Robson was always busy sewing, usually with a niece in attendance, and the floor of her room was littered with materials. She is an exquisite needlewoman with a special turn for patchwork; she likes to cover her own chair and sofa cushions with bits of silk and velvet wheedled from her dressmaker, and embarks without trepidation on a full-sized patchwork quilt.

Marlene Dietrich's VIP dressing-room, used when she was making *Knight Without Armour* with Robert Donat, was specially done over for her with pale wood, blue glass-topped tables, pink satin cushions and a continuous supply of pink long-stemmed roses. There she would receive her courtiers under an enormous hair-dryer, stretching out a white arm to be kissed in continental fashion; and many were the men who came to kiss it.

One very young star, who shall be nameless for obvious reasons, gave me a unique reception when I went to interview her. We hadn't met before, and my name obviously meant nothing to her. I tapped at the door. She called 'Come in!' and emerged from behind the shower curtain completely naked. This embarrassed her more than it embarrassed me. She blushed crimson, snatched a robe, and apologized with what I am sure was utter honesty. 'Oh,' she said, 'I really am most *terribly* sorry. I thought you were a *man.*'

NOTE: The young star referred to in the last paragraph – why shouldn't one say it now? – was June Duprez, who would have been at Denham making *The Thief of Baghdad*. – A.L.

Leslie Howard

Memories of early war days at Denham are inevitably mixed with memories of Leslie Howard. I learnt to know him well at that time, and came to be very fond of him.

We had met once, years earlier, briefly and entirely in the way of business. He had just come back from Hollywood, where he had been playing with Norma Shearer in *Romeo and Juliet*. The *Observer* wanted a story about him in his Surrey home; so did the *Boston Evening Transcript*, which reprinted most of it under the headlines, 'Leslie Howard at Ease on an English Estate'.

The 'English Estate' proved very hard to find. It was hidden in a leafy lane near Dorking, but nobody could tell me exactly *which* lane. They knew of only two actors thereabouts, I found: Mr Sydney Howard, the comedian, and Mr Charles Haughton, or some such name, who lived up along there on the hill. (It was May, and the bluebells were in a blaze of glory.)

In the end I discovered that Mr *Leslie* Howard, the one that I was asking for, was known locally as the mad fellow with the polo ponies. He kept sixteen of them at that time, six newly imported from America with a Californian polo-player and a Texan cowboy to train them.

When I arrived at what was presumably the 'English Estate' I found the lane blocked by errand boys with bicycles, chattering women in aprons, an ice-cream cart, a couple of tradesmen's vans, a string of polo ponies and a long, black American saloon flung haphazardly across the road, while what seemed to be the entire Howard household turned out to catch a brown mare who had gone berserk.

Leslie himself, looking oddly improbable in cowboy chaps, sat his pony in silence and watched while the Texan, with professional cries of 'Ho yo!' and 'Hi girl!', attempted to rope the unco-operative mare. Never, in the gravest of his screen epics, had the actor looked so worried. The other horses were getting too excited. There was a mare in the next field with a young foal, tossing her head nervously, neighing and cantering.

When the brown mare was eventually caught and saddled, Howard disappeared. He had a way of silently disappearing, as I was to find out later. I think it was an escape from instant pressure. Time and again he would be missing from the studio set; discovered at last, usually far away, reading or asleep in somebody's parked car. His comings and goings had an air of vague inconsequence, but when he was caught at last he was entirely at your behest, and could talk about his work with enthusiasm and authority.

His talk, on that long ago May morning, was mostly about Shakespeare. He naturally had a good deal to say about *Romeo and Juliet*.

'I always thought Romeo was a perfectly deadly part, except in the later scenes, when he is something more than just a man in love. A man in love is a stupid thing – he bores you stiff, in real life or anywhere else – but a woman in love is fascinating. She has a kind of aura. Shakespeare was obviously fascinated by Juliet, and it was the woman he enriched. Romeo acquires something in the late scenes, when he becomes the victim of a political feud, and in his tragic moments he is rather interesting, a kind of adolescent Hamlet.'

It was about *Hamlet* that he really wanted to talk. His mind was full of *Hamlet* at the time. He had plans to produce a *Hamlet* film in what he called a 'doll's house set'. The idea was to show the Hamlet family moving from room to room in the castle of Elsinore; to let us watch the cooks preparing the funeral baked meats in one corner, while the Queen was dallying with Claudius in another; to show the marks on the wall where the young prince had been measured as he grew; the casements he looked out of, the familiar stairs he trod. Elsinore, as far as I could understand it, was to be endowed with a special *genius loci*, and become a protagonist in the tragedy.

Leslie Howard's ideas for his screen *Hamlet* were original and exciting, but they stayed just ideas. That was the first and last time I ever heard of them. I cut my visit very short, for Leslie, although full of charm, was clearly absent of mind. Having forgotten the errant mare, he was following the movements of the adolescent Hamlet. I didn't see him again until the war.

Perhaps my first impression was superficial; possibly circumstance had altered character; at any rate, the Leslie Howard whom I came to know at Denham seemed a very different person from 'the mad fellow with the polo ponies'.

He looked a great deal older and a little frail. He had taken to wearing heavy, horn-rimmed spectacles; not always, and never on the set, but often enough to make them seem a part of him. There was still the gentle charm of manner (although one actor that I know insists the gentleness was a façade, and that as a director he was ruthless), but with it a new philosophy and purpose. It was as if the war had shown him where his heart lay; as if his passion to release a *genius loci* had passed from Elsinore to England.

When the airliner in which he was flying home from Lisbon was shot down over the Atlantic in June 1943 the news was received here with as much grief as shock. Perhaps no single war casualty gave the general public such an acute sense of personal loss. Leslie Howard was more than just a popular film star, who had endeared himself to audiences with *Pygmalion*, *Pimpernel Smith* and *The First of the Few*. He had become in an odd way a symbol of England, standing for all that is most deeply rooted in the British character.

I have sometimes wondered what Howard would have done if he had come back safely from that trip to Spain and Portugal. I had a long talk with him the day before he left. He was in a strange mood; overtired and overstrained; worrying, as he was far too apt to do, about his health. He had just turned fifty, and was acutely aware of it. He talked a great deal about youth, and youth's right to leadership.

He left me with an odd impression that he felt his special job was done. To be sure, he had plans; plans for a film about the Liberty Ship One Thousand and One, built in the Rockies and sailing in convoy to Murmansk; another film about Sir Christopher Wren and the building of St Paul's Cathedral; another very special one about the *feeling* of the English Downs. He was also toying with a fancy for a sequel to *Pimpernel Smith*, in which Professor Smith would meet a Mandarin. The essential characteristics of the British and the Chinese, he insisted, were curiously alike.

He could have been persuaded to appear in one or other of these films, I don't doubt. At the back of his mind, however, was the idea that it was time for him to stand aside as an actor. The public, he said, wanted young faces, and new voices. He may have been right about the faces, but about the voices – and his was one of the best-loved voices on the air at that time – he was supremely wrong.

I have just been going through my files and found a scribbled note from Robert Donat, dated 4th June 1943. 'How awful about L.H.', it says. 'I'd no idea how much he meant to our business until I realized he'd gone from it altogether. He had such subtlety and delicacy and style and I think he'd have developed into a first-class director.'

Subtlety, delicacy and style, all these; and with them a tremendous power of personal persuasion. I hope that nobody will ever try to film the Leslie Howard story. It would be, for many reasons, not only impertinent but impossible. His son Ronald, who looks so very like him, has properly refused to play the part, and anyone else would be unthinkable.

Leslie Howard was an odd man to encounter in the film business; not at all an easy man to understand; but I am very glad to have known him, however incompletely. He was a rewarding man to meet; he always set imagination working. He was a mass of apparent contradictions. He had the Kipling secret of the Cat Who Walked By Itself, and yet he was a born ambassador. He came, on one side, of Hungarian stock; he knew and loved America; but he was as much a part of England as Kipling's oak, ash and thorn.

Hitch

When I first met Alfred Hitchcock he was a chubby, rosy-cheeked young man with eyes like bright boot-buttons. He spent his time writing and designing subtitles for silent pictures. He used to announce 'Came the Dawn' in black letters on a white ground, or whisper that 'Heart spoke to heart in the hush of the evening'. He liked to embellish these moving words with slightly iconoclastic sketches, for he was a born draughtsman with an impish sense of humour.

By the time the Hitchcocks came out to dinner bearing a mass of tulips we had been good friends for nearly eleven years. Hitch – the full name is unthinkable to those who know him – was beginning to be famous as a director on both sides of the Atlantic. After the success of *The Man Who Knew Too Much*, *The Thirty-Nine Steps* and *The Secret Agent* even the more sober New York papers were not hesitating to call him 'brilliant'.

He had become a 'must' for visiting journalists, one of the compulsive sights of London. It seems strange now to remember that at that time hardly anybody knew what Hitchcock looked like. His fleeting personal appearance in a picture had not yet become a trademark, and of course there was no television.

My friends from overseas, almost without exception, envisaged this prince of melodrama as a lean, tough, saturnine fellow, a compound of Dashiel Hammett, Sherlock Holmes and Perry Mason. It used to be a constant source of entertainment to me to lead one of them up to the genial, rotund Hitchcock, and watch him as he found his hand engulfed in a vast directorial paw.

There were limits to Hitch's geniality, however. Affectation and stupidity enraged him. He could bellow on the set as well as coo. I have heard him thunder at a leading man who fumbled one entrance after another, 'Come on, So-and-So, you Quota Queen!' I have seen him startle animation into the face of some super-refined leading lady by whispering into her ear words which no refined girl would expect to hear.

He also had his teacup-smashing days. This used to be a great Hitchcock act, which he picked up, he told me, as a result of smashing crockery for sixpence a go at the Wembley Exhibition. I remember one day at Shepherd's Bush when I found him standing, rather like a malevolent kelpie, among a litter of broken china.

'Hullo, kid,' he said. 'You came five minutes too late.'

'What for?' I asked him.

'For the big scene.'

'Murder?' I asked.

'No, temperament. Me breaking china. Makes you feel good. Gets rid of inhibitions. That was a teapot once, executive model. I like to get up on a high rostrum and tip the tray over. Or push cups over the edge of a gantry. Or just open my hand and let the whole thing drop – like this. Wouldn't you?'

He kicked a sugar-bowl across the set and added, pleadingly: 'I got to have *some* fun, kid. I'm on a diet. And I don't do crazy things in my pictures any more. I've turned a technical ascetic, kid, no more luxuries or gimmicks. Surely you don't grudge me a bit of innocent fun?'

Hitchcock was a grandmaster of the art of wheedling. He could coax a performance out of the dumbest blonde in the industry, and make her look ravishing into the bargain. His methods were often cavalier, but his humanity was catholic. He loved to startle and still loves to startle, with the relish of a schoolboy who jumps at you out of a dark corner shouting 'Boo!'

For myself, I dislike Hitchcock in his moods of ghoulish glee. I used to tell him so, and he would sulk for days. We were on what René Clair once described as 'the not-so-speaking terms' (Clair's reference was to his current relations with Alexander Korda) for a long time after Hitch decided, in *Sabotage*, to blow up a schoolboy in a bus with a time-bomb he was carrying. I told him that it wasn't entertaining. He declared it was.

You can't skip the horrors in a moving picture as you can in a written thriller. They take you unawares. Hitchcock in particular has perfected the art of the sudden, unexpected body blow. He sickens you with the shock discovery of the shrivelled human head in *Under Capricorn*, the terrible onrush of murder in *Psycho*, before you can guard yourself against what's coming.

Time and again I could have taken him by the scruff of the neck and shaken him until his boot-button eyes popped out of his head for lending his naturally humane genius to cadenzas of inhumanity.

These touches of jocose, professional sadism aside, he was the gentlest of creatures. He has done more kindly turns to out-of-work actors, writers down on their luck and other friends in trouble than almost anyone I know of in the industry. At heart he is an old-fashioned man, a family character; believing in the importance of small, common courtesies, of promises given and habits formed; the trivial, ordinary event which alone make the big events extraordinary.

Up to the time when Hitchcock went to Hollywood it was an invariable custom for me to lunch with him on the day after the press show of one of his pictures. By that time I had sent in my review, and we were free to mull over his film, as well as to discuss prospects for the future.

Hitchcock was a connoisseur of food and drink; he understood the pleasures of the table. Sometimes increasing girth persuaded him to try a diet, but the diets in those days were of an eclectic kind. He never imposed a fast on guests, nor embarrassed them by an ostentatious abstinence. Perhaps his king-size steaks were rather smaller, perhaps he eschewed French-fried potatoes and cut down the cream on his strawberries. But he still lunched like an epicure, albeit an epicure restrained.

Most of my luncheon dates with Hitch took place in the now vanished Carlton Grill, where he ran an account and was allowed to scribble on the tablecloth to his heart's content. This was important, because he is a man who never can talk freely without scribbling.

He visualizes both by instinct and by training. The script of every film he makes is interspersed with diagrams and sketches, showing exactly how the shot should be taken and what it ought to look like. As he talks to you, his broad, draughtsman's pencil sneaks out and blocks in groups or figures on the napkin or the table-top.

Before me as I write I have his celebrated self-portrait, scribbled on the back of a menu, what four pouting lines, a hint of down-dropped eyelid and a sharp circumflex for the nose.

I also have a piece of blotting paper, on which my pencilled signature and his copy of it stand indistinguishably back to back. If all other means of livelihood had failed, Hitchcock might have made his fortune as a forger. 'It's only a trick, kid,' he told me; 'you don't think of it as writing, just drawing. It's easier to draw it upside down.'

For many years Hitchcock resisted all attempts to lure him out to Hollywood. He was a Londoner, a solid hunk of British bloodstock, who took a deal of moving. When at last he did agree to go, after the international success of *The Lady Vanishes*, he never broke his ties with friends in England.

After every London press show of a Hitchcock film I would get a telephone call from Hollywood. 'What did you think about it; honest, kid?' It was an echo of our traditional luncheon inquests, and I often wondered what he was scribbling at that instant.

When war broke out he lost no time in sending me a cable. Would Tony and I come out to California as his guests? He was almost certain he could get me a job on an American magazine. I am certain that he could and would have done so.

It was the action of a true friend, and I still remember the heaviness of heart with which I walked the mile to the nearest post office and sent back a refusal. Impossible to explain, in the scant words of a cablegram or even the phrases of a censored letter, exactly why I felt that I and mine were part of wartime Britain; why flight was inconceivable; why, when one's closest things are threatened, one has to stay and guard them. It was something too subtle to be expressed; one had to be on the spot to feel it.

I hope, but have never been quite satisfied, that Hitchcock understood.

Robert Donat

The Donats, both Robert and his wife Ella Voysey, were from my home town. I had known Ella very slightly as a girl, when she had lived for a time at Professor Rutherford's house as companion to his wife and daughter Eileen. Robert himself was born and grew up in Withington, only a few streets away from me, but I never came across him in those days. People say, 'But you *must* have known him,' rather as they might say to a native of Western Australia, 'I expect you know my sister-in-law in Sydney.' Manchester, to be sure, is not as big as Australia, but even in the early 1900s it was quite a considerable warren of its kind.

The great advantage of coming from the same place is the ease of conversation it induces with a stranger. Donat and I met for the first time as adults, but we quickly felt like friends, because our young days had so much in common.

He told me how he used to tear round the shops at the corner of Withington village on his tricycle, past the grocer's where there was a sharp slope to whizz down. The grocer's was called Seymour Mead's, and it was there that my parked pram once ran away and overturned, and a wailing Caroline had to be comforted with ginger biscuits at the counter.

He told me about the Presbyterian church where he went with his elocution master to give penny readings. Did I know the church? he asked. I did. I had good reason to, considering the number of tennis balls I had lost through its leaded windows.

He told me how he would walk home from drama classes, night after night, beside the tramlines along Wilmslow Road, declaiming Shakespeare as he went. 'I always saved the purple passages for the points,' he said. 'That was when you got the biggest clang. It was splendid, like hurling your voice in challenge to a great brass band.'

I always remember that story when I think of Robert Donat. I don't know whether the Manchester tramlines had anything to do with it, but his management of voice was Donat's special triumph. He cut a handsome figure on the screen or stage, but was never, in my opinion, a great actor.

As a speaker, however, he was remarkable. Even in the last years, when the voice grew thin and breathy with illness, he conserved and used it with mastery for what it had to do. He could recite Kipling's 'The Way Through the Woods' on the radio as if it were an enchanted poem (which I sometimes think it is). He could pay tribute to lost friends like Leslie Howard with a warmth that gave the tired voice more than volume; it managed in some way to speak for everybody, as if it had picked up our private thoughts.

VI

Envoi

By this time I was over sixty and had begun to realize that I was growing old. I dozed off easily – we are a sleepy family – and often had a job to keep awake during the afternoon's picture. I found too that I was stopping to take breath halfway up the stairs to the dress circle, and saying 'You go ahead' to the young critics who came leaping up the steps behind me.

I found the daily journeys up to town a weariness, and resented the long hours that had to be put in at lunchtime. I had no London club, could not afford the prices of the quiet restaurants which I preferred and spent most of my lunch-breaks on a bench in the Southwood Memorial Garden of St James's Church, sharing my sandwiches with the pigeons.

I can see now that, without consciously realizing it, I was losing my appetite for the cinema. Gone were the days when one met the challenge of each week with zest, hoping that something wonderful would happen. There were still films that I enjoyed, of course, and others that I admired without enjoyment; and I worked harder than ever on my Sunday column, trying to atone with clarity and justice for what it lacked in inspiration.

When a critic reaches this state of mind he should be thinking of retirement, for he is no longer giving full service to his readers. But I was obstinate; habit died hard; I knew my work was conscientious, even if it were no longer spirited. I shall go on until I'm sixty-five, I thought, and then retire and draw my old-age pension.

It wasn't to work out that way, however. One morning in the autumn of 1960, when I was sixty-three, I had a long letter from David Astor, saying, in the gentlest way possible, that he felt the time had come when my column should be handed over to 'a younger person'. He was quite right, of course, and looking back on it now, I hold his decision in nothing but gratitude. But at the moment it was a shock. I had been on the *Observer* for thirty-two years, and never known any professional life other than reviewing for the cinema.

I wrote my last article for the *Observer* on Christmas Day 1960. I was glad that Christmas should have fallen on a Sunday that year, for I had always tried to keep my Christmas articles distinct from the other fifty-one; to use them for a special message to my readers. That year I had a very special message, which was to bid them all goodbye; and add, as we were taught to say at the end of children's parties, 'Thank you for having me'.

Index of Films

Where a film is the main subject of a review, the page reference is given in **bold** type.

Index of Names

Rathbone, Basil, 17, 145, 155–6
Redgrave, Michael, 129, 170
Reed, Carol, 38, 170, 233, 234, 241, 242
Reed, Donna, 283
Reinhardt, Max, 97, 98
Richardson, Ralph, 34, 151–2, 155, 157–8, 166, 234
Robertson, Marjorie see Neagle, Anna
Robson, Flora, 166, 340
Rogers, Ginger, 31, 99, 123, 179, 226
Roman, Ruth, 247
Rooney, Mickey, 98, 173, 215
Rosmer, Milton, 26
Russell, Jane, 293
Russell, Rosalind, 34
Rutherford, Margaret, 213, 237
Ruttmann, Walter, 82
Ryan, Robert, 279

Sabatini, Rafael, 166
Sabu, 34
Saint, Eve Marie, 286, 301
Sanders, George, 172, 256, 257
Sarg, Tony, 127
Sargent, Malcolm, 281
Saunders, Terry, 292
Saville, Victor, 88, 92
Schertzinger, Victor, 149
Schulberg, Budd, 286
Scott, C. P., 9, 24–5
Scott, Martha, 177
Scott, Randolph, 178, 247
Scott, Zachary, 247
Sellers, Peter, 8
Selznick, David O., 172
Semon, Larry, 162
Sennett, Mack, 87, 109
Shakespeare, William, 98, 99, 107, 217, 218, 219, 342, 349
Shaw, G. B., 208, 209, 223
Shearer, Norma, 341
Sherriff, R. C., 151
Sherwood, Robert, 95, 336
Simmons, Jean, 231
Simon, Michel, 148
Sinatra, Frank, 215
Sjöstrom, Victor, 46, 50, 51, 299
Small, Edward, 190
Smith, C. Aubrey, 116, 120
Stevens, George, 278
Stevenson, Robert, 201
Stewart, James, 163, 164, 166, 167, 179, 236, 315
Stewart, J. I. M. (Michael Innes), 161
Stiller, Mauritz, 46, 50, 51

Stokowski, Leopold, 109
Stone, Lewis, 86, 116
Stroud, Gregory, 149
Sturges, Preston, 49, 202, 208, 215, 216
Sücksdorf, Arne, 51
Sullavan, Margaret, 167, 168
Sullivan, Arthur, 148, 149, 280
Sullivan, Francis, 180
Sullivan, Pat, 127
Sydney, Basil, 231

Tati, Jacques, 282, 283
Taylor, Alma, 44
Taylor, Robert, 123, 323–5
Taylor, Valerie, 196
Temple, Shirley, 215
Tester, Desmond, 107
Thorndike, Sybil, 170
Tilly Girls, 44
Todd, Ann, 221
Tone, Franchot, 102, 112, 113, 114
Tonge, Philip, 299
Toscanini, Arturo, 34
Toye, Geoffrey, 148, 149
Tracy, Spencer, 34, 143, 166, 172, 173, 174, 186
Trevor, Claire, 143
Trubshawe, Michael, 285
Truman, Ralph, 218
Tufts, Sonny, 226
Turner, Lana, 187, 240, 241, 293

Urquhart, Robert, 295

Valentino, Rudolf, 28, 45
Valli, Alida, 242
Van Dyke, W. S., 97
Vansittart, Robert, 138
Veidt, Conrad, 29, 52, 92, 216
Victor, Charles, 285
von Stroheim, Eric, 45, 53

Walbrook, Anton, 200, 201
Wallace, Edgar, 30, 47
Walsh, Kay, 284
Walton, William, 197, 218
Warner, H. B., 111
Warner, Jack, 251
Watt, John, 128
Wayne, John, 143, 249, 255, 269, 316
Wayne, Naunton, 129, 170, 237
Wegener, Paul, 91, 115
Weidler, Virginia, 214
Weismuller, Johnny, 250, 255
Welles, Orson, 49, 53, 201, 208, 216, 229, 242, 253

Wells, H. G., 27, 109, 110, 133, 339
White, Chrissie, 44
White, Ethel Lina, 129
Whitty, Dame May, 129
Wiene, Robert, 52
Wilcox, Herbert, 32, 136, 140, 226, 227
Wilder, Thornton, 176, 177
Wilding, Michael, 227, 243
Wilkinson , Geoffrey, 260
Williams, Emlyn, 170
Williams, John, 285
Willis, Constance, 149, 150
Wimperis, Arthur, 89, 95

Wolfit, Donald, 273
Woolcott, Alexander, 143
Woolland, Norman, 231
Wray, Fay, 14
Wright, Teresa, 229
Wyatt, Jane, 111
Wynyard, Diana, 170

Young, Harold, 96
Young, Robert, 112, 113, 114, 167, 178

Zinneman, Fred, 316
Zuckmayer, Carl, 105